Managing the Chinese Environment

中

Studies on Contemporary China

The Contemporary China Institute at the School of Oriental and African Studies (University of London) has, since its establishment in 1968, been an international centre for research and publications on twentieth-century China. *Studies on Contemporary China*, which is edited at the Institute, seeks to maintain and extend that tradition by making available the best work of scholars and China specialists throughout the world. It embraces a wide variety of subjects relating to Nationalist and Communist China, including social, political, and economic change, intellectual and cultural developments, foreign relations, and national security.

Series Editor

Dr Frank Dikötter, Director of the Contemporary China Institute

Editorial Advisory Board

Managing the Chinese Environment

Edited by

RICHARD LOUIS EDMONDS

OXFORD
UNIVERSITY PRESS

*This book has been printed digitally and produced in a standard specification
in order to ensure its continuing availability*

OXFORD
UNIVERSITY PRESS

Great Clarendon Street, Oxford OX2 6DP

Oxford University Press is a department of the University of Oxford.
It furthers the University's objective of excellence in research, scholarship,
and education by publishing world-wide in

Oxford New York

Auckland Bangkok Buenos Aires Cape Town Chennai
Dar es Salaam Delhi Hong Kong Istanbul Karachi Kolkata
Kuala Lumpur Madrid Melbourne Mexico City Mumbai Nairobi
São Paulo Shanghai Taipei Tokyo Toronto

Oxford is a registered trade mark of Oxford University Press
in the UK and in certain other countries

Published in the United States
by Oxford University Press Inc., New York

ISBN 0-19-829635-5

Antony Rowe Ltd., Eastbourne

Contents

Notes on Contributors

ROBERT F. ASH is the Chiang Ching-kuo Professor of Taiwan Studies in the Department of Economics, School of Oriental and African Studies, University of London.

JUDITH BANISTER is professor of demography at the Hong Kong University of Science and Technology. She is author of *China's Changing Population*.

RICHARD LOUIS EDMONDS is editor of *The China Quarterly* and senior lecturer in geography with reference to China at the School of Oriental and African Studies in the University of London. He has written extensively on mainland China, Japan, Taiwan, Macau and Hong Kong, and is the author of *Macau* (1989) and *Patterns of China's Lost Harmony: A Survey of the Country's Environmental Degradation and Protection* (1994). Currently, he is working on environmental problems in China and transition issues in Macau.

MARK ELVIN is a research professor at the Australian National University. He has written on the long-term economic history of China, the political and social history of China, China's historical geography, and the history of the environment in China (*Sediments of Time: Environment and Society in Chinese History*).

JAMES HARKNESS was a programme officer for the Ford Foundation in Beijing from 1995 to 1998. Since January 1999, he has served as Director of China Programmes for the World Wide Fund for Nature (WWF). His research interests include state-society relations and the environment, the "non-governmental" sector, resource tenure, community forestry, rural development, and the political economy of conservation.

ABIGAIL R. JAHIEL is adjunct assistant professor in the Department of Political Science at Illinois Wesleyan University where she teaches courses on Chinese politics and environmental studies. She has conducted substantial research on the implementation of environmental policy in China, focusing on China's water pollution policy and on the transfer of pollution.

LIU CHANGMING is a researcher at the Institute of Geography and the United Research Centre for Water Problems of the Chinese Academy of Sciences in Beijing. He is curently working on the North China Water Resources Dynamics, Allocation and Reallocation Project (for 1997–2000) and his most recent book (co-authored with He Xiwu) is *Water Problem Strategy for China's 21st Century*.

JAMES E. NICKUM is based in the Department of Advanced Social and International Studies, University of Tokyo. His most recent publication relating to China's water was *Dam Lies and Other Statistics: Taking the*

Measure of Irrigation in China, 1931–91, published as part of the East-West Center Occasional Papers: Environmental Series (No. 18, January 1995).

MICHAEL PALMER is a professor in the Department of Law, School of Oriental and African Studies, University of London, and director of its Centre for Chinese Studies.

LESTER ROSS is an attorney with the Beijing office of Paul, Weiss, Rifkind, Wharton and Garrison. His practice focuses on foreign direct investment, project finance, private equity, banking and financial services, and environmental law.

VACLAV SMIL is professor of geography at the University of Manitoba. He is the author of several books, including *Cycles of Life: Civilisation and the Biosphere* and *China's Environmental Crisis: An Enquiry into the Limits of National Development.*

BRUCE TREMAYNE is currently director of Pacific Consult Ltd which advises foreign businesses on their approach to Asia-Pacific markets. For the past five years he has been assisting the UK government in promoting the UK's environmental technology and service sector, particularly its exports.

EDUARD B. VERMEER is head of the Research and Documentation Centre for Contemporary China at the Sinological Institute, Leiden University, the Netherlands. His recent publications include *From Peasant to Entrepreneur: Growth and Change in Rural China* (editor and co-author), and *Co-operative and Collective in China's Rural Development* (co-editor and co-author).

PENNY DE WAAL is resident in Beijing with eight years experience working in the environmental sector in China including aid consulting, and providing technical assistance to multinationals and assistance to small- and medium-size enterprises developing environmental business in China.

Studies on China's Environment

The contributions to this Special Issue were first presented as discussion papers for a conference entitled "The Chinese Environment" convened by *The China Quarterly* and held in London at the School of Oriental and African Studies in January 1998. The papers benefited from the input of discussants and guests: Elisabeth Croll, Christopher Howe, and David Norse, and Fran Monks who served as rapporteur. James E. Nickum later wrote a general article on water issues which has enhanced and complemented the conference set. These combined efforts produced a volume which measures the state of the environment and pinpoints the environmental problems that China will face in the first decade of the 21st century.

The factors which determine environmental awareness are multifaceted. Although there are cultural components involved in the development of awareness of ecological degradation, some scholars prefer to emphasize the relationship between changes in environmental values and economic growth. For example, Hishida Kazuo of the Overseas Economic Co-operation Agency has pointed out that guaranteeing water supply seems to be the primary pollution concern in countries with annual GNP per capita of up to US$1,000. Once a society has reached the US$3,000 level, sewerage becomes a consideration, whereas waste disposal does not become a major concern until a GNP per capita US$10,000 level is reached.[1] The fact that water supply, sewerage, and air pollution are major concerns in China today, while solid waste and noise pollution remain secondary, suggests some truth to this universal economic argument.[2]

Such a view might suggest to some that there is nothing special about the Chinese case. However, while places and cultures may share similarities, each is also unique. If we look at the current management of the environment in China we can see clear links to the evolution of the Soviet-inspired communist Chinese state as well as to a traditional Chinese imperial management style. Culturally, the stereotypical idea that the Chinese look after their home environment but ignore the public domain has parallels with their image as family-oriented and disinterested in outsiders.[3]

Today, the post-1978 materialist view is the dominant environmental

1. Quoted in "Japan: China's largest donor," *China Environmental Review*, Vol. 1, No. 3 (1998), p. 11.
2. I have noted elsewhere (R. L. Edmonds, *Patterns of China's Lost Harmony* (London: Routledge, 1994), pp. 228–230) that water pollution was China's first environmental focus due to clear public health concerns and water shortage problems on the North China Plain. This is essentially part of the economic argument. Yet one must remember that water was seen as a crucial agricultural life-giving component in traditional Chinese culture and, with a government which was very seriously concerned with feeding its population in the early years of the People's Republic, agricultural values must have helped put water pollution high on the early pollution agenda in China.
3. One example of this stereotyping can be seen in Frank Ching, "China's attitude to the rest," *Far Eastern Economic Review*, Vol. 161, No. 28 (1998), p. 32.

attitude in China with one legacy from the Maoist era – that nature was seen as something to be conquered.[4] In fact, some authors feel that the materialist attitude towards nature predominated amongst environmental protection bureaucrats into the early 1990s at least.[5]

Despite the fact that the Deng Xiaoping-era leadership blamed some of China's environmental problems on the policies of that earlier period, a realization at the top leadership level that something had to be done to control environmental degradation was already apparent in the early 1970s. This realization is often credited to the personal support of Zhou Enlai, yet this viewpoint remained largely unimplemented in policy. It is fair to say that environmental protection and conservation have continued to have lower priority than political stability and economic growth during the last two decades.

To set the background for an understanding of the environmental issues it faces today, Mark Elvin looks closely at some aspects of the imperial legacy of China's environment in our first article – particularly those concerning the lower Chang (Yangtze) River delta. The main message for those interested in the contemporary period is that environmental problems are not new to China. Asserting that China has pushed its growth beyond sustainable limits on many occasions in the past, he notes that short-term rewards from nature were often sought at the cost of the environment. The result was serious degradation of parts of the Chinese environment prior to the modern era.

Contrary to the opinions of some authors, there has never been a single view of the human relationship to nature in China. For a start, there is today a divergence of opinion between rural and urban areas: urban Chinese are aware of environmental problems and "green" groups have begun to appear in cities in the last few years. Rural Chinese leaders espouse environmental reforms but stress the predominance of economic growth. Wong's and Chan's survey of workers in the environmental protection agencies of Guangzhou, Nanjing and Zhengzhou also indicates that there is not a consensus – even within the environmental protection bureaucracy – as to the relationship between environment and economic growth:

On the one hand, they [environmental protection bureaucrats] saw the need for a new form of co-existence between humans and nature. On the other, they professed that a strong emphasis should be placed on using nature to produce material goods to satisfy people's needs and wants.[6]

4. Rhoads Murphey, "Man and nature in China," *Modern Asian Studies*, Vol. 1 (1967), p. 319.

5. Koon-Kwai Wong and Hon S. Chan, "The environmental awareness of environmental protection bureaucrats in the People's Republic of China," *The Environmentalist*, No. 16 (1996), p. 215.

6. Koon-Kwai Wong and Hon S. Chan, "The environmental awareness," p. 215. For more on the Guangzhou case see Hon S. Chan and Kenneth K. K. Wong, "Environmental attitudes and concerns of the environmental protection bureaucrats in Guangzhou, People's Republic of China: implications for environmental policy implementation," *International Journal of Public Administration*, Vol 17, No. 8 (1994), pp. 1523–1554.

They also point out that the environmental bureaucracy in China is strongly influenced by the national culture, both in its organization and its viewpoint.[7] In her contribution to this volume, Abigail R. Jahiel argues that there are problems of insufficient authority and a lack of co-ordination amongst those involved in environmental protection, while the overall management ethos in China remains one in which sustaining economic growth is more important than sustaining the environment. This is a very timely study as Jahiel is able to comment on the administrative reforms and personnel cutbacks enacted in the spring of 1998. The National Environmental Protection Agency (NEPA) came out of this trimming and reshuffle rather well since it was upgraded to the ministerial level. It remains to be seen whether the overall cuts in China's bureauc-racy will limit the efficiency and impact of the newly-formed State Environmental Protection Administration (sometimes referred to as the State Environmental Protection Agency or SEPA). Jahiel draws attention to the limitations imposed by great regional variations in funding for environmental protection work, also noting the complicated division of responsibilities that sees much of the care for resource degradation and nature conservation placed outside of the hands of the former NEPA. It remains to be seen whether the upgrade of that agency, a rise in environmental concern amongst the top leadership, a heightened profile of environmental issues in Chinese foreign relations, and the appearance of independent domestic environmental organizations can reverse the trend towards further environmental degradation.

For most of the Chinese bureaucracy, the goals of economic growth and environmental protection are not seen as mutually exclusive: econ-omic growth will eventually help to pay for environmental clean up. Thus while a growing number of people in China are aware that science and technology have exasperated ecological problems in many cases, most of the leadership and much of society at large appear to believe that technological fixes can be found for most environmental woes.[8] This belief is likely to remain cemented in the minds of the leadership for some time as technocrats have only recently replaced party elders in some key political positions. One might expect that the younger North Ameri-can-, Western European-, and Japanese-trained technocrats will be more critical of technological fixes and end-of-pipe solutions than their elder Soviet- and Comecon-trained comrades and that their voice will increase if China continues to experience economic growth.

The stress on population control might be seen by some as a counter-point to the argument that environmental concerns remain secondary to economic growth. The famous one-child policy, however, was imple-mented for its potential to raise individual economic prosperity, not because it was thought that China's ecological "carrying capacity" had been exceeded. Today, population control policies are seen as having

---

7. Koon-Kwai Wong and Hon S. Chan, "The environmental awareness," p. 218.
8. This view was described by Tim O'Riordan, *Environmentalism* (London: Psion, 1981), pp. 376–77, as "technocentrism."

multiple benefits – one of which is environmental. The various benefits of population reduction are outlined in Judith Banister's paper. To some degree population control is seen as a way of hedging bets and tiding China over until it has the wealth to purchase and generate technological solutions to environmental problems.

The opinion in China today seems to be pollute first and pay later.[9] As several authors here note, however, China is increasingly placing the environment on its international agenda. A significant new development in this area was the role the environment played in President Bill Clinton's visit to China in July 1998 when a whole discussion session in Guilin was devoted to environmental issues and the U.S. President stated that he would do his best to increase Sino–American technical exchanges in this field.[10] With the change in domestic attitude and international support, we can expect to see China's attempts to clean up the environment gradually improve. Hopefully, the time lag will not mean that the damage done is irreversible.

Regulation plays a crucial role in the enforcement of environmental goals and it can go a long way towards halting China's worsening ecological situation. Michael Palmer's paper traces the evolution of this legal system. Palmer also goes beyond this to look at how environmental legal disputes are resolved, noting that a high proportion are settled outside of the courts. Those that do come to court are largely civil actions. Many governmental bodies have been involved in sorting out problems between provinces and agencies and in bringing cases to court. In conclusion, Palmer warns that the learning of legal traditions from the West is a mixed blessing as it may stunt China's ability to draw upon indigenous environmental protection traditions, stifling the development of local solutions by non-governmental environmental activists. So far, he concludes, the legal system has failed to halt the trend towards environmental degradation.

This discussion about the importance of Western-style "international" relations is amplified in the paper by Lester Ross who demonstrates how China's domestic environmental policy fits within international regimes. China's domestic environmental policy increasingly complies with international accords and China's top officials are cautious about the impact this may have on the country's development. To some degree China is forced into international accords out of fear of isolation. Whatever the case, Ross notes that China has gone from being a passive participant in international accords to taking a leading role in their adoption. The problem in regard to international standards and regulations in China is not their adoption but their implementation and enforcement. In his conclusion, Ross argues for foreign countries to adopt various policies to ensure China continues to strengthen its environmental efforts: sanctions, technical co-operation, cost-sharing, raising Chinese environmental con-

9. A counter-green attitude in China has been growing, especially in the last couple of years, but this remains largely outside popular culture and the power structure.

10. In a similar vein, French President Jospin's visit to China in the summer of 1998 also led to a string of environmentally-related accords.

sciousness to head off possible environmental "free-riding" or "extortion," granting aid for training environmental personnel to raise their status in the Chinese bureaucracy, as well as foreign investment which insists upon environmentally-friendly factories.

Robert F. Ash's and Richard Louis Edmonds' paper looks at concrete aspects of the environment within China – in this case the issues of land reduction and environmental degradation in agriculture since 1978. A regional analysis suggests that the north-east and north-west of China have shown less overall cultivated land loss than the coastal areas. While much new land is being reclaimed for agriculture, it is probably inferior to the land being taken out of cultivation. Under-reporting of farm land, presumably to avoid taxation, tends to be greatest in poorer interior regions where land is generally of inferior quality. Thus the quality and quantity of land actually being used for grain farming is declining. Yet much of the cultivated land reduction appears to concern fields that are being put into other forms of food production such as fish ponds or orchards. Such land uses can be reconverted to grain production and generally lead to less environmental damage than occurs in the conversion of arable land to industry or housing use. To some degree, land losses have been made up for by multiple cropping. These gains, however, have been achieved through increased use of pesticides and herbicides, especially in eastern portions of the country, and a majority of China's arable area is now likely to be suffering from some sort of environmental degradation. Various environmental problems have affected agricultural regions of China to greater and lesser degrees (i.e. erosion seems to be a greater problem away from the richer south-eastern provinces) and acid pollution and climate change are likely to have increasingly negative impacts on Chinese agriculture in the coming century.

James E. Nickum takes a close look at the issue of whether China is or is not facing a water crisis. His answer is "probably not," although he feels that some of the recent concern in the literature is justified. In order to understand the great variety of China's water problems (i.e. some places with too little and others with too much), Nickum regionalizes various water uses – particularly irrigation. His study suggests that irrigation has not been responsible for yield increases since the mid-1970s, which corroborates Ash's and Edmonds' view on the importance of agro-chemicals in recent years. Nickum sees future pressure on irrigation use coming from obsolescence in existing irrigation infrastructure rather than decline of arable area. The other major water use, aside from maintenance of stream flow, is for industry and energy generation. Nickum is cautiously optimistic about China's ability to reduce industrial water use by closing large inefficient factories. Moreover, he does not see increases in domestic use as posing a significant threat to water availability for some time. His suggestions that China's various water management organizations be co-ordinated and water fees be raised to reflect actual costs make good sense, and his conclusion is that China's "water crisis" remains localized (at its worst in Shandong and Shanxi on the

North China Plain) and that the problem is largely economic and institutional rather than one of a vanishing resource.

Liu Changming's paper discusses the proposed solution to deal with shortages in the most water stressed region of China, the North China Plain – the south-north water transfer project. He notes that the environmental costs of moving water from the Chang River valley to the Huang (Yellow) River valley are hard to measure and both regions will feel the impacts of the transfer. The three routes – western, central and eastern – are described. So far both the central and eastern routes have been approved but only the central route appears to be going ahead. Liu feels that many of the potential environmental problems these transfers could cause can be controlled by mechanical and management techniques such as lining the canal channels to reduce seepage and stopping the northward flow if waterflows in the Chang River fall below acceptable levels. He is concerned that wastewater output will rise with the availability of more water in the importing regions. Liu also points out that there is a need for the funding of these projects to be shared between central and local government, insuring that the water importing regions pay their share for construction and water delivery. While generally positive about the project, Liu concludes that north China cannot merely rely on transfers from the south to solve its water shortage problems.

James Harkness' paper traces recent trends in forestry and biodiversity conservation. While the growth of afforestation projects and nature reserves has been tremendous in recent years, adequate funds and personnel have often not been given to the organizations responsible for management of these natural resources. China faces several contradictions in this area. Forests are expected to produce enough revenue to provide a profit as well as pay for their management. This is usually quite difficult, given their depleted state. Nature reserves are often viewed as a drain on local resources rather than as a source of pride, a tourism magnet, or as sites with intrinsic biodiversity value. As a result forests and protected areas often exist merely in name and continue to be exploited in an unsustainable manner – sometimes financial necessity intensifies the level of exploitation. Harkness reiterates the point that while "forested area" appears to be increasing, the stored forest capacity or standing wood volume may actually be falling, both in state and collective forests. Much of the timber being cut, he notes, is primary and secondary growth rather than plantation trees. Harkness concludes that the planned phase-out of logging in natural forests by 2010 could result in the greatest re-orientation of forestry practice in the history of the People's Republic. Yet timber demands are such that China would have to import a considerable amount of forest products to make up for a short-fall and this could have serious environmental implications in other countries. Harkness' answer is for the central government to move away from grand forestry schemes and to create a system for local financial and regulatory support.

While most authors stress the level of change in environmental aspects of China in recent years, Vaclav Smil's article on energy also stresses continuity, in part because China's energy sources are fixed and also because of the long time it takes for a society to change from one energy source to another. The crux of the problem for China is the richness of its coal reserves and the relative poverty of "cleaner" sources of energy. The exception to this is hydropower, which is expensive in terms of dam and reservoir construction as well as in terms of transmission costs due to site concentration in sparsely-populated portions of the south-west. Smil points out that hydropower generation is not without its environmental costs – the most famous but by no means the only controversial project being the Sanxia (Three Gorges) Dam. The health risks associated with coal stem from particulate, sulphur and other forms of air pollution as well as slag generated and hazardous conditions in small mines. Nuclear power is seen by the Chinese as another alternative, but its development has been slower than anticipated and the environmental costs of this process can be enormous. Smil notes the recent improvements in energy efficiencies and calls for more to be done, especially in the small-scale industrial sector and in product design. In his conclusion he argues for increasing energy saving advocating a renewed emphasis on rail transport instead of the move towards automobiles we have seen in recent years.

The pollution generated by industrial production and energy usage is the subject of Eduard B. Vermeer's paper. He points out that while the number of national level environmental protection staff has doubled since the mid-1980s, salaries for workers have not kept pace and the problems facing SEPA today are greater than those facing NEPA a decade ago. Vermeer is pessimistic about the Chinese government's ability to meet its financial investment goals for pollution control and notes that state planners have lost their ability to control pollutants from many small enterprises. He also feels there is a large gap between the ability of the coastal areas and the interior to control pollution. He quotes surveys which suggest that Chinese citizens still are not as likely to complain about pollution as Westerners. While generally pessimistic about China's ability to solve pollution problems in the short run, Vermeer does think rapid economic growth could generate the funds necessary for prevention and clean up.

Judith Banister's paper tackles the tricky questions of the impact of population growth on the environment and the impact of environmental degradation upon China's population. She makes the point that the "economically active population" aged between 15 and 64 will increase dramatically during the coming decade and all this new economic activity itself will generate environmental problems. Although not clearly documented, various national indicators suggest that the health of the average Chinese has been affected by environmental degradation over the past 50 years despite the fact that improvements in infrastructure, public health, and medicine have largely offset the negative impact of degradation. The geography of public health, however, exhibits a tremendous contrast between the wealthy urbanized coastal areas and the poorer rural interior. If the wealth of China increases over the next decade, chronic diseases – in particular cardiovascular disease and tobacco smoking-related illnesses – will be the ailments most likely to cause health problems in the future.

In the closing paper, Bruce Tremayne and Penny de Waal consider the potential opportunities for foreign environmental businesses in China. They point out the problems of investing in an economy in transition and note that further legal, financial, and institutional reforms will be necessary if foreign investment is to become a straight-forward matter. Increasing environmental awareness may facilitate such reforms. As only a small proportion of domestic environmental protection equipment manufactured in China meets state-of-the-art standards, there is considerable room for the import of equipment and skills. Specific sectors for investment are discussed with emphasis on waste management. As with other businesses, foreign corporations need to take a long-term view towards expansion of environmental-related business in China.

In the coming decades environmental issues will play an increasing role in China's economic development drive, internal politics, legal development, international relations and regional development issues. While this Special Issue shows that there is lots of room for optimism, it also indicates that many environmental problems remain intractable and some are worsening. With these points in mind we hope that this Special Issue stimulates those working in other areas to be aware of the growing importance of environmental problems to the land and people of China.

RICHARD LOUIS EDMONDS

The Environmental Legacy of Imperial China

Mark Elvin

Introduction

China's long-term history – social, economic, political, and intellectual – has been interwoven from the start with its environment.[1] In counterposed fashion, the history of the Chinese environment has been entwined with that of anthropogenic forces. The Chinese landscape was one of the most transformed in the pre-modern world as the result of its reshaping for cereal cultivation, re-engineering by hydraulic works for drainage, irrigation and flood-defence, and deforestation for the purposes of clearance and the harvesting of wood for fuel and construction.

Two examples of this interdependence are provided by climate change and microbial diseases, which are cited here simply as illustrations of the point.

Chinese political history was linked, *grosso modo*, with alterations in the mean annual temperature.[2] Each downturn coincided approximately with a crisis. The most obvious examples are the ending of the culture of the Shang and early Zhou in the centuries following about 1050 B.C., the occupation of the North China Plain by non-Han peoples following the break-up of the rule of the successors of the Later Han empire in the early fourth century A.D., the fall of the Northern Song to the Jurchen in the 12th century A.D., and the Manchu conquest in the depths of the "Little Ice Age" in the mid-17th century. In counterpoint, the periods of the Han people's prosperity have tended to coincide with at least relative warming. Thus temperature at the height of the Middle Empire under the Tang was about 1° Celsius above the present, and the mid-Qing economic and demographic expansion of the 18th century was based on a climate relatively warmer than that of the 17th, with improved

1. See M. Elvin, "The environmental history of China: an agenda of ideas," *Asian Studies Review*, Vol. 14, No. 2 (1990), and M. Elvin, "Three thousand years of unsustainable growth: China's environment from archaic times to the present," *East Asian History*, Vol. 6 (1993). There is an overview in R. L. Edmonds, *Patterns of China's Lost Harmony, A Survey of the Country's Environmental Degradation and Protection* (London and New York: Routledge, 1994), ch. 2.

2. Long-term climatic trends are covered in Wu Chen, *Huabei pingyuan siwan nian lai ziran huanjing yanbian* (*Changes in the Natural Environment of the North China Plain During the Last 40,000 Years*) (Beijing: Zhongguo kexue jishu chubanshe, 1992). Wu shows that the dominant pattern of north China's climate in the late Quaternary has been an alternation between periods that are cold + dry and those that are warm + wet. For the historical era see Zhu Kezhen, "Zhongguo jin wuqian nian lai qihou bianqian de chubu yanjiu" ("Preliminary investigations into the changes in China's climate during the last 5,000 years"), *Kaogu xuebao* (*Journal of Archaeology*), No. 1 (1972). The pattern over the last 2,000 years is summarized in a chart in C. Blunden and M. Elvin, *A Cultural Atlas of China* (Oxford: Phaidon, 1983), p. 14.

insolation for rice-plants in the Chang (Yangtze) River valley and the far south.[3]

Turning to micro-organisms, it is evident that disease long limited the area of viable Han settlement. Malaria in much of lowland mainland far south China is an example. Though the danger was reduced by the spread of wet-field rice cultivation, possibly because this increased the exposure to sunlight of the water in which the mosquito larvae bred, even by the end of the imperial age there were places where non-locals could only move around with some safety during certain seasons of the year.[4] The spread of extensive settlement in northern Taiwan after the later 17th century had to contend with "miasma" disease (probably malaria), though it was eventually successful in diminishing it.[5]

On the contrary, some infections were made worse by the effects of settlement or economic development. Wet-field paddy cultivation, especially accompanied by the use of untreated night-soil as a fertilizer, facilitated the transmission of schistosomiasis, a close to incurable helminthic infection: the tailed swimming forms of the worm, released from snails in which they have developed, penetrate the bare feet of labourers, leaving the adult forms in the host's intestinal blood vessels, while passing the eggs out through the faeces to become new larvae, infect snails once more, and renew the cycle.[6]

The last two major epidemics in pre-modern China (whose nature is still to be established) occurred in the late 16th and mid-17th centuries just before the collapse of the Ming dynasty, causing heavy mortality in the densely populated areas of the North China Plain and the lower Chang valley, with a link formed by the Grand Canal.[7] It is not clear why these were the last outbreaks on such a scale, but their non-recurrence suggests an enhanced level of resistance to the disease(s) that may have contributed to the rapid increase in population during the 18th and 19th centuries.

Some diseases were probably also imported as a result of improved communications with the outside world. Syphilis, first reported in China from 1632, is said to have appeared in Guangdong – suggesting an overseas origin – before extending throughout the country.[8] It might be

3. On this last, see Li Bozhong, "Changes in climate, land, and human efforts: the production of wet-field rice in Jiangnan during the Ming and Qing dynasties," and R. B. Marks, "'It never used to snow:' climatic variability and harvest yields in late-imperial south China, 1650–1850," both in M. Elvin and T-J. Liu (eds.), *Sediments of Time: Environment and Society in Chinese History* (New York: Cambridge University Press, 1997).

4. E. Rosner, "'Gewöhnung' an die malaria in chinesischen Quellen des 18 Jahrhunderts" ("'Habituation' to malaria in Chinese sources of the eighteenth century"), *Sudhoffs Archiv*, Vol. 68, No. 1 (1984).

5 T-J. Liu, "Han migration and the settlement of Taiwan: the onset of environmental change," in Elvin and Liu, *Sediments of Time*.

6 G. J. Tortora, B. R. Funke and C. L. Case, *Microbiology. An Introduction* (Redwood City, CA: Benjamin/Cummings, 1989), pp. 568–69. On the present-day situation, see Zhejiang Province Anti-Parasitic Diseases Committee, *Jishengchongbing de fangzhi* (*Prevention and Cure of Parasitic Worm Diseases*) (Shanghai: Renmin chubanshe, 1972), pp. 1–45.

7 H. Dunstan, "The late Ming epidemics: a preliminary survey," *Ch'ing-shih wen-t'i* (now retitled *Late Imperial China*), Vol. 3, No. 3 (1975).

8 Li Ao, *Li Ao quanji* (*Complete Works of Li Ao*) (Taipei: Siji chubanshe, 1980), pp. 115–128.

hypothesized that the relatively "puritanical" nature of the Qing dynasty in sexual matters,[9] like the analogous situation detected by some writers in Europe,[10] was in part connected with the increased severity of micro-biological punishment for "misbehaviour." Slightly later, classic cholera reached south-east China in 1820 from Bengal, spreading up the coast and to some degree inland, with recurrent outbreaks from time to time thereafter.[11]

The incidence of some other diseases prior to effective modern therapy reflected characteristics of the built environment, chiefly of the workplace and residence. Thus the incidence of urban tuberculosis in China during the first half of the 20th century varied principally with the environment of the type of work performed by potential sufferers (not with their class or status as such).[12]

An awareness of environmental factors, of which these are but illustrative examples, is thus essential if we are to make full sense of most of the longer-term patterns of Chinese history.

The Environmental Legacy of the Past

Chinese-style pre-modern hydro-agrarian city-driven economic development was the main source of environmental difficulty and disaster in the historical period. Thus from the fourth to the sixth centuries A.D., when non-Han "barbarians" controlled the valley of the Huang (Yellow) River, and – partly out of deliberate pastoral policy,[13] and partly no doubt out of benign neglect – allowed the natural vegetation cover to re-establish itself, the frequency of hydrological disasters like breaches of the dykes and flooding (which were linked both to up-stream clearances and to hydraulic efforts to control the river downstream) dropped abruptly. The disaster rate rose again, at first gradually, later more rapidly, under the Sui-Tang empire, the Five Kingdoms and the Northern Song.[14]

It is hard for those familiar with the degraded, abraded and polluted developed parts of China at the present day, almost without wild animals or birds, to imagine the world of a millennium-and-a-half ago, when the banks of the Chang were covered as far as the eye could see with forests of sweet-gum trees, the river so clear that fish could be seen swimming along the bottom, the view eastward from the Tai Lake was one of

9. R. van Gulik, *Sexual Life in Ancient China* (Leiden: Brill, 1974; first edition, 1961), pp. 333–34.

10. Notably S. Andreski, "'The syphilitic shock:' puritanism, capitalism and the medical factor," *Encounter*, Vol. 55, No. 4 (1980). Also S. Andreski, "The syphilitic shock: a new explanation of the 'Great Witch Craze' of the 16th and 17th centuries in the light of medicine and psychiatry," *Encounter*, Vol. 58, No. 5 (1982).

11. K. L. MacPherson, "Cholera in China, 1820–1930: an aspect of the internationalization of disease," in Elvin and Liu, *Sediments of Time*.

12. Y. Zhang and M. Elvin, "Environment and tuberculosis in modern China," in Elvin and Liu, *Sediments of Time*.

13. See, in Blunden and Elvin, *A Cultural Atlas of China*, a map showing Toba Wei imperial pasture land, p. 95.

14. The complexities behind this summary formulation are discussed in Elvin, "Three thousand years," pp. 30–32.

hillocks rising from a green haze of water-chestnuts and reeds, the coasts were undyked tidal flats apart from a few salterns, and whales were so frequent on the seas that sailors had to beat drums to frighten them away.[15] By late-imperial times, however, much of the literature is giving expression to a vision of the exhaustion of resources, especially wood and mineral ores, shortages of water, erosion and lands ruined by salinization resulting from inappropriate development. While the picture is mixed, the main variables being the region and the personal perspective of the writer, the bleakness of the environmental descriptions that one sometimes encounters in the age just before modern times can be chilling.[16]

In some areas the local gazetteers allow one to follow the transformation. Thus the people of Jiaxing, in the lower Chang delta, made the transition from a demographically sparse, relatively technologically primitive, but relatively unpressured environmental affluence in Han times to a demographically overloaded, technically sophisticated, competitive, precarious and stressed existence in the late-imperial age, where they faced continual problems from resource shortages. Two thousand years ago the prefecture was reed-covered marshland where wild rice is said to have grown.[17] Cultivated rice was raised by the rough-and-ready method of "ploughing by burning, and weeding by flooding."[18] The other occupations at this time were fishing, hunting, boiling brine for salt and cutting timber in the hills.[19] This last is not mentioned for medieval times or later, which suggests deforestation. Food, including fruits and shellfish, was so abundant that the poor are said to have lived from day to day without keeping reserves.

Under the middle empire, the means of blocking off the sea with sea-walls and creating polders[20] was well advanced, but not technically perfected.[21] The newness of this hydraulic transformation emerges from such comments in the 13th-century gazetteer as that "recently" certain lakes had "all become enclosed fields," but that where more dykes and fields had been built at their edges there was the hazard that "the annual

15. Kitada Hideto, "Tōdai Kōnan no shizen kankō to kaihatsu" ("Natural environment and development in Jiangnan in the Tang dynasty"), in Gotō Akira et al. (eds.), Rekishi ni okeru shizen (Nature in History) (Tokyo: Iwanami, 1989), pp. 143–150.

16. See M. Elvin, "The Bell of Poesy: thoughts on poems as information on late-imperial Chinese environmental history," in S. Carletti, M. Sacchetti and P. Santangelo (eds.), Studi in Onore di Lionello Lanciotti (Napoli: Istituto Universitario Orientale, 1996).

17. Xu Yaoguang et al. revision of Wu Yangxian et al. comp., Jiaxing fuzhi (Jiaxing Prefectural Gazetteer) (Chengwen reprint of 1879 original, Huazhong #53. Taipei: Chengwen, 1970), p. 783 on wild rice; Shan Qing's revision of Xu Shi, comp., Zhiyuan Jiahe zhi (Gazetteer for Jiahe [≈ Jiaxing] in the Zhiyuan Reign-period), reprinted in Zhonghua shuju bianjibu (ed.), Song Yuan fangzhi congkan, 8 volumes (Beijing: Zhonghua shuju, 1990), Vol. 5, pp. 4422–423 for other items in this paragraph. Some of the material on the history of Jiaxing sketched here is drawn from M. Elvin, "Blood and statistics," in H. Zurndorfer (ed.), Chinese Women in the Imperial Past: New Perspectives (Leiden: Brill, 1998).

18. For a discussion of what this may actually have meant, see Watabe Tadayo and Sakurai Yumio (eds.), Chūgoku Kōnan no inasaku bunka (The Rice Culture of Jiangnan in China) (Tokyo: Nihon hōsō shuppan kyōkai, 1984), pp. 1–54.

19. See Gazetteer for Jiahe, p. 4500 on timber-cutting.

20. That is, enclosed land that at some time of the year may lie below the mean level of the water.

21. Gazetteer for Jiahe, pp. 4441–442.

floods are stored in an increasingly constricted space."[22] Keeping channels dredged and locks maintained proved an unending labour.[23] The sea
remained dangerous; every storm left the corpses of the drowned washed
up on the sands.[24]

In Haiyan county – in this same prefecture – there was no natural
source for irrigation water, which had to be drawn from official reservoirs. Ten days without rain could set all the pumps working in the fear
that the rice-fields would dry out.[25] Reeds had to be cultivated as fuel for
brine-boiling, pointing to a shortage of wood. Crops newly mentioned in
medieval times include wheat, beans, hemp and cotton. Apart from the
last, this does not mean that they were not known earlier, simply that they
had become more important. Silk was also now produced.[26]

In late-imperial times, economic, environmental and social stress is
evident everywhere. One probable symptom of this was what might be
called the "degendering of technology,"[27] especially in farming. In particular, women were, or had become, a crucial additional part of the
agricultural workforce.

It was a world of intensive rice-farming, with multiple cropping based
on dryland winter crops. In a good year these latter could provide half the
year's harvest, but the extra cost in labour was draining the paddies as dry
as possible before planting, just as the polder walls had to be rebuilt each
year to stop flooding.[28] The market provided some resilience in the face
of disasters, making it possible, for example, to buy new rice-seedlings if
it was necessary to replant after a flood.[29] In the busy season, it was said,
"women and children toil flat out" at planting wheat and beans, caring for
mulberry trees and building threshing-floors.[30] When water was distant
from the fields, double pumping was used.

The variability of the climate required constant adjustments in the
schedules of planting out and particular types of crops had to be painstak-
ingly matched to local variations in the soil. Applying supplementary
fertilizer to crops while they were growing, a refinement that improved
output, was also a delicate matter with critical timing.[31] The pressure of

22. *Ibid.* p. 4442.
23. *Ibid.* pp. 4444, 4450, 4452, etc.
24. *Ibid.* p. 4597.
25. *Ibid.* pp. 4451–452.
26. *Ibid.* pp. 4453, 4455.
27. Clearly the phenomenon, when it occurred, was multi-causal, and it was not the same everywhere. For example, it is explicitly recorded that women did not take part in the heavier tasks of farming in Zunhua, in the north-east, even at the end of late-imperial times, though they did weed, pick cotton and beans and carry food to the workers in the fields. See He Songtai *et al.* (eds.), *Zunhua tongzhi* (*Comprehensive Gazetteer of Zunhua zhou*) (Zunhua: 1886), *juan* 15, p. 3a. For an interesting overview of this subject, which for the most part takes rather different positions from those adopted here, see F. Bray, *Technology and Gender. Fabrics of Power in Late Imperial China* (Berkeley, Los Angeles, and London: University of California Press, 1996).
28. *Jiaxing Prefectural Gazetteer*, p. 789.
29. *Ibid.* p. 789.
30. *Ibid.* p. 783.
31. *Ibid.* pp. 784–85, 788.

demand on the supply of fertilizers is also evident, both as regards supply and the labour needed to collect them.

Producing silk yarn was primarily women's work,[32] but in areas like Haiyan, where "the land is constricted and people numerous, to the extent that exerting oneself at farming does not yield a sufficiency," rearing silkworms was an "urgent matter" in which men were also involved, mainly in the cultivation of mulberry trees. When the silkworms were feeding, "the men do not wash, and the women do not comb themselves."[33] It was said that if the silkworms failed the sericulturalists might have to sell their children,[34] another indication of the vulnerability of life and livelihood.

This is a cursory sketch of just one local case among literally hundreds, but it seems reasonable to think that late-imperial Jiaxing had become an over-densely settled world subject to social and environmental pressures, and – apart from its market network – without much margin in difficult times. In more recently settled regions such as parts of the south-west, the processes just described had proceeded less far and there were reserves of cultivable but unused land, of forests, and of wild animals, fish and plants that provided an environmental buffer against crises.[35]

With due allowance made for regional differences, we can hypothesize a general pattern of environmentally derived pressures intensifying over the imperial age but to some extent counterbalanced by increased technological ingenuity and improved market networks that allowed greater specialization and some insurance against local disasters – at a price.

The Primary Theoretical Problem

China's impressive pre-modern economic growth will be taken here as familiar.[36] The question that will be focused on is, why was this growth so often pushed beyond the limits of a sustainable and enriching co-existence with the rest of the natural world?

It should be noted at the outset, before looking at the probable causal pattern, that there is no good reason to presuppose any necessary prehistoric balance with nature.[37] The restraint preached by the environmental archaic wisdom found in certain Chinese classical texts is both familiar[38] and in all likelihood commonly misunderstood: it was probably not a

---

32. It was the women who sacrificed to the Goddess of Sericulture. See *ibid.* p. 803.

33. *Ibid.* p. 793.

34. *Ibid.* p. 793.

35. Thus, for example, the small group of Yanghuang people who lived in Guiyang in Guizhou province in Qing times made farming and textile production the basis of their livelihood, but "in their leisure time grasp their weapons and basket-traps for fish and devote themselves to fishing and hunting." *Guiyang fuzhi (Guiyang Prefectural Gazetteer)* (Guiyang: Prefectural Office, 1850), No. 89, p. 25a.

36. See M. Elvin, *The Pattern of the Chinese Past* (Stanford: Stanford University Press, 1973).

37. See M. Ridley, *The Origins of Virtue* (London: Penguin, 1997), ch. 11, although the argument therein is not without flaws.

38. See, for example, Elvin, "Three thousand years," pp. 16–21 on "Powerless wisdom: the ecological economy of archaic China."

symptom of any ancient harmony but, rather, of a rational reaction to an incipient but already visible ecological crisis. Nonetheless, the historical period witnessed a crucial change of tempo.

The hypothesis presented here is that the central driving force of environmental degradation has been the intensified exploitation of nature linked to the drive to acquire the means of political, economic and military power, at state and societal levels, and probably often even at the individual level, but we shall bypass this last. *Ceteris paribus*, the swift and effective short-term tapping of the potential of the natural infrastructure and resources, irrespective of sustainability, plus an analogous exploitation of the military, or quasi-military, force and the economic labour-power provided by subordinated human beings – in the familiar form of the agricultural-urban, literate, socially stratified society – and its pre-modern and modern high-technology derivatives, has proved irresistible, in a techno-cultural Social Darwinian sense, in all but a handful of environmental settings. Collectivities that did not go down this path, either because they did not want to, or did not know how to do so in the time available, either perished or were conquered. It should be noted, to avoid possible misunderstanding, that this argument applies to patterns of behaviour, not to genetically defined groups.

Donald Hughes glimpses something of this when he writes of the ancient west Eurasian classical world that "[a] most damaging aspect of Greek and Roman social organization as it affected the environment was its direction toward war ... Ancient cities and empires were warrior-dominated societies, never at peace for very long ... Non-renewable resources were consumed, and renewable resources exploited faster than was sustainable. As a result, the lands where Western civilization received its formative impulse were gradually drained ..."[39] The point that needs to be added is that this was due to competitive necessity.

Permanent sedentarization, based on farming, developed – by processes that still to some extent elude analysis[40]– into urban civilization with marked social stratification, proved as winning a formula in archaic China as in many other parts of the pre-modern world. The creation of the city, more than any other single change, forced a decoupling between the dominant and decision-making part of the human population, now living increasingly in a "built environment," and the greater part of the rest of natural world. It also required the invention of denaturing social and material structures to moderate and channel the increased rate of social interactions between different members of the population (which is also of course one of the attractions of the city), and, in parallel, techniques

39. J. D. Hughes, *Pan's Travail. Environmental Problems of the Ancient Greeks and Romans* (Baltimore, MD: Johns Hopkins University Press, 1994), pp. 198–99.

40. See, for example, R. Fletcher, *The Limits of Settlement Growth: A Theoretical Outline* (Cambridge: Cambridge University Press, 1995).

and institutions for controlling a larger compact demographic unit than any known before in human evolution.[41]

The scale and savagery of pre-imperial warfare in China is well-known, but it is worth recalling in order to underpin the point just made about competition. The Shang were constantly fighting other states and peoples, mobilizing thousands to some tens of thousands of troops on each occasion for the purpose. Since the population of the Shang at the start of the dynasty has been estimated to have been between 4 and 4.5 million,[42] this would not have been an impossible operation. The Zhou army that defeated the Shang towards the end of the second millennium B.C. had close to 50,000 soldiers. By the Springs and Autumns period, the forces raised by the separate individual states were of the same order of magnitude, and by the time of the Warring States, armies are frequently mentioned as having exceeded 100,000, sometimes several-fold. There were over 480 recorded wars in the 242 years of the Springs and Autumns period, and 590 in the 248 years of the Warring States period that followed.[43] These figures for the size of armies, huge by the standards of the archaic world, have understandably occasioned scepticism, but reference in the sources are numerous and broadly internally consistent. Irrespective of the precise magnitude of the armed forces involved, the economic strain and the continual military competition of this war-dominated human universe is not in question.

Chinese settlements acquired moats in the Yangshao period, probably mainly for defence against animals, since storage areas at this time could be outside the moat; walls followed in the Longshan period, presumably for protection against other people.[44] The *Record of the Rituals* (*Liji*) says of this period when the "Great Way had already fallen into obscurity" that "inner and outer walled cities and moats provided security; ritual behaviour and public-spirited principles provided discipline ... Thus whatever was advantageous was put into effect, but from this warfare came into existence."[45] Walls were of rammed earth, sometimes multiple, with substantial areas of non-urban land within them. A fairly standard urban spatial pattern developed under the Shang, with graves, and workshops for bone, ceramics and metal wares, for example, being just outside the defended area. Military control was based on each central city – above all, the principal capital – being surrounded by a network of satellite cities, and the development of "secondary capitals." [46]

The *Scripture of Songs* (*Shijing*) tells how Gong Liu, progenitor of the

41. Fletcher, *Settlement Growth*. On Shang urban drainage, see Song Zhenhao, *Xia Shang shehui shenghuo shi* (*A History of Social Life under the Xia and Shang Dynasties*) (Beijing: Zhongguo shehui kexue chubanshe, 1994), p. 26.

42. Song Zhenhao, *ibid.* p. 107.

43. Xu Jinxiong, *Zhongguo gudai shehui* (*Society in Ancient China*) (Taipei: Taiwan shangwu, 1988), pp. 408–411.

44. Yang Kuan, *Zhongguo gudai ducheng zhidu shi yanjiu* (*Researches in the History of the Systems of the Capital Cities of Chinese Antiquity*) (Shanghai: Shanghai guji chubanshe, 1993), pp. 10, 13, 16–17.

45. *Liji* (*Records of Ritual Behaviour*), "Li yun" (≈ "The evolution of ritual behaviour").

46. Yang Kuan, *Capital Cities*, pp. 19, 20, 23–25, 31–39. See also K-C. Chang, *Shang Civilization* (New Haven, CT: Yale University Press, 1980), pp. 134, 158–161, 268.

Zhou lineage, "mounted the southern ridge, discovering there [the site for] the Capital," and how "the farmed lands for the military cantonments of the Capital at the appropriate time spread everywhere." Furthermore, "his armies had three divisions, [so] he measured the wetlands and the uplands, and had the land share-cultivated to provide his tax-revenue in grain."[47] Nine generations later, Gong Tanfu, founder of the Zhou royal house, moved his capital to Zhouyuan, where "a hundred walls all rose up."[48] Though proof is for the moment unattainable, the driving force behind the agrarian-urban transformation seems to have been primarily military effectiveness. As the *Songs* say of Tanfu's city: "He raised the grand Earth-Altar whence the great armies marched forth."[49]

The multiplicity of walls spoken of by the *Songs* probably refers to internal walls around palaces and urban subdivisions. The Chinese city during the first two millennia of its existence was a cellular structure under tight control; only a few favoured mansions of the great opened directly onto the main thoroughfares, ordinary residences being confined within walled enclaves – the quarters – that were in effect culs-de-sac. During the first part of the imperial age that followed, locational subdivision by status and occupation seems to have been intensified and strict urban policing maintained. Life within the walls also ran to a time-schedule, including a ban on most movements around the city at night. Market areas, as is well known, had a monopoly of permitted trading and were walled and officially controlled during the early and middle empires up to the Tang.[50]

It seems possible that there was a political reaction against an over-concentration of population in some of the large cities in the early imperial age. For its technical level, parts of China at this time may actually have been over-urbanized.[51] The control system seems to have been in place long before the imperial age, though there is no way at the moment of saying from how early. He Xiu, a commentator of the second century A.D., noted of the *Gongyang zhuan* with reference to the 15th year of Duke Xuan [593 B.C.], that

in the spring and the summer the people went out to the fields. In the autumn and winter they went in to defend the inner and outer cities. In the seasons of agricultural work, the fathers and elders and chiefs of the urban quarters would open the gates at dawn, and sit at the surveillance posts. Those who left later than the proper time would not be allowed to leave; in the evening, those not holding a *qiao* [tally??] would not be allowed to come back in.[52]

---

47. Text from B. Karlgren, *The Book of Odes* (Stockholm: Museum of Far Eastern Antiquities; 1950), pp. 207–208 (Gong Liu); tr. M. Elvin.

48. Karlgren, *Odes*, p. 190 (Mian).

49. *Ibid.* p. 190 (Mian).

50. Yang Kuan, *Capital Cities*, pp. 209–211, 219, 224–26, 232.

51. Xiao Guojun, *Chunqiu zhi Qin Han zhi dushi fazhan (The Development of Cities from the Springs and Autumns Period to the Qin and Han)* (Taipei: Taiwan shangwu, 1984), pp. 251–54.

52. Cited in Yang Kuan, *Capital Cities*, p. 242, n. 2.

This provides a preliminary sketch of what early urban-agrarian life may have been like, though we could wish for more detail.

What seems clear is the association of agricultural development with the provision of the sinews of war. Thus the surveying of fields, pastures and water-channels, as well as fiscal planning was entrusted to the Minister of War in the state of Chu in the sixth century B.C., who calculated "the numbers of chariots to be supplied, and made a register of the horses, and determined the quotas of soldiers mounted in chariots and on foot, the numbers of [suits of] body-armour and of shields."[53] It was presumably in order to increase the flow of taxes and conscripts that the *realpolitik* theorists of the late pre-imperial age insisted on sedentarizing those who lived off the "mountains and marshes" by restricting access to these areas. As the *Book of the Lord of Shang* (*Shangjun shu*) said: "If they have nowhere to find something to eat, they will be obliged to engage in the cultivation of the fields."[54]

The linkage between hydraulic schemes and military logistics, both the supply of food and its cheap transport by water, was a commonplace in official thinking during the first millennium A.D.[55] In a somewhat analogous fashion, the social power of families and individuals was both partly founded on and partly reflected by the successful competitive appropriation and development of natural resources.

The Chinese search for power – both by the state and individual – was based, until very recent times, primarily upon an almost unending transformation of the lowland landscape to adapt it to an intensive agriculture, making use of hydraulic technology in the form of flood control, drainage, irrigation and seawalls to stabilize production in the face of irregularities in the weather, both seasonal and between years.[56] The huge and ever-rising levees along the lower course of the Huang River (until it broke them), and the creation of Jiangnan, a sort of "Chinese Netherlands," out of the alluvial mudflats and reed-covered salt-marshes at the mouth of the Chang River in Tang and Song times, are two of the most familiar examples of this process at work.[57] It has been the pay-off in power accruing to the "exploitation" of the environment at a rate overstressing its natural resilience and exceeding its capacity for self-renewal within a humanly relevant time-frame that has in the last analysis made

53. Discussed in Elvin, "Three thousand years," pp. 17–18.
54. *Ibid.* pp. 18–19.
55. For a famous example, see Chen Shou (ed.), *San guo zhi* (*Record of the Three Kingdoms*) (Beijing: Zhonghua shuju, 1969), "Wei shu," *juan* 28, pp. 775–76. This passage is also discussed in Sakuma Kichiya, *Gi Shin Nanboku-chō suiri-shi kenkyū* (*A Study of the History of Water Control under the Wei, the Jin and the Northern and Southern Dynasties*) (Kaimei shoin, 1980), pp. 13–14, and in Elvin, "Three thousand years," p. 24.
56. For an introduction to the complexities that lie behind these generalizations, see M. Elvin, "Introduction," in M. Elvin, H. Nishioka, K. Tamura and J. Kwek, *Japanese Studies on the History of Water Control in China. A Selected Bibliography* (Canberra and Tokyo: Institute of Advanced Studies, Australian National University, and Centre for East Asian Cultural Studies for UNESCO, 1994).
57. On the Huang River, see Elvin, "Three thousand years," and on Jiangnan, see Shiba Yoshinobu, *Sōdai Kōnan keizai shi no kenkyū* (*Researches on the Economic History of Jiangnan*) (Tokyo: Tōyō bunka kenkyūjo, 1988).

the process hard to restrain by conscious action, even when there has been a fairly widespread appreciation of its damaging effects.

It would be beyond the scale of this survey to pursue the details of the basic idea put forward here through the complete span of Chinese imperial history. It is, however, easy to find examples of the interlocking of economic development and the need of the state to enhance its military and other forms of power in later times, most commonly in frontier zones. Here, simply by way of illustration, is a characteristic example from the north-west in the second half of the 16th century, recorded by Liu Minkuan, the deputy military commissioner for Xining, on a stele, and describing the achievements of Tian Le when he was the military commander in charge of this region:[58]

Because of the peace negotiations in the past, the frontiers had long been in a slack state of preparedness. The northern frontier was repeatedly in difficulty with regard to transportation for the military, [the goods] for the most part deteriorating in transit. H. E. Tian [when governor of Gansu] pacified the five commanderies [of the Songshan region], stored up supplies and simplified and sharpened up [the system], apportioning out the matériel for the regular and auxiliary cavalrymen and foot-soldiers. There was no waste in the salt administration or in the [running of the] military colony lands.

Armour, spears, arrowheads, cannons, and swords are the means of attack and defence, but they are all matters that depend on metallurgy. Every year the province of Shaanxi supplied Ganzhou with more than 100,900 catties of wrought iron for military requirements; and every year Fengxiang supplied Xining with more than 7,500 catties of wrought iron. If there was a shortfall, then emissaries were sent to buy more east of the passes [that is, in Henan]. This was a journey of several thousands of *li* and took months or even years. Money was wasted on nothing more than travel and transport, and [doing this] was even so of no use in emergencies.

H. E. Tian therefore prepared plans with his senior subordinates, and had searches conducted everywhere in the mountains and scrublands [for ores]. He also requisitioned foundry-workers from Shaanxi and Shanxi who were capable of smelting metal and assisting in the [planned] operation.

I myself did not merely talk about this matter, but had already mobilized some soldiers and they had located ore at the foot of the Northern Mountains in Xiamuquan, in other words the present-day Five Peaks. [Ore] had in fact previously been obtained from the Great Defile, but the smelting workers told us that the Northern Mountain [seams] were wider and harder, much easier to work than those at the Great Defile. In these mountains the crystal clear rocks[59] were piled up in countless quantity. A few *li* away the mountain trees grew in profusion, providing fuel for burning [charcoal].[60] According to their report, it was possible to smelt iron [here].

58. In Qinghai sheng min wei shaoshu minzu guji zhengli guihua bangongshi (ed.), *Qinghai difang jiuzhi wuzhong (Five Old Local Gazetteers from Qinghai)* (Xining: Qinghai renmin chubanshe, 1989), pp. 627–28.
59. Haematite, the principal source of iron, has "glittering mirror-like surfaces" when well-crystallized. See A. Hallam *et al.* (eds.), *Planet Earth* (Oxford: Elsevier-Phaidon, 1977), p. 130 (and photograph).
60. Coke, or "charcoal coal," was also sometimes used for smelting iron ore in the north-west. See *Five Old Local Gazetteers*, p. 581.

I went in person to appraise the situation, after which I established a government office of six columns' width below the Northern Mountains, with two furnaces to smelt iron, barracks quarters of 50 units of space in extent, a signal beacon straddling the summit, with a beacon-lodge of four columns' width, surrounding this last with a wall and a moat in readiness for emergencies. His Excellency selected four hundred foot-soldiers from the various companies at Xining to supply the labour for the task of ramming down the earth [walls], picking Commander Lu Zhongai to lead the work to a successful conclusion. As before, personnel were chosen to become practised in this craft, and the order further given that, just as is recounted in the "Officials of the Zhou" [*Zhou guan*, the quasi-scriptural *Rituals of the Zhou*], they should draw maps by surveying and make them available. Both those to do forging and those to gather [fuel] were chosen. It was a scheme designed to last for a long time.

There are five advantages from this undertaking. The first is that in Hexi [the region west of the Huang River], the region where the wars are conducted, [iron] smelted in the morning can be put to use the same evening, being taken from an inexhaustible source. The second is that, since the toil of transporting [iron] for several thousands of *li* no longer exists, the commoner-civilians have obtained a respite. The third is immediate availability, with no delays of months and years. The fourth is that labour is provided by soldiers who would otherwise be eating in idleness; the charcoal and ore are taken from mountain forests not subject to official prohibitions [on felling], so that the village communities are not disturbed or the authorities bothered by demands for funds. The fifth is that the five commanderies supply the materials for their own needs, so that the neighbouring commanderies can stop supplying their quotas, and requirements for stores and weapons are made ready at a reduced price.

What is more, those [barbarians] within [our frontiers][61] have repeatedly been given a bloody nose in recent times by our forces, and have been sticking out their tongues in astonishment, speaking of "an iron wall!" When they now further hear that we are smelting iron here, won't they be inclined to behave themselves?

With his sturdy armour and keen-edged blades, like a blazing fire swiftly seizing its chances, as if about to stride across the Kunlun mountains or set the Qinghai's waters boiling, establishing benefits for countless generations without end, His Excellency may indeed be accounted loyal to Our Dynasty! ...

The links between military power, economic development and pressure on resources are illustrated by the above with a paradigmatic clarity.

Derivative Effects

Usually, of course, the effects were much less direct and invisible. As time went on, agrarian-urban economic growth also acquired more and more of its own logic and momentum, as the cascade effects of techno-logical and organizational innovations (like credit, and so on) prompting further such innovations became the most obvious driving forces unless inhibited in one way or another, as by the late-imperial "high-level equilibrium trap"[62] or the growing scarcity of technically accessible resources. What follows below is discussion of a possible effect that has

61. The stele text has a gap of a character at this point.
62. See Elvin, *Pattern of the Chinese Past*, pp. 312–15; M. Elvin, *Another History*, chs. 2 and 3 (for exceptions).

not, so far as I know, been identified before – that which might be labelled "the cash-in imperative." The basic idea is that the intensification of a market-orientated economy creates pressures to cash in natural resources at a faster rate. This can be illustrated by the case of forests.

By the end of the imperial period the residues of the forests that had once covered a great part of China were under pressures whose severity made their further survival, let alone self-renewal, problematic. The various factors typically at work in many localities may be illustrated from the section on "woods" in the 1909 gazetteer for Dan'ger subprefecture (later called Huangyuan county under the Republic), in Xining prefecture in Gansu, near the headwaters of the Huang River.[63] This was basically a pastoral region, and was probably never that heavily forested, at least in late-imperial times. The gazetteer section translated below makes plain the sparse distribution of the woods, their restricted extent, the small size of most trees, the degree to which forests' preservation depended on special factors such as public ownership, or monastic ownership, or the sacred nature of the groves, as well as the importance of a continuous, active silviculture and the difficulties in protecting growing trees from theft. Last, but not least, timber was a commercially valuable property. The *Domesday Book*-style accounting in this section – the listing of woods given here being nominally (though not actually) complete – is a reminder that, subject to the problem of getting accurate figures (on which more later), the meagre reserves of timber other than willow listed below had to meet the needs of a sub-prefectural population of at least 16,000 Han-Chinese people (besides some Tibetans and Mongols) as of 1890. The implications of many of the comments are worth close consideration, and key points have been italicized.[64]

Xiangher Wood ... On the mountain slopes south of the Huang River, from the base to the summit. It occupies about 40 *mu*. The trees range from 10 to over 20 feet in height, with trunk diameters of from 5 to 6 inches up to 8 to 9 inches.[65] These are the largest of the forest trees in the mountain passes, and consist solely of birches; *little of the material is suitable for* [making] *carts* [or barrows]. On the slopes to the east there is another wood, of somewhat more than 10 *mu*. Although the trees here are not large, they are dense and of an equal height. *It is apparent how well they flourish when the right methods are used to cultivate and protect them.* Both of these woods are *the public collective property* of the Xiangher village, and are cut and sold by the people of the community to provide for public purposes. Private persons are not permitted to take [trees] from them.

Ahadiu Wood ... In the curve of the mountains south of Ahadiu village. From the bottom of the mountain to the watershed it occupies more than 200 *mu*. The trees are over 10 feet tall, with trunk diameters from 1 to 2 inches up to 4 to 5 inches, with

---

63. *Five Old Local Gazetteers*, pp. 235–37. Note the "Huang" here was not the "Yellow" River. The Chinese character is a homophone but not a homograph.

64. *Five Old Local Gazetteers*, pp. 237–240. The figures seem to be doubtful. In addition to Han-Chinese there were Tibetans and Mongols.

65. Chinese "feet" and "inches." Conversion ratios varied locally, but were near enough to allow the terms to be left unadjusted here, since no guide to an exact local equivalent is available.

a sparse and not very flourishing distribution. There are both birches and poplars. To the south-east ... there is another wood of perhaps 40 *mu*, rather more thickly set but with trees of no great height. Both of these woods are owned by farming families in the neighbourhood; but even by making use of the strength of several households to safeguard their growth, *it has not proved possible to stop throngs of thieves coming in repeatedly.* In the area near the south mountain the ground is entirely sprouts and stumps on account of the difficulty of protecting it, and woods here are particularly few in number.

Qubutan Grove ... Occupies rather more than 10 *mu*. The wood is very densely set, and the trees likewise fairly large ... There is a small temple in the middle. *The elders of Qubutan village revere this grove as being of sacred trees,* and do not dare to collect the branches and twigs. Tradition has it that anyone felling a tree will meet with a supernatural calamity. They therefore keep a respectful watch over it ...

Lamole Wood ... Occupies about 200 *mu*. Of intermingling pines and birches. Although there are some large trees, it is not very dense. *This wood is the property of the Buddhist monks of the Dongke Temple,* and they have forbidden thieving and unauthorized felling. *For this reason it spreads about in luxuriant growth* ...

Yaoshui Gorge Grove: On the shaded slope of the Yaoshui Gorge mountains ... Discontinuous and not very dense. In recent years the temple monks have begun to propose that it be protected, this being because the timber can be encompassed in the span of one's hands and there are no large pieces. The trees are birch, and it will still be several decades before there is [usable] timber from a mature stand.

Dongke Temple South Mountain Wood: Covers about 200 *mu*. Pines and birches. Numerous large trees, especially pines. Diameters run up to more than 2 feet, with not a single horizontally growing branch broken off from bottom to top. For this reason they are twisted and swollen, coarse and knotted everywhere, so that the timber is, on the contrary, not of good quality. *The monks consider that trees before a temple are a means of showing reverence for the Buddha,* and for this reason since the time the temple was built until the present, *they have never cut one down.* The luxuriance of the growth is exceptional. Tibetan monks like cultivating woods, and since this one is near the temple, it is particularly easy for them to cultivate it.

Zhacang Temple Grove ... Rather more than a thousand pines, both large and small, and birch trees all told. Gathering [fallen branches] and felling is likewise forbidden. *The property of the Buddhist monks of the Zhacang Temple.* Nearby to the south-west ... are several tens of small cypresses *with no-one to tend them, which makes it hard to hope that they will grow into a mature wood.*

Willows on the Molin River: Spontaneously growing trees are very numerous in the floodplain of the Huang River and along its banks. *Once those near the watermills were protected by the people [there] they have been able to form a mature wood.* They are however only from 8 to 9 feet in height up to a little over 10 feet. The branches and twigs are luxuriant, affording a green shade that covers the ground ... They are not much use for timber. Branches are at times gathered from them and woven into large baskets to be filled with stones [as gabions] to serve as defence against floods ... Within the subprefecture over a hundred *mu* of land in all are occupied [by watermills] and trees of this sort are owned by the proprietors of the watermills in various places.

Planted willows: These are either along the dykes or the sides of the roads, or else beside fields and gardens ... There are plantings every year. The total of old and new, large and small, is at a casual estimate 400,000 to 500,000 trees. About 30 per cent of newly planted trees will find it difficult to stay alive; and approximately a further 50 per cent who have achieved a reduced span of life will not attain [a condition in which they are] fit for use as timber. Large trees with trunks whose diameters range from 5 to 6 inches up to a foot and some inches will only amount to 20 per cent. The general explanation for this state of affairs is that it is necessary for the trees planted by well-to-do families to wait until they have grown large before they are fit to be timber. *Those that do not wait to grow large but are cut down and sold to be beams for houses can fetch a mere 2 or 3 qian [tenths of an ounce of silver] for each one. This has* [even so] *caused large trees to be ever fewer in number.* Even though replacements are planted year after year, it is hard to have any hope that there will be woods of a flourishing appearance. These trees all belong to the common people.

Officially owned woods ... The sub-prefect of Dan'ger, Zhang Tingwu, contributed funds in 1907 for these to be planted. The two locations [concerned] have more than 10,000 trees all together, and they are already emerging as saplings. If it desired, however, that they stay alive and mature, there will have to be supplementary planting. There were no official trees in Dan'ger in times past; there have only started in the present day ... *If in the future these official trees are not safeguarded in a variety of ways ... they will gradually become fewer until finally none are left.*

Since the Qing-dynasty *mu* – the unit in which areas were recorded – was about 0.067 of a hectare, there were on the face of it about 47 hectares of forest, not all of them accessible for use, plus half a million willow trees, some pines and some saplings. Not counting the trees planted around farmers' fields, which may have been numerous and were not included, this was equivalent to about 0.003 of a hectare of trees, basically pines and birches, plus 31 willows, per person. Since, apart from large pine beams imported for the temples, Dan'ger is said to have met its own needs in timber, and these ran to several thousands of trees per year, it is clear that the listing is in fact far from complete. According to a note in the gazetteer, the people are said to have been so concerned that a tax per trunk would be imposed following an official survey, that they wanted to uproot all newly planted trees. As a result only a very limited percentage of the trees were reported, and the true figure for the area of woodland is unknowable. What has to be taken seriously is the desperate anxiety about the supply of wood, and its quantity and quality. Present-day China's problems with timber[66] had already become evident, in certain areas at least, by the eve of the modern era.

The critical problem would seem to be that once the rate of depletion, driven by perceived economic need, exceeds the rate at which stocks can renew themselves either solely "naturally" or with the help of an afford-able silviculture, the pressure to harvest immature trees starts a downward spiral (toward taking ever less mature specimens) that tends to be self-reinforcing, and perhaps ultimately breaks the continuity of an economically sustainable silvicultural production process, because of the long time-lags inherent in the biological nature of most trees. (Clearly, trees grown beside fields simply as by-products might to some extent

66. Discussed, for example, by S. D. Richardson, *Forests and Forestry in China. Changing Patterns of Resource Development* (Washington, DC, and Covelo, CA: Island Press, 1990).

escape from this trap, though still vulnerable to predation.) At the same time the higher prices for timber, though increasing producers' returns for material of a given quality, also make selling immature lower quality wood more economically acceptable, and, paradoxically, may further put up producers' costs in several ways: the cost of protecting growing trees against theft, prompted by greater economic rewards for crime, goes up, for example. The same is true for the costs of the prolongation of the time during which the crop is exposed to other risks (certainly including fire and perhaps not excluding the possible government imposition of levies), rather than being cashed in.

Since trees don't grow exponentially for long, once economic development has made it possible to invest the income securely at a given rate of compound interest, income will be foregone by deferring cutting after a certain moment. This moment depends on the pattern created over the years by the time-varying rate at which a tree of a particular species produces marketable timber, and on the interest rate. Thus, in over-simple terms, given a constant price per cubic metre, if cubic metres of saleable timber grown by a tree at the end of the first, second, third, fourth and fifth decade are respectively zero, five, 25, 40, 50, and the interest rate on money deposited is 10 per cent a year, it can be calculated that it pays to cut at the end of the third decade and invest the proceeds of the sale, rather than wait any longer. Although the quotation above is no more than an illustration for one place at one time, it suggests that an analysis of this sort is at least *a priori* a plausible one.

Thus, if the real rate of economic growth had risen in Dan'ger over time, perhaps because it had been little by little linked more closely to the main Chinese market economy,[67] the time-discount rate would probably have risen, increasing the value of timber at the present moment relative to that of the same timber kept in a more or less constant, or only slightly increased, quantity at some given point in the future.[68] Thus growth *in and of itself* can create a certain pressure to "cash in" resources, such as slow-maturing trees, as well as in other obvious indirect ways.

67. The Dan'ger mercantile economy was thought of as fairly conservative in the late 19th century, but putting money with merchants on deposit at interest was a standard practice. See, for example, *Five Old Local Gazetteers*, p. 351, and for background pp. 287–88.

68. The basic elements of this idea may be summed up in simplified form as follows. In an economy with markets and with banks that take deposits at interest, a resource R turned into cash of $\$x$ and deposited for n years at $r\%$ annual compound interest will yield a total of $\$x(1 + r/100)^n$ at the end of this period. Thus $\$100$ deposited for 10 years at 10% yields about $\$259$. This mechanism allows a comparison of values across time. It is also obvious that, in the example given, leaving R unconverted to cash on deposit creates a loss of $\$159$ in income foregone. If, however, $r = 0$, and if R is not subject to decay or increase, and the (real) exchange value of R in the market remains constant across time at the initial $\$x$, then there is no necessary loss over time. What enables the bank to pay interest at $r > 0$ is that it can lend the $\$x$ deposited with it to a business at a rate of $r + r'$ (r' positive), and that this business can (in general) utilize the $\$x$ to create a profit $p > r + r'$. In other words, the economy has to be growing. This is why growth *in and of itself* can create a pressure to "cash in" resources, such as slow-maturing trees.

Other Long-term Causes of Environmental Deterioration

Several other types of causes bear directly on decisions that affect the environment. The most obvious is ignorance of the results of human action. There are some areas where only an intuition at best could have existed about the true state of affairs in pre-modern times in China. The most obvious example is the nature of microbes, both helpful and pathogenic, though medieval Chinese were well aware that the largest cities tended to be sinks of disease,[69] and at least one late-imperial doctor came close to the microbial theory of infectious disease.[70] Another is the importance of preserving biological diversity as a sort of insurance of the resilience in the ecosystem when the latter is under strain.[71] A final, necessarily more speculative, instance is the so-called "biophilia hypothesis," the idea that humans, having evolved in close interaction with animals and plants, need this interaction to remain in some sense perceptually, spiritually and emotionally "fit."[72]

On the whole, though, a substantial number of Chinese had a fairly good idea of the disadvantages as well as the advantages of pre-modern economic development, though needless to say there were disagreements. In the Qing dynasty, Cheng Yaotian thought that the great Han-dynasty historian Sima Qian had already denounced the deleterious effects of hydraulic engineering, which is open to debate; but Cheng himself was unequivocal that "when the beneficial use of water is promoted ... disasters caused by flooding become increasingly fierce."[73] As far back as the third century A.D. Du Yu was already arguing against what he saw as the over-extension of reservoir barrages, which frequently broke and damaged fields, pastures and stands of trees – so Cheng's views on Sima Qian are not necessarily anachronistic.[74]

More important perhaps are the various ways in which aspects of pre-modern economic development increasingly separated the decisions to undertake certain types of action from the practical necessity of living,

---

69. One of the "riches" of the Tang capital Chang'an was said (in the tenth century) to be "illnesses." See Kitada Hideto, "Natural environment and development in Jiangnan in the Tang dynasty," p. 141. Cao Shuji, "Dili huanjing yu Song Yuan shidai de chuanranbing" ("Geographical environment and infectious diseases in the Song Yuan period"), *Lishi dili (Historical Geography)*, Vol. 12, p. 184, cites the *Songshi (History of the Song)* biography of Su Shi, *juan* 338: "Hangzhou, being the meeting-place of land and water [routes] constantly has more people dying of epidemics than other places."

70. Wu Youxing. See Dunstan, "The late Ming epidemics."

71. See B. Gustafsson, "Nature and economy," in M. Teich, R. Porter and B. Gustafsson (eds.), *Nature and Society in Historical Context* (Cambridge: Cambridge University Press, 1997), p. 358, and, for more detailed examination of the issue, C. Perrings, K-G Mäler, C. Folke, C. S. Holling and B-O. Jansson (eds.), *Biodiversity Loss: Economic and Ecological Issues* (Cambridge: Cambridge University Press, 1995).

72. See S. R. Kellert and E. O. Wilson (eds.), *The Biophilia Hypothesis* (Washington, DC: Island Press, 1993).

73. See M. Elvin and Su Ninghu, "Engineering the sea: hydraulic systems and pre-modern technological lock-in in the Hangzhen Bay area, circa 1000–1800," in Itō Suntarō and Yasuda Yoshinori (eds.), *Nature and Humankind in the Age of Environmental Crisis* (Kyoto: International Research Centre for Japanese Studies, 1995), p. 86.

74. See the discussion in Elvin, "Three thousand years," p. 45.

or living immediately, with the environmental consequences of these actions. This kind of separation can be in time: the full effect of forest clearance or overcutting, for example, may take generations to make itself felt. It may be in space: cities may import the timber they need from hundreds of miles away, unpenalized until prices rise, except relatively indirectly, by the damage resulting from the stripping. It may, more subtly, be a disjunction between what might be called separate "units of account." Thus the state (one "unit of account"), needing large timbers in a hurry for building ships to fight piracy, might order the cutting of huge trees that a monastery (another unit of account) owned, had preserved, and – perhaps aware of their ability to stabilize the soil and retain water – would otherwise have continued to preserve.[75] This sort of separation between units of account is familiar in modern times in the disjunction that sometimes occurs between a private firm that pollutes and a state authority that has to clean up, using taxpayers' money to do so.

The nature of property regimes has also had a major bearing on the nature of economic decisions with environmental consequences. The state, and collective institutions like monasteries and some large kin-groups, have tended on the whole to have much longer time horizons (or much lower present-future discount rates) than individuals and their immediate families. The long-term trend towards the privatization of non-farm property in China during the imperial period was closely associated with more rapid clearance and exploitation of forests and the related use of other non-farm resources.[76] In late-imperial times much of the forest that did survive in China was in fact that protected by "state prohibitions" or under some form of religious or kinship-based collectivity.[77]

The city was, and is, the epitome of most of these sorts of separation. Donald Hughes has suggestively observed of ancient Mesopotamia that "[i]t is as if the barrier of city walls and the rectilinear pattern of canals had divided human beings from wild nature and substituted an attitude of confrontation for the earlier feeling of co-operation ... [L]itera-ture ... often use[s] the image of battle to describe the new relationship with nature."[78] In his view most ancient cities in western Eurasia "placed too great a demand on available resources, depleted them within their sphere, and then went as far as they could to gain access to additional resources, until this effort also failed," leading to their eventual decline.[79]

Keeping the economic landscape in good order, a sort of housekeeping of the terrain, was a constant preoccupation among local officials and

75. For an example, see N. Menzies, "Forestry", section 42b, in J. Needham, *Science and Civilisation in China*, Vol. VI, No. 3 (Cambridge: Cambridge University Press, 1996), p. 661.

76. Examples are given in Elvin, "Three thousand years," pp. 25–29.

77. See *ibid.* on the traveller Xu Xiake; on Xu see also R. E. Strassberg, *Inscribed Landscapes. Travel Writing from Imperial China* (Berkeley: University of California Press, 1994), pp. 317–19.

78. Hughes, *Pan's Travail*, p. 33. Ancient Egypt was less confrontational.

79. *Ibid.* p. 168.

members of the gentry in late-imperial China. This obsession is well illustrated in the compendium called the *Complete Documents Relating to the "Summary of Regulations for Managing the Countryside"* (*Jing ye gui lüe quanshu*), mostly written by Liu Guangfu in 1603 for the Zhejiang county of Zhuji, where he was magistrate. It was reprinted in 1727, 1801, 1813 and 1865, and contains regulations for the management of the hydraulic installations designed to tame the alternate flooding and running dry of the Puyang River in its constricted mountain valley. Since these technical and organizational provisions have already been studied by Morita Akira,[80] the discussion here is limited to commenting on some of the prefaces that convey the attitude of mind that governed the actions of Liu and his successors. Here are his own words on what he saw himself as having done:[81]

The people of Zhuji rely entirely on their fields for a living, but half of these are in low-lying marshland. Though the soil of the high-lying fields is stony, these only suffer from drought once or twice every ten years. In places where dates, millet, tea, bamboo sprouts, hemp, wheat, silk and cotton are produced, the mountain folk can still obtain succour from all of these, so that crises are few in number, and they can avoid death for the time being. As for low-lying fields, [however,]they have to be concerned with the Wan [Puyang] River! The upper reaches come surging down in one knows not how many hundreds and thousands of tributaries with only a single belt [of river] to receive them and to discharge them below as through a throat. At the end of a morning of sudden rains, moreover, a hundred *li* will have become pools. Not two or three years out of every ten are free from disaster. There is no year in which the people of Zhuji are not anxious about floods. What is more, once they have been inundated, they have no hovels in which to live and a countryside empty of food, being placed amidst [overflowing] channels and pools on all sides. Every time they see an enclosure-dyke broken, the tragic cries of old and young continue day and night. How can those who govern the people endure to hear this, and watch it without lifting a finger?

... Both the elders and those who laboured in the fields declared that if the tasks of human beings [i.e. hydraulic maintenance] are not accomplished in full, there will constantly be disasters from Heaven. If officials and people do not make [such complete accomplishment] their habitual custom, great achievements will not be easy to attain. I wished to follow the encouragement given to me by the feelings of the masses, and plan a means of providing for them in perpetuity, praying that all disasters would be totally eliminated ... Thereupon they excavated channels, directed the flow of water, scythed vegetation clear, blocked up outlets, surveyed [for the building of] enclosure-dykes, distinguishing heights and widths in their construction, doubling [the strength of] both banks. Roads provided thoroughfares; nothing cluttered the foreshores. When a hundred days had passed a thousand *li* of dykes had risen up. Such indeed was the diligence of the people of Zhuji!

The heroically interventionist re-engineering of the landscape in the interests of what was seen as hydraulic efficiency and security was

80. Morita Akira, "Water control in Zhehdong during the later Ming," *East Asian History*, Vol. 2 (Dec. 1991), tr. M. Elvin and Tamura Keiko.

81. Liu Guangfu, *Jingye guilüe quanshu* (*Complete Documents Relating to the "Summary of Regulations for Managing the Countryside"*) (1603. Reprinted Zhuji: County Magistrate Hua Xuelie, 1865), *xu*, p. 13ab.

regarded by the writer of another preface as Liu's chief claim to celebrity:[82]

He also made a complete survey of the position-power of the water. In all the serpentine places, where a boat had to travel several tens of *li* but one could go directly on foot [between the same two points] in several tens of half-paces on land, he had them cut through [the land] in a straight line in order to remove the position-power of swift overflows [of the banks]. Where there were crooked flows in the territory of neighbouring counties that threatened us with disaster, he made an investigation to determine how urgent it was, and then summoned the people of that [area] to come to an agreement to cut through [the bends].

The attention to detail that he brought to what might be called hydrological orthopaedics can be seen, for example, in regulations governing the types of trees to be planted on the dykes, the permissible types of fishing-nets and their locations, bans on kilns and latrines that weakened dykes, and control of the dates during which it was permissible to float timbers on the waterways, as well as the more standard matters such as preventing encroachment by unauthorized cultivation on hydraulic installations such as overflow basins, surveying, registering, patrolling, dredging, clearing vegetation, labour-mobilization and maintenance, besides of course financing and controlling the use of the water.

The history of the upper Puyang River before Liu Guangfu's time is to a great extent a matter of speculation, but the floods and droughts were probably partly anthropogenic, due to the earlier clearing away of vegetation that had served to retain floodwater, and the construction of fields from the numerous natural storage-basins that lined the river. Both actions would have exacerbated the severity of hydrological fluctuations. Shallow lakes are also short-lived features, and sedimentation may have hastened their reduction in area or disappearance. The general point is, however, that while each locality has distinctive characteristics that can at times be decisive in the evolution of its hydrological systems, the development of hydraulic installations to improve farming tends to lead to natural and societal consequences that make recurring difficulties for their continued effective functioning. These tend to lock a society into the commitment to maintain them, often at a high and repeated expense in money, labour, raw materials and skilled management that might well in principle have been better directed elsewhere. This can be seen as a pre-modern form of path-dependency or technological "lock-in."

It goes without saying that the pressure on accessible resources that appeared in most areas of late-imperial China was also closely linked to the long-run expansion – not without reverses, it should be added – of the "Han" population across that space and its increasing in density within the space it occupied.[83] One of the most important features of late-

82. Liu Guangfu, *Summary of Regulations for Managing the Countryside, xu*, pp. 9b–10a.
    83. On the spatial expansion see the maps in Blunden and Elvin, *Cultural Atlas*, especially pp. 30–31, 34–35, 54, 62, 71, 92, 94. Also H. Wiens, *China's March Towards the Tropics* ... (Hamden, CT: Shoe String Press, 1954). The term "expansion" necessarily includes an unclear but significant amount of absorption.

imperial China was that it did not on the whole maintain internal political barriers to population movement. (Pre-1859 Manchuria under the Manchus was the only major exception, though the Han demographic "leakage" into the Liao River valley is well-known.)[84] If we think for a moment of a population as being not unlike a gas with human "particles," this absence of internal barriers tended to prevent regional populations from reaching a sort of approximate equilibrium with respect to the regional environment – at least so long as the option of out-migration remained open. The population history of Fujian in Tang and Song times, whereby a once sparsely settled area became an overpopulated one with substantial out-migration is a particularly clear and well-known illustration of this process from the period of the middle empire,[85] but it seems to have continued into late-imperial times in various forms. Two examples can sketchily illustrate something of this probable variety. Muramatsu Yūji long ago suggested that early 20th-century local settlement in the North China Plain had a comparatively shallow time-depth, resulting from continual readjusting movements by the population, "in a manner that as far as possible equalized pressure."[86] Recent work by James Lee on the population of the south-west in the mid-Qing times has shown the continuation of internal long-range migration processes.[87]

Because of empire-wide diffusion down demographic pressure-gradients, the only equilibrium that might have been possible – leaving overseas migration to one side – was thus an empire-wide one. One of the crucial aspects of late-imperial China was that, apart from Manchuria and a few other border areas, the empire had in fact begun to approach the point of being "full up," for its level of technological capability. For much of pre-modern China's history technology had continued to improve at something like an "adequate" rate, as we saw earlier in the case of Jiaxing. China's ancient and medieval rates of technological invention, innovation and diffusion had slowed down in late-imperial

84. The contrast indicated here is principally with early modern Western Europe where, *grosso modo*, it seems that with the crystallization of the nation-state the mutual reinforcement of political and cultural discontinuities greatly limited the possibilities of substantial *internal* movements of population. The large-scale movement of Russians into Siberia and Western Europeans into the New World and elsewhere overseas lies outside this formulation and does not have a Chinese parallel in terms of scale – except perhaps the expanded Han migration into Manchuria in the early decades of the present century.

85. See Shiba Yoshinobu, *Commerce and Society in Sung China* (Ann Arbor: University of Michigan, Center for Chinese Studies, 1970), pp. 181–89.

86. Muramatsu Yūji, *Chūgoku keizai shakai taisei (The Social Structure of the Chinese Economy)* (Tokyo: Tōyō keizai shinpōsha, 1949), p. 33. For a specific illustration, see S. Gamble, *North China Villages: Social, Political and Economic Activities Before 1933* (Berkeley and Los Angeles: University of California Press, 1963), Table 26, p. 331. In the village covered by this table, out of 276 families, 50% came to the village between 1483 and 1722, 44% between 1723 and 1902, and 6% between 1903 and 1933. In approximate terms, about half the population here thus lived in families settled for eight generations or more.

87. J. Lee, "Food supply and population growth in south-west China, 1250–1850," *Journal of Asian Sudies*, Vol. 41, No. 4 (1982), and J. Lee, "The legacy of immigration in south-west China, 1250–1850," *Annales de Démographie Historique* (1982).

times, however, to a degree that was beginning to create serious difficulties in the face of a continually growing population.[88]

In China, at least for the period for which detailed examination is possible (by and large, the 17th century and after), work by James Lee and his collaborators,[89] and by the present author,[90] has shown that, within the range of age-specific mortality rates that seem to have been characteristic of late-imperial China, under the prevailing conditions of all but universal early marriage of women (around 17 Western years of age in most cases), in a tightly clustered age-pattern, substantial, often very substantial, limitation of births *must* have been practised (if the underlying "natural fertility" of Chinese women was close to that determined by examining certain other populations in modern times). This probably took a variety of forms,[91] including abortifacients and social controls, as well as female infanticide (which is most conceptually conveniently included under this heading). In spite of this control, the long-term underlying rate of annual population increase crept up from well *under* 0.005 (that is, under half a per cent) to somewhat *over* 0.005 in the course of the last millennium. (This increase is all but imperceptible at a generational level, but it is easy enough to calculate that 500 years at, say, $r = 0.003$ will multiply a population by about 4.5 times.) Why this increase occurred (in the context of shorter-term fluctuations and spurts whose exact magnitudes are still controversial) is an unsolved question whose implications for China's situation on the eve of the modern age are obvious. Within the parameters of late-imperial technology, and with some regional variation, the Chinese population by 1850 had already come close to occupying and using most of the accessible economic space, particularly permanently cultivable land, often pressing hard enough on accessible resources to raise the cost of extracting them considerably.[92]

Lastly, a word on attitudes. Archaic China was rich in prescriptions for limiting the exploitation of wild animals, birds and fish, and in the

88. M. Elvin, *Pattern of the Chinese Past*, especially part 3; and M. Elvin, "Skills and resources in late traditional China," in D. Perkins (ed.), *China's Modern Economy in Historical Perspective* (Stanford: Stanford University Press, 1975), revised version in M. Elvin, *Another History: Essays on China from a European Perspective* (Sydney/Honolulu: Wild Peony/University of Hawai'i Press, 1996). The introduction of New World crops such as maize, sweet potatoes, peanuts and tobacco is of course a well-known example of non-inventive but economically crucial diffusion in the late-imperial period.

89. Li Zhongqing and Guo Songyi (eds.), *Qingdai huangzu renkou xingwei he shehui huanjing* (*The Demographic Activities of the Qing Imperial House and their Social Environment*) (Beijing: Beijing daxue chubanshe, 1994); J. Lee and C. Campbell, *Fate and Fortune in Rural China. Social Organization and Population Behaviour in Liaoning, 1774–1873* (Cambridge: Cambridge University Press, 1997); and J. Z. Lee and Wang Feng, *Malthusian Mythology and Chinese Reality: The Population History of One Quarter of Humanity* (forthcoming).

90. M. Elvin, "Blood and statistics: the population dynamics of late imperial China as reflected in the biographies of virtuous women in local gazetteers." Revised version of a paper given to the workshop "New Directions in the Study of Chinese Women. 1000–1800," University of Leiden, 1996. Available on request.

91. See Bray, *Technology and Gender*.

92. See S. A. M. Adshead, "An energy crisis in early modern China," *Ch'ing-shih wen-t'i* (now retitled *Late Imperial China*), Vol. 3, No. 2 (1974), pp. 20–28.

insights of philosophies that saw humankind as inextricably interwoven with natural processes in an organic universe. Under the Northern and Southern Dynasties from the fourth to the sixth centuries A.D., China saw the birth of some of the world's earliest landscape poetry – that is, poetry where the landscape and the meanings hidden in it are the central focus, not just a background or symbols that serve principally to express a human situation.[93] Some centuries later the poetry was followed by landscape painting, most of it implicitly expressive of the quasi-magical chthonic forces intuited by the pseudoscience of *feng shui* – geomancy – in mountains and waters. This wisdom was nonetheless powerless throughout the late pre-imperial and the imperial ages to stop the despoliation of the natural world.

A systematic study of Chinese views of nature, however – at least in late-imperial times for which materials are abundant – reveals almost the entire possible spectrum of attitudes.[94] There were Qing-dynasty enthusiasts for gigantic engineering projects, even more demented than Li Peng's Sanxia (Three Gorges) Dam.[95] There were those who believed that nature should be attacked in military fashion. Others argued that humans should accommodate themselves to the pattern of natural processes without forcing matters. Others again saw nature as savage towards humankind, or indifferent. Some, influenced by a moral meteorology, spoke of the weather as reflecting the judgement of Heaven on the populations affected. Others again saw nature as benevolent, or immersed themselves in it, beyond morality, in a kind of nature mysticism. By this time at least, there was no single set of attitudes towards nature that could legitimately be called "Chinese." We also need to be wary of looking too much for inspiration from pre-modern "China" in our present troubles.[96]

Conclusions

This survey has sketched and suggested, not proven. Broadly though, it has indicated that economic and technological growth were prerequisites in China for the military and other power that made possible what might be called a sort of "Social-Darwinian success" for these power-orientated ways of acting. Short-term rewards from the over-exploitation of resources tended to reduce any inclination to limit exploitation within

93. Described with numerous quotations by Obi Kōichi, *Chūgoku bungaku ni aratawareta shizen to shizenkan* (*Nature and the Concept of Nature in Chinese Literature*) (Tokyo: Iwanami shoten, 1963).

94. Examples are given in Elvin, "*Bell of Poesy.*"

95. See the analyses of the vulnerable mid-gorge rock-formations in Lin Chengkun, *Changjiang Sanxia yu Gezhouba de nisha ji huanjing* (*Sediments and Environment of the Three Gorges of the Yangzi and of Gezhou Dam*) (Nanjing: Nanjing daxue chubanshe, 1989).

96. See M. Elvin, review of J. B. Callicott and R. T. Ames (eds.), *Nature in Asian Traditions of Thought: Essays in Environmental Philosophy* (Albany, NY: State University of New York Press, 1989), *Asian Studies Review*, Vol. 14, No. 3 (1991). I draw attention here to the often neglected elements of environmental insight in the Western tradition, including the Old Testament (*Psalms, Job*), the classical world (Lucretius, for example), and early modern philosophy (especially Spinoza's *Ethica*).

sustainable limits at a given technological level. The development process further entailed a number of other changes that, overall, tended to weaken restraints on over-exploitation of the environment and impairment of the natural infrastructure underpinning human life. Urbanization and commercialization separated decision-makers from having to live with the direct environmental consequences of their behaviour. The economic growth process itself, especially the spread of markets and the possibility of safely depositing money at interest, altered what was semi-consciously perceived to be the appropriate discount rate applying to choices between present and future exploitation of resources, enhancing present values relative to future ones. In Social-Darwinian terms the Chinese techno-cultural style was highly successful for most of its imperial history, and its environment was – not accidentally – seriously degraded in many respects by the beginning of the modern era.

The Organization of Environmental Protection in China

Abigail R. Jahiel

In March 1998, the Ninth National People's Congress swept in a radical reform of government administration. When the dust had settled, the number of government ministry-level bodies had been reduced from 40 to 29, and 50 per cent of government employees had been slated for elimination from governmental payrolls within three years.[1] Amidst this massive effort to cut central government administration, the environmental protection administration emerged as a bureaucratic exception: after years of lobbying, it was finally upgraded to ministerial status.[2] With this unexpected promotion during a time of strict administrative austerity, the new Jiang Zemin–Zhu Rongji administration issued a clear signal that environmental problems were a serious central government concern in need of increased attention.

Degradation of China's environment has become increasingly severe over the past two decades – alarmingly so, by some estimates.[3] The high-growth, resource-intensive development strategy China has pursued, coupled with the norms and institutional relationships designed to support this development strategy, have no doubt played a critical role in the deteriorating quality of the environment.[4] Economic decentralization has given officials at the provincial level and below the means and incentives to develop their local economies.[5] The pervasive emphasis on development, consumerism and profit in government proclamations and throughout society has further provided local governments with the justification to intervene against regulations – such as environmental protection – deemed unfavourable to growth.[6]

1. Daniel Kwan, "Cutback tackles red-tape malaise: 'The government is handling many affairs it should not handle, cannot handle,'" *South China Morning Post*, 7 March 1998, p. 8; Erik Eckholm, "New China leader promises reforms for every sector," *The New York Times*, 20 March 1998, p A1.

2. Chan Yee Hon *et al.* "Green body upgraded to ministry," *South China Morning Post*, 2 April 1998, p. 10.

3. For recent reports of environmental conditions in China see *Clear Water, Blue Skies: China's Environment in the New Century*, (Washington, DC: The World Bank, 1997); Mark Hertsgaard, "Our real China problem," *The Atlantic Monthly*, Vol. 280, No. 5 (1997), pp. 97–114; "How the statistics stack up in the environmental crisis," *South China Morning Post*, 19 March 1998, p. 9; Nicholas D. Kristoff, "Across Asia a pollution disaster hovers," *The New York Times*, 28 November 1997, pp. A1 and A10; and Daniel Kwan, "NPC calls for action to curb urban pollution; inspection team says problem 'grave,'" *South China Morning Post*, 4 July 1996, p. 11.

4. For a case study of how the norms and institutional structures of the reforms affect implementation of one particular environmental policy, the discharge fee system, see Abigail R. Jahiel, "The contradictory impact of reform for environmental protection," *The China Quarterly*, No. 149 (1997), pp. 81–103

5. On the issue of decentralization of the Chinese economy see Susan Shirk, *The Logic of Economic Reform in China* (Berkeley: University of California Press, 1993).

6. Several scholars have observed this phenomenon of local government intervention in a variety of policy contexts. See, for example, Jean C. Oi, "The role of the local state in China's

But, as the central government's recent measures indicate, there is another factor at play as well. Although China has worked for more than a quarter of a century developing policies, promulgating laws and building an extensive institutional apparatus to address environmental problems, shortcomings *within* this system of environmental protection are also responsible for the country's ecological woes. Specifically, China's environmental protection apparatus has suffered from two lingering problems: insufficient authority and lack of co-ordination between institutional actors. Whether the administrative reforms of the 1998 National People's Congress will dramatically alter these problems remains to be seen. The following review of the organization of environmental protection, within the context of the larger Chinese state, sheds some light on the complexity of environmental management in China.

The Organization of Environmental Protection

The Chinese state is a multi-layered institutional structure with territorial divisions at the centre, province, city, county, township and village levels. It is composed of numerous government and Communist Party functional units (commissions, ministries, bureaus and departments), responsible for such diverse issues as education, finance, personnel, electric power and heavy industry. These functional units exist at the national level and typically replicate themselves (or their functions) in a vertical chain through successively lower territorial levels of government. Individual functional units within this system receive administrative guidance from their parent units above them; they are also subject to the leadership of the local governments to which they belong; but communication between functional units at the same territorial level has traditionally been very limited.

The organization of environmental protection reflects the basic features of the Chinese state (see Figure 1 and Table 1). A government unit solely responsible for environmental protection – the State Environmental Protection Administration (SEPA) – exists at the central level as the chief agency addressing the nation's environmental issues.[7] This unit falls under the direct leadership of the State Council, from which it receives almost all of its funding. It is supported in its efforts to formulate national policy by the Committee on Natural Resources and Environmental Protection under China's chief legislative body, the National People's Congress.

SEPA is replicated as Environmental Protection Bureaus (EPBs) or Offices (EPOs) down through successively lower levels of the administrative hierarchy at the provincial, city, district, county and, in some

footnote continued

transitional economy." *The China Quarterly*, No. 144 (1995), p. 1144, and Kenneth Lieberthal, *Governing China: From Revolution through Reform* (New York: W.W. Norton and Co., 1995), p. 316.

7. Prior to the 1998 administrative reforms, this agency was referred to as the National Environmental Protection Agency (NEPA).

places, township levels. The chief responsibility of these local environmental units is to enforce laws and implement policies designed by SEPA and to assist in drafting local regulations to supplement central ones. EPBs and EPOs thus work directly with local factories and other polluters, as well as with industrial bureaus and local government actors (including planning commissions, economic commissions, People's Congresses and mayors).

Like other local units, environmental protection organs must be responsive to two leaders: the administratively higher levels of the national environmental protection apparatus and the local governments where they reside. SEPA and provincial environmental protection agencies provide city and county environmental organs with policy directives and guidance for implementation. District and some county environmental protection units receive guidance from city organs as well. In all cases, however, it is the local government, not the higher levels of the environmental protection apparatus, that provides environmental agencies with their annual budgetary funds, approves institutional advancements in rank and determines increases in personnel and even allocation of such resources as cars, office buildings and employee housing.[8] Since environmental organs are so dependent on local governments, they must take these governments' concerns into account when regulating industry. It is the local government, therefore, that is the more powerful of the environmental agencies' two administrative leaders.

The vastness of the Chinese mainland and the decentralization of the Chinese economy have meant that there is great variability in size, funding, staffing and even work methods of environmental protection agencies in different parts of the country. Though the country as a whole suffers from a shortage of funds for environmental protection, environmental protection agencies in the wealthier coastal provinces and in large cities tend, as a rule, to have more personnel, be better funded and be staffed with more technically-trained people than those agencies in the poorer interior parts of the country, smaller cities, counties and townships.[9] Poor, remote regions, conversely, are less able to attract technically-trained, enthusiastic people: appointed staff often have no background in environmental protection or related fields and receive little motivational incentive as they are paid meagre salaries and are denied even basic resources such as vehicles to assist in conducting their work.[10]

---

8. The State Environmental Protection Administration and provincial Environmental Protection Bureaus do occasionally provide finances for environmental organs at lower levels of the administrative hierarchy. However, these grants are for specific projects, not operating funds, and they are certainly not funds that local environmental agencies can expect to receive on a yearly basis. In addition, local environmental agencies have developed ways of generating their own funds, but some of these financial sources create their own problems for environmental protection, as is discussed below.
9. Elsewhere in this volume, Vermeer provides a good discussion of investment in pollution control which stresses that investment levels for environmental protection differ markedly from province to province.
10. The piece by Harkness in this volume discusses the issue of regional differences and staffing in China's forest reserves.

Figure 1: **The Chinese Environmental Protection Apparatus (March 1998)**

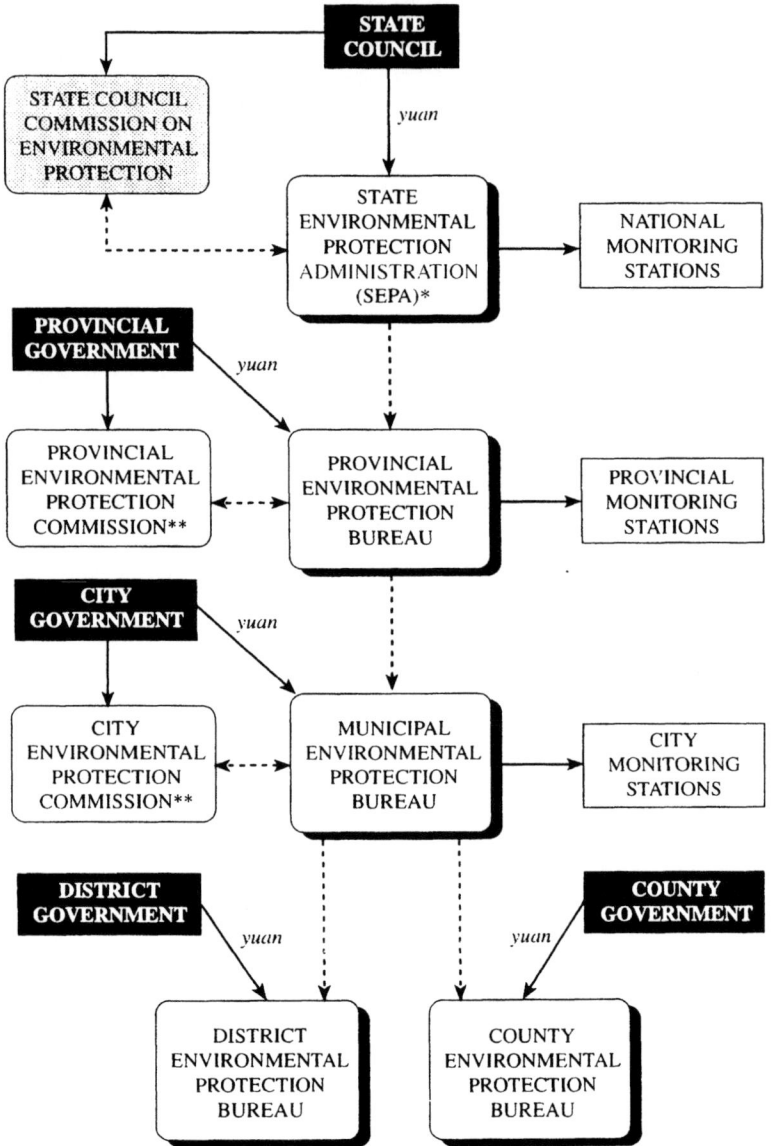

⬭ Defunct Agency	*Previously called the National Environmental Protection Agency (NEPA)
⬛ Regional Government Unit	
— Leadership Relationship	**The future of these commissions is in question.
---- Advisory Relationship	

Moreover, these regional differences in staffing and funding frequently influence the policy enforcement methods upon which EPBs in various parts of the country rely. Wealthier and more technically staffed EPBs,

Table 1: **The Organization of Environmental Protection**

SEPA (State Environmental Protection Administration)
The chief agency responsible for formulating and overseeing the administration of national environmental policy. Formerly called the National Environmental Protection Agency (NEPA), SEPA is responsible for developing environmental policies; drafting or assisting the National People's Congress Committee on Natural Resources and Environmental Protection in drafting environmental laws, regulations and standards; overseeing environmental management; designing and conducting environmental education and publicity programmes; hosting environmental meetings and symposia; promoting best available technologies; and co-ordinating international environmental exchanges and, as of the Ninth National People's Congress, interministerial environmental activities as well.

EPBs and EPOs (Environmental Protection Bureaus and Offices)
The primary local agencies responsible for enforcing national environmental laws and policies, setting local pollution standards, investigating environmental accidents and mediating environmental disputes.

Commissions on Environmental Protection
Interministerial umbrella organizations which co-ordinate interaction between environmental protection agencies and other government organs. Environmental Protection Commissions are composed of senior government officials (e.g. assistant governors, deputy mayors, county magistrates), environmental officials, and representatives of key government planning institutions including planning commissions, economic commissions, industrial ministries (or bureaus), and the media.

The National People's Congress Committee on Natural Resources and Environmental Protection
A central government committee, created in 1993, which now plays the lead role in drafting new environmental legislation and revising existing legislation.

Environmental Monitoring Stations
Professional units at all levels of the Chinese government which collect technical data on air and water quality, solid waste and noise pollution and provide this information to environmental agencies.

Environmental Offices in Industrial Ministries and Factories
Technical offices which monitor industry-specific pollutants and factory wastes and help develop industry- or factory-specific waste treatment regulations and procedures.

Environmental Research Institutes and Higher Education Programmes
Academic bodies responsible for environmental research and for the education of technical cadres for careers in environmental law, policy and science.

Environmental Protection Industry
Companies that have emerged in recent years that market environmental protection equipment to Chinese industry and government.

Other Ministries/Bureaus and Government Agencies
Administrative agencies responsible either solely or in concert with SEPA for various aspects of environmental protection.

for example, might be more likely to rely on technological solutions to environmental problems or on the legal system, whereas those with more limited resources might focus their energies on environmental education campaigns aimed at improving industrial management or on forging alliances with powerful local leaders and bureaus. It is important, nonetheless, to recognize that while poor areas often lack adequate resources to undertake environmental protection efforts, it is not necessarily the case that rich areas are more inclined toward environmental protection. Individual commitment to the environmental cause on the part of EPB officials (and local leaders) can often play a tremendously important role in policy implementation, independent of whether an area is rich or poor.

Environmental protection agencies at all administrative levels have for years been assisted in their regulatory work by a system of interministerial umbrella organizations, known as Environmental Protection Commissions. These Commissions have served as co-ordinating bodies between environmental protection agencies and other government organs at the same level of government in a system in which functional units at the same territorial level have traditionally maintained minimal communication.[11] Under the administrative changes introduced by the 1998 National People's Congress, however, the State Council's Environmental Protection Commission has been abolished, and the co-ordinating functions of the Commission transferred to the State Environmental Protection Administration.[12] As of summer 1998, the fate of local Environmental Protection Commissions was still to be determined.

Environmental agencies also receive support from a system of monitoring stations that provide the technical information to formulate and implement environmental regulations.[13] Monitoring stations fall under the leadership of the local environmental protection agency. However, they receive most of their funding from the local government via the local EPB, generating the rest through the professional services they perform. In addition, a National Environmental Quality Monitoring Network, composed of 200 stations located throughout the country, collects national data on air and water quality, acid rain, radioactive wastes and ecologically sensitive areas. This network of monitoring agencies reports directly to SEPA. Its funds come from professional fees as well as from

---

11. Interview 18, Summer 1991 and Professor Cheng Zhengkang, lecture for environmental law class, Beijing University, March 1991. All interviews referred to in this article were conducted by the author with central, provincial, city and county environmental protection officials in Beijing, Anyang, Shanghai, Wuhan, Xi'an and Xuzhou in 1991, 1992, 1995 and 1997. Interview notes are on file with the author.

12. Changhua Wu, World Resources Institute, personal correspondence with the author, 17 April 1998. David Biele, Consul, United States Embassy, Beijing, personal correspondence with the author, 28 April 1998.

13. As of 1996, China had 2,223 environmental monitoring stations throughout the country, of which one was national-, 37 were provincial-, 377 were city- and 1,808 were county-level. In total, 35,928 people were engaged in monitoring work, or 42.4% of all people engaged in environmental protection work in China. *Zhongguo huanjing nianjian 1996 (China Environmental Yearbook 1996)* (Beijing: Zhongguo huanjing nianjian, 1996), pp. 191–92.

money collected by SEPA from the environmental protection apparatus.[14] The quality of the data collected by China's monitoring stations varies across regions and sectors.

Affiliated with the environmental protection administration is a loose conglomerate of research institutions, university departments and companies that, among other tasks, perform environmental impact assessments (EIAs) and design and sell environmental protection equipment on a for-profit basis.

The national environmental protection network, including environmental protection agencies, commissions and monitoring stations, has assumed most, although not all, responsibilities related to environmental management – from air and water pollution to solid and hazardous (including nuclear) wastes, from wildlife conservation to wetlands preservation. In part because of the interconnections between the environment and a host of other activities, several other government agencies have also had jurisdiction over various aspects of environmental protection. Management of forests (including afforestation work) and nature reserves, conservation of wetlands and biodiversity, and desertification control have, until recently, been chiefly the responsibility of the Ministry of Forestry; management of water supply and water quality has been in part the responsibility of the Ministry of Water Conservation; the Ministry of Agriculture has been responsible for fisheries conservation, preservation of aquatic animals, various regulatory aspects of township and village enterprises and some land use decisions; the Ministry of Construction and Urban Development has held jurisdiction over zoos, parks and scenic sites, as well as many environment-related urban infrastructure projects, wastewater treatment plants and municipal solid waste management; various ministries have been involved in developing negotiating points for international environmental treaties, though ultimately agreements are finalized by the Ministry of Foreign Affairs; and the Ministry of Science and Technology (formerly the State Science and Technology Commission) has funded environmental research, co-ordinated scientific and technical exchanges related to the environment, and, along with the State Development Planning Commission (formerly the State Planning Commission), has solicited foreign funding for environmental projects. In addition, there are seven agencies responsible for monitoring China's seven major river systems. And this list is by no means comprehensive. The 1998 administrative reforms reduced the number of agencies involved in environmental protection, but did not completely eliminate the situation of fragmented authority. This complex arrangement of diffuse agencies, all with some responsibility for the environment, has several implications worth noting: first, the agency responsible for a given aspect of environmental work is not always strongly inclined toward environmental interests; secondly, this confluence of actors

14. Of the 200 stations in the national monitoring network in 1996, 135 monitored surface water, 103 urban air pollution, 113 acid rain, 55 noise, 31 radioactivity, and nine ecologically sensitive areas. *China Environmental Yearbook 1996*, p. 191.

creates competition for scarce environmental funds; finally, fragmented regulatory authority hinders the co-ordinated management of various, related environmental issues.

In addition to the agencies discussed above, industrial ministries (some now bureaus)[15] and some companies have assumed daily responsibility for industry-specific environmental management. Industrial ministries have developed their own environmental monitoring stations for specific pollutants as well as sector-specific environmental regulations to supplement national regulations. Moreover, most large and medium-sized factories have their own environmental protection divisions, responsible for monitoring factory wastes and developing factory-specific waste treatment procedures.[16] Though not part of the formal environmental protection apparatus, these divisions are often the critical interface between the factory and the local environmental agencies through which environmental policies are actuated. Small factories, including township and village enterprises (TVEs), do not as a rule have environmental divisions or even a trained individual for this job. Moreover, they are often private firms and as such have not fallen under the direct guidance of an industrial ministry or bureau. As a result of these differences, environmental protection agencies have had significantly greater difficulty monitoring the activities of small, privately-owned firms than they have large state-owned firms.[17]

Finally, the courts and the Chinese Communist Party are also involved in enforcement of environmental regulations, though not on a daily basis. Environmental Protection Bureaus turn to the courts as a last resort to administratively enforce (*qiangzhi zhixing*) environmental laws that polluters refuse to adhere to. Infrequently, the courts are also used by EPBs and individuals to sue firms for negligence over environmental accidents, as well as by aggrieved citizens or factory managers who feel wronged by EPB rulings. The role of the CCP in environmental protection is more nebulous. Holding no official function with regard to environmental protection, local Party secretaries are nevertheless often brought in by county and township EPBs in particular to help resolve environmental disputes. In these instances, the Communist Party's authority is often the decisive factor in convincing a recalcitrant firm to clean up, cease production, or compensate a party for wrongdoing. At the city level and

15. In the past, the Ministry of Chemical Industry played a particularly important role in monitoring factories within its sector and developing sector-specific environmental regulations. Under the 1998 administrative reforms, many industrial ministries were abolished. However, several were recreated as bureaus under the State Economic and Trade Commission (SETC), including the former Ministries of Chemical Industry, Metallurgical Industry, Coal Industry and Machine Building. Viven Pik-Kwan Chan, "Oil chief to head super ministry," *South China Morning Post*, 15 March 1998.

16. In 1994, 171,469 factory workers were responsible for environmental protection, including 48,069 specifically responsible for monitoring. *China Environmental Yearbook 1996*, p. 270.

17. Abigail R. Jahiel, "Policy implementation through organizational learning: the case of water pollution management in China's reforming socialist system," (PhD dissertation, University of Michigan, 1994), pp. 425–26.

above, the Communist Party's role in environmental protection is less visible.

In brief, environmental protection entails co-ordinated efforts between environmental agencies, various other government units, industrial bureaus, factories, research institutes, courts, and even the Chinese Communist Party. Still, the primary responsibility for environmental quality falls to the environmental protection apparatus itself. It is the local EPB that must ensure that factories install pollution prevention technology, operate waste treatment facilities, reduce harmful emissions, or pay fees if these emissions exceed standards – even if the factories view these extra costs as unreasonable. It is the local EPB, too, that must ensure that city planning agencies reject proposals from heavily polluting foreign and domestic firms seeking to invest in the area or that counties wishing to turn wetlands into farmland conduct environmental impact assessments – even if these projects promise to be lucrative for the local economy. In an atmosphere in which economic growth is the primary state goal, these are not small tasks.

Accordingly, environmental protection agencies must have sufficient authority to carry out their responsibilities. In the Chinese political system, formal authority relations play an important role in influencing the power distribution among government agencies, often affecting whether or not policies are enforced. Authority is predominantly wielded in two ways, through superior administrative ranking and through financial control. Ranks are assigned to governments and functional departments at each level of the political hierarchy. A government office of lesser rank has no bureaucratic authority to compel compliance from one of superior rank; nor can government units of equal rank issue binding orders to each other.[18] A functional unit's rank within the local government is influenced by its parent organ's rank at the central level, but is ultimately determined by the local government to which it belongs. As such, this rank in great part reflects the local leadership's perception of the importance of the unit within the local government.

Financial control further defines authority relations and concentrates even more power at the local level. As mentioned, most local government agencies report directly to two leaders, their immediate functional superior and the local government in which they reside. Since the reforms that began in the late 1970s, local governments have held the purse strings, providing the annual budget for functional offices; functional superiors have simply provided administrative and professional guidance. The more a functional department depends on the local government for its funding

---

18. In most cases ranking is clear. For example, provinces are of higher rank than cities, and ministries of higher rank than bureaus. In some cases, however, rank orders are not so obvious. For example, provinces have the same rank as ministries; thus, a central-level ministry cannot command a province to comply with its policy mandate – it can only recommend it do so. The importance of bureaucratic rank and commensurate status is discussed in Kenneth Lieberthal and Michel Oksenberg, *Policy Making in China: Leaders, Structures and Processes* (Princeton: Princeton University Press, 1988), pp. 142–45, and in Lieberthal, *Governing China*, pp. 159–170.

(i.e. the fewer outside sources of funding it possesses), the greater the local government's authority over the department.

Government agencies that lack high administrative ranking and reliable sources of funding are often forced to develop on an individual basis their own ways to attain the nominal levels of ascribed authority necessary to conduct their jobs. For example, they may undertake educational drives to convince other agencies of the importance of their work, they may court powerful local actors on a personal basis, or they may turn to the legal system as a means to enforce policy when access to formal authority fails. Attaining ascribed authority when formal authority is lacking is thus not impossible, but it does require considerable effort. This effort is magnified the more the aims of the particular agency conflict with the dominant goals of the Chinese state.

The primary goal of the Chinese state over the last two decades has been rapid economic growth. The state supports this goal through institutional arrangements, such as the decentralization of the political economy to stir up local initiative, and through the creation of growth-oriented and consumerist social norms. Moreover, contribution to rapid economic growth is the lens through which the state has defined authority relations: greater authority has been vested in those organizations that support this primary state goal.

In relation to the organization of environmental protection in China, the structure, distribution of authority and primary goal of the Chinese state carry several implications. First, the functionally fragmented nature of the state highlights the challenges of regulating state agencies, particularly when the targets of regulatory policy are numerous. Secondly, the importance of rank as a designator of authority within the matrix of local government organs indicates that powerful government organs can ignore the demands of weaker ones. Thirdly, local government budgetary control of regulatory agencies suggests that local interests may have more influence on how policy is implemented than do the interests of central-level regulatory agencies responsible for formulating policy, and, therefore, that the central government's ability to co-ordinate policy across regions may be seriously limited. Finally, primary concern for economic growth may place competing interests in a disadvantaged position in their fight for authority.

A historical overview of the institutional development of the environmental apparatus highlights the strengths and weaknesses of the organization today with regard to establishing a position of authority.

Institutional Development and Authority-building

Virtually from its inception, the history of environmental protection in China has been a continuous effort to build institutions and vest them with the authority necessary to implement policy. This effort has focused predominantly on increasing bureaucratic rank and commensurate size. Efforts to develop independent sources of funding have been more limited. Periods of institutional advancement (such as those in 1979,

1984, 1988 and 1998) have been punctuated by periods of institutional setbacks (such as those in 1982 and 1994).

National environmental protection efforts in China have their origins in the months just prior to and following the 1972 United Nations-sponsored Stockholm Conference on the Human Environment. During the 1970s relatively few steps were taken to establish an environmental protection organizational network. The central government agency which acted as the chief locus of environmental policy activity until 1981 was designated an "office." This rank meant that it could not issue orders to subordinate levels of government. Therefore this central office maintained little contact with local environmental protection units, established in parts of the country in the early 1970s as "three wastes offices."[19]

With the advent of the reforms in the late 1970s, attention to environmental issues increased notably.[20] The promulgation of China's first Environmental Protection Law in 1979 signalled a new level of central government interest in environmental matters. In response, several provincial and city governments took the initiative between 1979 and 1982 to increase the rank of Environmental Protection Offices to that of bureaus, making them first-tier organizations. As such, new Environmental Protection Bureaus (EPBs) were granted additional personnel, direct access to local government leaders, the power to call meetings and issue orders without supervisory approval, and the right to establish specialized subunits and functionally divide up work. This markedly increased regulatory activity.[21]

Still, at this early stage, even where institutional structures existed, the local environmental agency's actual authority position was extremely limited. Industrial bureaus and local factories resisted EPB efforts to implement policy by delaying or simply refusing to take action; and local governments, in the interests of the local economy, frequently intervened on behalf of firms.[22] This weakness was compounded by the fact that the central government Environmental Protection Office remained a second-tier organ (with a staff of only 30), incapable of issuing mandates to industrial sectors. Although a few leaders in the central government recognized the importance of environmental protection enough to allow for the passage of environmental laws and regulations and to include environmental protection in such key documents as the nation's five-year

19. Although steps taken to establish an environmental protection organization in the 1970s were minimal, they were not insignificant. At the national level, the Environmental Leadership Small Group, established in May 1974, brought together 20 leaders of various industrial ministries to consider environmental issues. Though this small group met only twice in nine years, it was responsible for the creation of the Environmental Protection Office. At the local level, "three wastes offices" of one or two individuals, and later slightly larger Environmental Protection Offices were gradually established in some Chinese cities and became the precursor of today's institutional apparatus. *Zhongguo de huanjing baohu shiye: 1981–1985 (China's Environmental Protection Work: 1981–1985)* (Beijing: Zhongguo huanjing kexue chubanshe, 1988), p. 155.
20. For insights into the reasons behind this shift in focus, see Jahiel, "Policy implementation through organizational learning," pp. 82–86.
21. Interviews 33, 56 and 83, autumn 1991
22. Jahiel, "The contradictory impact of reform," pp. 86–87.

plans and its constitutions (1978 and 1982), the large majority of central leaders and even more local leaders were either ignorant of the environmental problem or believed economic growth was far more important. As a result, even institutional advances were followed by set-backs.

The most critical set-back came in 1982–1983 when the Deng administration initiated the first of its structural reforms aimed at reducing the size of the Chinese bureaucracy. Among the institutional changes was the consolidation of three previously existing administrative units into the new Ministry of Urban and Rural Construction and Environmental Protection. With this change, the Environmental Protection Office was placed under the newly created ministry. Although its status was raised to that of a bureau and its personnel increased from 30 to 60 people, it was not made an independent agency. In this regard its position was somewhat weaker than previously, as it was now embedded in another bureaucracy. These changes quickly revealed serious and long-term negative impacts for environmental protection.

The immediate effect of the 1982 reforms was that many areas which had previously created independent Environmental Protection Bureaus under the direct administration of the local government now placed them under their Bureaus of Urban and Rural Construction and Environmental Protection and cut back their personnel. This reduction in status and personnel "subjected an originally fragile environmental management organization to a serious assault and generally weakened managerial power."[23] In Sichuan province, for example, an independent, first-tier organization had been established by 1982. With the central government changes, the Sichuan EPB was demoted and placed under the authority of the Ministry of Construction. It was not until 1990 that this EPO was able to muster the political support necessary to re-emerge as an independent, first-tier administrative organ.[24]

While the impact of the 1982 reforms continued to thwart environmental protection efforts in many counties into the 1990s, the negative consequences of the 1982 change were relatively short-lived for most cities and for some provinces. During the Second National Environmental Protection Conference in the winter of 1983–1984, complaints from both environmental personnel about the 1982 decisions and from scholars, concerned about the deteriorating state of China's environment, led the central government to make two significant changes that resulted in an increase of EPB status. First, in May 1984, the State Council announced its creation of an inter-organizational body, the Environmental Protection Commission, to aid the EPB in directly communicating with industrial ministries. Secondly, in December 1984, the State Council formally

23. *Zhongguo huanjing nianjian 1990* (*China Environmental Yearbook 1990*) (Beijing: Huanjing kexue chubanshe, 1990), p. 7.

24. Interview 27, summer 1991. Without a strong provincial body, city and county environmental organs lack an advocate for increases in personnel or institutional status; moreover, there is no organization to write environmental laws specific to provincial needs. Sichuan's delay in establishing an independent environmental agency may help explain its poor performance in managing its acid rain problem and enforcing its environmental policies.

increased the bureaucratic authority of the Environmental Protection Bureau by changing its name to the National Environmental Protection Bureau (NEPB) and raising its personnel allowance from 60 to 120 people. The NEPB was now essentially higher in rank than other second-tier organizations and had correspondingly more independence. Because the national agency now had two superiors, the Ministry of Construction and the State Council's Environmental Protection Commission, the NEPB could seek approval from the Commission to issue documents rather than going through the Ministry of Construction, which had previously treated environmental protection more like "… an append-age … than an integral component."[25] Moreover, unlike rules approved through the Ministry of Construction which only held for those within the ministry itself, the NEPB ministerial rules and regulations approved by the Commission applied externally to other ministries, such as industrial ministries associated with factories. In addition, the change in status meant the NEPB could now issue orders directly to provincial EPBs; it could decide upon and conduct its own meetings; and it now received Ministry of Finance funds directly earmarked for environmental protec-tion, rather than having to wait for these funds to be channelled through the Ministry of Construction.[26] Finally, the Bureau gained virtually independent status to deal with international affairs. All of these changes vastly enlarged the central-level Bureau's capabilities.[27]

The 1984 changes in Beijing also encouraged many provincial and municipal environmental protection organs in particular, but also some counties, to establish Environmental Protection Commissions. Moreover, local governments began to rebuild EPB strength, and some actually increased strength over 1982 levels. It was at this time that several cities began to establish county and district environmental protection organs, or to expand existing ones.[28]

A further change at the central level served to shore up the institutional authority at the city level. In March 1988, as part of a second round of administrative reforms, the NEPB was granted independence from the Ministry of Urban and Rural Construction and Environmental Protection and renamed an Agency. Its bureaucratic rank was raised to a half-notch below a ministry, it now reported directly to the State Council, and its personnel allotment was significantly increased from 120 people to 321.[29]

25. Lester Ross, *Environmental Policy in China* (Bloomington: Indiana University Press, 1988), p. 141.

26. This was an important change because monies transferred through other agencies were subject to misappropriation for functions unrelated to environmental protection. Interview 27, autumn 1991.

27. Interview 11, spring 1991, and Interview 18, summer 1991.

28. *China Environmental Yearbook 1990*, p. 8, and Interviews 31 and 98, autumn 1991.

29. Although NEPA was granted a personnel allotment of 321, it never actually filled all of these positions. In 1994, as a result of a third round of government-wide reforms, discussed below, NEPA reviewed its personnel, and reassigned them. In the process a total of 196 people were retained, 76 people were transferred out of NEPA and the agency tried to fill the vacancies with technically qualified people with advanced degrees. *Zhongguo huanjing nianjian 1995* (*China Environmental Yearbook 1995*) (Beijing: Zhongguo huanjing nianjian, 1995), p. 228.

As a result the National Environmental Protection Agency (NEPA) expanded its functional divisions and, by 1994, had ten different divisions of second-tier rank with 43 subdivisions, a stark contrast to the ten subdivisions of third-tier rank it had prior to the 1988 change.[30] As reported by several street-level officials, local EPBs and EPOs benefited greatly from this functionalization; NEPA now provided them with training, technical advice on pollution control equipment, and educational materials, in addition to the legal and policy guidance it previously gave.[31] In addition, NEPA was able to expand the national monitoring station network and to successfully see to the creation of the new National People's Congress committee in March 1993, now known as the Committee for Natural Resources and Environmental Protection. This committee has been responsible for revising and drafting anew a series of environmental laws and assuring their rapid promulgation. Local environmental protection officials in 1997 indicated that this spate of law-making in the mid-1990s had notably increased their authority and eased their work.[32]

As a consequence of these institutional developments – as well as the legal and policy advances they inspired[33]– in many cities and several provinces throughout China, the modicum of authority necessary to routinize policy implementation had been established by the late 1980s: as a rule, pollution discharge fees were being collected, local EPB officials were being included in government meetings to consider the viability of proposed large-scale development projects, and the environmental impacts of such projects were receiving at least cursory consideration.[34] Moreover, by the early 1990s, industries were referring to city Environmental Protection Bureaus as one of the five hegemonic powers (*wuge bawang*) of local government because they possessed the ability to veto new industrial ventures.[35] An ironic but telling sign of this increase in authority is reflected in the increase in certain parts of the country of bribery by industries (including joint ventures) to convince EPBs to accept flawed environmental impact assessments or approve new construction projects.[36] Overall, however, the increase in authority and

---

30. The ten offices were the General Office; the Department of Planning and Finance; the Department of Policies, Laws and Statutes; the Department of Administrative System and Personnel; the Department of Science, Technology and Standards; the Department of Pollution Control; the Department of Supervision and Management; the Department of Nature Conservation; the Department of International Co-operation; and the Department of Publicity and Education. *Zhongguo huanjing nianjian 1994* (*China Environment Yearbook 1994*) (Beijing: Zhongguo huanjing nianjian, 1995), p. 223.

31. Interview 38, autumn 1991.

32. Interview 312, July 1997.

33. During the 1980s several media-specific environmental laws and regulations were promulgated, covering oceans, inland water pollution, air pollution and noise pollution. By the end of the 1980s, China had also developed a series of eight policy implementation mechanisms. For details, see Barbara J. Sinkule and Leonard Ortolano, *Implementing Environmental Policy in China* (Westport: Praeger, 1995), pp. 25–42.

34. Interviews 39b and 87b, autumn 1991.

35. Interview 42, autumn 1991.

36. Eduard Vermeer, comments at *The China Quarterly* conference on China and the Environment, January 1998, School of Oriental and African Studies, University of London.

expansion of personnel has benefited urban EPBs. It has allowed them to broaden the scope of their work from monitoring immediate pollution problems to trying to prevent future ones. Technically-staffed, large, urban EPBs in cities such as Shanghai and Wuhan have focused some of their efforts, in the second half of the 1990s, on large scale engineering projects and economic incentive schemes to encourage pollution abatement rather than solely on administrative means and factory-specific projects. They use the legal system to enforce laws more than they did in the past. And they have expanded their educational efforts, beyond the special training programmes developed in the early 1990s for government and industrial leaders, to encompass high-tech, mass-scale educational efforts, including the airing of weekly environmental television shows and the establishment of environmental phone hotlines.

A noticeable impact of these cumulative changes has been an increased environmental awareness among the Chinese populace. Urbanites in particular now often serve as the eyes and ears of EPBs, performing a watchdog function that relieves EPB staff to concentrate on policy enforcement. Even more striking, strong citizen participation on environmental hotlines has increased pressure on local leaders to take action on long-standing environmental problems. The impact of citizen input was not lost on NEPA, which in recent years has urged the media to expand its role in environmental education and has encouraged the development of environmental non-governmental organizations.[37]

Although there has been a general improvement in environmental protection work in cities, the situation for counties has been far more difficult. There, the 1982 creation of the Ministry of Urban Construction and Environmental Protection had the greatest impact. Since very few counties had begun to establish environmental protection agencies by the early 1980s, county governments automatically placed them under the administration of construction departments when they did so in greater numbers later in the decade. Not surprisingly, this created problems. A county environmental official in Henan described the situation as follows: "... We were just a division (*gu*), so no-one listened to us ... We only had ten people ... People at the top [the head of the Construction Commission and city government leaders] didn't take us seriously and neither did people at the bottom [the factories]."[38] It took a full eight years for this EPB to extricate itself from under the Construction Commission and establish organizational independence. A Hubei county official in 1991 recorded a typical experience: he noted that his EPO was still under the Construction Commission and, although the county government had allotted the Commission personnel and commensurate salaries specifically for its environmental division, the environmental division

37. Jasper Becker, "All systems go for a green prophet," *South China Morning Post*, 18 April 1998.
38. Interview 16, summer 1991.

Table 2: **Local Environmental Protection Organs by Rank, Year-end 1992**

Country	Province	City	County	Entire
First-tier (independent)	14	176	877	1,067
Second-tier (independent)	5	18	41	64
Under Department of Urban Construction	3	66	1,002	1,071
Under other Departments	8	55	257	320
Total	30	315	2,177	2,522

Source:
  Based on data provided in *China Environment Yearbook 1994*, (Beijing: Zhongguo huanjing nianjian, 1995), p. 226.

"never saw a penny of it;" instead the money went to construction projects.[39]

An examination of the institutional status of county environmental agencies nation-wide demonstrates quite clearly that until very recently institution-building at the county level has been a slow and laborious process. By 1992, 58 per cent of all county environmental protection organs were still divisions of local Construction Commissions or other agencies; only 42 per cent were independent (see Table 2).

Ominously, it was in that year that Deng Xiaoping delivered his Shenzhen speech, calling on localities to take risks to speed economic development. This kicked off a new burst of economic growth that reverberated throughout the Chinese countryside, creating numerous heavily polluting TVEs. By 1996, the Chinese government was reporting that rural industries had become one of the main sources of pollution and the problem was rapidly growing worse.[40] Yet as one Chinese scholar reported a year before:

Since the surge in development of township and village enterprises in 1992, nothing has been done to thwart the problem of dealing with these heavily polluting enterprises. No new policies have been developed and no progress made ... The emphasis is on economic development and particularly the development of central and western China. If you start to clamp down on environmental issues, you impede economic growth. The policy is to take economic growth first, so no-one is willing to take strong measures against polluters. As a result, the environment is not considered at all.[41]

In fact, rather than undertake measures to combat rapidly worsening rural environmental problems, central government policy directives actu-

39. Interview 74, autumn 1991.
40. The report noted that town and village enterprises (TVEs) accounted for 68.3% of all air pollution particulate emissions, 46.5% of all chemical oxygen demand (a measure of organic pollutants in waste water), and 38.6% of solid wastes in China during 1995. "1996 Zhongguo huanjing zhuangkuang gongbao" ("1996 report on China's environmental situation"), *Zhongguo huanjing bao* (*China Environmental Daily*), 7 June 1997.
41. Interview 201, May 1995.

ally exacerbated them. In 1993 and 1994, a third round of administrative reforms took place throughout the Chinese government. Again the goal was to reduce the size of the bureaucracy. Counties in particular were singled out to pare down the size of their administrative apparati. The State Council placed limits on the number of first-tier units they could have and identified 18 administrative units as essential for all county governments. Notably, environmental protection was not among the 18. The immediate effect in many counties was that Environmental Protection Bureaus were demoted to second-tier organs and, in a few cases, actually abolished. This significantly reduced the status of environmental protection work at the county level and demoralized those within this area who saw their most difficult challenge as coming from the rural industrial sector.[42]

Unlike the 1982 setback, the confluence of several events has served to limit the duration of this 1994 institutional setback – though not necessarily to fundamentally alter the situation in the countryside. In recent years, deteriorating environmental conditions throughout China – and particularly in the countryside – have drawn a much higher level of central attention to environmental issues than previously.[43] Throughout 1995, the environmental protection apparatus emphasized strengthening county environmental organs; a few provinces (including Guangdong, Jiangsu and Henan) responded by making environmental protection a required unit for all county governments.[44] When the Fourth National Environmental Protection Conference convened in July 1996, it attracted a new level of central leadership attention: for the first time, both the heads of the Communist Party and the Chinese State (at the time Jiang Zemin and Li Peng respectively), attended an environmental conference. At the conference, several environmental officials and local leaders voiced distress over the severe shortage of environmental staff and lack of funding to support staff increases. Though the central government did not respond directly to this financial concern, the State Council issued a statement following the Fourth Conference calling for localities to strengthen their environmental protection apparatus so as to assist in a massive campaign, discussed below, to close heavily-polluting TVEs.[45] By July 1997, 75–80 per cent of county environmental protection organs were reportedly independent, about half of these first-tier.[46]

This development, however, does not necessarily indicate that environmental conditions in the countryside will rapidly improve. First, the number of first-tier organizations is virtually the same as it was in the

42. Interviews 201, 202, 203, 207, May 1995. In 1995, a senior NEPA official complained that "the fact that well over 50% of county EPBs now have only second-tier status is a huge impediment to environmental work." Interview 203, May 1995.

43. A June 1996 report warned that China's environment had further deteriorated during the previous year, with problems spreading from urban to rural areas. See "Report warns of worsening pollution," *China Environment News*, 15 July 1996.

44. *China Environmental Yearbook 1996*, p. 242.

45. See "Guanyu huanjing baohu ruogan wenti de jueding" ("Decision concerning several problems related to environmental protection"), August 1996.

46. Interview 307, July 1997.

early 1990s, when the environmental regulation of counties was already extremely difficult. Secondly, although there are now many more second-tier independent organizations than in the past, the fact that they are second-tier still limits their authority. Thirdly, in general, county environmental units, even more than city units, are dependent on local governments for funds. As several scholars have noted, local governments have entrepreneurial interests in TVEs and act as their advocates, rather than their regulators.[47] Thus, regardless of their formal position of authority, county environmental agencies are often forced to overlook environmental regulations. Finally, the 1998 National People's Conference did nothing to discourage the continued growth of TVEs; in fact its strong emphasis on dismantling the state sector and building up private industry may actually end up further encouraging the development of TVEs.

Perhaps partially because of the continued inability to shore up commitment to environmental protection in the countryside, and partially, too, because of the notably deteriorating quality of China's urban environment under rapid economic growth, the 1998 National People's Congress decided to formally increase the authority of the National Environmental Protection Agency despite a strong climate of administrative austerity. To this end, several changes were made. First, NEPA was promoted to ministerial status and officially renamed the State Environmental Protection Administration (SEPA). Symbolically, this promotion indicates to Chinese government agencies and the public alike the increased central government attention to environmental protection. Secondly, SEPA's functional domain was notably enlarged. The Administration took over full responsibility for biodiversity, nature reserve management, wetland conservation and desertification control from the newly abolished Ministry of Forestry; from the State Oceanographic Administration it acquired the right to regulate marine pollution within approximately two miles from shore; it took control of the environmental effects of mining from the now defunct Ministry of Minerology; and it assumed responsibility for nuclear safety – and an important role in influencing China's emerging nuclear energy programme – from the China Atomic Energy Agency.[48] These changes have allowed for an increased level of functional integration and comprehensiveness essential to environmental protection work. Finally, the National People's Congress abolished the State Council Committee on Environmental Protection, allowing SEPA to turn its proposals into legislation much more rapidly. As a result of these changes, SEPA has decisively emerged as the main government body in the area of Chinese environmental protection and one with significantly

---

47. Jean C. Oi, "The role of the local state in China's transitional economy," p. 1144.
48. Chan Yee Hon et al. "Green body upgraded to ministry," p. 10. According to sources at SEPA, the National Nuclear Safety Administration (formerly part of the China National Nuclear Corporation and the China Atomic Energy Agency) will now be a bureau associated with SEPA: Biele, personal correspondence with the author, 28 April 1998. The decision to place nuclear safety under SEPA's domain reflects the administration's desire to project nuclear energy as a "clean" source of energy that will contribute to China's efforts to reduce global warming. *China Environmental Review*, Vol. 1, No. 4 (1998), p. 3

increased bureaucratic authority. The hope among government officials is that this increase in central authority will, among other things, filter down and translate into increased authority for local EPBs as they enforce environmental policy.

In sharp contrast to the extensive efforts to raise institutional status, there has been notably less change nation-wide in assuring ample funding. Recent promises of increased spending on environmental protection have neither addressed where this money is to come from nor guaranteed that local governments will in fact foot the bill. Instead, structural reforms designed to cut bureaucracies during the 1980s and continuing into the late 1990s have translated into greater limits on the availability of local government funds. Environmental protection agencies in some areas have developed individual means for coping with a shortage of funds so as to support their growing organization and its activities, but it would be wrong to speak of these means as a reliable solution to the problem.

The most common source of supplementary funds for EPBs and EPOs in cities, districts and counties has been the collection of discharge fees, money paid by enterprises who have exceeded pollution discharge standards. By law, up to 20 per cent of fees may be retained by local environmental agencies to support the work of their existing organizations. In fact, many EPBs and EPOs – particularly prior to achieving independent status – have enlarged their organizations on the basis of discharge fees, and a significant portion of base-level environmental protection officials are supported solely through funds collected from the discharge fee system (a practice referred to as "eating discharge fees," *chi paiwufei*). This practice has clearly created a contradiction for environmental protection: relying on discharge fees instead of government funds, EPBs respond to the incentive to collect fees rather than reduce pollution; indeed, pollution reduction could dry up this important source of funds.[49]

In some areas over the past decade, EPBs have also become entrepreneurial. In line with trends throughout the government, environmental agencies have set up subsidiary research institutes and engineering companies and have supplemented their government budgetary allocations through fees for services such as Environmental Impact Assessments (EIAs) and technology consultation or design.[50] The problem here is that not all environmental agencies throughout the country are equally equipped with technically-trained personnel to pursue such strategies; poorer areas, and rural areas, are at a disadvantage. Moreover, a question of conflict of interest arises when the regulating agency is being paid by the company to perform EIAs or design pollution prevention equipment. What happens if the equipment fails? Will the EPB still hold the firm responsible for pollution accidents? And if a company pays an EPB subsidiary to conduct an EIA, will the EPB then be more likely to

---

49. Jahiel, "The contradictory impact of reform."
50. For a good discussion of this phenomenon in the Special Economic Zones of Guangdong province see Sincule and Ortolano, *Implementing Environmental Policy in China,* pp. 161–185.

overlook some of the environmental short-comings of the proposed project? Thus, although these entrepreneurial forms of income generation may reduce one form of financial dependence that favours economic interests at the expense of environmental interests (dependence on local governments), they may well create another.

A final and recent development is the creation, encouraged by NEPA, of EPB-based "environmental protection funds" (*huanjing baohu zijin*). Discharge fees create the capital that initiates these investment funds; in turn, investment funds generate profits to support EPB work and loans for firms wishing to install environmentally-friendly technology. This development is still in its nascent phase. To date, however, 20 provinces and municipalities have established environmental protection funds or special foundations and have accumulated over 3 billion *yuan*.[51] The future impact of these funds with regard to creating sources of independent financing for environmental agencies remains to be seen. Again, however, it seems likely that poorer areas will be disadvantaged.

In sum, the institutional history of efforts to develop authority for the environmental protection apparatus is mixed. Clearly, the past 15 years in particular has seen the assembly of an extensive institutional system nation-wide and the increase of its rank. With these gains has come a commensurate increase in EPB bureaucratic authority – particularly in cities. Efforts to build formal authority through financial strength have had more ambiguous results. In certain areas of the country developments have reduced financial dependence on local governments (although not necessarily on local economies, nor without creating potential conflicts of interest); however, not all areas have succeeded in developing significant financial channels independent of these governments.

However, even where EPBs have acquired formal authority – where they have achieved independent status, diversified their functions, properly staffed themselves, succeeded in basically routinizing policy implementation and developed a source of outside funds – environmental policy remains at times difficult to implement. Two factors are at play here. First, irrespective of formal authority, powerful local actors still regard environmental interests as secondary to economic interests and, consequently, intervene against the enforcement of environmental policies.[52] Secondly, advances in formal authority do little to overcome structural features of the Chinese political system that tend to isolate government agencies at the same administrative level from one another – be they EPBs in different geographic locales or various government agencies within one locale. To overcome these shortcomings, environmental protection agencies at both the national and local level have recognized that they must assure the active assistance of other govern-

51. Interview 310, July 1997.

52. In 1995, a senior NEPA official complained that "city, county, and village officials still protect their enterprises and intervene on their behalf against environmental regulations." He reported further that "... in the last couple of years, city governments have started to use the discharge fees to pay salaries and to build roads and other such things. They act in the short term and don't consider the long term." Interview 203, May 1995.

ment actors through various efforts aimed at co-ordination between EPBs and other government agencies.[53]

Co-ordination with Other Government Agencies

Perhaps the earliest recognition of the need for co-ordinated management is reflected in the application of the contract responsibility system to the environmental realm. Initiated in various locales in the mid-1980s, the environmental responsibility system (*huanjing baohu mubiao zerenzhi*) became official government policy in the 1989 revised Environmental Protection Law. Under this system, local government leaders (including provincial governors, city mayors and county magistrates) have signed annual contracts with Environmental Protection Bureaus, agreeing to help EPBs achieve certain pollution reduction targets and specifying precise projects to meet these goals. The incentive for compliance with these contracts lies in the fact that, at year's end, the leader's environmental performance is evaluated and, in some places, publicized; poor performance ratings can negatively impact on political careers.[54]

During the early 1990s, environmental responsibility contracts were signed *en masse* at all levels of local government, from the province to the county.[55] Evidence from several cities and counties suggests that where local government leaders willingly signed such contracts, there was a noticeable impact on EPB work. They reduced local government attempts to intervene on behalf of polluting factories; they granted EPBs the authority to issue deadline clean-up orders to egregious polluters without first receiving government approval; they placed increased government pressure on enterprises, causing them to adopt more stringent pollution control measures; and they led local governments to assign responsibility for some environmental monitoring tasks to other agencies (for example, the monitoring of automobile exhaust and noise pollution in Wuhan is now the responsibility of the Bureau of Public Security).[56] In all these ways, they helped EPBs overcome their institutional weakness *vis-à-vis* the local power brokers.

In recent years, the environmental protection apparatus has pursued several other means aimed at drawing important local government actors

53. Jahiel, "Organizational learning through policy implementation," pp. 277–334, and Sinkule and Ortolano, *Implementing Environmental Policy in China*, pp. 152–54. Economy draws similar conclusions about the necessity of co-ordinated efforts for another relatively weak institution with environmental responsibilities, the Water Resources Bureau. Elizabeth Economy, *Environmental Scarcities, State Capacity, Civil Violence: The Case of China* (Cambridge, MA: American Academy of Arts and Sciences, 1997), p. 47.

54. Interview 31, autumn 1991, and interview 312, July 1997. Also see Sinkule and Ortolano, *Implementing Environmental Policy in China*, p. 37.

55. Some of the enthusiasm for environmental responsibility contracts appears to have waned recently, notably at the provincial level. Nevertheless in some locales – especially at the district and county levels, where economic pulls are most immediate – these contracts continue to play a significant role in boosting EPB or EPO efforts. Interviews 203 and 207, May 1995; Interviews 310, 312 and 317, July 1997.

56. Interviews 60b, 69, 75, 80, 85, 89, 91 and 98, autumn 1991.

into the policy process. In 1995, the National Environmental Protection Agency forged an alliance with the People's Bank of China and its local affiliates. Under the compact reached, the Bank agreed to refuse credit to firms that "could not correctly dispose of their industrial waste or failed to meet state standards for environmental protection."[57]

During the following year, NEPA reached an agreement with several government agencies, most importantly, the General Customs Agency, to work jointly to prevent the import of hazardous wastes to China. For several years prior, China had faced an influx of foreign wastes, fraudulently marketed as recyclables, imported by Chinese firms eager to make money. The environmental protection apparatus, as a rule, did not learn of these wastes – some of them hazardous – until they manifested themselves as local pollution problems. In 1996, NEPA worked with the General Customs Agency, the Commodity Inspection Bureau, the Industrial Commerce Administration and the Ministry of Foreign Economic Relations and Trade (MOFERT), to jointly issue specific "Methods for the environmental management of imported wastes," and to include mention of this issue in the Solid Waste Law about to be promulgated. The result was that rather than being solely NEPA's responsibility, the General Customs Agency became actively involved in regulation. The NEPA division chief responsible for solid wastes saw this alliance as an extremely successful one: in 1996 alone, 200 European and American ships carrying solid waste headed for China were turned back, sending a message to the international community that China would no longer complacently allow itself to be a dumping ground. Since then, similar incidents have decreased dramatically.[58]

A final case in which the environmental protection administration has allied with other government agencies involves the recent nation-wide effort to close small, heavily polluting firms. The relatively successful closure of 67,000 firms by July 1997 is in part attributable to the fact that the environmental protection apparatus was not working alone. Rather, local commerce bureaus revoked firms' operating permits; electric companies cut their electricity; banks withdrew loans; and in the end, in several places, local governments, with the assistance of public security bureaus, simply bulldozed the sites to prevent firms from reopening. Clearly, in enforcing policy, the environmental protection apparatus had the support and assistance of the agencies most crucial to industrial activity.[59]

57. Additionally, the People's Bank of China agreed to increase its financial lending for environmental protection technologies and programmes. Economy, *Environmental Scarcities, State Capacity, Civil Violence*, pp. 47–48.

58. Interview 308, July 1997.

59. The closure of firms is somewhat more complicated than this overview suggests. First, in some cases economic factors and not environmental ones may be primarily responsible for firm closures. Closure of firms may be a response to market failures or may serve to rid localities of unprosperous factories and allow firms to create economies of scale through mergers. Secondly, while 75% of the firms slotted to be shut down have been closed, in some cases firms have reopened, though apparently the problem is easing. Finally, even if the majority of small-scale, heavy polluters that have been closed remain closed, new polluting firms continue to open. Interviews 305 and 312, July 1997.

Jurisdictional Divides

Unfortunately, as the National People's Congress decision to merge regulatory functions suggests, the environmental apparatus has not been successful in *all* cases necessitating co-ordinated management. One type of institutional weakness in the organization of environmental protection appears to be, as yet, insurmountable: the lack of co-ordination across jurisdictional boundaries – both between EPBs in different geographic locales and between EPBs and other government organs within the same region. Two examples illustrate this problem; one involves the transfer of polluting industries or waste matter from one part of the country to another; the other the destruction of watersheds shared by neighbouring cities or provinces. In both cases, institutional fragmentation and lack of sufficient authority, combined with prevailing local interests in economic development, prevent co-ordination.

The transfer of polluting industries and wastes from one region in China to another is a subject that the Chinese are hesitant to discuss. Nevertheless, there is evidence that over the past decade, polluting firms – particularly when banished from prosperous coastal cities – have relocated to less-developed inland locales. In many of these areas, local government officials have courted any kind of investment, regardless of environmental impact, so long as it appears profitable, and opposition by environmental officials has been thwarted. For example, officials in Wuhan in 1991 reported that a few years earlier, heavily polluting electroplating firms from Shanghai had been relocating there in droves.[60] In the mid-1990s, Chongqing environmental officials found themselves unable to prevent a heavily polluting factory from migrating to their city after it failed to meet stringent environmental regulations in Qingdao.[61] And Xi'an officials in 1997 reported that one of the reasons they would never be finished with their task of closing the 15 types of heavily polluting small enterprises slotted for elimination by the central government was that there were always new polluting factories relocating to Shaanxi province unbeknownst to environmental officials.[62] In addition, several areas in China, particularly poorer, rural ones, have now become the repository for wastes from wealthier urban areas where consumerism has taken hold. Though this transfer often involves China's richer coastal regions, it is not restricted to these areas. In 1995, authorities in the interior Ningxia Autonomous Region discovered nearly 200 railcars of municipal garbage and construction waste; investigation revealed the waste had come from Xi'an city, capital of neighbouring Shaanxi province.[63]

60. Interview 56, autumn 1991.

61. Interview 301, June 1997.

62. Interview 312, July 1997. While some argue that less prosperous locales should have the right to pursue their economic interests by sacrificing the health of their environment, others, this author among them, contend that a real question of environmental justice is brought to play when environmental sacrifice becomes a dominant means of economic advancement.

63. Interview 306, July 1997. Ellen Spitalnik, "The long, arduous path towards effective waste management," *Asia Environmental Business Journal*, Vol. III, No. 5 (1997), p. 12.

The severity of the jurisdictional boundaries problem mounts when entire watersheds are involved. Often faced with pressure from local governments to ease environmental regulations for the sake of economic development, environmental agencies have in many instances approved environmentally harmful projects by requiring that they be sited downstream from the drinking water intakes for the city under their jurisdiction.[64] In essence, environmental organs have aimed to avoid a pollution problem within their regulatory domain by moving the problem to a neighbouring domain. With local environmental agencies in virtually all locales behaving in this way, and with water bodies crossing county, municipal and provincial lines, management of river basins necessitates co-ordination between environmental protection agencies (and often local governments) in different jurisdictions.

When major river bodies are concerned, moreover, multiple regulatory authorities are also involved. The Chinese refer to this situation as the problem of "many dragons" (*duolong*). As a deputy director of the Wuhan EPB explained,

... several different government organs all have rights to control the nation's. waters ... the Ministry of Agriculture, the Ministry of Water Conservation, the Ministry of Navigation, the Ministry of Transportation and Communications, and the EPB ... The problem is that when everyone is responsible, in actuality nobody is responsible! [*sheidou guan, sheidou buguan!*][65]

The jurisdictional impediments to watershed management are thus extremely difficult to overcome.

An illustration of this was the Huai River disaster. In 1994 the cauldron of environmental disaster brewing along the Huai River finally boiled over.[66] Over 150 million Chinese live along this river, which, along with its tributaries, traverses four provinces (Shandong, Henan, Jiangsu and Anhui). For the past few decades the Huai River has been a site of industrial development and accompanying industrial pollution. Beginning in 1974 and continuing into the next decade, central leaders repeatedly urged local leaders to take action to control industrial pollution of the watershed, but with only minimal results.

With the growth of small-scale TVEs in the region during the late 1980s, the pollution problems became more severe. By 1990, water that flowed through the cities of Xuzhou, Yangzhou and Huaiyin was seriously polluted, destroying fish and shrimp stock. Concern over the loss to the fisheries led to efforts to force immediate clean up or closure of factories, but again with little success. The number of inter-provincial disputes over polluted water continued to rise; meanwhile, the director of

64. In one city in Sichuan province, the city government had actually institutionalized this tendency by issuing a city ordinance requiring all new chemical plants to be located downstream so as not to pollute the city's water supply. Interview 81. autumn 1991.

65. Interview with the Deputy Director of the Wuhan EPB, International Conference on Environmental Economic Policy, Shandong, PRC, July 1991.

66. This discussion draws extensively on Li Kefeng, "Huai: health hazard," *China Environment News*, July 1993, p. 4–5, and Economy, *Environmental Scarcities, State Capacity. Civil Violence.*

the Bureau of Water Resources Protection of the Huai River, responsible for co-ordinating efforts among the four provinces involved, conceded that his bureau had no real authority to force action. In 1993, senior officials and journalists surveyed the Huai valley during a fact-finding investigation of local environmental conditions and reported the extent of the pollution problem along the Huai River.[67] As one senior NEPA official later said, "economic development had just occurred blindly."[68] Small paper mills had multiplied in the preceding years, with 600 in Henan alone.[69] In response to the situation, in May 1994, the State Council's Environmental Protection Commission convened a meeting to discuss the problem of provincial co-operation on the Huai River. The meeting was a failure, with each of the provinces blaming the other three for polluting the river and demanding that the others pay for the cleanup. Meanwhile factories continued to ignore central government directives that they stop disposing of wastes directly into the water, and local officials ignored earlier pleas to shut down paper, leather, and dyeing factories.[70]

In mid-July, pollution of the Huai River reached crisis proportions. The river turned black. More than 11.7 million kilograms of fish were killed, dozens of fish farms were destroyed, and factories were forced to close for over a week, with cumulative economic losses estimated at US$75 million. By 16 July, the primary waterworks in the region was no longer functioning properly and contaminants in the treated water exceeded minimum safety standards by several dozen times. Several thousand people became seriously ill with dysentery, diarrhoea and vomiting. Water could no longer be used for drinking, cooking or irrigation. The disaster was exacerbated on 20 July, when local authorities in Bengbu, Anhui, acting without consultation or warning to the downstream cities or fish farms, released additional polluted water detained by the Bengbu Dam. Hundreds of thousands of people were left without drinking water, in some cases for weeks.

Social unrest was immediate and drew rapid central government response. High-level investigations were conducted, an interministerial sub-commission was established, and 999 paper mills and untold numbers of other factories were closed.[71] According to the Chinese government, not only did these immediate measures restore drinking water to the community, but long-term efforts have improved the quality of the Huai River.[72] Still, even if these reports are accurate – and there is some reason

67. Plato Yip, "Green campaigning takes off," *One Earth* (Winter 1996), pp. 15–16.
68. Interview 207, May 1995.
69. *Ibid.*
70. Hertsgaard, "Our real China problem," p. 104.
71. *Ibid.* p. 104.
72. Kang Ren, "Huaihe survey finds better water quality," *China Environment News*, 15 December 1997, p. 1.

to question this[73]– the fundamental problem that led to the situation, and could easily affect other regions, does not appear to have changed: local governments continue to pursue economic self-interest first; and co-ordination across regional jurisdictions and between various agencies responsible for water quality has not improved.

Organizational Strengths and Weaknesses

The above examination of the organization of environmental protection in China and the way it has evolved leads to several conclusions. First, China has built an extensive, nation-wide environmental protection apparatus, complete with monitoring networks and interagency co-ordinating bodies at all levels of government. Growth at the national level has extended the range of activities environmental officials perform. Secondly, chiefly by raising its bureaucratic rank, the environmental agency has markedly enhanced its formal position of authority relative to other powerful actors. SEPA is now finally a ministerial body; most city environmental organs are now first-tier units; 27 out of 31 of China's provincial EPBs have first-tier rank (with the other four having bureaucratic independence); and as many as 75–80 per cent of county environmental organizations are independent.[74] This increase in authority has notably eased efforts to implement policy. Thirdly, in some parts of the country, environmental agencies have found ways to generate funds, allowing them to expand their employee payrolls. Fourthly, recent administrative changes have enlarged the environmental protection apparatus' regulatory domain, further enhancing interagency co-ordination and increasing formal authority. Finally, where formal authority has been insufficient, the environmental apparatus has, in recent years, increased its ability to work with other government units, forging alliances with powerful government agencies to overcome implementation hurdles.

Still, many of these advances are relative. Although environmental agencies in many locales have now achieved equal bureaucratic rank with finance bureaus, bureaus of industry and commerce, and industrial bureaus, they, as equals, remain unable to issue binding demands. It is not clear whether the 1998 NPC decision to abolish industrial ministries and incorporate their functions within the State Economic and Trade Commission (SETC) will help improve this situation. Two factors suggest otherwise. First, the designation of the SETC as a commission indicates a rank higher than the newly promoted SEPA, suggesting that new institutions at the local level responsible for economic development and trade will also have a higher rank than first-tier environmental agencies.

---

73. Reports indicate that some of the firms shut down secretly re-emerged, even after equipment was seized. "Polluting paper mills die hard," *China Environment News,* 15 March 1996, p. 2. Moreover, environmentalists report that actions taken to shut down firms have not achieved a fundamental change for the better. Kang Ren, "Huaihe survey finds better water quality," p. 1.

74. Interview 307, July 1997.

Secondly, the diminishing role for the state in industrial matters suggests that the ranking of environmental agencies relative to industrial bureaus may increasingly be irrelevant, and ascribed authority vested in EPBs by industry even more significant than in the past.

More importantly, EPB dependence on local governments continues to be a fundamental structural impediment to consistent enforcement of environmental policy, as local governments continue at times to pressure EPBs to ease regulations in the interest of economic concerns. Furthermore, sources of funding for environmental protection are still inadequate. Even solutions aimed at overcoming financial shortages and dependence on local government through the generation of outside funds do not necessarily free environmental protection agencies from dominance by local economic interests – or aid in the reduction of pollution.

The two chronically weak links in the organization of environmental protection in China are those at the county-level, and those involving inter-jurisdictional domain. County agencies are still short of staff, funds, equipment and technically-trained cadres; in many areas their low bureaucratic rank continues to deprive them of the authority to enforce policy. Yet it is precisely the rural industrial sector that is both the most polluting sector and one of the fastest growing sectors of the Chinese economy – and it remains the most difficult sector to regulate.[75] The problem of inter-jurisdictional domain – whether between EPBs in different geographic regions or between EPBs and other government agencies within a locale – is in many ways even more intractable because it is intrinsic to the traditional relationships of the Chinese administrative system. Further, it is compounded by the fact that the central government, in its efforts to invigorate the Chinese economy through decentralization, has relinquished considerable control over localities.

The Future

What impact will the 1998 NPC administrative reforms and work platform be likely to have on the problems identified above? The historical overview of the environmental protection apparatus demonstrates clearly that increased formal authority at the central level has traditionally benefited the environmental protection apparatus as a whole. It has meant an increase in personnel and in funds, as well as bureaucratic promotions for local EPBs. However, whether SEPA's recent promotion to ministerial status will have as great an effect, particularly in the short term, is unclear. Uncharacteristically for newly promoted organizations, but consistent with the Ninth NPC decision to reduce all government staff by 50 per cent, SEPA is to see an overall reduction in staff. Although the agency will receive an influx of personnel to work on nuclear safety

---

75. Reports exist of county environmental officials actually being beaten up when they have tried to collect discharge fees. Not surprisingly, of the 1,190,000 polluting TVEs conservatively estimated to exist, only 30–40,000 are actually charged fees. Interview 305, June 1997.

issues, half of its existing personnel are to be dismissed. In total, SEPA will have over 200 employees compared with the more than 300 people it had previously been allotted.[76] Moreover, no promises of increased funding have yet been made, and the general message of the Ninth NPC to government agencies throughout China was to tighten their belts.

Nevertheless, the purpose of raising SEPA's status and consolidating environmental functions under one agency was to increase the Administration's authority to assert control over environmental protection work. The NPC decision to expand SEPA's functional domain will, no doubt, ultimately reduce interagency competition for limited environmental funds; moreover, it will ease environmental efforts in certain respects – most notably with regard to control of biodiversity, forestry, wetland conservation, coastlines and nuclear safety. However, there are still critically important regulatory domains related to environmental protection that remain under the purview of other agencies and hence beyond SEPA's control. First, decisions regarding the energy profile of the Chinese economy – a critical issue with regard to addressing global warming – are still well beyond SEPA's reach (even as the central government continues to regard development of fossil fuels as critically important to relieve bottlenecks to industrial development). Secondly, SEPA continues to have little say over decisions made by the Ministry of Foreign Economic Relations and Trade which encourage investment by foreign firms even when these firms are harmful to the environment. Thirdly, SEPA still lacks regulatory jurisdiction over oceanic pollution, conservation of fisheries and preservation of marine animals. Finally, there is still no resolution to the jurisdictional problems that produce watershed management conflicts, a particularly pernicious problem given the mounting concern over water scarcity in China.[77]

As for the decision to abolish the State Council's Committee on Environmental Protection, the implications of this administrative change are at present difficult to assess. While abolition of the Committee strengthens SEPA's position of sole responsibility for environmental protection, it potentially weakens its ability to achieve compliance from other agencies. A critical function of the Commission on Environmental Protection was its role as a neutral ground for government agencies outside the environmental protection network to hammer out their differences with regard to environmental legislation, under pressure from a senior member of the State Council. The responsibility for interministerial environmental co-ordination now falls to SEPA alone. SEPA's success in this regard will depend greatly on the ascribed authority it, as a newly promoted ministry, is able to garner.

Reforms in the broader economic sphere also have implications for environmental protection work. Under the austerity measures announced at the 1998 NPC, faltering state enterprises are to be closed once and for

76. Changhua Wu, correspondence with the author.
77. For further information on the problem of water shortage in China see articles by James E. Nickum and Liu Changming elsewhere in this volume.

all. This may pose some environmental benefit as such enterprises would have had very limited funds to deal with pollution. But small-scale private industry – the hardest sector to regulate – is to be encouraged. Even more significantly, the main platform of the 1998 National People's Congress made clear that the primary goal of the Jiang Zemin–Zhu Rongji administration remains rapid economic growth. There is no indication in the decision to pursue annual growth rates of 8 per cent that a transformation in the leadership's thinking regarding the relative importance of environmental management *vis-à-vis* economic growth is likely.

What conclusions can we draw, then, for the future? Incidents like the Huai River disaster are sobering reminders of the serious shortcomings that still exist within the organization of environmental protection in China. Their broader implications for political stability are real. During the next ten years, assuming current trajectories and similar growth rates for the Chinese economy, China's environmental problems are only likely to grow worse. Should several environmental catastrophes similar to the Huai River situation develop, however, public protest could shake the regime. Even individual environmental incidents could conceivably conjoin with other social problems, such as unemployment, in an explosive mix. This is the pessimistic outlook.

The more optimistic forecast suggests that the recent changes made at the Ninth NPC reflect the fact that the environmental situation in China is already so severe that major changes are in the offing. Clearly, environmental concern among the top leadership, particularly since the Huai River incident, has risen noticeably and central-level leaders realize the potential political and economic crises environmental catastrophe can entail.[78] A recent report by the Chinese State Science and Technology Commission contains a severe assessment of environmental degradation in China which concludes with the remark "the alarm bell is not frightening, but having heard it, not to heed its warning would be truly frightening!"[79] Furthermore, recent studies suggest that economic losses due to pollution may actually be outstripping gains from rapid economic growth.[80] And senior economists have publicly acknowledged that "inadequate ecological protection" could impede future growth.[81]

If catastrophic disaster does not sound the wake-up call, and if pursuit of short-term economic gain continues to be the *modus operandi* of the Chinese political leadership, however, two other emerging forces may provide the necessary catalysts for change. In recent years the organization of environmental protection has expanded outwards in two ways.

78. Interview 305, June 1997.
79. Summary of report entitled "Science and education for a prosperous China," State Science and Technology Commission, published in Changhua Wu and Jeffrey Logan (eds.), *China Environment Reporter*, Vol. 2, No. 3, (1997). Full report available at http:// www.redfish.com/USEmbassy-China/
80. Vaclav Smil has estimated economic losses due to environmental degradation at 10–15% of the annual Chinese GDP. This compares to the average annual growth rate of just under 10%. Vaclav Smil, *Environmental Problems in China: Estimates of Economic Costs* (Hawaii: East West Center Special Report 5, April 1996).
81. Li Yining quoted in Hertsgarrd, "Our real China problem," p. 102.

First, international concern for the environment has had an increasing bearing on environmental politics in China.[82] International environmental conferences (such as the 1992 Rio Conference, the 1997 Kyoto Conference, and so on) and international funding for environmental control have begun to motivate many of China's most powerful government agencies, such as the State Development Planning Commission and the Ministry of Science and Technology, and to send them scrambling for a piece of the environmental pie.[83] In addition, international environmental organizations such as the World Wide Fund for Nature (WWF) are dramatically expanding their programmes in China, further attracting government attention to and interest in the environment.

Secondly, in the last few years, independent domestic environmental organizations – including Friends of Nature, the Global Village Environmental Culture Institute of Beijing, Green Earth Volunteers and the Beijing Environmental Protection Foundation – have begun to emerge in China.[84] In addition to these organizations, student-organized environmental groups are sprouting up on college campuses.[85] At present environmental groups in China are still in their infancy, but depending on political developments over the next decade, this force could grow significantly stronger.

What would the Chinese have to do to overcome some of the organizational hurdles to effective pollution control? To begin, they would have to elevate the status of the environmental protection apparatus at *all* levels of the government hierarchy, ideally giving it status comparable to commissions and therefore of at least equal par with state economic interests. Secondly, they would have to break the local governments' hold over local environmental protection agencies by assuring a source of

---

82. Interview 13, July 1997.

83. From 1992–1997, according to the World Bank, approximately 5% of all World Bank loans to China have been directed toward environmental protection. China receives loans or funds for environmental protection from other development agencies such as the Asia Development Bank and foreign governments as well. See The World Bank homepage, Country Brief China, http://www.worldbank.org/html/extdr/offrep/eap/china.htm.

84. Friends of Nature is the largest of these groups. Established in 1994, it had 350 members by 1997; it and the Global Village Environmental Culture Institute of Beijing, established in 1996, emphasize environmental education. Green Earth Volunteers, founded in 1997, organizes environmental activities such as tree-planting in the Engebie Desert. The Beijing Environmental Protection Foundation was established in August 1996 and has since focused its efforts on recycling and on educating women and children about the environment. Interview 310, July 1997. Elizabeth Knup, "Environmental NGOs in China: an overview," in *China Environment Series* (Washington, DC: Woodrow Wilson Center, 1997), pp. 9–15. Cai Fang, "Beijing Environmental Foundation's environmental enthusiasts," *China Environment News*, April 1998, p. 8.

85. In Beijing, as of July 1997, there were over 20 such groups, and at least ten campus organizations had been established in other parts of the country, some with as many as 400 members. For obvious reasons, all of these groups have taken a non-confrontational stance toward government policy, emphasizing education and volunteerism instead. Nevertheless, their budding activism is indicated by the (unofficial) establishment in March 1996 of The Green Student Forum (*lüse daxuesheng luntan*). Green Forum acts as a network among college environmental groups, publishing a newsletter and organizing summer "Green Camps" for projects such as protecting the Yunnan snub-nosed monkey and opposing logging in Tibet. Interview 309 with member of Green Forum, July 1997.

consistent and sufficient funds from a channel as removed from local politics and economics as possible. This would best be achieved through central government budgetary allocation of funds. Thirdly, they would have to significantly weaken the regional economic interests that make environmental inter-jurisdictional co-ordination so complex and contentious. The key question is whether or not the government can undertake such reforms without re-prioritizing its goal of rapid economic expansion, abandoning its consumer-oriented growth strategy, and significantly altering the structure of China's current political economy. After all, the main platform of the 1998 National People's Congress made clear that the primary goal of the Jiang Zemin–Zhu Rongji administration remains market-driven, rapid economic growth, and that a transformation in the leadership's thinking regarding the relative importance of environmental management *vis-à-vis* economic growth has not yet occurred.

Environmental Regulation in the People's Republic of China: The Face of Domestic Law

Michael Palmer

Introduction

In the post-Mao era, one highly significant dimension of China's official programme of reform and integration into the international economy has been a commitment to legal construction. This commitment has included a sustained effort to fashion a basic corpus of environmental protection law alongside supportive institutions, administrative norms and policies, in order to create a "basic legal system of environmental protection" (*huanjing baohu de jiben falü zhidu*).[1] In the eyes of the authorities in the People's Republic of China, such efforts reflect a degree of environmental concern that is unusually strong for a developing society.[2] China's achievements, we are often told, must be placed in the context of the considerable difficulties the PRC faces in terms of the pressing need to raise living standards, a serious problem of over-population, a shortage of natural resources, an outdated industrial infrastructure and poor industrial management.[3] Of course, viewed comparatively, the PRC's embrace of environmental protection law was somewhat belated,[4] only properly commencing after its participation in the 1972 United Nations Conference on the Human Environment held in Stockholm. The subsequent expansion of environmental legislation and enforcement has been somewhat erratic. Nevertheless, there appears to be a continuing intent to fashion a substantial body of environmental law, and concern with the construction and revision of this was further enhanced by China's participation in the 1992 UN Conference on Environment and Development,

1. Wang Jin, "Zhongguo huanjing baohu de jiben falü zhidu" ("The basic legal system of environmental protection in China"), paper presented at the China-Europe Legal Seminar, Beijing, 13–14 November 1997, p. 1.
2. In particular, the PRC's commitment is reflected in the fact that the Environmental Protection Law 1979 (for trial use) was one of the seven major law codes promulgated by the National People's Congress and its Standing Committee after the decision by the Chinese leadership to revert to more orthodox modes of legal development and to govern through a "rule of law." This raft of legislation was thus regarded as a symbol of the beginning of a new era of legal construction, and it is particularly significant that environmental protection was one of the areas of social life to be given priority in the legislative programme. In addition, at the second national working conference on environmental protection held in 1983, environmental protection was made a basic national policy (*jiben guoce*) – see Yang Chaofei, *Huanjing baohu yu huanjing wenhua* (*Environmental Protection and Environmental Culture*) (Beijing: Zhongguo zhengfa daxue chubanshe, 1994), p. 6.
3. Wang Jin, "The basic legal system of environmental protection in China", p. 1.
4. That is, it only effectively commenced in the mid-1970s, significantly later than many Western societies that were already beginning to address environmental issues in a sustained manner in the 1960s.

held in Rio de Janeiro. Following this, Premier Li Peng "made a commitment to conscientiously implement resolutions adopted at the Conference"[5] and, given the PRC's very substantial size and population, a positive embrace of internationally acceptable standards of environmental welfare is highly significant for future global environmental protection. This article examines the principal features and significance of the PRC's domestic environmental protection law, and considers briefly the implications of the Chinese approach to environmental law for understanding the development of law more generally in post-Mao China.

The efforts that the PRC has made towards environmental protection through law over the past two decades have, however, been made against a background of deepening environmental degradation. The problems that have manifested themselves most obviously include extensive water and air pollution, deforestation and desertification. The apparent ineffectiveness of the legal regulatory regime for environmental protection reflects, to a significant extent, the relatively late start that the PRC made in adopting legal measures for environmental welfare. In the development of a socialist legal system in the 1950s, inspiration came primarily from the Soviet Union, and it is therefore perhaps not surprising that only limited attention was given to environmental legislation. But an embryonic concern for environmental interests can be located in a very restricted number of statutes. For example, the 1956 Regulations of the Protection of Mineral Resources stipulated that local water was not to be polluted in the exploitation of mineral resources, and the 1956 Regulations on Factory Safety not only promoted a safe working environment by requiring, for example, that "covered spittoons be provided at working places and be cleaned at least once a day" but also contained potentially important provisions on gas, dust and dangerous materials which, *inter alia*, stipulated that "waste materials and waste liquids shall be properly disposed of so as not to endanger the health of workers or the local inhabitants."[6] Other important developments included the introduction in 1956 of a policy for comprehensive utilization (*zonghe liyong*) of industrial waste, the 1957 State Council Provisional Programme on Water and Soil Protection (which initiated efforts at preventing and dealing with soil erosion problems), the 1962 State Council Directive Concerning the Active Protection and Rational Use of Wildlife and Natural Resources, and the mid-1960s State Council Directive on Strengthening the Work of Purchase and Utilization of Waste Products. The latter directive introduced the concept of management and recycling of the "three wastes" (*sanfei*) namely, gaseous emissions, water discharges and industrial residue.[7]

Although there is something of a debate on the attitude taken in

5. *China's Agenda 21 – White Paper on China's Population, Environment, and Development in the 21st Century* (Beijing: China Environmental Science Press, 1994), p. 2.

6. Jin Suilin, *Huanjing faxue* (*Environmental Law*) (Beijing: Beijing daxue chubanshe, 1990), p. 51

7. See Zhang Zitai, *Huanjing baohu fa* (*Environmental Protection Law*) (Nanjing: Hehai daxue chubanshe, 1994), pp. 20–21, and Luo Huihan, *Huanjing faxue* (*Environmental Law*) (Guangdong: Zhongshan daxue chubanshe, 1986), pp. 23–24.

classical Marxism to the relationship between safeguarding the environment and economic development,[8] the position inspired by Mao in China in the late 1950s and for the second half of the 1960s appears to have been rather unambiguous. It is true that Mao showed some concern for the promotion of afforestation and other aspects of "green agriculture",[9] and apparently believed that collectivization could help to overcome environmental problems in the countryside.[10] However, this interest in environmental welfare was vastly overshadowed by the vigorously pursued utopian ideal of the Great Leap Forward which led to extensive deforestation, pollution and many environmentally-unsound infrastructure projects such as the filling of lakes to create arable land.[11] Subsequent natural disasters and famine conditions were interpreted in terms of the vagaries of the climate and the errors of lower-level cadres, rather than as reflecting the central leadership's insufficient attention to environmental welfare concerns.

It was not until the early 1970s that concern with environmental protection was revived. In 1973, at the first national conference on environmental protection held in Beijing by the State Council, a firm decision was taken on the need for environmental safekeeping. The tentative and draft 1973 Several Rules on Protecting and Improving the Environment (*Guanyu baohu he gaishan huanjing de ruogan guiding* (*shixing caoan*)), provided a basic programme for environmental protection, and in 1974 this protection was extended to the maritime sphere through the Provisional Regulations on the Prevention of Pollution of Coastal Waters (*Fangzhi yanhai shuiyu wuran zanxing guiding*).[12] In due

---

8. See, for example, David Goldblatt, *Social Theory and the Environment* (Cambridge: Polity Press, 1996), pp. 5–6, 9–11, and David Harvey, *Justice, Nature and the Geography of Difference* (Oxford: Blackwell, 1986), pp. 197–204.

9. See, for example, Roderick MacFarquhar, Timothy Cheek and Eugene Wu, *The Secret Speeches of Chairman Mao* (Cambridge, MA: Harvard University Press, 1989), pp. 379, 384.

10. See, for example, Mao Zedong, "Introducing a co-operative," in *Selected Readings from the Works of Mao Tsetung* (Beijing: Foreign Languages Press, 1971), pp. 499–501, especially editorial note 1 at pp. 500–501.

11. As Schwartz has pointed out, this had been preceded by the enthusiastic campaign against the Four Pests in which a "war" was waged against rats, flies, mosquitoes and sparrows – see Benjamin I. Schwartz, "Thoughts on the late Mao – between total redemption and utter frustration," in MacFarquhar, Cheek and Wu, *The Secret Speeches of Chairman Mao*, p. 33. The mass extermination of the latter, however, permitted other insect pests to burgeon and in 1960 sparrows were replaced by bedbugs as a target – see *ibid.* p. 379. The official view of the environmental impact of the Maoist approach may be illustrated as follows: "such stupidities as draining lakes and ponds, building dykes in the sea, cutting down forests and destroying pastureland in order to reclaim land for planting grain ended up causing inestimable damage to forestry, animal husbandry and fishery. Grave imbalances appeared in the rural economy and the natural ecology" (Luo Hanxian, *Economic Changes in Rural China* (Beijing: New World Press, 1985, tr. Wang Huimin), p. 92).

12. Jin Suilin, *Environmental Law*, pp. 52–53. The renewed concern for protecting the environment was further reflected in the creation in May 1974 of a specific organ for environmental welfare, the Environmental Protection Leading Group (Guowuyuan huanjing baohu lingdao xiaozu) which drew for its membership on a wide range of government departments and commissions and operated under the leadership of the State Council. The latter body introduced a number of environmentally relevant provisions including the above-mentioned 1974 Provisional Regulations on the Prevention of Pollution of Coastal

course, this programme manifested itself in the 1979 Environmental Protection Law (for trial implementation). The general drift towards safeguarding environmental welfare was accelerated by the embrace of the concept of environmental protection in the 1978 Constitution which declared, at Article 11, that "the state protects the environment and natural resources, and prevents and eliminates pollution and other hazards to the public." This constitutional commitment was reaffirmed and expanded in the 1982 Constitution with Article 26 proclaiming that "the state protects and improves the environment in which people live and the ecological environment. It prevents and controls pollution and other public hazards. The state organizes and encourages afforestation and the protection of forests;" Article 9 states: "the state ensures the rational use of natural resources and protects rare animals and plants. Appropriation or damaging of natural resources by any organization or individual by whatever means is prohibited."

A conservative ideological feature significantly inhibiting the embrace of environmental rights is the idea of "co-ordinated development." Until the 1992 Rio Earth Summit, the PRC was reluctant to accept the important concept of "sustainable development" that had emerged in international environmental jurisprudence in the 1980s – that is, "development that meets the needs of the present without compromising the ability of future generations to meet their own needs."[13] The PRC, characterizing itself as part of the developing world, gave explicit priority to "economic development" for many years in order that it might first solve basic problems of over-population and poverty before adopting a more environmentally-sensitive approach. The conceptual device for this attitude to environmental protection was the principle of *xietiao fazhan* or "co-ordinated development," under which environmental protection is given the same importance as the development of the national economy. Thus environmental welfare and economic growth are congruent. An essential difference between the concept of "sustainable development" and "co-ordinated development" appears to be the former's emphasis on the rights of future generations. In addition, the notion of "co-ordinated development" means that environmental protection is regarded as one sector or dimension of the economy, and is therefore in essence an *economic* issue, rather than a social issue. This in turn encourages a *short-term view* of environmental degradation, with administrators concentrating on some sort of immediate cost balance between the needs of economic growth and environmental protection. It also encouraged the view in China that the PRC must avoid "negative protection of the

---

footnote continued

Waters, and a number of environmental standards for such objects as industrial emissions, drinking water and food. Together with its Office (*bangongshi*), this Group became the Bureau or Agency of Environmental Protection (Huanjing baohu ju) in 1982: see Yang Chaofei. *Environmental Protection and Environmental Culture*, p. 32.

13. G. H. Brundtland, *Our Common Future – the Report of the World Commission on Environment and Development* (Oxford and New York: Oxford University Press, 1987), p. 8. See also the discussion of "sustainable development" (*chixu fazhan*) in Jin Suilin, *Environmental Law*, pp. 94–97.

environment" at the expense of developmental needs – in other words, development was, in reality, given priority over the needs of the environment.[14] The principle of co-ordinated development was manifested most prominently in Article 4 of the 1989 Environmental Protection Law:

the plans for environmental protection formulated by the state must be incorporated into the national economic and social development plans; the state shall adopt economic and technological policies and measures favourable for environmental protection so as to co-ordinate the work of environmental protection and economic construction and social development.

The policy of co-ordinated development now appears to have been supplanted to a significant extent by the concept of sustainable development as a result of China's participation in the 1992 Rio Earth Summit and the State Council's adoption of Agenda 21 for China. The latter has been integrated in the PRC's Ninth Five-Year Plan of National and Social Development and the Outline of Long-Term Targets for the Year 2010. Although the Chinese approach remains relatively conservative, with an emphasis on economic development, the responsibility of more developed countries for shouldering a larger part of the costs of environmental protection, and state sovereignty as a basis for international co-operation,[15] nevertheless there is a clear commitment to promote and enforce sustainable development through law.[16] It is acknowledged that reform of environmental law is needed in a number of areas including population control, environmental impact assessment, the environmental dimensions of economic planning, the standardization of national and local legislation to international levels, public consultation, environmental research and education, and the supervisory role of the National People's Congress and the Chinese People's Political Consultative Conference.

The constitutional and policy support for the right to a healthy environment noted above finds particular expression in the 1989 Environmental Protection Law. In Chinese environmental law its relationship to the Constitution is characterized in the following terms: "the Constitution is the core and the Environmental Protection Law is the foundation" of the system of environmental regulation. Whereas Article 1 of the 1979 Law merely reaffirmed the principle laid down in the 1978 Constitution that "the state protects the environment and natural resources and prevents and eliminates pollution and other hazards to the public," Article 1 of the 1989 Law not only declares that the Law is an implementation of Article 26 of the 1982 Constitution, placing a heavy burden of responsibility on the state for environmental welfare, but also states that the 1989 Law is intended to safeguard human health and facilitate socialist modernization.

14. See, for example, Zhang Kunmin and Jin Suilin, *Huanjing baohu fa jianghua (A Guide to Environmental Law)* (Beijing: Qinghua daxue chubanshe, 1990), pp. 20–26.

15. See, for example, Li Peng, "Preface," in *China's Agenda 21 – White Paper on China's Population, Environment, and Development in the 21st Century*, p. 2.

16. Chapter 3: "Legislation for sustainable development and its enforcement," in *China's Agenda 21—White Paper on China's Population, Environment, and Development in the 21st Century*, pp. 14–21.

In addition, the 1989 Law stipulates that all units and individuals have a duty to protect the environment, and empowers them to "report on or file charges against units or individuals that cause pollution or [otherwise] damage the environment" (Article 6). This provision also reflects the general PRC jurisprudential principle of "mutuality of rights and obligations" (*quanli yiwu xiang yizhi*) – the right to a healthy environment is a matter that places significant obligations not to damage the environment on citizens, enterprises and others. These obligations are reinforced by a system of environmental responsibility that includes criminal, administrative, and civil liability.

The Institutional Framework

In order to promote the constitutionally-guaranteed system of environmental protection a substantial array of institutions has been created over the past 25 years. Many of these bodies are encouraged by the provisions of Articles 9 and 16 of the 1989 Environmental Protection Law which impose on local people's governments the obligation to establish environmental standards to maintain the quality of the environment in areas under their jurisdiction, and to take measures to improve the quality of the local environment. From the point of view of legal regulation of the environment, however, most environmental disputes are resolved by extra-judicial processes.

Perhaps the most important body is the NPC's State Commission on Environmental and Natural Resources Protection (formerly the State Commission on Environmental Protection) or *Quanguo renda huanjing yu ziyuan baohu weiyuanhui*.[17] As the highest body responsible for environmental welfare in the PRC, the Commission deals with general policy matters in the area of protection of the environment and natural resources, and assists the NPC's Standing Committee in its supervision of other environmental agencies. It also aids in the drafting of regulations and guidelines on issues of environmental welfare. However, as this body was only established in 1993, it has yet properly to define its role in the PRC's system of environmental regulation.

Secondly, there is the State Council Committee for Environmental Protection (*Guowuyuan huanjing baohu weiyuanhui*). This Committee, which is the Secretariat for the Commission, is an administrative organ with responsibilities for such matters as drafting legislation, producing plans for and reports on environmental protection for the State Council, conducting investigations into serious incidents of pollution, handling conflicts over environmental problems between provinces through mediation processes, the registration of dangerous chemical products, the issue of emission licences and fines for industrial effluent, and promoting research and wider awareness of environmental welfare.[18]

17. Yang Chaofei, *Environmental Protection and Environmental Culture*, p. 6.
18. Han Depei and Xiao Longan (eds.), *Huanjing baohu fa jiben zhishi (Basic Knowledge of Environmental Law)* (Beijing: Zhongguo huanjing kexue chubanshe, 1990), pp. 62–63.

A third key central body is the State Environmental Protection Administration (formerly known as the National Environmental Protection Agency) or SEPA as it is often characterized in English. This agency is funded by and operates under the direct leadership of the State Council. Established in 1988 as the National Environmental Protection Agency, having been a component of the Ministry of Urban and Rural Construction and of Environmental Protection until being upgraded in March 1998, SEPA works to the orders of the State Council Committee on Environmental Protection, and is primarily responsible for unified creation and management of the system, the prevention and control of pollution, enhancing environmental welfare, and promoting sustainable development. It has a wide range of specific functions including the development of state policies and laws on environmental protection, assisting subordinate departments in the formulation of administrative regulations, setting of environmental standards, assisting in dealing with such problems as international and trans-provincial boundary pollution, and co-ordination of the PRC's responses to the United Nations Environment Programme and other international environmental developments.

At the level of the provincial government and below,[19] the key institutions are the local Environmental Protection Bureaus (EPBs), whose main tasks are the implementation of policies and laws specified by SEPA and supervision of the work of the local Environmental Monitoring Stations. The latter, *inter alia*, gather data on pollution and provide reports on environmental assessment. Monitoring stations' knowledge of local environmental circumstances is an important strength in their administrative mediation and dispute resolution functions. The EPBs are often compromised by government policies of economic growth and local pressures to ignore environmental standards. Operating under a dual leadership system in which financial support is provided by the relevant level of local government rather than SEPA, EPBs – like the people's courts[20]– are often placed in a difficult position of sanctioning their own "almoner."

The post of Inspector of Environmental Protection, created in 1989, has responsibility for conducting independent investigations into cases of pollution, supervizing compliance with environmental standards by state enterprises, issuing warnings or fines to polluters on behalf the EPBs, and bringing suits in the people's courts on behalf of the state or citizens. Although the post remains largely experimental, there is qualitative evidence that increasing importance is being attached to this role, largely in attempts to redress the vexed problem of enforcement. Thus, inspectors have been despatched by the NPC to investigate the enforcement of environmental laws and regulations in the municipalities of Beijing, Tianjin and Shanghai, and to the provinces of Shanxi, Liaoning and

19. Except at the township level, where environmental welfare is often the concern of an appointed "environmental protector."

20. See Donald Clarke, "The execution of civil judgments in China," in Stanley B. Lubman (ed.), *China's Legal Reforms* (Oxford: Clarendon Press, 1996) for an insightful analysis of the impact of local court funding on judicial work in enforcement.

Hainan. In addition, NPC inspectors were sent out in early 1997 to assess the enforcement of forestry law in a number of provinces including Jiangxi, Fujian, and Yunnan, and to monitor enforcement of the Water Law (which, *inter alia*, deals with flood prevention and control).[21]

Another key institution is the environmental research institute, an organ ordinarily sponsored by the SEPA and a university or educational department. Three particularly important research institutes are those at Nanjing, Wuhan and Xinjiang, and these come directly under the leadership of the Research Division of the State Bureau of Environmental Protection. The most prominent of these bodies is the Environmental Law Research Institute at Wuhan University, sponsored by both the University and SEPA. The Institute has been involved in the drafting of many major items of environmental legislation.

This account of the institutional framework for environmental welfare is, of course, very public sector-orientated. There are few NGOs or pressure groups in the environmental field, partly because PRC authorities continue to characterize the environment as an internal matter, an essential element of China's "own right to existence." As a result, the legal framework of the PRC does not favour the promotion of environmental standards protection by international non-governmental organizations (NGOs) and other pressure groups such as Greenpeace, Friends of the Earth, and so on.

In addition, the political and legal milieu in the PRC is inimical for indigenous NGOs. Elsewhere in the world NGOs have often proved critical in the development of environmental awareness and the utilization of legal mechanisms for promoting environmental standards. In China, the authorities are not keen to encourage an organizational form that is often associated with political dissent. Overall responsibility for management and regulation of voluntary associations or "social organizations" (*shehui tuanti*) lies with the Ministry of Civil Affairs and its regional bureaus, a body that is politically very conservative. The key legislation governing NGOs is the 1989 Regulations on the Registration and Administration of Social Organizations (*Shehui tuanti dengji guanli tiaoli*)[22] which, at Article 3, require that voluntary associations "respect the Constitution and the laws and regulations, and uphold the unity of the [various] peoples of the state." It stipulates that such bodies "may harm neither the interests of the state, society, or organizations, nor the lawful rights and interests and liberties of other citizens." The Ministry's rigorous registration system requires prior permission for a registration

---

21. Dong Songqiao, "Yi fa baohu huanjing, jianshe meihao jiayuan" ("To protect the environment in line with the law and to beautify our homeland"), *Zhongguo falü* (*China Law*), No. 3 (1997), pp. 4–6, at p. 5. See also, more generally, Mei Hong, "Legal gateways for environmental protection in China," *Review of European Community and International Environmental Law*, Vol. 4, No. 1, pp. 22–32.

22. "Shehui tuanti dengji guanli tiaoli" ("Regulations on the registration and administration of social organizations), in Zhongguo falü nianjian bianjibu, *Zhongguo falü nianjian 1990* (*Law Yearbook of China 1990*) (Beijing: Falü chubanshe, 1991), pp. 253–55. The law is currently undergoing revision, although the redrafting is apparently proving to be a difficult process because of the political sensitivity of such legislation.

application to be obtained from the relevant government department or Party body (Article 9), detailed information and personnel, membership, organizational rules, funding sources and so on to be supplied in the application itself (Article 10), while the activities of the organization are closely supervised by the civil affairs authorities. Not surprisingly, this leaves very little scope for the emergence and development of genuinely autonomous NGOs and, in reality, the vast majority of bodies in the PRC that might be thought of as non-governmental in nature are "GONGOs" or governmentally-organized voluntary associations. That said, a variety of quasi-NGOs do exist either by adopting indirect methods of registration or by simply not registering at all, and the authorities are perhaps now more tolerant of such bodies as they are willing to provide services that the state itself is unable to afford. Nevertheless, this has not helped significantly the position of environmental NGOs as they remain fundamentally suspect to the authorities. An indication of this hostile attitude is the new provision in Article 24(6) of the 1994 Regulations on Administrative Penalties for Public Security prohibiting the establishment of organizations "in violation of the regulations on the administration of registration of public organizations, carrying out activities in the name of a public organization without having been registered or in the name of the former public organization after its registration has been cancelled, or after the organization has been officially dissolved or banned, when the circumstances are not serious enough for criminal punishment."[23] The few environmental NGOs that have emerged in recent years have often done so by concentrating their efforts on environmental education and by refraining from adopting an overly-critical stance towards the authorities.

Environmental Legislative Framework

As noted above, the corpus of environmental law has been greatly expanded since 1979, with new impetus given to producing a comprehensive range of laws and revising some of the relatively early legislation by the PRC's apparent acceptance of the policy of sustainable development. The principal sources of the body of environmental law are the Constitution, the basic laws, international environmental treaties that have been ratified by the NPC, State Council Regulations and regulations promulgated and enforced by bodies subordinate to the State Council, local laws and interpretations of law.

As is also observed above, the significance apparently attached to environmental protection and natural resources is reflected by several provisions in the 1982 Constitution. Thus, Article 9 of the Constitution requires, among other things, that "the State ensures the rational use of natural resources and protects rare animals and plants. The appropriation or damage of natural resources by an organization or individual by

23. "Zhonghua renmin gongheguo zhi'an guanli chufa tiaoli" ("Regulations of the PRC on administrative penalties for public security"), in Zhongguo falü nianjian bianjibu, *Zhongguo falü nianjian 1995 (Law Yearbook of China 1995)* (Beijing: Falü chubanshe, 1995), pp. 169–174.

whatever means is prohibited." In addition, Article 26 declares: "the State protects and improves the living environment and the ecological environment. It prevents and remedies pollution and other public hazards."[24]

In addition to these Constitutional provisions, two laws of fundamental importance in the PRC scheme of legislation are in part concerned with environmental issues. Thus, the 1986 General Principles of the Civil Law[25] provides a number of environmentally relevant provisions, as Articles 80 and 81 require that those who lease state-owned land or other natural resources are obliged to "manage, protect, and properly use" the land or natural resources, and Article 83 obliges neighbours to "maintain proper neighbourly relations over such matters as water supply, drainage, passage-way, ventilation and lighting." In addition, in the section of the Law dealing with personal rights, it is provided that citizens enjoy the right to life and health. Civil liability will arise if damage is caused by hazardous operations – such as those involving use of high pressure, high voltage, combustibles, explosives, highly toxic or radioactive substances (Article 123), or where damaging pollution occurs in violation of the state provisions on environmental protection and pollution prevention (Article 124).

The Criminal Law 1979[26] defined a number of offences and punishments relating to environment damage, and the Environmental Protection Law (1989) at Article 43 imposes criminal responsibility for "serious environmental pollution." Industrial accidents, misuse of dangerous materials or products, and unlawful use of forestry resources, aquatic assets and wildlife could also give rise to criminal liability under the 1979 Law. That Law was augmented by various special rules introduced by the Standing Committee of the National People's Congress.[27] The revised Criminal Law which came into force on 1 October 1997 contains new provisions in a special section that specifically deals with "the crime of sabotaging the protection of the environment and resources" for the first time. These provisions clearly define the crimes and heavy punishments (*yanli de xingfa*) involved in polluting or destroying land, water, air, forests, mineral deposits, or wild animals and illegally importing hazardous wastes, and so on. In addition, officials responsible for supervising and managing the protection of the environment may be liable for criminal punishment (*xingshi chufa*) for deviant acts committed in the course of duty. The provisions in the revised Criminal Law which specifically address "the crime of sabotaging the protection of the

---

24. Dong Songqiao, "To protect the environment in line with the law and to beautify our homeland," p. 5.

25. "Zhonghua renmin gongheguo minfa tongze" ("General principles of the civil law"), in Zhongguo falü nianjian bianjibu, *Zhongguo falü nianjian 1987* (*Law Yearbook of China 1987*) (Beijing: Falü chubanshe, 1987), pp. 68–76.

26. "Zhonghua renmin gongheguo xingfa" ("Criminal law"), in Zhongguo falü nianjian bianjibu, *Law Yearbook of China 1987*, pp. 142–151.

27. For example, the 1988 Supplementary Provisions of the Standing Committee of the Standing Committee of the National People's Congress Concerning the Punishment of the Crimes of Catching or Killing Precious and Endangered Species of Wildlife Under Special State Protection.

environment and resources" are particularly significant in that the failure to carry out one's legal responsibilities in the area of environmental law is now likely to be characterized as a criminal offence, carrying criminal punishment rather than administrative penalties. The idea is that this will strengthen the deterrence force of the criminal law and enable the authorities to crack down (*yanli chengzhi*) more effectively on environmentally-related criminal acts. In the eyes of the Chinese authorities, this development is a manifestation of the determination to punish criminal sabotage of the environment.

In addition, there is a substantial quantity of national legislation that provides various environmental regulatory rules. These include the 1990 Joint Venture Law, and the 1994 Foreign Trade Law. Thus, Article 17 of the Foreign Trade Law specifically prohibits the export or import of goods or technology where these impair environmental welfare or endanger the life or health of citizens. Moreover, there is now a substantial body of local legislation dealing with environmental protection – rules for Shanghai[28] and Xiamen,[29] for example, are detailed and rigorous legislative efforts. The laws issued by local bodies, it should be noted, may not conflict with national legislation, and local governments may determine their own environmental standards provided that these do not fall below national standards.

The Environmental Protection Law 1979 (for trial use) was one of the seven major law codes promulgated by the NPC and its Standing Committee after the decision by the Chinese leadership to revert to more orthodox modes of legal development in the post-Mao era. As already noted, this re-emergence of legislation was regarded as symbolic of a new era of legal construction. In this light, it is significant that special attention was given to environmental protection. The 1989 Law provides basic principles and methods to protect the environment, prevent pollution, and afford rehabilitation possibilities for existing problems of pollution. One significant feature stipulates the rights and obligations of the state and, in particular, enterprises and institutions in regard to environmental protection. Article 4 requires the incorporation of state environmental protection plans into national economic and social plans, and stipulates that the state co-ordinate the work of environmental protection with economic construction and social development. Article 6 provides that it is a general duty of all units and individuals to protect the environment, conferring a general right on citizens to report on or file charges against those who pollute or otherwise damage the environment. Article 7 imposes on "the competent departments of environmental administration under the State Council (that is, the State Council Committee for Environmental Protection and NEPA (now SEPA)) to super-

28. "Shanghai shi huanjing baohu tiaoli 1995" ("Regulations of Shanghai municipality for environmental protection"), *China Economic News*, 10 April 1995 (Supplement No. 2).

29. "1994 Xiamen shi huanjing baohu tiaoli" ("Regulations of Xiamen municipality for environmental protection"), Xiamen shi renda weiyuanhui bangongting, Xiamen shi renda weiyuanhui yanjiushi (compilers), *Xiamen shi difang fagui huipian (1994–1995)* (*Collected Regulations of Xiamen Municipality (1994–1995)*).

vise and manage environmental protection work throughout the country." Similarly, that article – together with Article 16 – requires that provincial, municipal and autonomous governments supervise and manage environmental protection work within the areas under their jurisdiction. Units causing pollution are obliged by Article 24 to incorporate environmental protection into their plans, establish an environmental responsibility system, and adopt effective measures for the prevention and control of pollution. A polluting unit is required by Article 27 to register with the relevant authorities. The "polluter pays" principle is expressed in Articles 28,[30] 39,[31] and 41.[32] Criminal liability for pollution and damage to natural resources is specified in Articles 43 to 45. Finally, the Environmental Protection Law (1989) provides that the provisions of international environmental law treaties to which China has concluded or acceded apply in the PRC even if they differ from those of Chinese domestic law unless the PRC has announced reservations in regard to the relevant provisions (Article 46).

Alongside the Environmental Protection Law, the Criminal Law and the constitutional provisions, a number of legislative provisions have been introduced steadily throughout the 1980s and 1990s. In the Chinese characterizations of this additional legislation, five enactments are particularly important: the Water Pollution Prevention and Control Law 1984 (revised, 1996),[33] the 1995 Law on the Prevention and Control of Environmental Pollution by Solid Wastes; the 1987 Law on the Prevention and Control of Atmospheric Pollution (amended in 1995 by the Decision of the Standing Committee of the National People's Congress on Revising the Law of the People's Republic on the Prevention and Control of Atmospheric Pollution); the 1997 Law on Control and Treatment of Noise Pollution (in force 1 March 1997, replacing the 1989 Regulations on Noise Pollution); and the 1982 Marine Environmental Protection Pollution Law.[34] Other important items of legislation include: the 1985 Grassland Law; the 1986 Forestry Law; the 1986 Mineral Resources Law; the 1988 Land Administration Law; the 1988 Water Law; the 1988 Law on Protection of Wildlife; the 1990 Regulations on the Control and Treatment of Pollutants; the 1990 Regulations on the Construction of Coastal Projects; the 1991 Law on Water and Soil

---

30. "Enterprises and institutions discharging pollutants in excess of the prescribed national or local discharge standards shall pay a fee for excessive discharge ... and shall assume responsibility for eliminating and controlling the pollution."

31. "An enterprise or institution that has failed to eliminate or control pollution by the deadline as required shall ... pay an excessive discharge fee; in addition, a fine may be imposed on it on the basis of the damage incurred, or the enterprise may be ordered to suspend its operations or close down."

32. "A unit that has caused an environmental pollution hazard has the obligation to eliminate that hazard and to make compensation to the unit or individual that has suffered direct losses."

33. "Zhonghua renmin gongheguo shui wuran fangzhi fa, 1996" ("Prevention of water pollution law of the PRC, 1996"), in Zhongguo falü nianjian bianjibu, *Zhongguo falü nianjian 1997 (Law Yearbook of China 1997)* (Beijing: Falü chubanshe, 1997), pp. 272–76.

34. Dong Songqiao, "To protect the environment in line with the law and to beautify our homeland," p. 5.

Conservation; the 1995 Food Hygiene Law; the 1996 Law on the Prevention and Control of Environmental Pollution caused by Solid Waste, and the 1997 Flood Control Law.

In addition, administrative regulations and rules governing environmental welfare may be issued by the State Council and ministries and other bodies under the State Council such as SEPA. These are often elaborations of laws introduced by the National People's Congress and its Standing Committee. Among the most important of the administrative regulations introduced in the past decade or so are the 1984 Provisions on Strengthening Environmental Management of Rural, Township and Neighbourhood Enterprises, the 1985 Regulations on Ocean Dumping, the 1986 Regulations on Environmental Management in Special Economic Areas Open to the World, the 1989 Regulations on the Implementation of the Law on the Prevention and Control of Water Pollution, the 1990 Administrative Regulations on the Prevention and Control of Pollution and Damage Caused to the Marine Environment by Coastal Construction Projects, the 1990 Decision on Further Strengthening of Environmental Protection Work, the 1993 Regulations on the Emergency Management of Nuclear Accidents, and the 1994 Regulations on Nature Reserves.[35] Moreover, a wide variety of departmental provisions were enacted in the 1980s and 1990s to regulate the dumping of waste and to provide emission standards for air, water and noise pollution.

Environmental Liability and Dispute Resolution

There is a broad range of "environmental liabilities" in PRC law – criminal, civil, economic and administrative sanctions may be imposed by a variety of law enforcement agencies according to the circumstances of each particular case. In many circumstances, however, a pattern of dispute resolution prevails utilizing the relatively informal mechanisms of administrative or people's mediation. Court proceedings are taken only as a last resort. Of course, it should also be pointed out that in a cultural milieu that has long favoured *rang* or "yielding" in dispute situations, and a legal and political milieu that does not encourage the assertion of rights, many environmental grievances are not transformed into disputes[36] but, rather, simply endured.

The most serious cases of environmental pollution are dealt with as criminal issues. These are prosecuted by the procuracy in accordance

35. Among the most important administrative rules are the 1986 Provisions on Environmental Protection Management in Capital Construction Projects, the 1990 Administrative Measures for Supervising Pollution by Exhaust Fumes from Automobiles, the 1991 Implementing Provisions on the Prevention and Control of Air Pollution, the 1992 Measures on Administrative Penalties for Environmental Protection, and the 1992 Administrative Measures for Marks of Environmental Supervision and Management and Enforcement of Law.

36. For a general account of the process of dispute transformation see William Felstiner, Richard Abel and Austin Sarat, "The emergence and transformation of disputes: naming, blaming, claiming," *Law and Society Review*, Vol. 15 (1980–1981), pp. 631 ff. See also Michael Palmer and Simon Roberts, *Dispute Processes: ADR and the Primary Forms of Decision Making* (London: Butterworths, 1998), pp. 7–14.

with the provisions of the Criminal Procedure Law 1979 (and in revised form, 1996). The principal substantive law applied in environmental cases involving criminal liability is the criminal code, together with a variety of supplementary provisions typically found in specific environmental protection laws and the decisions of the Standing Committee of the National People's Congress. As discussed above, the 1979 Criminal Law – in force until 1997 – contained a number of provisions penalizing various kinds of environmentally threatening conduct. These included endangering public property such as rivers, forests and the air (Articles 105 and 106), causing danger to public safety (Articles 114 and 115), undermining the socialist economic order (Articles 126, 128, 129 and 130), and destroying scenic or historic sights (Article 179). In addition Articles 187 and 188 stipulate liability for maladministration and abuse of power in relation, *inter alia*, to environmentally polluting conduct. There are circumstances in which the death penalty may be applied such as killing an endangered species,[37] but the punishment for many of the environmentally-related offences is between one and seven years' fixed-term imprisonment.

In addition to the Criminal Law itself, a number of provisions in substantive legislation expand the scope of the criminal law in matters of environmental welfare. Thus, the Forestry Law (Article 36), the Air Pollution Prevention Laws (Article 38) and the Wildlife Protection Law allow for the Criminal Law to be applied where damage has been very serious. As already noted, the newly-revised Criminal Law is intended, *inter alia*, to provide a more comprehensive regime for environmentally-related "serious" offences. These include causing pollution by the dumping of hazardous waste products – an offence that carries a penalty of three to seven years' fixed-term imprisonment (Article 338). Importing solid waste "in violation of state regulations" is an offence bearing the possible punishment of both a significant period of imprisonment and a fine (Article 339). Catching aquatic products in forbidden areas or during prohibited periods of the year, or by using illegal methods of capture, is punishable by up to three years' fixed term imprisonment (Article 340). The killing of endangered species, or trading in endangered species and the products manufactured from such creatures, ordinarily carries a punishment of up to five years' imprisonment; serious cases may attract up to ten years' in jail (Article 341). Illegal occupation of farmland, illegal mining operations and illegal logging (as well as dealing in timber resulting from such activity) are offences which may lead to punishment by both imprisonment and a fine (Articles 342–345).

The Environmental Protection Law (1989), as outlined above, requires units causing pollution to carry out a variety of corrective administrative

37. "Quanguo renda changweihui guanyu chengzhi busha guojia zhongdian baohu de zhengui pinwei yesheng dongwu fanzui de buchong guiding, 1988" ("Supplementary provisions of the Standing Committee of the National People's Congress on punishment for the crimes of killing precious wild animals and endangered species, 1988"), in Zhongguo falü nianjian bianjibu, *Zhongguo falü nianjian 1989 (Law Yearbook of China 1989)* (Beijing: Falü chubanshe, 1990), p. 137.

actions. These administrative remedies and penalties are justified by Article 38 of the Environmental Protection Law 1989: "an enterprise or institution ... shall be fined by the competent department ... authorized by law to conduct environmental supervision and management in accordance with the resulting damage in serious cases, the persons responsible shall be subject to administrative sanction by the unit to which they belong or by the competent department of the government." In addition, according to Article 41, a polluting unit has a duty both to eliminate the pollution and to compensate the individual or unit that has suffered *direct* losses. Environmental regulation bodies and the Public Security Bureau are authorized by the 1994 Regulations on Administrative Penalties for Public Security (revising the 1987 provisional regulations) at Article 25(6) and (7) to impose an administrative penalty, especially a fine, for relatively minor environmentally deviant conduct. This represents one manifestation of the principle of "administrative liability for polluters," and is an application of the "polluter pays" principle. The latter finds much fuller expression in other legislation including, most recently, the 1995 Law on Environmental Pollution by Solid Waste. Thus, under the provisions of this Law an administrative penalty of up to 100,000 *yuan* may be imposed by the relevant administrative department for failure to eliminate or control pollution within a specific period of time. Under the system of Administrative Review (*xingzheng fuyi*), a party that has been fined in this manner may appeal to an environmental organ at one level higher than the decision-maker (Administrative Review Regulations 1991,[38] Articles 12–18), and may also apply for review of the administrative decision by the court (Article 47). In addition, it should be noted that administrative organs with responsibility for environmental protection may apply to the people's court to secure an order compelling the defendant to submit to administrative sanctions.

Under the process of Administrative Review prevailing in the PRC, it is possible for a local EPB to investigate an environmental dispute and mediate between the parties. If mediation fails, the particular Bureau may impose a decision – this is in effect a system of environmental arbitration[39] – and the decision may include an order for payment of compensation to the other party. An appeal can be made to a higher administrative authority, or a new case brought in a civil or economic chamber of the local people's court. There is an additional and more overtly mediation-based system of dispute resolution by environmental protection organs, such as those in the local urban planning department or environmental monitoring station. Finally, the long-standing mechanism

38. "Xingzheng fuyi tiaoli, 1990" ("Administrative review regulations, 1990"), in Zhongguo falü nianjian bianjibu, *Zhongguo falü nianjian 1991 (Law Yearbook of China 1991)* (Beijing: Falü chubanshe, 1992), pp. 252–56.

39. Arbitration proper is another possible mode of proceeding in civil cases, and there have been some calls in the Chinese legal press for the establishment of special arbitral bodies that would deal with environmental issues. However, at the moment, formal arbitration is only used in the PRC in cases of foreign-related ocean pollution – the arbitral body in such cases is the China Maritime Association Commission, and the governing law is ordinarily the 1982 Marine Environmental Protection Law and the Maritime Arbitration Rules.

of the "Letters and Visits" system should be noted – any party can submit a written or oral complaint (*shangfang*) to the Letters and Visits Offices, found in Party and government organs and media bodies. It is ordinarily the case that in these circumstances the aggrieved party has reported her or his complaint to a specific environmental protection organ but failed to secure appropriate redress. This is, however, something of a last ditch attempt to put pressure on the relevant administrative organ to deal with the problem in a satisfactory manner.

Judicial review of administrative decisions affecting the environment is similarly possible under the Administrative Litigation Law 1989 (in force, 1 October 1990). This is a relatively new system – although, in the 1980s, the Civil Procedure Law could be used to bring administrative actions – and only very specific decisions may be reviewed (Article 11). In addition, Article 12 specifies that certain kinds of administrative decision may not be reviewed – including acts of state in areas such as national defence and foreign affairs, and administrative decisions with general binding force. Thus, a general decision by the State Council, for example, empowering a local government to build a nuclear power station, or to develop a surface coal mine, may not be reviewed. In particular, this article precludes the possibility of aggrieved citizens bringing an administrative suit against the government in respect of possible environmental degradation caused by the Sanxia (Three Gorges) Dam project. Moreover, Article 12 states that the courts may not have jurisdiction in respect of decisions made by an administrative organ on awards and punishments for its personnel or on the appointment or relief of duties of its personnel. Consequently, the administrative disciplining of the manager of an enterprise for that enterprise's pollution may not be reconsidered by a court. Instead, specific decisions may be reviewed under Article 11 of the Administrative Litigation Law: pollution fines imposed by an environmental protection body; refusal by a relevant governmental agency to issue emissions licences; refusal to allow regulation of a company on the ground that it has failed to install equipment necessary for pollution prevention or recycling; harm or losses caused as a result of maladministration, and failure to fulfil statutory obligations (Sections 4, 5, and 8). Applications for judicial review of administrative sanctions are governed by the provisions of Article 40 of the 1989 Environmental Protection Law. These specify that an aggrieved party must apply for judicial review of the case within 15 days of receiving the administrative sanction or the results of a review by a higher administrative body. The administrative review procedures also require submission of an application within 15 days of receiving the administrative penalty.

That such conflicts often involve many parties, some of whom it is impossible to identify at the commencement of legal proceedings, is one of the most important complicating factors in environmental disputes in any jurisdiction. In order to deal with problems of this nature, Article 6 of the Environmental Protection Law 1989, apparently encourages individuals or units to bring "class actions" against polluters: "all units and individuals ... have the right to report on or file charges against units or individuals that cause pollution or damage to the environment." In other parts of the world, particularly the U.S., this form of proceeding has of course been an important mechanism in promoting environmental welfare.[40] It appears to be gaining some ground in the PRC, too, although in reality it is still relatively experimental. The Civil Procedure Law 1991 provides for such cases under Articles 53–56. Thus, Article 53 permits the use of class or joint actions (*gongtong susong*) in cases in which one or more of the parties consists of two or more persons, and the cause of action is the same. Article 54 provides that in joint actions in which one party consists of numerous persons, a representative (or representatives) may be chosen to conduct the litigation. The difficult situation in which one party consists of an unknown number of persons is dealt with in Article 55 – in such cases the court should issue a notice stating the relevant details of the case, and requesting potential claimants to register. Such persons are then expected to elect a representative. All judgments and rulings made by the court in respect of the action are effective for all the claimants. Article 56 allows third parties with no independent right of claim, whose legal interests will be affected by the outcome of the claim, to be joined to the action. The class action is still an incipient development, with the additional complication that the financial costs of bringing such an action are prohibitive. But it does appear to be gaining in significance in a number of different types of case, including pollution, and has been extended on an experimental basis to cases of judicial review heard under the Administration Litigation Law.[41]

Most environmentally-related disputes have been brought to the people's courts in the form of ordinary civil litigation – the proceedings are therefore the same as for divorce, for example. Plaintiffs typically seek an injunction, an order for the removal of pollutants, or damages in compensation. Civil actions concerning environmental problems are processed under the Law of Civil Procedure 1991 and are handled by the civil chambers of the people's courts. Civil liability is a common form of remedy in cases of pollution, and Articles 28 and 41 of the Environmental Protection Law embody the "polluter pays" principle. Thus, Article 28 stipulates payment of a fee for excessive discharge of pollutants, the income being used to prevent and control pollution only, and Article 32 and Article 41 provide for civil liability. Damages may include both direct and indirect loss – actual damage and loss of income resulting from the harm. The General Principles of the Civil Law 1986 provide in Articles 124 and 134 the right for any unit or individual to apply to the courts for an order requiring the polluter to remove the source of pollution and pay damages. However, in civil cases the typical outcome is a mediated agreement between the parties. Mediation is favoured as a

40. See, for example, David Robinson and John Dunkley (eds.), *Public Interest Perspectives in Environmental Law* (London: Wiley Chancery, 1995).

41. See Note, "Class action litigation in China," *Harvard Law Review*, Vol. 111 (1998), pp. 1523–1541.

mode of decision-making as it produces less socially divisive outcomes, is relatively easily effected as most cases concern damages, and enhances prospects for enforcement of the outcome.[42]

Many relatively routine civil disputes are, however, dealt with by means of the mechanism of people's mediation (*renmin tiaojie*). The Chinese system of people's mediation is considered at some length in other sources[43]– suffice it to say here that the overwhelming majority of civil disputes in the PRC are dealt with by people's mediation, and that this highly organized system of informal dispute settlement continues to grow in importance and sophistication. However, because many mediation committees use only very crude categories for characterizing the kinds of dispute that they deal with, and because many local disputes are often polycentric[44] in nature and, therefore, not easy to classify, the vital role played by mediation committees in settling environmental disputes tends to be overlooked by Western scholars analysing processes of environmental dispute resolution. There is evidence that a great deal is done by way of environmental dispute resolution at the local level by people's mediation committees. Most important, the case load of such committees often includes disputes over *feng shui* or geomancy claims, with such claims being perhaps a manifestation of a "traditional culture of environmental welfare" which has been marginalized in socialist China on the ground that it is "feudal" (*fengjian*) in nature.

Another dispute resolution mechanism which is potentially very important is "lawyers' negotiations" – that is, direct negotiations between lawyers as partisan representatives of disputing parties. The importance of this development in China should not be exaggerated, because many lawyers continue to avoid involvement in environmental disputes, feeling that such cases will frequently bring them up against government interests. However, there is evidence that in environmentally-related disputes between medium-sized and larger enterprises in urban areas, lawyers are increasingly called in to assist the parties in reaching a negotiated settlement of their dispute. This development reflects the emerging importance of lawyers, an importance given legislative underpinning by the new Lawyers' Law which, *inter alia*, allows Chinese lawyers to form partnership law offices.[45]

In environmental matters, as in other areas of the law, the manner in which the official system of environmental liability operates is clearly deficient in a number of important respects. There is little doubt that enforcement of legal rules and court judgments and orders is a serious

42. See Michael Palmer "The revival of mediation in the People's Republic of China: (2) judicial mediation," in W. E. Butler (ed.), *Yearbook on Socialist Legal Systems 1988* (Dobbs Ferry, NY: Transnational Books, 1989).

43. See, for example, Michael Palmer "The revival of mediation in the People's Republic of China: (1) extra-judicial mediation," in W. E. Butler (ed.), *Yearbook on Socialist Legal Systems 1987* (Dobbs Ferry, NY: Transnational Books, 1988).

44. On the concept of "polycentric dispute" see Lon Fuller, "Mediation – its forms and functions," *Southern California Law Review*, Vol. 44 (1971), pp. 305–339.

45. "Zhonghua renmin gongheguo lüshi fa, 1996" ("Lawyers' Law of the PRC, 1997") in force 1 January 1997, in Zhongguo falü nianjian bianjibu, *Zhongguo falü nianjian 1996* (*Law Yearbook of China 1996*) (Beijing: Falü chubanshe, 1997), pp. 276–280.

problem and that it is particularly difficult to persuade local officials to sacrifice economic interests in order to enhance standards of environmental protection. The administration still has very considerable powers, and can use its discretion to influence local environmental protection to suit itself. Take, for example, environmental impact assessment – this is a requirement that is not always imposed on those industries that are owned by the local government, but it will invariably be imposed on joint ventures and private businesses. If the local government makes a profit from the operation of local industries that pollute, it often does not worry too much about that pollution. Indeed, in some respects the system appears to encourage or at least tolerate pollution – such as in instances where effluent fees are a critical source of finance for local environmental monitoring stations. Local environmental protection authorities do not worry too much about the fact that the penalties that they impose are not financially stringent – they are as much concerned with securing an income from the fines as they are with protecting the environment, and they therefore do not wish to see polluting enterprises made bankrupt. Also it is not always clear where the income from the fines goes to – there is evidence to suggest that the money is filtered off for personal gain. More generally, environmental matters are still very much seen as a matter of policy – which is variable and ambiguous – rather than law. Sometimes the authorities stress a particular problem as a matter of policy, but because there is no law there is no real continuity of approach. Decentralization and the rise of consumerism have exacerbated problems. Violations of environmental law often go unpunished, especially in cases in which enforcement is required by a body from outside the immediate area – the local government often has a direct interest in the financial health of local enterprises, and the development of township and village enterprises has worsened the situation. Environmental law is an area in which problems of distorted decision-making stemming from Party influence, corruption, selective implementation of rules, the difficulties of confronting local political leaders, the low status of those involved in administering the system and so on appear to be particularly serious. One response, mentioned above, has been to develop the environmental inspectors system. But in addition, the State Environmental and Resources Protection Committee and the State Council's Environmental Protection Committee have made joint attempts to assess the enforcement of the Environmental Protection Law in most parts of China and are reported to have ordered or encouraged local authorities to investigate and prosecute some 6,000 apparent violations of the Law.[46]

Conclusions

In retrospect, the development of environmental law in the PRC is noteworthy for its relatively early embrace of the notion of environmental

---

46. Dong Songqiao, "To protect the environment in line with the law and to beautify our homeland," pp. 4–6, at p. 6.

welfare. Although a late starter compared to many other jurisdictions, there are indications that some efforts were being made to develop a corpus of environmental law even before the Cultural Revolution, and it is significant that efforts were made to protect the environment through law at that stage. The efforts of the 1970s, too, culminated in the 1979 Environmental Protection Law – one of the seven major codes that, in a very real sense, marked the Chinese leadership's decision to pursue more orthodox policies of socialist legal development.[47] There has also been an obvious, albeit cautious, willingness to learn from foreign experience, and although the reality may well be less convincing than the rhetoric, some of China's most senior environmental officials claim that the PRC has quickly become a major player in international conventions on environmental protection – "since 1979 China has successively participated in nearly 30 international conventions ... [and] ... as a matter of fact has always earnestly carried out its obligations in the international conventions and agreements on environmental protection it has signed, approved or participated in." [48] However, the willingness to be an international player and to learn from the West in this area of law is not an entirely unmixed blessing. It seems that there may also be something of an anti-democratic impulse at work here, for this embrace of Western and international standards stems in part from a reluctance to draw on either China's indigenous traditions of environmental protection or on the ideas of non-governmental environmental activists. That is, willingness to learn from abroad in the matters of environmental law is not to be read as simply an expression of modern ideas and standards of environmental welfare, but also as an attempt to limit the political role of environmental activists and to avoid a genuine degree of public participation in environmental decision-making. Environmental law seems to fit as comfortably with the quasi-paternalistic Chinese Party-state as it does with Western-style liberal democratic political systems. Indeed, in some respects it may be easier to impose more rigorous standards of environmental protection in a non-democratic milieu such as that of the PRC. The promotion of environmental welfare, and the introduction of laws that do enable elements of civil society to aspire to higher standards of environmental protection, are very important developments, but it is also significant that the line between environmental regulation and social control may sometimes be difficult to draw in the authoritarian political context of the PRC.

Moreover, the body of environment protection legislation is proving insufficient for safeguarding environmental welfare. Despite the very considerable body of recently enacted legislation on environmental protection, and membership of a number of important environmental protection international conventions, the condition of the Chinese environment continues to deteriorate. Although Chinese environmental lawyers feel that China has basically established its system of environmental legal regulation and resources protection to a level that suits the PRC's national

47. See above, note 2.
48. Dong Songqiao, "To protect the environment in line with the law and to beautify our homeland," pp. 4–6, at p. 6.

conditions, it remains a system with serious flaws. It is still essentially administrative rather than legal in nature, with courts and lawyers playing only a minor role; it does not deal with the difficult issue of historical land contamination; there is a real need to establish clearer parameters of liability, and the system places too much emphasis on punishment as opposed to material incentives in order to secure compliance. In addition, it is a system in which Party and local interests all too often intrude into the proper functioning of the regulatory regime. As in other areas of Chinese law, there are pronounced elements of coercion in the environmental protection system, based on the misguided notion that compliance with the law is best secured by severity of penalty rather than certainty of detection. It might well be argued that without the democratic impulse that has informed much environmental law and practice in the West, enforcement in the PRC will remain a serious issue. Perhaps more importantly, the system of environmental regulation that has emerged may wear a modern, sophisticated countenance, but it still bears significant imprints from older, Chinese socialist ideas. In addition to the administrative ethos of the system as a whole, it is important not to overlook the ideological influence of Mao's theory of contradictions in which a sharp distinction is drawn between non-antagonistic and antagonistic contradictions. This tends to encourage, on the one hand, the use of the consensual methods of education, persuasion and mediation for the resolution of routine environmental problems and disputes and, on the other, a reliance on coercive methods to solve more fundamental problems. The "Law," occupying something of an interstitial position, still plays an uncertain and ambiguous role.

China: Environmental Protection, Domestic Policy Trends, Patterns of Participation in Regimes and Compliance with International Norms

Lester Ross*

Environmental protection in the international context constitutes a type of soft or functional regime directed at the control of behaviour by states which generally does not present an overt threat to their neighbours. Rather, the principal danger is one of everyday social or economic activity presenting risks within the state in which it originates, to that state's neighbours and, possibly, the global commons. Thus, it is typically the activity's externalities rather than any intent to cause harm or encroach on neighbours' territory which is the cause of concern. Control is complicated by sovereignty issues, which become paramount when externalities cross a country's boundaries and affect the originator's neighbours and/or the wider international community. Although there have been cases of countries obtaining judicial relief for environmental harms that originated in another country, such issues are overwhelmingly non-justiciable.[1] It is more likely that any international regimes that are established will provide no avenue for judicial relief.

Despite the paucity of judicial means of dispute resolution, international regimes have been established in increasing numbers in the environmental area. The issue then becomes one of why states establish and participate in such regimes and, because the activity of member states is not well-monitored,[2] why they comply with the norms of such regimes after they become participants. Keohane *et al* argue that the key variable is "the degree of domestic environmentalist pressure in major industrialized democracies, not the decision-making rules of the relevant international institution."[3] Moreover, even when violations are subject to an international regime, they are not necessarily readily subject to sanctions because the regime relies on consensus, the harm originates in the externality rather than the behaviour itself, sovereignty limits the reach of

---

* The views expressed herein are those of the author and not necessarily those of the law firm with which he is associated. An earlier version of this article was published in Michel Oksenberg and Elizabeth Economy (eds.), *China Joins the World: Progress and Prospects.*

1. The North American Agreement on Environmental Co-operation among the United States, Canada and Mexico is an exception. Adopted as part of the NAFTA accord, this agreement provides that one party may submit to the Commission that another party is failing to enforce its own environmental laws. It also requires that each party provide private judicial remedies for environmental harms.

2. U. S. General Accounting Office, *International Environment: International Agreements are not Well-monitored* (Washington: GAO/RCED-92-43, January 1992).

3. Robert O. Keohane, Peter M. Haas and Marc A. Levy, "The effectiveness of international environmental institutions," in P. M. Haas, R. O. Keohane and M. A. Levy (eds.), *Institutions of the Earth: Sources of Effective International Environmental Protection* (Cambridge, MA: The MIT Press, 1994), p. 14.

punishment and proof of causation is subject to considerable scientific uncertainty. As Chayes and Chayes and others have argued, this tends to place environmental issues within the ambit of "co-operative" or positive sum regimes that are more suitable to a managerial or consensual style of diplomacy in which states are encouraged to adhere to international norms through suasion and because it is in their own best interests to do so, rather than fear of sanctions.[4]

Despite nearly two decades of rapid industrialization and a measure of political reform, China ranks well below the advanced industrialized countries of the world on a per capita basis with respect to economic development. It is also an assertive defender of national sovereignty, both its own and as a principle, against external interference. Thus, for China, where low income levels and restrictions on political participation limit the present-day potential for domestic environmentalist pressure and external interference is treated warily by the state, the questions are whether and why China has become more participatory in international environmental regimes; whether the quality of China's participation varies by substantive area, the threat of sanctions or other variables; and whether constructive engagement can shape China's participation.

China: The Domestic Context

If solutions to international environmental issues are predominantly of the co-operative type, then the predisposition of the state in question assumes major importance. If the state lacks knowledge or is impervious to information concerning the existence of particular problems, their salience and the most effective means for their resolution, the prospects for co-operation are correspondingly limited. Conversely, if the state exhibits a tendency to acknowledge the existence of environmental problems internally and take action on them domestically, then the prospects for international progress through co-operation and encouragement of the state's environmental policy-making capacity are enhanced.

China began to manifest an awareness of environmental problems in the early 1970's, during the latter stages of the Cultural Revolution. This was at approximately the same time that the People's Republic of China was awarded China's seat in the United Nations and in the midst of the early stages of normalizing relations with the U.S. Specifically, in 1971, a leading small group for environmental protection was established informally under the State Council to supervise preparations for the June 1972 United Nations Conference on the Human Environment ("UNCHE") in Stockholm. Thus, China's first high level environmental policy body was established in direct and urgent response to an impending international conference, the planning for which had commenced in

4. Abram Chayes and Antonia Handler Chayes, *The New Sovereignty: Compliance with International Regulatory Agreements* (Cambridge: Harvard University Press, 1995), pp. 6–8; see also the discussion of the non-zero sum game or co-operative principle in Wang Yi, *China's Position and Role in the Global Environmental Challenge*, paper presented to the 1997 China Environment Forum (Beijing: 24–28 February 1997), p. 9.

the United Nations in 1968 before the PRC had become a member. China did not play a particularly constructive role at UNCHE. Like developing countries in general, it assigned principal responsibility for pollution control to the advanced industrialized countries and defended the right of developing countries to exploit their own resources without external interference. Going further, the delegation attempted unsuccessfully to inject such tangential and divisive issues as the Vietnam War and nuclear testing into the Conference declaration. Although the declaration was eventually approved by consensus, in part to avoid a recorded vote, China publicly announced that it had not taken part in the voting.[5] In other words, China was a "laggard" participant in this international regime, avoiding international obligations by shunning treaty commitments or exhibiting a disdainful attitude towards compliance obligations.[6]

UNCHE is widely regarded as the origin of international environmental diplomacy. Of particular importance is the impetus it gave China and other developing countries to create an environmental policy, notwithstanding their fear that advanced industrialized countries would make use of environmental concerns to curtail their economic potential. The growth and elaboration of China's environmental bureaucracy both have their origins in China's participation in UNCHE. In particular, international emphasis on the unique nature of environmental policy accelerated China's elaboration of a bureaucracy separate from the Ministry of Public Health, which had previously and ineffectually exercised overall responsibility for environmental matters, and later from the former Ministry of Urban and Rural Construction.

Formal establishment of the leading small group under the State Council in 1974 was followed by the elaboration of administrative responsibilities and the establishment of a small Environmental Protection Office.[7] The two bodies evolved into the State Commission on Environmental Protection (SCEP) chaired by Song Jian, chair of the State Science and Technology Commission until 1998, and the State Environmental Protection Administration (SEPA)[8] under Xie Zhenhua. The elevation of Xie Zhenhua, the head of SEPA, to ministerial rank in 1998

5. Lynton Keith Caldwell, *International Environmental Policy: Emergence and Dimensions* (Durham: Duke University Press, 1984); *Peking Review*, 23 June 1972, p. 8; Lester Ross, *Environmental Policy in China* (Bloomington: Indiana University Press, 1988), p. 137.

6. Keohane, Haas and Levy, "The effectiveness of international environmental institutions," p. 16, classifies states by four categories of behaviour: "laggards" which (1) avoid international obligations or (2) accept such obligations but fail to comply with them; and "leaders" which (3) comply with such obligations or (4) lead others to exceed such obligations and assume additional obligations.

7. State Council, "Environmental protection structure and the scope of environmental protection responsibilities and key work items of concerned departments," *Guo huan ban (State Environmental Document)* [74] No. 1, reprinted in State Commission on Environmental Protection (SCEP) and People's University Research Office on Population, Environment and Development, *A Complete Work on the Policies, Laws and Regulations Concerning China's Environment and Natural Resources* (Beijing: Zhongxin chubanshe, 1996), p. 14. The SCEP was abolished in March 1998.

8. Guo Nei, "Agency given greater powers," *China Daily*, 1 April 1998, p. 1. Until March 1998, SEPA was known as the National Environmental Protection Agency. SEPA as used herein will refer to SEPA both under its present and former names.

will enhance its power, although it will still have to overcome limitations created by staff shortages, conflicting local government priorities and rivalries with other government agencies.[9]

The origin of environmental regulation can also be traced to the UNCHE era. China's first set of environmental regulations (excepting a few occupational health and safety norms adopted from Soviet models), "Some regulations on protecting and improving the environment,"[10] was circulated in 1973. From 1972, China stated the need to incorporate the environment in the national planning process, although environmental protection did not receive treatment as a separate chapter in such national plans until the Sixth Five-Year Plan (1980–1985). Environmental policy made slow progress during the next five years because of institutional weakness and the leadership succession crisis. Since the late 1970s, however, China has enacted or promulgated over a dozen environmental and related statutes, dozens of regulations and several hundred standards – all of which exercise an increasingly important role within the economy. The legislative and regulatory processes in the National People's Congress and SEPA have also become relatively open to international influence, with many policies such as discharge and emission permits modelled on practice in the U.S. and other advanced industrialized countries. The China Council for International Co-operation on Environment and Development, established with financial support from Canada in 1992 and currently chaired by Vice-Premier Wen Jiabao, provides a formal avenue for the communication of international advice to the Chinese government.

Much of the impetus for expanding the scope, comprehensiveness and stringency of environmental regulation is domestic. For example, the largest cause of citizen complaints to environmental protection bureaus is noise pollution – a purely domestic concern. This eventually led to the enactment of a noise pollution law, a statute not always found in advanced industrialized countries.[11] Moreover, China has begun to take stringent action to address various pollution problems in specific areas, particularly water pollution in key water bodies, sulphur dioxide and acid rain, under the so-called "Three Rivers," "Three Lakes" and "Two Regions" controls policy.[12]

9. U.S. and Foreign Commercial Service, "The fading of Chinese environmental secrecy" (Hong Kong: American Consulate General, 23 March 1998), paragraphs 13–17. There has been speculation that SEPA will be further elevated to ministerial status in a later round of government restructuring.

10. State Council, "Some regulations on protecting and improving the environment (provisional draft) (29 August 1973)," in China Environmental Management, Economics and Law Society et al. (eds.), Huanjing fa cankao ziliao xuanbian (Compendium of Reference Materials on Environmental Law), Vol. 1 (1982), p. 41, circulated as Appendix 2 to State Council, "Approval of the circulation of the State Planning Commission's report on conditions at the national environmental protection conference."

11. Law on Environmental Noise Pollution Prevention and Control (1996).

12. The Huai, Hai and Liao rivers; Lakes Tai, Dianchi and Chao; and sulphur dioxide and acid rain emissions controls in parts of every province except Hainan, Tibet and Qinghai. State Council, "Instructions concerning the plan for demarcating the acid rain control regions and the sulphur dioxide pollution control regions submitted for approval" (28 January 1998). On recent developments, see "Environmental protection," in Chen Mianhua (ed.), 1998 nian

However, international environmental diplomacy has become more salient in China as environmental issues have gained importance in international relations in general, and in bilateral relations with the United States and Japan in particular.[13] Even in the absence of an international regime, global influences shape the policy process by disseminating scientific knowledge and expanding awareness of environmental harms, thereby strengthening SEPA and related agencies and fostering the emergence of a nascent environmental constituency. Spending on environmental protection is also increasing at a relatively fast pace, further signifying government recognition of the importance of environmental protection.[14]

However, leading officials remain cautious with respect to the potential constraints on development imposed by environmental policy or by other countries or international regimes. The core principle from the Second National Environmental Protection Work Conference in 1984 through 1996 held that economic development and environmental protection must advance in tandem.[15] While this principle acknowledged the importance of protecting the environment, it became all too common for environmental protection to be relegated to the sidelines to maintain economic growth. Not until 1996 did a top leader, in Jiang Zemin's speech to the fourth National Environmental Protection Conference, criticize this tendency and emphasize that environmental protection (like populatiuon planning) was a core policy that could not be subordinated without affecting long-term development.[16] By contrast, senior officials with environmental portfolios, such as Qu Geping, chair of the Environmental and Resources Protection Committee of the National People's Congress and former director-general of SEPA, have long stated that economic development may have to be restrained in some respects in the interest of environmental protection.[17]

Thus China resists the imposition of obligations that are deemed to be

---

footnote continued

Zhongguo guomin jingji he shehui fazhan baogao (*1998 Report on China's National Economic and Social Development*) (Beijing: Zhongguo jihua chubanshe, 1998), pp. 282–290. The focus on particular areas reflects the Chinese government's penchant for implementing policies on a trial basis before applying them nation-wide, as well as the practical constraints presented by funding and other factors.

13. On environmental and energy issues in U.S.–China relations, see Wang Yi, Zhang Jiqiang, Wu Changhua and He Kebin, "Co-operation of energy and environment on global background: strategic capitals in Sino–American Relations," *Zhanlüe yu guanli* (*Strategy and Management*), No. 6 (1997), pp. 54–59.

14. These and other accomplishments in this regard are recited in the "White paper on China's environmental protection," *People's Daily*, 5 June 1996, pp. 1 ff. Spending is projected to increase to 1.5% of GDP by 2000, up from 0.7–0.8% in the Eighth Five-Year Plan. Ma Chenguang, "Plan for greener future," *China Daily*, 16 December 1995, p. 1.

15. Li Peng, "Protecting the environment is a major task facing China," translated in Lester Ross and Mitchell A. Silk, *Environmental Law and Policy in the People's Republic of China* (Westport, CT: Greenwood Press, 1987), pp. 35–43.

16. Jiang Zemin, "Speech at the Fourth National Environmental Protection Conference," *People's Daily* (overseas edition), 19 July 1996, p. 1.

17. Ma Chenguang, "Plan for a greener future." (China can realize its environmental goals "only ... if necessary caution is taken in the nation's rapid development.")

incompatible with its development level, and opposes environmental diplomatic initiatives if they threaten to constrain its development potential or unjustifiably interfere in its internal affairs. This position was articulated in advance of the 1992 United Nations Conference on Environment and Development ("UNCED") when China somewhat vainly convened a forum attended by some 41 developing countries. This forum resulted in the promulgation of the "Beijing ministerial declaration on environment and development." The declaration acknowledged the need for international co-operation to promote environmental protection and sustainable development while demanding financial assistance, and asserted the right to development and to oppose interference in the internal affairs of developing countries.[18] This position gained ground in the mid-1990s and was reaffirmed by President Jiang Zemin in his address to the Fourth National Environmental Protection Conference on 16 July 1996.

In that address, Jiang acknowledged that environmental protection had entered the arenas of international politics, economics, trade and culture, and expressed China's willingness to play a positive role in global environmental protection. However, any such role had to be commensurate with its level of economic development, and he rejected any interference in domestic politics in the name of environmental diplomacy. In an impor-tant directive issued in 1996 in conjunction with the Ninth Five-Year Plan (1996–2000) and the Long-Term Development Plan (1996–2010), the State Council shifted the emphasis towards environmental protection by establishing stricter deadlines for environmental regulation and enforcement, particularly on a regional basis and with respect to new pollution sources. Although the concept of parallel economic development and environmental protection was preserved, its prominence was reduced and modified to apply to an overall balance of economic, social and environmental interests.[19]

Such a policy tendency, born in China's response to UNCHE but developed more fully in the domestic arena, suggests that China is not unalterably opposed to international environmental regimes: on the contrary, China is prepared to embrace many environmental norms. However, it will be more likely to be a leader with respect to those international environmental regimes that are perceived not to constrain its development potential, and less likely to be a leader if the international environmental regime is perceived to impose such constraints. Such a distinction should be reflected in domestic policy and regulation. If so, it suggests that international organizations and other states may have to provide a combination of incentives and disincentives to elicit the desired behaviour from Chinese agencies with respect to those obligations that are perceived to constrain development. As discussed above, however, there does appear to be a long-term policy trend in China in support of

18. 14–19 June 1991.
19. State Council, "Decisions concerning certain issues in environmental protection (August 3, 1996)," *Zhongguo huanjing bao* (*China Environment News*), 13 August 1996, p. 1.

environmental protection and correlated with economic development. If so, the determination to resist certain obligations would be expected to diminish over time through the spread of knowledge, rising incomes and the expansion of environmental awareness in China.

International Environmental Diplomacy

International environmental agreements, addressing external effects both on the global commons and within another country's frontiers, have increased in number and entered into force more rapidly since UNCHE and UNCED.[20] These trends have emerged primarily because of the heightened salience of environmental issues and a greater reliance on momentum-building processes involving conventions and scientifically-based accretions to agreements rather than an uncompromising insistence on binding international treaties.[21]

Although initially an environmental laggard, China has become a more active participant. One study has traced the origins of the term environmental diplomacy (*huanjing waijiao*) to former SCEP Chairman Song Jian's address at the 16th meeting of the SCEP in 1989.[22] Environmental diplomacy was deemed an important element in China's external relations by the SCEP in 1990. The Ministry of Foreign Affairs began to train environmental specialists in its international department and treaties and law department in 1989, and in December 1990 the State Council directed relevant departments and units to play an active role in international co-operative efforts to resolve global environmental problems under the co-ordination of the Ministry of Foreign Affairs and SEPA – provided that China's principled positions were articulated and the interests of China and developing countries were protected.[23] The Ministry of Foreign Affairs has tended to be more sensitive to issues of national sovereignty and economic development than SEPA.

A recent compendium edited by SEPA's Policy and Law Section listed 29 multilateral environmental agreements to which China has become a party.[24] Although the data do not permit definitive conclusions with respect to patterns of China's participation in international agreements, it

20. Peter M. Haas with Jan Sundgren, "Evolving international environmental law: changing practices of national sovereignty," in Nazli Choucri (ed.), *Global Accord: Environmental Challenges and International Responses* (Cambridge, MA: The MIT Press, 1993), pp. 405, 410–11.

21. Haas, "Evolving international environmental law," pp. 416–17.

22. Address of state councillor and SCEP (19 October 1998), in SCEP Secretariat (ed.), *Guowuyuan huanjing baohu weiyuanhui wenjian huibian* (*Compendium of SCEP Documents*) (Beijing: China Environmental Sciences Press, 1995), Vol. 2, p. 72, cited in Zhang Haibing, *Lun Zhongguo de huanjing waijiao* (*On China's Environmental Diplomacy*) (unpublished PhD dissertation: Beijing University, 1997), p. 7.

23. State Council, "Decisions on further strengthening environmental protection," in SEPA and Ministry of Forestry, *Quanguo huanjing baohu zhifa jianchao zhinan* (*Investigation Guide to the Implementation of Nationwide Environmental Protection Laws 1993*), p. 132, cited in Zhang Haibing, *On China's Environmental Diplomacy*, p. 13.

24. SEPA Policy and Law Section (ed.), *Zhongguo huanjing baohu fagui quanshu (1982–1997)* (*Complete Book of China's Environmental Protection Laws and Regulations (1982–1997)*) (Beijing: Chemical Industry Press, 1997).

appears that, over time, China has generally become more willing to participate in such agreements and to do so at an earlier date. Regarding this, it may be noted that the Republic of China government, which previously occupied China's seat in the United Nations and specialized international organizations, was not an active participant in international environmental law at that time. Moreover, China's adherence to international obligations has become more pronounced in recent years as international environmental diplomacy has accelerated and as China's own capacity to participate has increased.

All environmental agreements impinge on national sovereignty to some extent in that they require the parties to ensure that activities within their jurisdiction or under their control do not damage the environment of other states or the global commons.[25] There is, however, some perceived variation. The Convention on Biodiversity, adopted at UNCED, was seen to impose substantial constraints on development in selected, generally undeveloped areas in order to conserve biological diversity within and in some cases outside a jurisdiction. This would not impose broad constraints on development in an economy as a whole. In this respect, it is perhaps not surprising that China not only participated in the Convention, but that Premier Li Peng endorsed the Convention in his address at UNCED and that China was the first major state (and fifth overall) to ratify the Convention. The Biodiversity Convention nevertheless does present potential constraints on China's development, and these may not have been fully appreciated within China's government at the time.

Beyond becoming a party, China has taken active measures to implement the Biodiversity Convention. Even before it was adopted, the State Council had organized the Co-ordinating Group on Establishing the Biodiversity Convention, consisting of 13 ministries and agencies led by SEPA. By the end of 1993, China had adopted the China Biodiversity Conservation Action Plan, implementation of which commenced in 1994. Subsidiary action plans that have been adopted include the Forestry Action Plan under the Ministry of Forestry, the China Panda Migration Conservation Plan under the Ministry of Construction, and the China Agro-Biodiversity Action Plan under the Ministry of Agriculture. In 1997 China submitted its National Report on Sustainable Development. SEPA has conducted a national survey of biodiversity under UNEP sponsorship since 1995. Nature reserves have been established at a rapid rate – by the end of 1995, 799 nature reserves with a total area of 71.85 million hectares had been established, amounting to 7.19 per cent of the country's surface area.[26] Although the quality of management in nature reserves is generally deficient, major efforts are underway to upgrade management and protect reserves against despoliation and encroachment. Of particular importance is the promulgation of the "Regulations on nature reserves."[27] Management and administrative organizations with responsibility for

25. Principle 21, United Nations Conference on the Human Environment.
26. "Priority given to animal, plant sanctuaries," *China Daily*, 5 June 1996, p. 4.
27. State Council 1994.

nature reserves are authorized to accept domestic and foreign donations, providing a direct avenue for international influence at the administrative level, although Article 31 of the Regulations perversely provides that approval is required before foreign nationals can enter nature reserves. Penalties, including potential criminal responsibility, are provided for violations.

China took a less prominent position at the Rio United Nations Framework Convention on Climate Change (the "Framework Convention"). Soon after its adoption, however, the SCEP directed the Office of the Climate Change Co-ordinating Group to prepare a draft analysis of the Framework Convention's impact on China for the Co-ordinating Group on 2 July 1992. The Office convened representatives of responsible agencies – notably the State Science and Technology Commission (SSTC), the former Ministry of Energy, SEPA, the China Meteorological Administration (CMA)[28] and the Ministry of Foreign Affairs – to draft a document analysing China's obligations and assigning responsibility for the various components to different agencies. Importantly, lead responsibility was assigned to the SSTC, SEPA, CMA and the Chinese Academy of Sciences, not to the Ministry of Energy or any other production-oriented agency.[29] China ratified the Framework Convention on the same date as the Biodiversity Convention – again, the first major state and fifth signatory overall. After ratification, the CMA was designated as the lead agency, with the Office of the Climate Change Co-ordinating Group beneath it.

China moved more cautiously on the Framework Convention than the Biodiversity Convention, although in this respect its position was not necessarily different from that of most other states, including the U.S. China participated in the UNEP/Global Environment Facility (GEF) project on greenhouse gases and sinks (absorbents of greenhouse gases, such as forests or oceans), completed a paper assessing the impact of climate change on China using Global Circulation Model results, conducted various pilot studies and became an active participant in the UNDP project on least-cost emissions reduction.[30] Preparation of its national action plan on climate change is still underway.

Legislative action on issues raised in the Framework Convention has been uneven. In 1995 China amended its Air Pollution Prevention and Control Law, originally enacted in 1987. The revised statute calls for coal washing and the designation of acid rain or sulphur dioxide control districts. The Environmental and Resources Conservation Committee of the National People's Congress took note of the international obligations that China had assumed under the "Vienna convention for the protection

---

28. Then known as the State Meteorological Administration.

29. Office of the State Climate Change Co-ordinating Small Group, "Conditions for developing follow-on work to the Framework Convention on climate change" (20 December 1992), in *Compendium of Documents of the SCEP*, Vol. 2, p. 569.

30. Jan Fuglestvedt *et al.* "A review of country case studies on climate change," *Global Environment Facility Working Paper* (Washington: The World Bank, 1994), No. 7, p. 30.

of the ozone layer," the "Montreal protocol on substances that deplete the ozone layer" and the Framework Convention when drafting amendments to the Air Pollution Law.[31] On the whole, however, the statute falls short of satisfying these obligations. The Electric Power Law, also enacted in 1995, establishes a preference for clean and renewable fuels in electric power generation, and the Law on the Prevention and Control of Pollution of the Environment by Solid Wastes (1996) establishes controls on ash content, which would tend to discourage further the use of high ash-content fuels. The Energy Conservation Law was also enacted in 1997 after several postponements, but is largely hortatory in nature and requires a stronger regulatory foundation before its provisions can be operationalized.

At the Kyoto global warming summit in 1997, China strongly resisted the imposition of any binding or even voluntary obligations on developing countries – including itself – with respect to greenhouse gas emissions. Only the 38 Annexe B (or developing) states of the 159 participating states (consisting primary of OECD states and Eastern European transitional economies) were assigned such obligations under the Kyoto Protocol.[32] Not all of the latter have welcomed such obligations, which call for an aggregate 5.2 per cent reduction in greenhouse gas emissions below 1990 levels by Annexe B countries by 2008–2012.

The indefinite maintenance of a laggardly or obstructionist position was unlikely: China is already a major contributor to global warming, with 800 million tonnes of carbon emissions in 1995, placing it second behind only the U.S. in aggregate (but not per capita) greenhouse gas emissions. The World Bank has forecast that such emissions will nearly treble by 2020 to 2,380 million tonnes unless China takes corrective action.[33] Emissions approaching such levels would bring much greater pressure to bear on China in the future, and it would not be able to count on the support of developing countries such as the small island states that are especially vulnerable to global warming, or those that are more responsive to environmental influences. Furthermore, certain domestic constituencies are increasingly concerned with environmental issues and alarmed at the risks that global warming presents to China in terms of coastal flooding and other problems.[34] Thus, on 30 May 1998, China

---

31. Lin Zongtang, "Explanation of the 'Air Pollution Prevention and Control Law of the People's Republic of China (Revised Draft)'" (21 October 1994), in *Gazette of the National People's Congress of the People's Republic of China* (1995), p. 547.

32. Tom Korski, "Chinese official says Western nations attempting to shirk climate responsibility," *BNA: Daily Report for Executives*, 10 December 1997, p. B-5.

33. The World Bank, *Clear Waters, Blue Skies: China's Environment in the New Century* (Washington, DC: The World Bank, 1997), p. 34.

34. Although the principal concerns are domestic and even local, a survey by Friends of Nature also found increased coverage of global issues in the media. Liu Yingtang, "Newspapers fix environment," *China Daily*, 20 May 1998, p. 1; State Science and Technology Commission Chinese Research Centre on the Advancement and Development of Science and Technology, "Zhongguo jumin de huanjing zhishi zhuangkuang ji qi duice" ("The state of environmental knowledge among residents of China and corresponding countemeasures"), *Diaoyan baogao (Research Report)*, No. 7 (5 May 1995). For a concise

subscribed to the Kyoto Protocol on the basis of a prospective accommo-
dation along the lines of the ozone depleting substances (ODS) control
regime, whereby the developed countries would assume larger and/or
earlier control obligations and finance part of developing countries'
control costs. Under the ODS provision, although as of 1996 China was
the largest producer and consumer of ODS, it committed to phasing out
use in aerosols by 1998 and in all sectors by 2005 under the leadership
of its Ozone Protection Leading Group. Reflecting China's cautious
approach to restrictive obligations, however, China was only the 37th
state to sign the Kyoto Protocol,[35] in contrast to its alacrity in signing both
the Biodiversity and Framework conventions.

To the extent that China seeks to minimize costs associated with
control of greenhouse gas emissions, placing a higher priority on the
control of sulphur dioxide and acid rain, the outside world can also foster
the forces of change within China by supporting SEPA, the Environmental and Resources Protection Committee of the NPC and China's
nascent environmental non-governmental organizations (NGOs). SEPA
has consciously sought to enhance both its influence and the popular
awareness of environmental issues by improving the flow of information
– e.g. the publication of urban air quality indices became a staple press
item in 1997–1998. Although such information will be primarily directed
to issues of domestic and local concern, such as total suspended particulates, the resulting overall rise in consciousness is likely to accelerate
China's willingness to participate in international regimes and contribute
to the solution of environmental problems.

The fear of international isolation cannot be ignored. China can
take shelter behind the reluctance of such major countries as the U.S.
and Australia to accept compulsory controls on their own greenhouse
gas emissions: it would fear much more pressure to control its own
emissions if all of the world's leading countries took action as well.
Because of resistance to doing so, particularly in the United States
Congress, a simultaneous or near-simultaneous commitment to obligations of differing magnitude and time sequences may be the most feasible
solution.[36]

China thus appears to have become more of a leader in the area
concerned with the Biodiversity Convention than global climate change.
This does not necessarily mean it has been obstructionist in the latter

---

footnote continued

summary of the risks facing China, see Michael B. McElroy and Chris P. Nielsen, "Energy,
agriculture and the environment: prospects for Sino–American co-operation," in Ezra F.
Vogel (ed.), *Living with China: U.S.–China Relations in the Twenty-first Century* (New York
and London: Columbia University Press, 1997), pp. 225–27.

35. "China signs Kyoto Protocol on climate change," *Asian Wall Street Journal*, 1 June
1998, p. 16.

36. Robert Repetto and Jonathan Lash, "Planetary roulette: gambling with the climate,"
Foreign Policy (Fall 1997), p. 97; Cheryl Hogue, "U.S. not ready to reject Kyoto deal,
Eizenstat tells House Science Committee," *BNA: Daily Report for Executives*, 6 March 1998;
"Forecast is dim in the Senate for global warming treaty," *Congressional Quarterly Weekly
Report*, 13 December 1997, pp. 3068–69.

instance, but rather that it has been more reluctant to assume obligations beyond the extent of research or pilot projects. As a sign that global warming issues are acquiring greater policy import, policy co-ordinating responsibility in the Climate Change Co-ordinating Group was transferred in the spring of 1998 from the relatively weak CMA to the State Development Planning Commission.

The Role of the Private Sector in International Environmental Regimes

International bodies characterized by substantial involvement of the private business sector and contractual provisions governing global transactions play an increasingly important role in environmental policy. The source of such regimes and contractual practices lies in advanced industrialized countries where business and creditor concern about environmental issues has been heightened by increasingly stringent and comprehensive regulation, judicial decisions and public pressure. Many companies have adopted corporate policies requiring compliance with all applicable requirements and sometimes demanding performance in excess of these regulations. Corporations with international operations tend to impose such internal policies on a system-wide basis, regardless of location or enforcement, because the costs of adapting production and pollution control technologies to local regulatory requirements generally outweigh any cost savings. They also anticipate that regulatory requirements will become more stringent, are averse to long-tailed Superfund-type and other environmental risks, and respect public and investor concern over environmental liabilities. Companies such as Ciba-Geigy, ICI, Mobil and Shōwa Denkō have adopted such internal policies on a world-wide basis.[37] In some cases, aware of the risks posed by investments in joint ventures such as those encountered by Union Carbide at Bhopal, companies insist on a disproportionate right to exercise control over environmental matters. In other instances, including some in China, they have sometimes walked away from prospective deals because of environmental concerns.

For similar reasons, lenders in international transactions increasingly tend to impose strict contractual covenants on borrowers regardless of an investment's location. Environmental liabilities jeopardize a borrower's repayment capability – a risk which has aroused great concern in OECD countries and which is magnified in the non-recourse and limited-recourse lending particularly common in project finance. Lenders are also concerned about their own liability should they participate in management in a workout or foreclosure context, a concern which originated

---

37. United Nations Conference on Trade and Development ("UNCTAD"), *Self-Regulation of Environmental Management* (Geneva: United Nations, 1996). The United States has encouraged United States businesses to adopt and implement voluntary codes of conduct for doing business around the world including such areas as environmental protection and environmental practices. *Model Business Principles* (26 May 1996).

from domestic loans in the United States.[38] Loan covenants with respect to environmental matters may be even more stringent when the lenders include multilateral development institutions which have more rigid loan (and where applicable, investment) approval procedures and, in the case of The World Bank, environmental guidelines addressing project technology and environmental impact.[39]

It is as a consequence of its economic reforms that China has become subject to external influence by the private sector. These have in turn increased its dependence on foreign trade, investment and credit. One prime example that is emerging in this regard involves standardization. China has long had a standard-setting process which serves to promote business, science and technology, and social welfare throughout society. The process of standardization was accorded a legislative basis with the enactment of the Standardization Law (1988) and the subsequent promulgation of the Implementing Rules Concerning the Standardization Law (1990). The Standardization Law particularly authorizes the formulation of standards for the safety and hygiene of industrial products and their manufacture, transportation and storage; technical requirements and monitoring methods governing environmental protection; and technical terms, symbols, codes and drafting methods for environmental protection.[40] The Standardization Law also provides that the State shall encourage the active adoption of international standards[41] and, as of August 1988, approximately 36 per cent of all standards were international.[42]

Standards protecting human health and property are mandatory.[43] Standardization under the statute is encouraged to protect people's health and safety, the rights of consumers and the environment;[44] to promote resource efficiency, popularize scientific and technological advances, and facilitate product interchangeability;[45] and to promote economic and

---

38. Approximately 90 banks have subscribed to the United Nations Environment Programme's Statement by Banks on the Environment and Sustainable Development (1992); National Wildlife Federation, *Global Survey on Environmental Policies and Practices of the Financial Services Industry: The Private* Sector (Washington, DC: 1997); *United States* v. *Fleet Factors*, 901 F.2d 1550 (11th Cir. 1990); Jaret Seiberg, "Banks learn clean-up liability fears the hard way," *American Banker*, 6 June 1995, p. 3. Lender concern in the United States has been alleviated in part under the Asset Conservation, Lender Liability and Deposit Insurance Protection Act of 1996, enacted into law as Title II. Subtitle E of the FY 1997 Defense Appropriations Act. This statute exempts lenders from the definition of "owner or operator" under Superfund so long as the lender does not "participate in the management" of the property prior to foreclosure. Fiduciary liability also is limited under the new law. U.S. Cong. Conf. Rpt. 104–863 (Sept. 28, 1996). ("Superfund" is the more commonly-used name for the Comprehensive Environmental Response, Compensation and Liability Act (1980) (CERCLA), the fund governing the clean-up of abandoned disposal sites, for example.)

39. The World Bank, *Operational Manual*, Part 4; The World Bank, *Industrial Pollution Prevention and Abatement Handbook* (preliminary version, July 1995). Multilaterals in China are, for example, increasingly reluctant to finance thermal power plants and, when they do, tend to demand stringent compliance with environmental regulations.

40. Article 2, Standardization Law (1988).

41. Article 4, Standardization Law (1988).

42. *China Law and Practice*, Vol. 3, No. 2 (1988), p. 54.

43. Article 7, Standardization Law (1988).

44. Article 8, Standardization Law (1988).

45. Article 9, Standardization Law (1988).

technological co-operation with foreign entities and foreign trade.[46] The production, sale and import of nonconforming products and products which bear an improper certification symbol are punishable under law.[47] Additional details on the standard-setting and implementation process are provided in the Implementing Rules. Under the Implementing Rules, the State Bureau of Quality and Technology Supervision (SBTS)[48]– as the administrative department in charge of standardization, metrology and quality – supervises and co-ordinates the process. However, the drafting, examination and approval of standards is actually led by the relevant departments of the State Council.[49] Thus, SEPA co-ordinates standard-setting with respect to environmental matters, increasing its influence over the process relative to production-oriented ministries. Further, under the Procedures on Administering the Adoption of International Standards (for trial implementation),[50] China has a well-established process for encouraging and regularizing the adoption of international standards to promote technical exchanges, raise product quality, promote international trade and meet domestic needs. Under the Procedures, international standards can be adopted in three forms: in whole, with approximately the same content, or by reference.

The International Organization for Standardization (ISO) has adopted the ISO 14000 Series of environmental management standards.[51] ISO is an international organization based in Geneva that was established in 1946. It has a staff of less than 200, and, independent of the United Nations, it is constituted by designated national standard-setting bodies. The nature of such bodies ranges from private to governmental, and, at last count, ISO had 118 national standard-setting bodies as members, including 85 full members with voting power. All OECD member countries have standard-setting bodies which are full members of ISO

---

46. Article 11, Standardization Law (1988).
47. Chapter 4.
48. Formerly the State Bureau of Technology Supervision.
49. Article 12, Standardization Law (1988).
50. State Economic Commission, State Science and Technology Commission and former State Administration of Standards 1982. The scope of international standards provided therein includes: (1) international standards set by (a) international standard-setting organizations, namely the International Organization for Standardization and the International Electrotechnical Commission, and (b) United Nations agencies such as the International Telecommunications Union and standards established by international agreement; and (2) advanced foreign standards set by (a) regional standard-setting organizations such as the European Committee for Standardization, (b) national standard-setting bodies in advanced industrialized countries such as the United States and (c) internationally recognized standard-setting organizations such as the American Society for Testing and Materials, the American Petroleum Institute and Underwriters Laboratories.
51. This section draws heavily on UNCTAD, *ISO 14000: International Environmental Management Systems Standards: Five Key Questions for Developing Country Officials* (Geneva: United Nations, 1996, draft). For a more practice-oriented introduction, see John Voorhees and Robert A. Woellner, *International Environmental Risk Management: ISO 14000 and the Systems Approach* (Boca Raton, FL: Lewis Publishers, 1998).

but, unlike China, most developing countries are not even correspondent members or subscriber members.[52]

ISO issues two kinds of standards: (1) specification standards which normalize product standards and (2) meta-standards which standardize procedures. For most of its history, ISO activity was confined to specification standards and highly technical meta-standards. The contribution of such activity is readily apparent when one compares the portability of automatic teller machine cards – which can be used worldwide – and electric plugs – which vary greatly between and sometimes even within countries.

ISO's character began to change in 1987 with adoption of the ISO 9000 Series, the first series of "soft" meta-standards, directed in this instance towards quality management.[53] Revised in 1994, the significance of the 9000 Series included its impact on foreign trade. A rising number of companies in advanced industrialized countries decided to adopt the standard, which requires certification of compliance by an accepted auditing agency. Such certification is conducted on a facility-by-facility basis and typically requires annual, biennial or triennial audits.

As companies adopted ISO 9000, particularly ISO 9001 which governs design and manufacturing, they began to demand that their suppliers also be certified. As such requirements spread more widely, exporters in developing countries as well as suppliers in advanced industrialized countries were required to become certified if they were to maintain and expand their markets. Furthermore, many public procurement agencies, particularly in Europe where the impetus for ISO 9000 had originated, increasingly required that bidders and their suppliers be certified. Hong Kong, for example, will not accept bids on public contracts valued in excess of HK$10 million unless the bidder has ISO 9000 certification.[54]

This diffusion of the ISO 9000 Series also impacted on accrediting agencies. Although certification may be and is commonly conducted by an auditing agency from the country where the facility is located, this is not an ISO requirement. Thus companies, particularly in developing countries, desirous of ISO 9000 certification could and do obtain certification from foreign auditing agencies, whose certification may be more widely accepted than local certification. Thus governments and, to the extent that they differ, standard-setting bodies encourage the development of a national accreditation industry.

ISO 9000 certification is endorsed by China's central government and has become increasingly popular in China. As CSBTS director Li Chuanqing explained, ISO 9000 certification is promoted by the central government as a means of raising product, construction and service quality;

52. Correspondent members are organizations with observer status that do not qualify as national standard-setting bodies. Subscriber members are national standard-setting organizations from small countries and have limited participation rights.

53. For more on ISO 9000, see Robert W. Peach (ed.), *The ISO 9000 Handbook* (Fairfax, VA: CEEM Information Services, 1992).

54. *International Environmental Systems Update*, Vol. 3, No. 4 (1996), p. 20.

avoiding the imposition of trade and technical barriers against Chinese exports; and raising the quality of enterprise management.[55] Standard GB/T 19001 was adopted in 1992 in conformance with ISO 9001. The China Council for the Quality System (ISO 9000) of the Export Manufacturers, established by the State Administration for the Inspection of Import and Export Commodities and 15 other government agencies and commissions,[56] encourages exporters to seek ISO 9000 certification. Accrediting bodies have been established under the China National Accreditation Committee for Quality System Certification Bodies, which determine if applicants merit the issuance of a Certificate of Conformity of Quality System Certification. By the end of 1994, more than 120 state-owned and foreign-invested companies were reported to have ISO 9000 certificates.[57]

While ISO 9000 has no direct bearing on environmental quality, it constitutes the first systematic international effort by business and/or government to establish management standards on a global basis, and such standards serve to upgrade management practices. Although voluntary, adoption and compliance carry not just moral weight but also the potential for exclusion from important international markets. The ISO 14000 Series of Environmental Management Standards reflects a comparable process. In 1991 ISO's Technical Management Board (TMB) created the joint Strategic Advisory Group on the Environment (SAGE) with the International Electrotechnical Commission (IEC),[58] reflecting the desire among some member bodies and ISO staff to explore whether and how ISO should respond to environmental issues. Such concern was emphasized by the Business Council for Sustainable Development, an organization of international business leaders, which suggested that ISO play a role at UNCED. SAGE convened four times between June 1991 and June 1993 with participants including business people, consultants, academics, government officials and others, as well as representatives of national standard-setting bodies. Asked to assess the need for international standardization of sustained industrial development and environmental performance and/or management, SAGE unanimously recommended formation of a new ISO technical committee at its third meeting in October 1992.

The TMB surveyed national standard-setting bodies on the proposal and all 29 respondents voted in favour. ISO subsequently formed Technical Committee TC 207 with responsibility for standardization in

55. Ma Zhiping, "Revised ISO 9000 Series discussed," *China Daily*, 22 April 1995, p. 2.
56. Announcement No. 1, 1995, *China Daily*, 26 April 1995, p. 3. The CSBTS has its own mandate to verify that products satisfy quality standards. "Products must attain standards of quality," *China Daily* (28 September 1995), p. 4.
57. Qiu Qi, "100 Chinese firms aim for ISO quality standard," *China Daily*, 29 May 1995, p. 5.
58. Established in 1906, the IEC sets international standards for electrical equipment and electronic products. China is a member of the IEC. Vice Premier Wu Bangguo stated in an address to an IEC advisory body that China must adopt international standards and raise product quality to be successful in international markets. Ma Zhiping, "Experts discuss standardization," *China Daily*, 23 May 1995, p. 2.

environmental management and systems. TC 207 was directed to liaise with existing technical committees responsible for acoustics (TC 43), air quality (TC 146), water quality (TC 147), soil quality (TC 190), solid wastes (TC 200) and quality management and quality assurance (TC 176), as well as competent international industry and NGO organizations. TCs 43, 146, 147 and 190 retained exclusive authority over testing methods for pollutants, while TC 207 was barred from drafting standards concerning pollution limits, environmental performance levels or product standardization, and directed to focus on environmental management tools and systems.

Like ISO activity in general, TC 207 was dominated by the advanced industrialized countries. Working groups convened by sub-committees to prepare working drafts were similarly chaired by individuals from advanced industrialized countries, and developing countries generally did not even participate in proportion to their overall membership in ISO.

The drafting process proceeds on a consensus basis, thereby providing veto power to any member. Working drafts that achieve consensus proceed to formal reviews by the technical committee which, in a two-stage process, first issue Draft International Standards and then International Standards. In this instance, TC 207 was formed in 1993 and ISO 14001 ("Environmental management system – specifications with guidance for use") was adopted first as a Draft International Standard at Oslo in June 1995, and then as an International Standard at Rio de Janeiro in June 1996. ISO 14000 drew heavily on environmental management standards adopted in Great Britain (BS 7750) and the European Union's Eco-Management and Audit Scheme (EMAS). China participated throughout the process, sending seven delegates to the Oslo meeting and 14 to the Rio de Janeiro meeting.[59] Several other standards in the ISO 14000 Series have been adopted, at least one has been returned for further consideration, and others remain at various stages in the drafting process. Thus, China did not exercise its right of veto under the consensus system, either on its own behalf or as a representative of developing countries.

ISO 14001 establishes five requirements for certification: (1) the existence of an appropriate environmental policy for each facility – including commitments to continual improvement and prevention of pollution and compliance with relevant environmental legislation and regulations and voluntary requirements – is documented and communicated to all employees for implementation and is available to the public; (2) conformance assessments with respect to environmental objectives, and legal and voluntary requirements; (3) management systems to check compliance with the environmental policy statement; (4) periodic internal

59. On the standard-setting process including China's role therein, see Office of the China Steering Committee for Environmental Management Certification, "Jianli tongyide guojia guanli zhidu baozheng ISO 14000 biaozhun zai woguo youxiao shishi" ("Establish a unified national management system, ensure that the ISO 14000 standards are effectively implemented in our country"), *Zhongguo huanjing bao* (*China Environment News*), 11 December 1997, p. 3.

audits and reports to top management; and (5) a public declaration of ISO 14001 status. Thus, ISO 14001 commits a certified party to establish a meaningful and verifiable policy of compliance with applicable regulatory requirements, as opposed to a policy vacuum or a policy without content. ISO 14001 is the foundation of the ISO 14000 Series but it has been subject to criticism from several quarters, particularly environmental NGOs who did not recognize its potential significance until relatively late in the process and were handicapped in their ability to participate by the ISO structure, the complexity of the subject matter and the logistics of attending many meetings held at various locations around the world over the course of several years (see Table 1 for the complete ISO 14000 Series in its current formulation).[60]

Environmental NGOs have also criticized ISO 14000, particularly 14001, because it outlines a management rather than a performance standard. ISO 14000 focuses on management rather than compliance except regarding a compliance commitment by management – and this commitment is bounded by applicable regulations and voluntary obligations. Therefore, a company and/or any of its facilities could be ISO 14001-certified notwithstanding the fact that it does not comply with applicable standards, is subject to compliance obligations that themselves fall short of international standards or otherwise fails to provide adequate assurances with respect to environmental quality. Conversely, some industry leaders have objected to ISO 14000 because it imposes an additional, quasi-regulatory burden, particularly for those companies that already have stringent environmental management systems in place, and may benefit companies with only weaker policies to be implemented.[61]

Such criticism is largely misplaced with respect to China where the problem is no longer one of a failure to adopt appropriate environmental legislation and regulations. China has enacted more than a dozen major environmental statutes, several of which have been amended to make them more stringent and applicable to a wider range of actions. Similarly, the number of regulatory personnel has been increased to more than 80,000 with over 200,000 additional persons employed in regulated industries and other sectors of society, although SEPA itself remains understaffed at the national level. And, although the standard-setting process is less open than that of the United States where any interested party from industry, government, business or NGOs may participate in the Technical Advisory Group,[62] the process is open to experts as well as government officials and business.

60. See, e.g. Daniel C. Esty, *Greening the GATT: Trade, Environment and the Future* (Washington, DC: Institute for International Economics, 1994), p. 173, n. 30 ("ISO procedures have only limited opportunities for public involvement. More disturbingly, the only representatives at many meetings are invited business representatives from the industry to be regulated").

61. "ISO 14001 should not be required by law or regulation, attorney says," *BNA: Daily Executive Report,* 14 February 1996, p. A-23.

62. U.S. Environmental Protection Agency, *ISO 14000: International Environmental Management Standards* (Washington: EPA/742-F95–006, May 1995).

Table 1: **The ISO 14000 Series**

Organization Evaluation Standards

ISO14001:	Environmental Management System – Specification with Guidance for Use (GB/T 24001)
ISO14004:	Environmental Management System – General Guidelines on Principles, Systems and Supporting Techniques (GB/T 24004)
ISO14010:	Guideline for Environmental Auditing – General Principles on EA (GB/T 24010)
ISO14011/1:	Guideline for Environmental Auditing – Audit Procedures Part 1. Auditing of Environmental Management Systems (GB/T 24011)
ISO14012:	Guideline for Environmental Auditing – Qualifications Criteria for Environmental Auditors (GB/T 24012)
ISO14013:	Management for Environmental Audit Programmes (Deleted from TC 207 Agenda – No further work scheduled)
ISO14014:	Initial Reviews (Deleted from TC 207 Agenda)
ISO14015:	Environmental Site Assessments
ISO14031:	Evaluation of the Environmental Performance of the Management System and its Relationship to the Environment
ISO 1403x:	Evaluation of the Environmental Performance of the Operational System and its Relationship to the Environment

Product Evaluation Standards

ISO 14020:	Goals and Principles of All Environmental Labelling
ISO 14021:	Environmental Labels and Declarations (ELD) Self-Declaration Environmental Claims – Terms and Definitions
ISO 14022:	ELD – Self-Declaration Environmental Claims – Symbols
ISO 14023:	ELD – Self-Declaration Environmental Claims – Testing and Verification
ISO 14024:	ELD – Environmental Labelling Type I Guiding Principles and Procedures
ISO 1402X:	ELD – Environmental Labelling Type III
ISO 14040:	Life Cycle Assessment – Principles and Practices
ISO 14041:	Life Cycle Assessment – Life Cycle Inventory Analysis
ISO 14042:	Life Cycle Assessment – Impact Assessment
ISO 14043:	Life Cycle Assessment – Interpretation
ISO 14050:	Terms and Definitions – Guide on the Principles for ISO/TC 207/SC6 Terminology
ISO 14060:	Guide for the Inclusion of Environmental Aspects in Product Standards (reassigned to ISO Guide 64 – no longer a standard)

The biggest problem in the estimation of Chinese officials is a lack of effective and consistent implementation or enforcement.[63] Recognition of this deficiency led to the issuance by SEPA in early 1998 of a document

---

63. Chan Yee Hon, "Law fails to punish polluters," *South China Morning Post*, 4 April 1998, p. 8; Oksenberg and Economy, *China Joins the World: Progress and Prospects*.

on the strengthening of environmental enforcement.[64] ISO 14001 and the entire ISO 14000 Series are expected to help this process by encouraging Chinese companies, directly and through pressure from purchasers of their products and services, to commit to compliance with applicable regulatory requirements and publicly declare their ISO 14001 status.[65] Such self-implementation can ease the burden on regulators and foster corporate cultures of compliance and sustainable development, while enhancing the competitiveness of Chinese enterprises in international trade. SEPA established an office of Environmental Management Systems to lead such work and conducted trial certifications in five enterprises. With the CSBTS it established the State Leading Committee on the Certification of China's Environmental Systems,[66] resulting in adoption on 1 April 1997 of five ISO 14000 standards under the GB/T 24000-ISO 14000 Series.[67]

Subsequently, the China Steering Committee for Environmental Management System Certification was established under SEPA with two operating arms – the China Accreditation Committee for Environmental Management System Certification Bodies (covering accreditation, supervision and management of relevant certification bodies), and the Environment Management Committee of China Registration Board of Auditors (responsible for training and registering environmental management system auditors).[68] Environmental auditing had originated with a pilot programme established with UNEP and World Bank support to conduct cleaner production audits under the auspices of the China National Cleaner Production Centre. This new entity was established under the Chinese Research Academy of Environmental Sciences and helped to serve as a foundation for the establishment of an environmental audit service industry, adopting GB/T 24010–1996 Guidelines for Environmental Auditing: General Principles.[69] This was quickly followed by the establishment of the Environment Management Committee of China Registration Board for Auditors. Environmental management and consulting centres have been established in part to conduct ISO 14000 certification and environmental auditors have been certified.[70]

Twenty-seven enterprises achieved ISO 14001 certification during the

64. SEPA, "Guanyu jiaqiang huanjing xingzheng zhifa gongzuo de ruogan yijian" ("Some opinions on strengthening the work of environmental administration and law enforcement" (March 26, 1998)), in *Zhongguo huanjing bao* (*China Environment News*), 2 May 1998, p. 3.

65. For a similar analysis with respect to the diffusion of ISO 9000 certification in China, see Jane Parry, "New environmental standards introduced as ISO craze hits China firms," *China Joint Venturer*, Vol. 2, No. 4 (December 1996/January 1997), pp. 1 ff.

66. "Our country develops environmental management systems standards and certification," *People's Daily*, overseas edition, 13 July 1996, p. 5.

67. CSBTS Standards Section and National Environmental Management Standards Technical Committee, GB/T 24000-ISO 14000 (1997).

68. *China Daily Business Weekly*, 24 May 1998, p. 1.

69. SEPA, China National Cleaner Production Centre, United Nations Environment Programme Industry and Environment and the World Bank, *Cleaner Production in China: A Story of Successful Cooperation* (Paris: 1996).

70. Motorola (China) Electronics Ltd's large Tianjin plant is among the earliest facilities to be ISO 14000 certified in China. "Motorola Tianjin plant receives ISO 14000 certification," *Zhongguo huanjing bao* (*China Environment News*), 28 April 1998, p. 1.

first year following promulgation of the GB/T 24000-ISO 14000 Series by inspectors certified by the China Accreditation Committee for Environmental Management System Certification Bodies.[71] According to an official of SEPA's Environmental Management Systems Audit Centre, these early certifying enterprises could be classified as either active or passive: active enterprises were eager to implement ISO 14000 and saw environmental management systems auditing as a tool for raising their competitiveness. The environmental consciousness of these enterprises was attributed to their attention to product quality and their appreciation of the benefits of a good environmental image in international and domestic marketing. The passive enterprises fell into two categories: those which were impelled by environmental regulators and regulatory requirements to adopt ISO 14001, despite their tendency to focus on cost reduction and neglect product quality; and those which adopted ISO 14001 at the demand of their customers, even though they themselves lacked strong environmental consciousness. Thus, market requirements, particularly those of the global marketplace, as well as regulatory pressures created the impetus to seek ISO 14001 certification.[72]

About half of the 27 enterprises were foreign-invested enterprises, indicating their higher sense of environmental responsibility. More than half were in the electronics and household appliances industries – both heavily export-oriented and conscious of their public image. The third largest response came from the chemical industry, which faces complex environmental issues.[73]

Leaving standards aside, contractual provisions are even more a function of private business. A borrower in a loan contract or indenture will typically be required to represent that it is in compliance with all applicable laws and regulations and covenant that it will indemnify the lender against all environmental liabilities. Absent any restriction on freedom of contract with respect to such provisions, a lender has the power to declare a default in the event of noncompliance, and to require the borrower to indemnify the creditor for any environmental liabilities. There do not appear to be any provisions under Chinese law that would render such provisions unenforceable, subject to the practical barriers to enforcement in general.

Indeed, under pressure from SEPA and others, the Chinese government itself has sought to harness its power over creditors to induce borrowers to raise their compliance consciousness. Under the General Provisions on Loans (People's Bank of China 1996), China's state-owned banks are

71. Xiao Zhu, "Environmental exams awaiting Chinese firms," *China Daily*, 20 May 1998, p. 2.

72. Dong Wenxuan, "Woguo shishi ISO 14000 xilie biaozhun de dongtai fenxi" ("An analysis of the trends in China for implementing the ISO 14000 series standards: part I"), *Zhongguo huanjing bao* (*China Environment News*), 28 April 1998, p. 4.

73. Dong Wenxuan, "Woguo shishi ISO 14000 xilie biaozhun de dongtai fenxi" ("An analysis of the trends in China for implementing the ISO 14000 series standards: part II"), *Zhongguo huanjing bao* (*China Environment News*), 12 May 1998, p. 4.

prohibited from extending credit to borrowers if business operations or investment projects lack environmental approvals.[74]

China is also encouraged to support ISO standards and enforce contractual provisions by potential economic disincentives. ISO standards may constitute trade barriers to the extent that exporters from developing countries such as China are required to become certified. The Final Agreement of the GATT (1994) provides, however, that international standards (voluntary guidelines approved by a recognized body) are deemed to make an important contribution to production efficiency and the conduct of international trade.[75]

The Final Agreement, the foundation for the new World Trade Organization for which China's membership application is still pending, also provides that appropriate standards promulgated by other relevant international organizations open for membership to WTO members may apply to sanitary and phytosanitary measures with respect to human, animal and plant health not otherwise addressed by the Codex Alimentarius under FAO and WHO, the International Office of Epizootics or the International Plant Protection Convention.[76] Although the ISO 14000 Series has not yet been determined to qualify under WTO, it would appear that standards set by a national standard-setting body that conform to or are less stringent than ISO 14000 in foreign countries and by multinationals could be used to restrict imports from China or other developing countries. Similarly, with respect to contracts governing international transactions, were China to determine that such provisions were unenforceable and that environmental and related regulatory risks must be borne by lenders, interest rates would rise and the availability of foreign capital would diminish.

Policy Implications

This study indicates that China is now a ready participant in international environmental regimes and has procedures in place establishing the policy-making bodies that will co-ordinate the positions of various agencies in formulating positions and implementing strategies with respect to such regimes. Yet it is concerned lest such regimes infringe on its sovereignty and hamper its development potential. China is not a simple naysayer or violator of its international obligations. Rather, it has embarked on a long-term course to formulate and implement increasingly stringent environmental policies. Because of China's importance with respect to the solution of global and regional problems, it is particularly important that it continue along this track and further expand its participation in international environmental agreements on a positive basis. From this perspective, the following policy implications emerge.

74. Article 24(2) (v). This provision is more stringent than Article 25(3) (iv) in the version previously adopted for trial implementation in 1995 which prohibited loans only in case of actual violations of environmental regulations.

75. *Agreement on Technical Barriers to Trade*, MTN/FA II-A1A-6 (1994), p. 1.

76. *Agreement on the Application of Sanitary and Phytosanitary Measures*, MTN/F II-A1A-4, Annexe A.

Sanctions. China's determination to develop its economy by safeguarding its access to export markets and enhancing its attractiveness for foreign investment can make sanctions an effective incentive for participation and compliance. The Montreal Protocol[77] and the Convention on International Trade in Endangered Species of Wild Flora and Fauna, as well as domestic legislation of importing countries such as the United States,[78] contain provisions for such sanctions. As noted earlier, however, such sanctions are unusual and difficult to apply under international environmental regimes. The standard-setting process provides a less direct, more private means for discouraging non-conformist behaviour by imposing trade barriers to substandard and otherwise non-conforming products. The ISO 14000 Series takes the sanctioning potential of standards to a new level with the possibility of restricting trade in products and services from non-certified facilities.[79] Except for certain labour standards and standards applicable to products derived from wildlife, international standards generally do not govern the process of manufacture (and would be of questionable enforceability under GATT and now WTO) and in that sense do not address pollution arising in the manufacturing process. ISO 14000, however, has the potential to reduce environmental harms by addressing management deficiencies.

Scientific and technical co-operation. China continues to maintain barriers to the free flow of information, as evidenced by the expulsion of foreign Greenpeace activists in 1996 and restrictions on the reporting of negative news. Nevertheless, information is more widely available with respect to scientific and technical matters, and there are relatively few barriers to receiving such information and acting upon it. The standard-setting process illustrates novel ways of managing production and fostering compliance with little if any dispute, even though their efficacy is largely untested and compliance behaviour would become more discretionary. Under such circumstances, maintaining and expanding scientific and technical exchanges would help to influence Chinese policy-making further in accordance with the norms and practices of international environmental regimes, while minimizing conflict with ideological and nationalistic barriers.

Sharing the costs of environmental protection. In R. H. Coase's classical treatment of externalities, equally efficient outcomes could be obtained regardless of whether the polluter or the victim took or financed remedial action. This seemingly amoral analysis of environmental prob-

---

77. See Oksenberg and Economy, *China Joins the World: Progress and Prospects.*

78. U.S. sanctions under the Pelly Amendment to the Fishermen's Protective Act of 1967, 22 U.S.C. § 1987, were applied against Taiwan in 1994 and lifted on 11 September 1996. Regulations to curb illicit international trade in endangered species are being drafted by the Endangered Species Import and Export Managing Office under the State Council. Chen Chunmei, "State curbs illicit wildlife trade," *China Daily,* 17 May 1996, p. 2.

79. Stephen L. Kass, "ISO plans uniform standards," *National Law Journal,* 6 November 1995, p. C4 ("ISO 14000 sponsors can have considerable confidence that their efforts will survive challenges under both the Uruguay Round agreements and NAFTA").

lems may be ethically or politically objectionable if the quest is for a division of the costs of environmental pollution based on culpability – e.g. the "polluter pays" principle, to which China itself subscribes. The Coase Theorem may be morally acceptable as well as efficient if transaction costs are high because the issues are fundamentally nonjusticiable or the procedures for adjudicating disputes are so cumbersome as to be impractical, as is typically the case in international environmental disputes. This is particularly likely when the victim is both richer than the polluter and less tolerant of environmental harms. China has established the Trans-Century Green Project to solicit funds to this end, and claims to have received a total of US$3 billion in foreign financial support from multilateral development institutions, including the GEF, and bilateral programmes.[80] Such costs can be financed through external assistance and export credits on a bilateral basis, as Japan,[81] the United States[82] and other countries are doing, or multilaterally through the GEF and facilities like the Montreal Protocol Fund,[83] the scope of which has been expanded to include climate change and biodiversity to varying degrees. Therefore, if the advanced industrialized countries wish to foster environmental protection in China, they should be prepared not only to share knowledge with China, but also to provide training on a subsidized basis to enhance China's technical capacity and provide funds to ease the financial burden of environmental protection.[84] As others have noted, the U.S. can do more in this regard by relaxing Cold War restrictions on the involvement of the U.S. Agency for International Development and the United States–Asia Environmental Partnership in China.[85] Such programmes can also provide support for exporters of environmental goods and services.[86] But this does

80. Zhu Baoxia, "China seeks bilateral protection initiatives," *China Daily*, 11 May 1998, p. 2; "Mr. Xie goes fishing," *Business China*, 16 February 1998, pp. 3–4; Liu Yingang, "Green fund increasing," *China Daily*, 24 November 1995, p. 1.

81. "Japan: China's largest donor," *China Environmental Review*, Vol. 1, No. 3 (1998), p. 10; Peter Evans, "Japan's green aid," *The China Business Review*, Vol. 21, No. 4 (1994), p. 39.

82. Vanessa Lide Whitcomb, "A cleaner tiger," *The China Business Review*, Vol. 21, No. 4 (1994), p. 44.

83. Instrument for the Establishment of the Restructured Global Environment Facility (September 1994). On the United States decision to fund the Montreal Protocol Fund under pressure from other countries, see Richard J. Smith, "The ozone layer and beyond – towards a global environmental diplomacy," presented to the American Chemical Society (24 August 1994). China was among the few developing countries participating in the establishment of GEF to support the principle that all participants should contribute to the core fund, regardless of their level of development. See Helen Sjöberg, "From idea to reality: the creation of the global environment facility," *Global Environment Facility Working Paper* (Washington: 1994), No. 10, p. 30. China's contribution is the minimum amount of 4 million SDRs (special drawing right from the IMF).

84. Chayes and Chayes, *The New Sovereignty: Compliance with International Regulatory Agreements*.

85. David M. Lampton, "Chinese security objectives and U.S. interests in policy," testimony presented before the House Committee on National Security (20 March 1996).

86. Other examples are the Environmental Trade Working Group co-chaired by the Department of Commerce and Environmental Protection Agency, and the Office of Environmental Technologies Exports within the Department of Commerce. *Trade Promotion Co-ordinating Committee Environment Trade Working Group, China: Environmental Technologies Export Market Plan* (Washington: U.S. Department of Commerce, International Trade Administration March 1996).

not necessarily provide any direct solace to poorer victims, and to the extent that Chinese externalities harm poorer neighbours such as Laos, Burma and Vietnam, it is unlikely that such countries could share China's costs of environmental protection. However, China's commitment to compliance not just with national environmental regulations but also bilateral and multilateral environmental agreements and the environmental requirements of multilateral development banks in the Tumen River Economic Development Area and relevant areas of North-East Asia indicates a determination to co-operate with its neighbours in at least some respects on behalf of environmentally responsible economic development.[87] Furthermore, this recommendation does not call for the issuance of blank cheques, but rather for providing assistance carefully targeted to achieve the goals of international environmental regimes,[88] while gradually weaning China away from such subsidies as its economy develops.

Preventing free-riding and extortion. Although sharing the costs of environmental protection may be attractive to China because of its cost-sharing promise, it presents potential free-rider and extortion problems and is subject to resource limitations. With respect to free-riding, China – like any other polluter – could act with impunity in the face of problems affecting its neighbours or the world at large in the expectation that richer countries or the world as a whole would then reduce their own international damage, enabling the planet to absorb the impact of China's conduct without exceeding any threshold of injury. In terms of extortion, a polluter could threaten to increase its harm to its neighbours or the global commons unless payments were made to induce better behaviour. China could be in an excellent position to make such threats because of its size and strategic importance. As we have seen, it has demanded that developed countries make larger financial contributions and reductions in pollution in order to resolve global environmental problems, as in the control of ODS and greenhouse gas emissions. From China's perspective, however, such behaviour does not constitute free-riding but rather reflects a demand for a more equitable sharing of global resources and additional time to develop its own economy. This perspective has been reflected in international environmental agreements.[89] In other words, China generally has not denied the existence of particular environmental problems, challenged the merits of consensual solutions to such problems or denied its obligation to contribute to their resolution, but has disputed the amount and terms of those contributions. Evidence against any proclivity to

87. Framework Agreement for Environmental Protection Governing the Tumen River Economic Development Area and North-East Asia (19 December 1995); Memorandum of Understanding on Environmental Principles Governing the Tumen River Economic Development Area and North-East Asia (30 May 1995).

88. See also Oksenberg and Economy, *China Joins the World: Progress and Prospects.*

89. Article 4(2) of the Framework Convention establishes different commitments for developed country parties and other parties. See also the discussion of the equity principle in Wang Yi, *China's Position and Role in the Global Environment Challenge,* p. 9.

extortion may be found in its general tendency to become party to international agreements, the paucity of reservations in Chinese accession and ratification instruments with respect to environmental agreements, and domestic environmental statutes which contain express treaty supremacy provisions. China has in fact criticized the United States and other countries on environmental grounds for exporting harmful products to China, resulting in a tightening of controls on the import of waste products.[90]

To address this issue from another angle, China's domestic policy has, over time, attached greater importance to environmental protection. While the pace and breadth of China's policy changes are far from sufficient, they constitute substantial progress and are occurring at an earlier stage of economic development than has generally occurred in advanced industrialized countries. This is partly a matter of self-interest because China itself will almost always be the biggest and most immediate victim of its own behaviour, thereby creating a domestic constituency in favour of environmental control.[91] Part of the reason for this is the diffusion of knowledge. To the extent that environmental quality is a universal value rooted in scientific knowledge, the Chinese elite and, less directly, the population at large have become more supportive of environmental protection programmes and more accepting of some restrictions on their own behaviour. There is even some evidence that certain Chinese leaders would prefer to create a highly sanitary and environmentally clean (albeit politically controlled) society like Singapore.[92] Of course, some of China's environmental burdens will continue to increase as the population and economy expand, and new environmental concerns will emerge. Monitoring of China's compliance with international environmental agreements by Traffic and international NGOs can supply critical and even embarrassing information that can further spur compliance in a manner that neither domestic environmentalists nor the overseeing Environmental and Resources Protection Committee can accomplish at present.[93] On the whole, enhancing communication with China through both official and unofficial channels is likely to raise environmental consciousness and thereby reduce any tendency toward free-riding or extortion.

Influencing China's environmental diplomats. China's United Nations diplomacy and, by extension, its participation in international regimes has generally been characterized by a high degree of passivity or aloofness. Because of China's size, such conduct may impede the negotiation of international agreements and therefore preserve the status quo at the expense of environmental quality. Although other countries do not have direct influence over Chinese foreign policy, the technical nature of

90. "Emergency meeting lays down garbage law," *China Daily*, 30 May 1996, p. 2.
91. SEPA, State Planning Commission, UNDP and The World Bank, *China: Issues and Options in Greenhouse Gas Emissions Control* (Washington: The World Bank, 1994), Summary Report, p. 56.
92. Jasper Becker, "Journey through Jiang's utopia," *South China Morning Post International Weekly*, 3 February 1996, p. 7 (describing Zhangjiagang county).
93. Oksenberg and Economy, *China Joins the World: Progress and Prospects*.

environmental issues provides some opportunity to shape the perspective of Chinese diplomats. Specifically, some members of China's diplomatic teams involved in environmental issues are seconded from SEPA and other agencies such as the State Oceanic Administration which tend to be more favourably disposed to environmental protection than the government as a whole. For example, SEPA shared co-ordinating responsibility with the Ministry of Foreign Affairs during the Agenda 21 negotiations. SEPA also generally welcomes international attention to enhance its own influence within China's government. Senior officials of SEPA have indicated interest in training programmes in international relations to enhance their capabilities and to increase SEPA's leverage at home against rival agencies, e.g. those concerned with nuclear power. Such programmes are likely to be most effective when sponsored by multilaterals or NGOs, and if established or expanded, may indirectly influence both individual diplomats and China's positions on environmental issues and other areas with environmental components.

Foreign investment. In addition to opportunities in the environmental industry itself,[94] many transnational businesses already recognize the necessity and even the desirability of establishing and adhering to high standards of environmental compliance. Their motivation is a product of heightened environmental awareness, risk aversion, public and investor relations consciousness, increased pressure to disclose material environmental facts to the investing public, and competitive pressures. One way that transnational businesses can influence China is by insisting that their facilities in China adhere to the same high standards that they impose elsewhere. Another way may be to impose an ISO 14000 certification requirement on their suppliers, which will encourage Chinese businesses to become certified and qualified as vendors of goods and services to other companies. This is particularly important to the extent that China's present problems are due to implementation shortcomings, as opposed to statutory and regulatory deficiencies. Furthermore, as foreign investment has increased, many foreign investors themselves have become more aware of the compliance burdens issued by the current Chinese regulatory regime. For example, some American companies, particularly concerned about potential long-tail Superfund-style liability, were storing their toxic and hazardous wastes on site or disposing of them very carefully even before enactment and implementation of the Solid Waste Law. As the amount of foreign investment increases, the growing market for waste treatment and disposal services is encouraging the establishment of appropriate facilities which will be available to domestic as well as foreign-invested enterprises. To foster such private sector involvement, foreign companies should continue to share information on an informal basis and work with their Chinese counterparts to address common problems and, not incidentally, prevent Chinese companies from acquiring competitive regulatory advantages.

94. See, for example, Sun Hong, "Foreign investment sought for ecology protection," *China Daily,* 7 August 1995, p. B8.

China's Land Resources, Environment and Agricultural Production*

Robert F. Ash and Richard Louis Edmonds

Success in agriculture depends on many factors embracing the natural environment, economic and demographic policy, institutions and technology. China's agricultural resource endowment has long encouraged reliance on land-intensive methods to raise farm outputs. Indeed, the record of agricultural growth in China since 1978 is most remarkable for the overwhelming debt it owes to increases in yields per hectare.

At the same time, the intrusion of highly polluting industries into rural areas has been the source of major crop losses that have entailed significant economic costs.[1] Soil erosion, waterlogging, arid land degradation (desertification), and salinization-alkalization have reduced agricultural productivity in China. Natural disasters are also responsible for the loss or reduction of arable land every year.

While the rapid growth of chemical fertilizer use has made a notable contribution to China's agricultural growth in recent years, land, water[2] and labour remain the most fundamental inputs underlying farm production. Under the twin impact of decollectivization in the 1980s and productivity improvements associated with institutional and other economic reforms, a massive labour surplus has emerged in the countryside. By contrast, even allowing for serious under-reporting in official statistics, China's arable land base and water resources have continued to contract.[3] As industrialization and urbanization lead to further encroachment on this minimal farmland base, there is a strong economic case for arguing in favour of the formulation of policies expressly designed to increase manufactured exports in order to pay for imports of land-intensive products. Such an approach does not, however, accord with the Chinese government's perception of the situation. Rather, the government continues to reserve a fundamental economic role for agriculture and, in particular, it remains committed to a policy of grain self-sufficiency.[4]

* The authors would like to thank the following for their comments and supply of data: Claude Aubert, James Harkness, Peter Lindert, David Norse, Scott Rozelle and Vaclav Smil.

1. See for example, Richard Louis Edmonds, *Patterns of China's Lost Harmony: A Survey of the Country's Environmental Degradation and Protection* (London: Routledge, 1994), pp. 188–190.

2. Although we recognize the critical constraint imposed by water shortages in China, we have deliberately chosen not to focus on this issue, since it is examined in detail elsewhere in this volume. The most recent apocalyptic prediction for water shortages in China is that of Lester R. Brown and Brian Halweil, "China's water shortage could shake world food security," *World Watch* (1998), pp. 10–18.

3. "The role of sustainable agriculture in China: environmentally sound development," Seventh Report for the Fifth Conference of the China Council for International Co-operation on Environment and Development (CCICED) presented in Shanghai, 23–25 September 1996, p. 3 suggests that the current rate of land losses would, if continued unchecked, result in a 10% reduction in arable area by 2045.

4. In the words of a famous slogan which still enjoys wide currency in China, "agriculture is the foundation of the economy; grain is the basis of that foundation."

This paper seeks to address some of the issues relating to the availability of arable land in China. It charts changes in the supply of farmland at national and regional levels since 1978, as revealed by official statistics and recently-released revised estimates of farmland. It also analyses the sources of land loss and additions to arable land at both levels during this period. Bearing in mind that increases in multiple cropping can compensate for a shrinking land base, consideration is also given to changes in total sown area through adjustments in the multiple cropping index.

This is not, however, merely an exercise in quantitative analysis. Yields are, after all, determined by temperature, moisture, insolation, soil and seed quality, and past cropping patterns, as well as access to fertilizers and other chemical inputs. Nor should the potential impact of land degradation and natural disasters be underestimated. In short, qualitative analysis is also required. Accordingly, we seek to investigate not only the changing availability of arable land, but also the impact of various forms of environmental degradation on its quality.

Trends in Arable Area

Shrinkage of China's arable land base is not a phenomenon which has only emerged since 1978. Even allowing for easy gains associated with early rehabilitation, the expansion in cultivated area from 97.88 to 107.92 million hectares – an increase of 10 per cent – between 1949 and 1952 was a remarkable achievement.[5] To have raised cultivated acreage to what may have been a new historical peak level[6] is testimony to that achievement. Even more noteworthy is that under the subsequent First Five-Year Plan (1953–1957) a period of unprecedented rapid industrialization – the expansion of arable area continued. Between 1953 and 1957, a further 4 million hectares was added to the cultivated land base (a further rise of 3.6 per cent).[7]

As in so many respects, the Great Leap Forward was a watershed for arable land availability. During just two years (1958–1959), 7.25 million hectares were lost to farming and by 1962, China's national arable area was lower than at any time since 1950.[8] Even more significantly, 1958 marked the beginning of a secular contraction in arable land availability

5. Ministry of Agriculture (Planning Department), *Nongye jingji ziliao, 1949–83 (Materials on the Agricultural Economy, 1949–83)* (no publisher: internal document), p. 120.

6. Problems of statistical analysis and interpretation make it difficult to set this figure in its historical context. One perspective is provided by an authoritative estimate, indicating a total "mainland" arable area of 102.25 million hectares in 1933. (Ta-Chung Liu and Kung-Chia Yeh, *The Economy of the Chinese Mainland: National Income and Economic Development, 1933–1959* (Princeton, NJ: Princeton University Press, 1965), p. 129). For other estimates of arable area in the late 19th and early 20th centuries, see Xu Daofu (ed.), *Zhongguo jindai nongye shengchan ji maoyi tongji ziliao (Statistical Materials on Agricultural Production and Trade in Modern China)* (Shanghai: Renmin chubanshe, 1983), especially ch. 1.

7. Ministry of Agriculture (Planning Department), *Materials on the Agricultural Economy, 1949–83*, p. 120. Note that increases in areas under paddy and dry crops shared in the arable land expansion between 1949 and 1957 (*ibid*).

8. *Ibid.*

that has continued to the present day.[9] The average rate of contraction between 1957 and 1978 was 0.5 per cent per annum, implying an annual loss of 540,000 hectares. Such calculations are, however, misleading and underestimate the impact of the Great Leap Forward. During 1958–1963 alone, the arable area fell by more than 9 million hectares (an average annual loss of 1.8 million hectares).

Ignoring the special circumstances of the Great Leap Forward, even against the background of arable land contraction that had occurred consistently since 1958, the acceleration of land loss after 1978 remains a notable feature of China's agricultural development in the last two decades.[10] Table 1, based on official statistics, indicates that between 1978 and 1996 the total arable area fell by almost 4 per cent (from 99.39 to 95.47 million hectares) – an annual loss of 218,000 hectares.

The years from 1979 to 1985 constitute a period of rapid deterioration in terms of accelerating arable land shrinkage. In three of these years – 1981, 1984 and 1985 – China suffered a gross annual loss of more than a million hectares. Although a further million hectares (gross) were lost in 1986,[11] the period of the Seventh Five-Year Plan (1986–1990) saw this accelerating trend reversed and in 1990, for the first time since the beginning of economic reforms, more new land was brought into cultivation than was lost. Thereafter, however, conditions once more began to deteriorate – a situation that has only been halted since 1994–1995. It is tempting to ascribe the recent reversal to the impact of the "grain bag" policy and associated efforts to halt serious land loss associated with rapid industrialization and urbanization in southern and eastern coastal provinces. But even allowing for significant improvements in conserving land by some of these provinces in 1995 and 1996,[12] the reality is that the burden of recovery was carried by the northern half of the country (above all, by land reclamation activities in Heilongjiang, Inner Mongolia and Xinjiang).

Table 2 provides estimates of cumulative gross reductions in (additions

9. Official Chinese statistics suggest that increases in arable area have been recorded in eight out of 39 years (1958–1996):1960, 1964–1965, 1978–1979, 1990 and 1995–1996 (ibid. and Ministry of Agriculture, Zhongguo nongye fazhan baogao (China Agricultural Development Report) (Beijing: Nongye chubanshe), 1995, p. 179; 1996, p. 179; 1997, p. 111.

10. The institutional framework within which land is used has also changed dramatically since 1978. At the end of the Mao period (1976), 5% of the total arable area was stated-owned, 6% was absorbed by peasants' private plots (ziliudi) and 89% was collectively-owned and collectively-worked (Ministry of Agriculture (Planning Department), Materials on the Agricultural Economy, 1949–83, p. 122). By the mid-1980s, the disbanding of the collective sector and its replacement by household-based farming via production responsibility systems had laid the foundation for a much greater degree of autonomous farm decision-making (including land use), albeit practised in the context of predominantly collective land ownership.

11. In net terms, the level of arable land loss in 1986 remains worse than in any other year, except 1985, since 1978. Indeed, the extent of such losses in 1985 and 1986 combined was almost as great as during the previous five years.

12. Most notably, in the south-east (Fujian, Guangdong, Guangxi and Hainan), where in contrast to the loss of over 200,00 hectares in the previous four years, 1995–1996 saw the disappearance of a mere 3,270 hectares (data from Ministry of Agriculture, Zhongguo nongye nianjian (Chinese Agricultural Yearbook) (Beijing: Nongye chubanshe), various issues).

Table 1: **Trends in Arable Area, 1978–1996**

Year	Total arable	Loss of arable land	Addition to arable area	Net change in total arable area
		(All figures in 1,000 hectares)		
1978	99,389.5	800.9	1,042.5	+ 108.5
1979	99,498.0	934.0	748.0	-192.8
1980	99,305.2	940.8	754.8	-268.2
1981	99,037.0	1,023.0	432.0	-431.0
1982	98,606.0	863.0	521.6	-246.4
1983	98,359.6	768.0	1,077.0	-505.9
1984	97,853.7	1,582.9	590.5	-1,007.4
1985	96,846.3	1,597.9	491.9	-616.4
1986	96,229.9	1,108.3	476.3	-341.2
1987	95,888.7	817.5	477.8	-166.9
1988	95,721.8	644.7	451.7	-65.8
1989	95,656.0	517.5	484.3	+ 16.9
1990	95,672.9	467.4	468.7	-19.3
1991	95,653.6	488.0	510.9	-227.8
1992	95,425.8	738.7	408.0	-324.4
1993	95,101.4	732.4	513.9	-194.7
1994	94,906.7	708.6	686.7	+ 67.2
1995	94,973.9	621.0	1,116.8	+ 492.6
1996	95,466.5	625.5		

Sources:
Ministry of Agriculture, *Zhongguo nongye fazhan baoguo* (*China Agricultural Development Report*) (Beijing: Nongye chubanshe, various years): 1995, p. 179; 1996, p. 179; 1997, p. 110.

to) China's arable area during selected periods since 1978. The estimates underline the serious impact, in terms of arable land loss, of the early post-1978 reforms. In the first half of the 1980s, an average of almost 1.2 million hectares was being lost each year. In its own terms, this was serious enough. In reality, the situation was even worse, for the underlying accelerated *gross* decline in cultivated acreage occurred at a time when the rate of new additions to arable land was itself declining – a trend which was to continue until the 1990s. As a result, the 1980s saw a cumulative net loss of some 3.6 million hectares of farmland – more than the entire arable area (1990) of Hubei or Liaoning province.[13] For the entire period (1979–1996), the cumulative net loss was 3.9 million hectares – comparable with the total arable area of Jilin province.

Such is the determining influence of the sheer size of China that the significance of these developments cannot properly be understood without reference to regional breakdowns. Accordingly, Table 3 contains a summary of cumulative net changes in the arable area in six regions of the country.[14]

What emerges from these data is that were it not for net additions to arable land in the north-east and north-west – in the latter case, a reflection of large-scale reclamation activities – in the 1990s, the decline in national cultivated acreage would have been a good deal worse. It is also clear that together the north and centre-east accounted for the largest share (about two-thirds) of the cumulative national decline in the entire period. These two regions indeed are unique in having experienced a net arable area contraction in every year since 1979.[15] The seriousness of land losses in centre-eastern provinces is highlighted by the fact that this region – traditionally, a major source of surplus grain[16]– enjoyed levels of agricultural productivity well in excess of the national average.[17]

Considered in terms of the relative importance of each region as shown by its share of national cultivated acreage, the estimates in Table 3 are revealing. Data up to 1995 would highlight the disproportionately small

13. Some 2.5 million hectares of arable land disappeared during 1981–1985; a further 1.2 during the second half of the decade

14. The regional breakdown used in this paper is as follows: north-east [NE]: Liaoning, Jilin, Heilongjiang; north [N]: Hebei, Henan, Shandong, Shanxi, Beijing, Tianjin; centre-east [CE]: Hunan, Hubei Jiangxi, Jiangsu, Anhui, Zhejiang, Shanghai; south-east [SE]: Fujian, Guangdong, Guangxi, Hainan; south-west [SW]: Sichuan, Guizhou, Yunnan, Tibet; and north-west [NW]: Inner Mongolia, Shaanxi, Ningxia, Gansu, Qinghai, Xinjiang.

15. In 1995–1996, the north and centre-east accounted for 86% of the gross decline in national arable area.

16. Until 1984, centre-eastern provinces contributed the biggest share of incremental grain production throughout China. See Robert F. Ash, "Grain self-sufficiency in mainland China: a continuing imperative," in Robert F. Ash, Richard Louis Edmonds and Yu-ming Shaw (eds.), *Perspectives on Contemporary China in Transition* (Taipei: National Chengchi University, Institute of International Relations, 1997), p. 62.

17. In terms of crop value-output per hectare of arable land in 1996, centre-east China (20,796 *yuan*) was second only to the south-east (26,844 *yuan*). The national figure was 14,340 *yuan*, while that for north China was 13,875 *yuan* (estimates derived from Guojia tongjiju (State Statistical Bureau), *Zhongguo tongji nianjian* (*Chinese Statistical Yearbook*) (Beijing: Tongji chubanshe, 1997), p. 369; and Ministry of Agriculture, *Chinese Agricultural Yearbook 1997*, p. 287.).

Table 2: **Cumulative Changes in China's Arable Area: Selected Periods, 1979–1996**

Period	Cumulative decline in arable area	Cumulative addition to arable area	Cumulative net change in arable area
		(All figures in 1,000 hectares)	
1979–1980	1,874.8	1,790.5	-84.3
1981–1985	5,834.8	3,375.9	-2,458.9
1986–1990	3,555.4	2,382.0	-1,173.4
1991–1995	3,288.8	2,589.8	-699.0
1979–1995	14,553.8	10,138.2	-4,415.6
[1979–1996]	[15,179.3]	[11,255.0]	[-3,923.0]

Source:
Table 1.

Table 3: Cumulative Changes in Arable Area: A Regional Perspective

| Period | North-east | North | Cumulative net change in arable area (+/-) in each of the following regions (in 1,000 hectares) | | | |
			North-west	Centre-east	South-east	South-west
1981–1985	-15	-525	-796	-522	-266	-334
1986–1990	-142	-424	-56	-321	-67	-19
1991–1995	+101	-389	+457	-545	-227	-97
1996	+179	-81	+455	-56	-2	-3
1981–1996	+123	-1419	+455	-1444	-562	-453

Note:
Inconsistencies between the estimates in Table 3 and those shown in Tables 1 and 2 are attributable to the use of different Chinese sources.
Source:
Appendix Table A.

share of land losses (1.3 and 9.4 per cent respectively) suffered by the north-east and north-west, each of which accounted for 17 per cent of the national farmland area. But such was the pace of land recovery and new reclamation in 1996 that the inclusion of such figures shows that the cumulative impact of the two regions was in fact to offset arable area declines taking place elsewhere in China. In other words, thanks to massive land reclamation in Inner Mongolia and Heilongjiang (and to a lesser extent, in Xinjiang) during 1996, the overall contribution of the north-east and north-west to the net incremental change in China's arable area during the entire period 1981–1996 is positive. Given its designated role as a major source of current and future grain surpluses, the performance of the north-east in this regard is especially noteworthy.

By contrast, however, the record of centre-eastern, northern and south-eastern provinces has been more disappointing. With 21 per cent, 26 per cent and 7 per cent of China's arable area, the centre-east, north and south-east were each responsible for disproportionately large shares (44 per cent, 43 per cent and 17 per cent) of national cumulative net losses.[18] From one perspective, such findings are no surprise, for these are precisely the regions where the most rapid industrialization, urbanization and structural change have taken place in the 1980s and 1990s.

Analysis of the land issue in China reveals that the changes in arable area shown in Table 1 are the net result of two processes. One reflects the absolute loss of land; the other, new additions to the existing land stock. In evaluating the relative importance of these forces, it must be remembered that offsetting quantitative changes between them do not necessarily reflect equivalent qualitative adjustments. Most cultivated land that has disappeared as a result of industrial, urban and infrastructure development is likely, by definition, to have been fertile land on the periphery of major cities and towns.[19] By contrast, a high proportion of reclaimed land probably constitutes relatively inferior land, whose productivity is for the time being inferior to much of what has been lost. It would be misleading to assume that a hectare of newly-added land in north-west China, where most new reclamation has taken place but where irrigation facilities are notably deficient, is an adequate replacement for a hectare of arable land lost to a province in northern, central or south-eastern China.[20] Urbanization and population increase do, however, increase the total supply of potential soil nutrients and may thereby help to offset the loss of fertile farmland by improving the supply of nutrients to land which remains in agricultural use.

18. With 12% of China's arable area, the south-west was responsible for 14% of those losses.

19. We also are aware that some abandoned cultivated land was marginal agricultural land.

20. In a personal communication, James Harkness rightly warns against merely assuming that new additions to farmland in recent years have been uniformly low-quality. Even in the north-west, government and multilateral donor investment in major projects has facilitated the reclamation of high-quality irrigated land. For a discussion of contradictions in irrigated land statistics see James E. Nickum, *Dam Lies and Other Statistics: Taking Measure of Irrigation in China 1931–91* (Honolulu: East-West Center Occasional Paper, 1995).

Official and Revised Estimates of China's Arable Area: A Brief Note

It has long been known that official estimates of China's arable area and pollution levels contain a significant downward bias. In an obvious sense, acknowledging this constitutes a major qualification to the analysis above. At the same time, assuming that the degree of bias is unlikely to have changed significantly during the last 20 years, the trends and relationships with which we are mainly concerned in this paper are also unlikely to have been much affected by the problem.

Nevertheless, the issue of statistical veracity clearly needs to be addressed.[21] It deserves to be said that environmental statistics for rural pollution are no more than "guesstimates" and are usually ignored in official statistics which are concerned with state-owned and urban industry. Quantitative indicators of land degradation statistics often only reflect rural conditions and are based on rural scientific surveys and areal photographs. As such, information on rural land degradation is more reliable than that addressing rural pollution.[22] Here, however, we are concerned with arable areas statistics which are officially recognized by the Chinese government to be underestimates.

Table 4 presents official estimates of national and provincial arable areas in 1985, as used in the previous section, together with revised figures based on a land census undertaken in the mid-1980s. The variation in the degree of understatement of arable area contained in official statistics is clearly enormous. At the extremes – and ignoring Beijing and Shanghai, whose contributions to national arable area are insignificant – the figures in Table 4 range from under-reporting by 19 per cent for Jiangsu to 163 per cent for Guizhou.

The estimates are, however, more usefully considered from a broader regional perspective. Thus, Table 5 summarizes the data contained in Table 4 in terms of regional groupings used earlier in this paper.

The principal finding to emerge from Tables 4 and 5 is that the degree of under-reporting has tended to be greater in hilly and mountainous regions of China than in lowland areas. This is of course an important finding, suggesting that official estimates of arable area may approximate to reality more closely in richer, more productive regions. There is a strong supposition that much unrecorded land may be quite marginal in nature, whether because of its physical disposition (for example, as remote hillside supporting minor, supplementary crops) or because it constitutes land that has been only partially recovered for crop use. Consideration should also be given to the extent to which various sources use a consistent definition

21. On this question, see also Hou Jiandan *et al.* (eds.), *Zhongguo gengdi dijian wenti de shuliang jingji fenxi (An Economic Analysis of the Progressive Decline in the Amount of China's Arable Land)* (Beijing: Jingji kexue chubanshe, 1992), especially ch. 2; Ziping Wu and Alan W. Kirke, *Farmland in China: Quantity, Quality and Potential* (mimeo); Frederick W. Crook, "Underreporting of China's cultivated land area: implications for world agricultural trade," in United States Department of Agriculture (USDA), *International Agriculture and Trade Reports: China* (Washington, DC: USDA, Economic Research Service, July 1993), pp. 33–39; Edmonds, *Patterns of China's Lost Harmony*, p. 42 *et passim*.

22. The first survey of rural industrial pollution was undertaken in Shandong in 1989.

Table 4: **Revised Estimates of Provincial Arable Areas (in 1,000,000 hectares, 1985)**

	Official (1)	Census (2)	Ratio ((2)/(1) × 100)
Heilongjiang	8.93	11.36	127.2
Jilin	4.00	5.36	134.0
Liaoning	3.59	4.51	125.6
Beijing	0.42	0.53	126.2
Tianjin	0.45	0.62	137.8
Shanxi	3.76	6.14	163.3
Hebei	6.60	7.51	113.8
Henan	7.03	8.96	127.5
Shandong	7.04	9.14	129.8
Shaanxi	3.63	5.59	154.0
Inner Mongolia	4.93	6.83	138.5
Gansu	3.49	5.88	168.5
Ningxia	0.80	1.84	230.0
Qinghai	0.57	0.88	154.4
Xinjiang	3.08	4.06	131.8
Shanghai	0.34	0.39	114.7
Jiangsu	4.60	5.48	119.1
Anhui	4.42	6.11	138.2
Zhejiang	1.78	2.62	147.2
Hubei	3.59	4.44	123.7
Hunan	3.34	4.99	149.4
Jiangxi	2.37	2.76	116.1
Fujian	1.26	1.65	131.0
Guangdong	3.04	5.49	180.6
Guangxi	2.56	4.34	169.5
Sichuan	6.37	11.14	174.9
Guizhou	1.87	4.91	262.6
Yunnan	2.78	5.79	208.3
Tibet	0.22	0.38	172.7
China	**96.86**	**139.70**	**144.2**

Sources:
Official 1985 figures taken from Kenneth R. Walker, "Trends in crop production," in Y. Y. Kueh and Robert F. Ash (ed.), *Trends in Chinese Agriculture: The Impact of Post-Mao Reforms* (Oxford: Clarendon Press, 1993), pp. 189–190. Census data reproduced from Frederick W. Crook, "Underreporting of China's cultivated land area: implications for world agricultural trade," in United States Department of Agriculture (USDA), *International Agriculture and Trade Reports: China* (Washington, DC: USDA, Economic Research Service, July 1993), p. 34.

of arable land.[23] In short, it is possible that the economic implications of statistical deficiencies associated with official land statistics may be less serious than they would superficially appear to be.

23. For example, Wu and Kirke note that the area of ridges and roads accounted for 11.7% of the national cultivated area, as measured by the National General Land Census (1985).

Table 5: **Official and Revised Estimates of China's Arable Area by Region (in 1,000,000 hectares 1985)**

	Official (1)	Census (2)	Ratio ((2)/(1) x 100)
CHINA	**96.86**	**139.70**	**144.2**
North-east	16.52	21.23	128.5
North	25.30	32.90	130.0
North-west	16.50	25.08	152.0
Centre-east	20.44	26.79	131.1
South-east	6.86	11.48	167.3
South-west	11.24	21.22	197.7

Source:
    Table 4.

The preceding discussion is a necessary preliminary to consideration of the main sources of reductions in (additions to) land that have taken place in China in recent years. Relevant data are far from complete, nor are they always consistent. Nevertheless, even if a comprehensive picture cannot be given, the trends seem clear enough.

The Loss of Arable Land

Table 6 examines the contribution of domestic and industrial construction activities to the gross reduction in national cultivated acreage in China.[24]

The estimates indicate that encroachment on cultivated land by both state and collective sectors has been steadily rising in recent years. Since 1985, construction activities carried out under state auspices have resulted

Table 6: **Sources of Arable Land Loss in China, 1985–1996**

Period	Gross arable land decline	of which: State capital construction	Collective construction	Peasant housing
		(Figures in 1,000 hectares)		
1985	1,597.9	134.3	92.3	97.0
1986–1990	3,555.4	438.4	212.8	243.7
1991–1995	3,288.8	609.5	348.4	133.1
1996	625.5	105.3	55.7	30.4

Sources:
    Ministry of Agriculture, *Zhongguo nongye fazhan baogao* (*China Agricultural Development Report* (Beijing: Nongye chubanshe, various years): 1995, p. 179; 1996, p. 179; 1997, p. 110.

24. Lack of data makes it impossible to include detailed information for years before 1985 and explains the periodization used in the table.

in the loss of almost 1.3 million hectares.[25] The same basic trend was in evidence at town and township levels, where collective construction removed over 700,000 hectares from the arable area. Taken together, the share of total land loss accounted for by state and collective activities rose from 18 per cent (1986–1990 cumulative) to 29 per cent (1991–1996). Meanwhile, however, the impact of peasant house-building appears to have been in decline, its share of national land losses falling from six to 4 per cent during the same period.

The point has already been made that land encroachment resulting from capital construction activities and from peasant house-building has often resulted in the loss of farmland of above-average productivity. It must also be emphasized that such losses are irrevocable in the sense that land that is built over is difficult to return to agriculture. Paradoxically, however, there still exists a considerable amount of waste land, especially in the south-eastern and centre-eastern regions, which has been abandoned or is unused as a result of damage from mining or industrial activities. If appropriate funding could be made available, much of this could be restored to agricultural use.

But even allowing for the increasing impact of state and collective construction activities, the most striking finding to emerge from Table 6 is surely that other factors have continued to contribute far more to land loss in China during recent years.[26] The two most important sources of this residual are likely to have been structural change within agriculture – for example, transfers of land out of cropping and into animal husbandry, aquaculture or forestry – and environmental change – such as the destruction of soil quality, possibly following flooding or soil erosion. The rapid development of township and village enterprises (xiangzhen qiye) may also have been responsible for the abandonment of arable land, as farmers have moved from crop cultivation to employment in factories. Where pollution from these factories has damaged land and crops, the same source may have had a further negative effect on farming.

Fragmentary information relating to the impact of structural change within the farm sector, as well as that of natural disasters, is available for 1987–1991. This is reproduced in Table 7 and confirms the growing importance of state construction and collective activities – especially those associated with the development of township and village enterprises – as sources of arable land loss. Much more striking, however, is the indication that structural change within the agricultural sector itself has made by far the most significant contribution to such losses, accounting typically for well over half of the shrinkage of China's cultivated acreage between 1987 and 1991. More detailed analysis of this important finding is provided below.

25. A further 300,000 hectares were lost to the same source during 1980–1984 (Ministry of Agriculture, *China Agricultural Development Report 1997*, p. 100).

26. By way of comparison, during 1972–1974 (the only years for which we have found such data) basic capital construction by the state and by commune and brigade authorities accounted for about 35% of arable land loss. See Ministry of Agriculture (Planning Department), *Materials on the Agricultural Economy, 1949–83*, p. 121.

Table 7: **The Impact of State and Collective Construction, Peasant House-building, Structural Adjustment in Agriculture, and Natural Disasters on Arable Land Availability: China, 1987–1991**

| Year | *Proportion of arable land loss resulting from:* | | | | |
	State construction	*Collective construction*	*House building*	*Structural adjustment*	*Natural disasters*
1987	11.2	5.8	5.1	63.5	14.4
1988	11.4	4.5	3.4	57.1	23.6
1989	2.3	5.4	3.7	55.4	23.2
1990	13.1	7.2	3.5	60.0	16.3
1991	13.0	7.5	2.3	52.4	24.9

Source:
    China's Agriculture in 1996 (Japan-China Economic Association, 1997), p. 154, citing *Ziran ziyuan* (*Natural Resources*) No. 5 (1994), p. 2.

It is interesting too that natural disasters have become an increasingly important source of arable land loss. Indeed, if the figures in Table 7 are to be believed, natural disasters may still be the second most important single cause of land loss after structural adjustments in agriculture.

That natural disasters reduce agricultural productivity is obvious, but the extent to which such disasters have removed cultivated land from use for more than one season is much less clear. Nor is it apparent whether the estimates shown in Table 7 include the impact of long-term environmental degradation resulting from factors such as erosion and salinization-alkalization.[27] While drought, hail, pests and frost can reduce yields, they are unlikely to permanently remove agricultural land from cultivation. By contrast, longer-term or even permanent loss of cultivated land may result from flooding, earthquakes, mud flows and – in coastal areas – subsidence and coastal erosion.

Table 8 indicates that in many Chinese river systems, both the incidence and intensity of floods appear to have been increasing, especially in central and southern parts of the country. At the same time, the area covered by flood prevention measures increased by 8 per cent between 1985 and 1995. Table 9 suggests that notwithstanding major flood control efforts in western China since 1985, the populous and flood-susceptible regions of northern and central-eastern China have remained the most effectively protected regions. The most impressive progress was made in the north-east (especially in sparsely-populated Heilongjiang province) where the protected ratio of the flood-prone area has risen from less than

27. On the basis of production growth estimates for 1984–1995, a recent report by the World Bank (*At China's Table: Food Security Options* (Washington: World Bank, 1997), p. 14), takes the view that the effect of natural disasters on rice production in southern China and corn production in the north has been less serious than that of changes in input-output prices and labour prices. The dynamic multi-sector output response model employed by the World Bank suggested that for corn production in north China, erosion-salinization was a more significant negative factor influencing growth than natural disasters, whereas the reverse was true for rice production in southern China. It is a pity that the World Bank report provides no details of how this model was constructed nor how these conclusions were reached.

Table 8: **Years of Extremely Severe Flooding in China by Region**

Region	Year				
North, north-east and	1553	1604	1760	1819	1991
north-west China	1569	1613		1822	1995
		1652		1848	
		1653		1864	
Centre-east China				1831	1915
				1848	1931
				1849	1954
					1981
					1983
					1991
					1995
					1996
					1998
South-east and south-west	1478	1582	1647	1713	1839	1994
China	1485					1995
						1996
						1998

Source:
    Modified and updated from Zhang Jiacheng and Lin Zhiguang, *Climate of China* (New York: Wiley, 1992), p. 291.

60 per cent to more than three-quarters.[28] Interpreting flood data, however, is bedevilled by the problem of how to assess the impact of damage and the effectiveness of prevention facilities on land of differing quality.[29] We would suggest that land in the west is likely to be of inferior quality and have inferior flood prevention measures than in the east.

    We have been unable to find comprehensive regional data on sources of land loss. Quite detailed statistics on some aspects, however, are available for years since 1988 and these are reproduced in Table 10. These estimates reveal the wide variety of conditions that lie concealed beneath the national picture. In some areas, state and collective-sponsored construction has accounted for a significant proportion of arable land loss. In particular, in the north and centre-east, such activities were responsible for 40 per cent and 46 per cent, respectively, of the contraction of

---

    28. As Table 9 shows, this impressive record owes most to improvements made in the second half of the 1980s. They no doubt contributed significantly to the role of the north-east as a major source of national incremental grain production during this period.
    29. Y. Y. Kueh, *Agricultural Instability in China, 1931–1991: Weather, Technology, and Institutions* (Oxford: Clarendon, 1995), p. 112, draws attention to the differentiation, in Chinese disaster data, between *shouzai* ("covered") and *chengzai* ("calamitously affected"). *Chengzai* refers to agricultural land which has lost 30% or more of its crop and is included within the larger *shouzai* category. Kueh weights the *chengzai* category as averaging 60% crop loss and the *shouzai* area minus the *chengzai* area category as averaging 15% crop loss. Huang Jikun and Scott Rozelle ("Environmental stress and grain yields in China," *American Journal of Agricultural Economics*, No. 77 (1995), pp. 856–57) found that there was an increase in the area classified as *yilao* ("easily flooded and drought damaged") during the late 1980s. *Yilao* means that an area cannot withstand floods or drought with a frequency of once in three years without suffering a reduction in yield.

Table 9: **Regional Distribution of Flood Prevention Measures**

Region	Percentage improved of area liable to floods (Percentage of national improved area in parentheses)					
	1985		1990	1995		
North-east	**57.3**	(22.1)	**74.6**	**76.0**	(23.7)	
North	**79.0**	(33.3)	**79.5**	**85.0**	(32.3)	
Centre-east	**85.4**	(37.2)	**85.8**	**88.0**	(36.2)	
South-east	**67.3**	(4.2)	**68.6**	**69.6**	(4.0)	
South-west (excluding Tibet)	**54.0**	(1.4)	**59.8**	**65.5**	(1.7)	
North-west (excluding Qinghai and Ningxia)	**62.4**	(1.8)	**63.0**	**68.3**	(2.1)	

Sources:
Calculated from Guojia tongjiju (State Statistical Bureau), *Zhongguo tongji nianjian* (*Chinese Statistical Yearbook*) (Beijing: Tongji chubanshe, various years), 1986, p 158; 1991, p. 334; 1996, p. 363.

Table 10: **Arable Land Loss Under the Impact of State and Village Construction and House Building, 1988–1996**

Region	Proportion of arable land loss in each of the following categories (per cent)		
	State construction	Collective construction	House building
CHINA	100.0	100.0	100.0
North-east	10.7	10.2	6.5
North	26.3	21.3	24.6
North-west	7.9	13.4	23.0
Centre-east	29.6	35.0	29.3
South-east	14.4	6.9	4.8
South-west	11.1	13.2	11.9

	Contribution to total arable land loss in each region of the following categories			
	State construction	Collective construction	House building	TOTAL
CHINA	16.9	9.2	4.6	30.7
North-east	15.1	7.7	2.5	25.3
North	27.8	12.1	7.0	47.0
North-west	4.8	4.4	3.8	13.0
Centre-east	28.2	18.0	7.5	53.7
South-east	17.8	4.6	1.6	24.0
South-west	14.8	9.6	4.3	28.7

Note:
The time period covered in this table is dictated by the availability of data.
Sources:
Appendix, Table A; Ministry of Agriculture, *Zhongguo nongye nianjian* (*Chinese Agricultural Yearbook*) (Beijing: Nongye chubanshe, various issues), 1989, pp. 238–39; 1990, pp. 243–44; 1991, pp. 275–76; 1992, pp. 268–69; 1993, pp. 235–36; 1994, p. 291; 1995, p. 309; 1996, p. 270; 1997, p. 287.

Table 11: **Sources of Arable Land Loss by Region, 1988–1992**

| Region | Proportion of arable land loss accounted for by: | | | |
	Construction (state and collective)	Afforestation	Animal husbandry	Other
CHINA	28.6	23.8	14.1	33.5
North-east	20.8	22.8	17.0	39.4
North	59.1	30.0	4.5	6.4
North-west	10.2	25.2	28.6	36.0
Centre-east	54.0	17.3	0.9	27.8
South-east	17.7	17.2	1.4	63.7
South-west	20.7	29.5	19.0	30.8

Sources:
Ministry of Agriculture, *Zhongguo nongye nianjian* (*Chinese Agricultural Yearbook*) (Beijing: Nongye chubanshe, various issues), 1989, pp. 238–39; 1990, pp. 243–44; 1991, pp. 275–76; 1992, pp. 268–69; 1993, pp. 235–36; 1994, p. 291; 1995, p. 309; 1996, p. 270; 1997, p. 287.

cultivated acreage (1988–1996). The geographical concentration of such activities is reflected in the fact that these two regions accounted for 56 per cent of national land loss deriving from state and village construction during this period.

Elsewhere in China the impact of these activities has been much less pronounced. The most extreme example comes from the north-west, where little more than 9 per cent of arable land loss was attributable to state and collective construction in the same period. In the remaining three regions, the corresponding figure was around 22–25 per cent.[30]

Examination of the impact of house-building by rural residents reveals a similar profile. In the north and centre-east, housing construction accounted for 7 per cent or more of arable land loss. Elsewhere, the figure ranged from a low of 1.6 per cent (south-east) to a high of 4.3 per cent in the south-west.

In any case, the most striking finding to emerge from Table 10 is one that underlines a point made earlier: namely, the major contribution to arable land loss of factors other than state and collective construction and house-building. The north and centre-east apart, such residual factors were typically responsible for about three-quarters of area contraction – and in one notable instance (the north-west), some 87 per cent. Indeed, the centre-east was the only region of China in which construction and housing consistently accounted for more than half of land loss.

The two main categories of residual factors are likely to be natural disasters and structural changes that have taken place within the farm sector itself. In the absence of relevant data, it is impossible to estimate the permanent loss of cultivated land resulting from climatic and other

30. The minor role played by state and (especially) village construction as a source of land loss in the south-east is at first glance surprising. Part of the explanation may lie in the activities of overseas entrepreneurs in parts of south-east China and it would be interesting to know how much farmland has disappeared in Guangdong under the impact of the cross-border re-siting of Hong Kong and Macau factories and associated developments.

forms of natural disaster.[31] Information on structural changes in farming is also far from complete, although a partial data set is available for 1998–1992 which offers interesting insights into the impact of such changes on arable area in each region of China. The relevant data are presented in Table 11. For comparative purposes, we have also included information on construction and housing during the same period.

For China as a whole, the figures suggest that 38 per cent of the land withdrawn from cultivation during 1988–1992 was transferred to forest and animal husbandry.[32] In absolute terms, such restructuring absorbed more than a million hectares of arable land. From a regional perspective, the corresponding figure was less than 20 per cent only in the centre-east and south-east. Elsewhere, it ranged from a low of 34.5 per cent (north) to a high of 53.8 per cent in the north-west. Bearing in mind that arable land transferred to fishponds and orchards is not included, we may infer that transfer of land from crop cultivation to a different agricultural use was a significant contributory factor to arable land loss throughout China – and was the single most important such factor in several regions.[33]

This finding has important policy implications. A major debate about the relative merits and weaknesses of a strategy designed to maintain grain self-sufficiency in China has occurred in recent years.[34] Future conditions will depend on many unknowns, some of which (such as global climate change) are beyond China's control. Moreover, given appropriate assumptions, almost any outcome can be forecast and predictions of the future balance between domestic demand and supply range from estimates of near self-sufficiency throughout the first quarter of the 21st century to import levels which surpass current global international flows of grain. One strand in the argument of some who predict that China will be compelled to enter international markets in order to make large-scale purchases of foreign grain is that encroachment on arable land resulting from industrialization and urbanization will have a severely negative effect on domestic grain production. The most extreme

31. By contrast, information on the immediate impact of such disasters on sown area is readily available in Ministry of Agriculture, *Chinese Agricultural Yearbook* and State Statistical Bureau, *Chinese Statistical Yearbook*. A valuable compendium is State Statistical Bureau, *Zhongguo zaixing baogao, 1949–1995* (*Report of Disasters in China, 1949–1995*) (Beijing: Zhongguo tongji chubanshe, 1995).

32. This figure is significantly smaller than what would appear to be the corresponding figure shown in Table 7. Part of the explanation may lie in different sources that have been used in order to compile the two tables. A more important factor is likely to be that the contribution of "structural adjustment," as revealed by Table 7, includes land converted to fishponds, whereas such land transfers are captured in the residual (under "other") in Table 11.

33. Vaclav Smil cites data showing that between 1987 and 1995, 59% of national arable land loss resulted from conversion to forest, pastures, orchards and ponds ("China's agricultural land," mimeo).

34. Recent studies in English include: Lester Brown, *Who will Feed China? Wake-up Call for a Small Planet* (London: Earthscan, 1994); Vaclav Smil, "Who will feed China?" *The China Quarterly*, No. 143 (1995), pp. 801–813; Pierre Crosson, "Who will feed China?" *Perspectives on the Long-Term Global Food Situation*, No. 2 (1996), pp. 1–8; Dawn Stover, "The coming food crisis," *Popular Science* (August 1996), pp. 49–54; and Fan Shenggen and Mercedita Agcaoili-Sombilla, "Why do projections on China's future food supply and demand differ?" (Washington: International Food Policy Research Institute, Environment and Production Technology Division Working Paper 22, 1997).

proponent of this view is Lester Brown who has used the analogy of major contractions in arable land in Japan, Taiwan and South Korea under the impact of modernization to argue that China is likely to lose a significant proportion of its cultivated acreage during the next two or three decades.[35]

There are clear dangers in seeking to extrapolate from the experience of small polities to that of the People's Republic of China, where there has been – and will continue to be for the foreseeable future – a strong regional dimension to the twin processes of economic development and structural change. Such dangers apart, the estimates presented in Tables 10 and 11 indicate that even allowing for the increasingly important role played by state and collective construction activities, changes taking place in the farm sector itself – above all, those associated with agricultural re-structuring – promise to make the more significant contribution to land loss.

This is an important finding, suggesting that policy-makers may enjoy greater flexibility in addressing the land issue, structural adjustments in agriculture being more susceptible to policy manipulation. By the same token, it would be easy to exaggerate the impact of land loss on food availability suggested by crude macro-estimates of arable area contraction. The disappearance of crop land via afforestation is bound to be accompanied by a reduction in crop output, although this negative effect may be offset by improvements in productivity on existing land that is better protected and irrigated as a result of tree plantings. Afforestation also promises to enhance arable land conservation by inhibiting degradation. Moreover, crop land that has been converted to fishponds, fruit orchards and animal husbandry remains an important source of energy. Indeed, in its new guise it may generate significantly more calories and protein than the grain land it has replaced.[36]

New Additions to Arable Land

Reference to Table 1 reveals how important the addition of new land has been in compensating for China's losses of arable land since 1978. It is noteworthy that only four years during this period – 1979, 1990, 1995, and 1996 – saw such additions more than offset losses, thereby generating a net expansion of the cultivated acreage. The real significance of new land extension is, however, best gauged by calculating how much greater the contraction of farmland would have been in its absence.

The estimates in Table 1 suggest that if no new land had been brought into use after 1978, China's arable area would have fallen to 84.21 million hectares by 1996 – 10 million hectares less than the official figure. Stated differently, some 15.18 million hectares of farmland was lost in gross terms after 1978 – the physical equivalent of the entire combined current arable area of Henan and Hebei. At the same time,

35. Brown, *Who will Feed China?* especially ch. 4.
36. For such reasons, Smil has argued that fishponds and orchards ought to be included as part of China's farmland total (see Smil, "China's agricultural land").

Table 12: **New Addition to Arable Land, 1988–1996 (cumulative)**

Region	Newly-added arable land 1,000 heactares (per cent)		Of which, reclaimed land 1,000 hectares (per cent)	
China	**5.199.4**	**(100.0)**	**2,367.8**	**(100.0)**
North-east	855.9	(16.5)	371.4	(15.7)
North	247.3	(4.8)	117.6	(5.0)
North-west	2.683.6	(51.6)	1,061.3	(42.9)
Centre-east	227.3	(4.4)	98.5	(4.2)
South-east	558.6	(10.7)	361.8	(15.3)
South-west	626.7	(12.1)	402.2	(17.0)

Sources:
Ministry of Agriculture, *Zhongguo nongye nianjian* (*Chinese Agricultural Yearbook*) (Beijing: Nongye chubanshe, various issues) 1989, p. 238; 1990, p. 243; 1991, p. 275; 1992, p. 268; 1993, p. 235; 1994, p. 291; 1995, p. 309; 1996, p. 279; 1997, p. 287.

more than 11 million hectares was brought into cultivation during the same period – more than the arable land base of Heilongjiang province.[37]

A comprehensive regional analysis of new additions to arable land is hindered by a lack of data. However, on the basis of information made available by the Ministry of Agriculture since 1988, the picture in Table 12 emerges, suggesting that the regional distribution of land newly brought under cultivation has not only been very unequal, but in many cases has also been disproportionate to the importance of individual regions in terms of their share of national cultivated acreage. What emerges most strikingly is that since 1987, the north-west – with a mere 17 per cent of China's arable area – has accounted for more than half of all "new" farmland.[38]

This is an important finding, for it underlines the point made earlier that losses of (additions to) arable land must be interpreted in terms of quality, as well as mere physical extent. Data would indicate that the productivity of arable land, as measured in terms of gross value-output of cropping per arable hectare, is lower in the north-west than in any other region of China.[39] Similarly, average yields of cereals have also tended to be lower in the north-west than elsewhere. In short, we may conclude that the impact on production of land newly brought under cultivation has been mitigated by its probable poor quality and/or need for extensive irrigation and other infrastructure investment – an argument that is

37. A point ignored in this paragraph concerns the quality of land lost to, and newly brought under cultivation.
38. By contrast, the north, containing a quarter of all arable land, accounted for less than 5% of newly-added land during the same period.
39. In 1995, cropping GVO per arable hectare was 7,520 *yuan* – 53% of the national level (data derived from State Statistical Bureau, *China Statistical Yearbook 1996*, p. 369; Ministry of Agriculture, *China Agricultural Development Report*, 1995, p. 1 and 1996, p. 1; and regional arable area estimates, as given in Appendix Table A).

underlined by the loss of substantial amounts of fertile land in the moister central and south-eastern coastal provinces of the country.

Indeed, except for the south-east – a rich agricultural region[40] that has also accounted for a disproportionately large share of "new" arable land (albeit to a lesser extent than in the north-west) – the figures in Table 12 point to an inverse relationship between the inherent value of cropping land in any region and the physical extent to which new land has been brought under cultivation in it.

The evidence of Table 12 also warns against equating new land extension with land reclamation. The estimates suggest that except for the south-east and south-west, where almost two-thirds of newly-cultivated land did result from reclamation, the corresponding figure elsewhere ranged from only 38 to 48 per cent.[41] Nationally, therefore, up to about half of all "new" arable land may have been returned to agricultural use rather than being opened up from "virgin" lands.

The Role of Multiple Cropping in Offsetting Arable Land Loss

A shrinking arable land base can be offset by higher multiple cropping. Between 1978 and 1990, the total sown area in China fell from 150.1 to 148.4 million hectares. Recovery took place in the early 1990s, although it was temporarily halted in 1993–1994. By 1996, however, thanks to a startling increase in a single year (by 2.5 million hectares during 1995–1996),[42] the total sown area had expanded to 152.38 million hectares – higher than in any year since 1957.[43]

From a policy perspective, the contraction of arable area, which has been such a striking characteristic of China's rural scene in recent years, has major implications for the level of multiple cropping that will be required in order to fulfil future plans.[44] The previous analysis has shown that since 1978, the pressures arising from encroachment on farmland have been more powerful than forces working in the opposite direction. A simple comparison of 1978 and 1995 reveals that during these 19 years the decline in total sown area (225,000 hectares) was more than offset by that of the arable area (4.4 million hectares). The implication is that an increase in the multiple cropping index (MCI) from 150 (1978) to 158 (1995) compensated for, but did not entirely offset, the loss of cultivated land during this period. This observation is not altered by the remarkable

40. In terms of cropping GVO per arable hectare.

41. Note too that only in the north-east and north-west did *state-sponsored* reclamation contribute more than marginally to total reclamation. Relevant data can be found in Ministry of Agriculture, *Chinese Agricultural Yearbook*, as detailed in the sources to Table 10.

42. See Ministry of Agriculture, *Chinese Agricultural Yearbook*, p. 299.

43. In 1957, the total sown area was 157.24 million hectares. Sown area time series data are available in Ministry of Agricultural (Planning Department), *Zhongguo nongcun jingji tongji daquan (1949–86)* (*A Compendium of Chinese Rural Economic Statistics, 1949–86*) (Beijing: Nongye chubanshe, 1989), p. 130.

44. The multiple cropping index is a measure of the extent to which a piece of arable land can be used in order to raise more than one crop in a year. Sown area differs from arable area by the extent to which such multiple cropping is practised.

Table 13: **Arable, Sown and Multiple Cropped Area in China and its Regions: 1979, 1985, 1990, 1995, and 1996**

				Arable area (1,000,000 hectares)			
Year	China	North-east	North	North-west	Centre-east	South-east	South-west
1979	**99.17**	16.15	25.89	17.44	21.03	7.12	11.54
1985	**96.85**	16.52	25.30	16.49	20.44	6.86	11.24
1990	**95.68**	16.24	24.88	16.44	20.11	6.79	11.22
1995	**94.97**	16.34	28.13	16.89	19.56	6.56	11.13
1996	**95.47**	16.52	24.41	17.35	19.51	6.56	11.12
				Total sown area (1,000,000 hectares)			
1979	**148.48**	16.55	36.49	17.90	43.60	14.74	19.20
1985	**134.64**	16.35	36.40	16.88	42.12	12.88	19.01
1990	**147.55**	16.22	36.74	17.61	42.66	13.56	20.76
1995	**149.85**	16.30	36.72	17.92	41.93	14.76	22.22
1996	**152.44**	16.57	37.16	18.46	42.31	15.30	22.64
				Multiple cropping index			
1979	**149.7**	100.5	140.9	102.6	207.3	207.0	166.4
1985	**148.3**	99.0	143.9	102.4	206.1	187.8	169.1
1990	**154.2**	99.9	147.7	107.1	212.1	199.7	185.0
1995	**157.8**	99.8	149.9	106.1	214.4	225.0	199.6
1996	**159.7**	100.3	152.2	106.4	216.9	233.2	203.6
				Multiple cropped area (1,000,000 hectares)			
1979	**49.31**	0.40	10.60	0.46	22.57	7.62	7.66
1985	**46.79**	− 0.17	11.10	0.39	21.68	6.02	7.77
1990	**51.87**	− 0.02	11.86	1.17	22.55	6.77	9.54
1995	**54.88**	0.04	12.23	10.3	22.37	8.20	11.09
1996	**56.97**	0.05	12.75	1.11	22.80	8.74	11.52

Notes:
All figures in million hectares, except the multiple cropping index, which is given as a percentage. The regional breakdown follows that shown in Appendix A.
Sources:
Ministry of Agriculture, *Zhongguo nongye nianjian* (*Chinese Agricultural Yearbook*) (Beijing: Nongye chubanshe, various issues) 1980, p. 100; 1986, p. 177; 1991, p. 293; 1996, p. 291; 1997, p. 299.

developments in 1996, when substantial increases in both arable and sown areas raised the multiple cropping index to 160.

The context in which such developments have unfolded is shown in Table 13.

Quite detailed analysis of changes in multiple cropping practice and of their implications for arable and sown areas in China for the early post-1978 period is already available elsewhere.[45] Suffice to say that the

45. See Kenneth R. Walker, "Trends in crop production" in Y. Y. Kueh and Robert F. Ash (eds.), *Trends in Chinese Agriculture: The Impact of Post-Mao Reforms* (Oxford: Clarendon, 1993).

estimates shown in Table 13 indicate that until the mid-1980s, the effects of a contracting arable area were exacerbated by a similar decline in total sown area.[46] Thereafter, however, a consistent rise in multiple cropping throughout the country played a major role in mitigating the impact of the continuing decline in arable area (see Table 14).

The background to these estimates is that in the early post-1978 years, the decline in arable area was unrelieved by any offsetting increase in the multiple cropping index, resulting in a parallel contraction in China's total sown area.[47] By contrast, the figures in Table 14 highlight the much more positive role played by extended multiple cropping in subsequent years. They suggest that since the mid-1980s, the decline in arable area has been tempered by a significant increase in the multiple cropping index. Between 1985 and 1996, the national index rose by more than 11 points while the multiple cropped area expanded by over 10 million hectares.

In the second half of the 1980s, this trend was common to all regions in China in varying degrees. In the 1990s, the provinces of south-west and, more surprisingly, south-east China have contributed disproportionately to the continued national expansion of the multiple cropped area. In the south-east, between 1985 and 1996, the multiple cropping index increased by a remarkable 45 points to reach 233 per cent, although part of the increase reflected recovery from a substantial decline in multiple cropping which had occurred in the region during the first half of the 1980s. From this perspective, an even more remarkable achievement was that of south-west China, where a consistent expansion of the multiple cropped area raised the multiple cropping index from 166 (1980) to 204 per cent (1996). Whether such increases in multiple cropping reflect the operation of economic forces or are more a response to the dictates of policy – not least, those associated with the "grain bag" strategy and institution of a provincial "governor responsibility system" – is a subject that deserves further consideration.[48] It is also noteworthy that the expansion of the multiple cropped area has been accomplished by a substantial increase in the use of chemical fertilizers and pesticides, as well as by a much more modest expansion of irrigated area.[49]

An interesting question is to what extent the multiple cropping index can be further increased, subject to economic (cost) constraints. Evidence

---

footnote continued

esp. pp. 162–67; and R. F. Ash, "Agricultural reform since 1978," in R. F. Ash and Y. Y. Kueh, *The Chinese Economy Under Deng Xiaoping* (Oxford: Clarendon, 1996), pp. 77–82.

46. In the first half of the 1980s, only the north and south-west experienced increases in the multiple cropping index.

47. The single, marginal exception to this trend was the north-east. Consideration of the regional dimension of changes during the early post-1978 years is provided by Ash (see "Agricultural reform since 1978," p. 78).

48. It has been argued that in the early 1980s, higher costs associated with high multiple cropping indices had an adverse effect on farm incomes and incentives – such factors encouraging a reduction in the multiple cropped area (see Ash, *ibid.*).

49. Chemical fertilizer use has more than quadrupled since 1978, whereas irrigated area has expanded by 7.8%.

Table 14: **Changes in Arable, Sown and Multiple Cropped Area: 1985–1990, 1990–1995, and 1990–1996**

	China	North-east	North	North-west	Centre-east	South-east	South-west
				Change during 1985–1990			
AA	**-1.17**	-0.28	-0.42	-0.05	-0.33	-0.07	-0.02
TSA	**3.91**	-0.13	0.34	0.73	0.54	0.68	1.75
MCA	**5.08**	0.15	0.76	0.78	0.87	0.75	1.77
				Change during 1990–1995			
AA	**-0.71**	0.10	-0.39	0.45	-0.55	-0.23	-0.09
TSA	**2.30**	0.08	-0.02	0.31	-0.73	1.00	1.46
MCA	**3.09**	0.06	0.37	-0.14	-0.18	1.43	1.55
				Change during 1990–1996			
AA	**0.50**	0.18	-0.08	0.46	-0.05	0.00	-0.01
TSA	**2.59**	0.27	0.44	0.54	0.38	0.54	0.42
MCA	**2.09**	0.01	0.52	0.08	0.43	0.54	0.43

Note:
All figures in million hectares. AA stands for arable area, TSA for total sown area, and MCA for multiple cropped area.
Source:
Table 13.

for 1996 suggests that the national index (159.7 per cent) is already higher than what in the mid-1980s was considered to be a notional optimum level.[50] With the index already at record levels in many southern provinces, where natural conditions favour multiple cropping, it is difficult to believe that the recent upward trend will be easily sustained. There is perhaps scope for further increases in parts of the centre-east and north, although it is noticeable that recent years have seen a slowing in the rate of expansion of the multiple cropped area in these regions. This may, in part, reflect severe water shortages in many areas of north China and along the east coast – factors which are likely to constrain future efforts to raise the multiple cropping index here. By contrast, dam construction is likely to have eased water constraints in the south-west where the index has risen by 18 points in the 1990s (exceeding 200 for the first time in 1996).

If the secular trend of a declining arable area is maintained and if further rises in the multiple cropping index are difficult to achieve, it is possible that the total sown area will once more start to contract. Even in such a worst-case scenario, policy-makers will retain a degree of flexibility to the extent that they can control the use to which available land is put. Consideration of this aspect is beyond the confines of this discussion. It can, however, be observed that since 1978, significant structural change has already taken place within the cropping sector itself. Food grains now account for a significantly smaller share of the total sown area (74 per cent in 1996, compared with 80 per cent in 1980). The share of cotton has meanwhile fluctuated within less than a single percentage point, while the shares of other major economic crops – oil-bearing crops, sugar, tobacco, vegetables, tea and fruit – have all risen substantially.[51] Against the background of rising per capita incomes, such structural adjustments could have been expected and are likely to continue. If necessary, however, adjustments of the cropping pattern in a different direction could yet be susceptible to policy decisions.

The Inter-relationship Between the Environment and Agricultural Productivity

Environmental degradation, like arable land contraction, is not a phenomenon peculiar to the period since 1978. Worsening resource degradation and pollution characterized the Mao period, although inaccessibility and/or lack of detailed data on rural degradation has made it

50. In the mid-1980s, a multiple cropping index of 156% to 158% was considered optimal. In their projections for the 1990s, studies carried out under the auspices of the Chinese Academy of Agricultural Sciences anticipated the re-establishment of a MCI at the 1977 level of 155: see "Woguo liangshi he jingji zuowu de fazhan" ("A study of the development of food grains and economic crops in China"), in Chinese Academy of Agricultural Sciences, Research Group for the Development of Food Grains and Economic Crops, *Zhongguo nongcun fazhan zhanlüe wenti* (*Strategic Issues Relating to China's Rural Development*) (Beijing: Nongye kexue chubanshe, 1985), p. 395.

51. Relevant data can be found in State Statistical Bureau, *Chinese Statistical Yearbook 1997*, pp. 380–82.

Table 15: **Major Causes of Arable Land Degradation in China, 1996**

Category	(1,000,000 hectares) Area	Per cent
Erosion	40	48.1
Arid land degradation (desertification)	15	18.0
Salinization-alkalization and water-logging	>6	7.3
Pollution	10	12.0
Total	**83.2**	**100.0**

Source:
"The role of sustainable agriculture in China: environmentally sound development," seventh report for the fifth conference of the China Council for International Co-operation on Environment and Development, presented in Shanghai, 23–25 September 1996, pp. 9–10.

difficult to move beyond generalizations. Huang and Rozelle's quantitative study, largely based on official statistics, concluded that the positive impact of productive inputs on yields during the second half of the 1970s and throughout the 1980s was offset by the effects of soil erosion on irrigation, increases in soil salinity and worsening damage to land caused by flood and drought.[52] Today, although expert estimates vary greatly, environmental degradation is thought to be affecting around 83.2 million hectares or 60 per cent of China's revised total arable area.[53] Table 15 shows the estimated areal amounts for various types of land degradation throughout China.[54]

Much of the damage shown in Table 15 has resulted from farming on marginal land in water-deficient areas where soil conservation measures have not been properly implemented. In general, the impact of environ-

52. Huang and Rozelle, "Environmental stress and grain yields," pp. 860–61. They suggest that "[e]nvironmental degradation may have cost China as much as six million metric tons per year during the late 1980s." Remedial measures proposed by Huang and Rozelle include continued research into new techniques and the possibility of new labour mobilization schemes. The latter suggestion seems to be echoed in the massive afforestation projects of the 1990s. A literature is also emerging which suggests that the reforms of the 1980s have sped up environmental degradation of agricultural land. For example, see Joshua S. S. Muldavin, "The political ecology of agrarian reform in China: the case of Heilongjiang province," in Richard Peet and Michael J. Watts (eds.), *Liberation Ecologies* (London: Routledge, 1996), pp. 227–259; Joshua S. S. Muldavin, "Impact of reform of environmental sustainability in rural China," *Journal of Contemporary Asia*, Vol. 6, No. 3 (1996), pp. 289–321; and Richard Smith, "Creative destruction: capitalist development and China's environment," *New Left Review*, No. 222 (1997), pp. 3–39.
53. The figure is taken from "The role of sustainable agriculture in China," p. 10. See Table 20 for revised arable area. The "Strategy and Action Project for Chinese and Global Food Security: Final Report of the February 18–19, 1998 Working Meeting" (Washington, DC: unpublished draft report of 21 April 1998, p. 14), points to a much worse situation in its suggestion that 163 million hectares are affected by water erosion (especially in eastern China and in Sichuan) and 122 million hectares affected by wind erosion We share the cautionary note struck in the draft report – notably so in the case of wind erosion – to distinguish between human-induced and "natural" erosion.
54. Note, however, that the estimates provide no measure of the extent to which each factor reduces agricultural productivity. It would, for example, be wrong to assume that erosion has caused more yield reduction than pollution.

mental degradation has been most severe in terms of yield reductions rather than permanent loss of arable land.

Soil erosion in China often results from deforestation, cultivation on slopes,[55] overgrazing and poor management of industrial land use. National-level statistics suggest that erosion has become more serious since the mid-1980s. Despite intensified soil conservation efforts, the problem is likely to deteriorate before it improves.[56] Over three-fifths of China's soil loss through erosion has resulted from arable topsoil loss[57] totalling 3,300 million tonnes annually.[58]

The impact of erosion on yields depends on the initial soil fertility and structure, as well as the amount of topsoil removed. In general, however, finer, nutrient-rich soil particles are the first to be washed or blown away by erosion, which hardly ever benefits cultivated land.[59] Recently, Lindert, Lu and Wu, as well as van Lynden have cast doubt on the role of erosion as the major cause of fertility loss on China's cultivated land.[60] Huang and Rozelle point out, however, that erosion has a considerable indirect impact on Chinese agriculture through damage to irrigation

55. In a survey of the 287 counties and municipalities conducted in 1985, Huang Zhanbin and Zhang Ximei found that average grain yields on the Loess Plateau were 4,470 kg per hectare (298 kg per *mu*) compared with a national average of 5,460 kg per hectare (364 kg per *mu*). Counties on the Plateau with low yields (below 3,000 kg per hectare or 200 kg per *mu*) were concentrated in the hilly, eroded central portion ("Huangtu gaoyuan diqu zhuyao zuowu shengchanli ji tigao tujing de chubu fenxi" ("Preliminary analysis of productivity and realization approaches of main grain crops on the Loess Plateau"), *Xibei shuitu baochi yanjiu jikan (North-west Soil Erosion Research Quarterly)*, Vol. 10 (1989), p. 168). It is significant that virtually all cultivation was on land with a slope of more than 10 degrees. Li, J. and Cheng, K. ("The erosion process in the middle and upper reaches of the Yangtze River," *International Association of Hydrological Science Publication: Erosion and Sedimentation in the Pacific Rim*, No. 165 (1987), p. 486), cite an investigation based on north-east Guizhou along the Wu River, which indicated that farming on slopes of 30–35 degrees resulted in all the topsoil being washed away within five or six years.

56. See Appendix Table C. The view expressed here is shared by Scott Rozelle, Huang Jikun and Zhang Linxiu, "Poverty, population and environmental degradation in China," *Food Policy*, Vol. 22, No. 3 (1997), pp. 233–34.

57. "The role of sustainable agriculture in China," p. 10.

58. Bi Yuyun, *Zhongguo gengdi (China's Cultivated Land)* (Beijing, Zhongguo nongye chubanshe, 1995), p. 129.

59. In theory, topsoil can wash down from slopes and have a positive impact upon lowland soil fertility. Equally, poor quality soil can wash down and have a negative impact. "The Strategy and Action Project for Chinese and Global Food Security" points out that half of all wind erosion causes a loss of topsoil, whereas 43% causes terrain deformation (p. 14).

60. Peter H. Lindert, Joann Lu and Wu Wanli, "Trends in the soil chemistry of south china since the 1930s," *Soil Science*, Vol. 161, No. 5 (1996), pp. 339–340 suggest that losses of topsoil do not directly correspond to reductions in organic matter levels nor amounts of nitrogen, phosphorous or potassium in soils in China's rice growing regions between 1930 and 1980. They propose that increases in cropping intensity could be more important. Similarly the same authors found that during the same period, changes in organic matter and total nitrogen levels showed no significant trend in north China. Total levels of phosphorus and potassium appear to have increased significantly except in the Shaanxi-Shanxi winter wheat and millet region. (See "Trends in the soil chemistry of north China since the 1930s," *Journal of Environmental Quality*, Vol 25, No. 4 (1996), pp. 1168–1178.) The authors again express doubts about the impact of erosion upon cultivated soil fertility loss. Goder van Lynden's report is summarized in "The Strategy and Action Project for Chinese and Global Food Security," pp. 14–15.

Table 16: **Official Estimates of the Regional Distribution of Soil Erosion in China (1991, 1994 and 1996)**

Region	Eroded area (1,000,000 hectares)		
	1991	1994	1996
North-east	7.936	14.248	22.766
North	14.387	28.447	28.461
North-west	12.304	37.330	56.230
Centre-east (excluding Shanghai)	8.591	17.936	22.737
South-east	2.527	4.764	5.275
South-west (excluding Tibet)	5.016	37.612	45.194

Sources:
Calculated from Ministry of Agriculture, *Zhongguo nongye nianjian* (*Chinese Agricultural Yearbook*) (Beijing: Nongye chubanshe, various issues) 1992, p. 426; 1995, p. 434; 1997, p. 424.

infrastructure (for example, siltation of reservoirs and erosion of dikes).[61] Huang, Rosegrant and Rozelle concluded that during the 1980s and the first half of the 1990s the most severe effects of erosion in north China were on maize, wheat and cash crops.[62]

In the absence of relevant provincial-level statistics, we can only speculate about the relationship between erosion and farm yields. We do know, however, that there are great variations in the regional incidence of soil losses (annual and cumulative), as well as in the causes of the erosion. For example, the severity of soil erosion in the Huang (Yellow) River valley and especially on the Loess Plateau, as well as the increase of erosion in the Chang (Yangtze) River valley prior to the afforestation campaigns of the 1990s, is well-documented as the most severe of such damage in China.[63] The second most seriously

61. Huang and Rozelle, "Environmental stress and grain yields," p. 856.
62. Huang Jikun, Mark W. Rosegrant and Scott Rozelle, "Public investment, technological change and reform: a comprehensive accounting of Chinese agricultural growth," working paper (Washington, DC: International Food Policy Research Institute, 1996) as reported in Rozelle, Huang, and Zhang, "Poverty, population and environmental degradation in China," p. 235.
63. William Y. B. Chang, "Human population, modernization, and the changing face of China's eastern Pacific lowlands," *China Exchange News*, Vol. 18, No. 4 (1990), p. 4, estimated the damage to be 10,000 million tonnes per annum with a loss of fertility equal to about 80,000,000 tonnes of chemical fertilizers. Bi Yuyun (*China's Cultivated Land*, p. 128) gives a figure of 40 million tonnes of nitrogen, phosphorous and potassium equivalent lost through soil erosion annually. For more on general erosion conditions see Edmonds, *Patterns of China's Lost Harmony*, pp. 62–72. While erosion levels have remained lower in the Chang River valley and the south in general compared to, say, the Loess Plateau, the soil layer above bedrock in much of the Sichuan Basin is very thin (less than 20 centimetres) and the red soil hilly region of south China centred on Jiangxi also has particularly serious erosion problems. Soil erosion in the exposed red soil hills causes a serious loss of nutrients – in particular nitrogen (277.94 kg per hectare) and phosphorus (2.981 kg per hectare). In the mid-1990s, China started the second phase of a red soil reclamation programme with a total investment of 2,500 million *yuan* which included a World Bank loan. According to "Unproductive red

affected area has been farmland on the Yunnan-Guizhou Plateau in the south-west.[64]

The official perception of the regional impact of erosion in China, as revealed in Table 16, is likely to be exaggerated (these figures suggest unreasonably high increases in eroded area during the 1990s). Even allowing for such exaggeration, the estimates allow little room for doubt that the south-east has been least affected by soil erosion, the most serious impact of which has been in western China. It is, however, important to bear in mind that such regional data may conceal considerable local variation. It is clear too that much of the erosion highlighted in Table 16 has not affected arable land[65] and, therefore, may not have had an effect on farm production commensurate with its physical extent. This is not to underestimate its impact: one Chinese source indicated that soil erosion on cultivated land is the single most serious form of erosion in China.[66]

Although somewhat dated, the data in Table 17 confirm that the problem of erosion is most severe on the Loess Plateau and in the south-west. They also suggest a correlation between erosion and cultivation of sloping land. In areas of high population density or where existing cultivated land is being transferred to other uses, we would expect more sloping land to be brought under cultivation, thereby increasing the likelihood of a higher incidence of soil fertility loss in the future.[67] This matter is also more complicated than it seems with recent years seeing some abandonment of farming on sloping land in areas where out-migration is severe.

Most sources suggest that semi-arid and sub-humid regions of China are becoming less productive for cultivation and grazing, although the relationships between cultivation, grazing, topsoil loss and various nutri-

---

footnote continued

soil reclaimed," *Beijing Review*, Vol. 39, No. 51 (1996), p. 27, over 58,000 hectares of red soil land are to be reclaimed, but not all of it will be used for agriculture since forestry, animal husbandry and fishpond development are also part of the plan. In the mountainous areas of the south-east, the outwash of boulders and debris from the mountains has affected the agricultural potential of existing farmland. Although generally not a problem, erosion in the north-east can be quite serious in the spring and summer if melting snow is accompanied by heavy rain and examples of serious erosion already exist.

64. Bi Yuyun, *China's Cultivated Land*, p. 129, states that according to the second national soil survey, some 24.85% of eroded cultivated land in China was located in the Loess Plateau region, and 22.39% in the south-west Plateau region. Eroded arable land in these regions accounted for 71.30% and 52.53% of the cultivated areas respectively. After these two regions the north-east and the North China Plain experienced the most serious problems of cultivated land erosion.

65. In every region except the south-east, erosion covers an area greater than the cultivated acreage.

66. Bi Yuyun, *China's Cultivated Land*, p. 129.

67. Rozelle, Huang and Zhang, "Poverty, population and environmental degradation in China," p. 249, suggest that in some parts of rural China where population pressure is intense, there is insufficient time available to implement appropriate institutional changes that would encourage sustainable agriculture. They argue that areas where local leaders have controlled population growth and sought to raise incomes have had better success at controlling the rural environment than those which have focused on environmental clean-up.

ent levels in the soil are far from clear.[68] In 1997, the pace of desertification was officially estimated at 2,460 square kilometres per annum.[69] This figure is greater than indicated in earlier periods, suggesting that desertification is becoming an increasingly serious problem. The total areal extent of desertified land is thought to be about 176,000 sq. km.

Dry land degradation – often also called desertification – is largely confined to the northern half of China. As one moves from the north-west to the north-east, the potential for rectification of degraded arid land improves. The literature is generally in agreement that agricultural activity accounts for about one-quarter of China's arid land degradation.[70] Desertification of grasslands, especially in eastern Inner Mongolia, has also affected neighbouring land that has long been under cultivation.[71] In some areas the rectification efforts of earlier periods have been undone.[72] Dry land degradation is a more serious problem for those involved in animal husbandry than for crop farmers, although it also defines the limits

68. Chinese sources indicate that desertified land (including "latent desertified land" – i.e. land which has the potential to become fully desertified in the near future) accounts for 15.9% of the national cultivated area. According to Guo Huancheng, Wu Dengru and Zhu Hongxing ("Land restoration in China," *Journal of Applied Ecology*, No. 26 (1989), p. 790), and Han Chunru ("Recent changes in the rural environment of China," *Journal of Applied Ecology*, No. 26 (1989), p. 805), desertification threatens the livelihood of nearly 55 million people and 3.9 million hectares of cropland, in addition to 10 million hectares of pasturage, 4.9 million hectares of rangeland and more than 2,000 kilometres of railway lines. Lindert, Lu and Wu ("Trends in the soil chemistry of north China," p. 1176), found that topsoil loss in cultivated portions of the desert-steppe region was insignificant between the 1950s and 1980s. Inner Mongolia did experience a reduction of total nitrogen and total organic matter. In contrast, phosphorus and potassium levels rose in Inner Mongolia during the same period. See also Rozelle, Huang and Zhang, "Poverty, population and environmental degradation in China," pp. 232–33, who suggest that while revegetation programmes such as the Three Norths project (*Sanbei fanghulin*) have alleviated dust problems in northern China, the situation continues to deteriorate overall.
69. Jiang Wandi, "Will sand drift to our doorstep tomorrow?" *Beijing Review*, Vol. 40, No. 28 (1997), pp. 24–25.
70. Kōno Michihiro, "Chūgoku ni okeru sabakuka to sono bōchi ni tsuite no gakusho" ("A note on desertification and its counterplan in China"), *Chirigaku hyōron* (*Geographical Review of Japan*), Vol. 61, No. 2 (1988), p. 187. Other causes and the proportion of area affected are overcutting of forests 31.8%, overgrazing 28.3%, misuse of water resources 8.3%, industrialization and urbanization 0.7%, and wind-blown sand dune encroachment 5.5%. Committee on Scholarly Communication with the People's Republic of China (ed.) (*Grasslands and Grassland Sciences in Northern China* (Washington, DC: National Academy Press, 1992), pp. 14–15), states that "in the mesic eastern regions, inappropriate conversion to agriculture is probably the leading cause" of grassland degradation in northern China. Wood-harvesting and overgrazing are more serious in the north-west.
71. In grassland areas of Inner Mongolia, creation of reservoirs to offset water deficiencies has led to a further reduction of agricultural land and pasturage, thereby increasing the pressure on remaining land. In some areas such as northern Shaanxi, the extent of degradation on cultivated lands is intensifying rather than the areal extent of the affected area expanding so that land is being removed from cultivation. Elsewhere in China, the evidence points to yield reductions rather than land being taken out of cultivation.
72. Zhang Yun, "Renkou qianru yu Gansu, Qinghai jingji fazhan" ("Immigration of population and economic development of Gansu and Qinghai Provinces"), *Jingji dili* (*Economic Geography*), Vol. 11, No. 2 (1991), p. 30, states that attempts to institute cultivation on fixed and semi-fixed dunes in Gansu between 1958 and 1990 resulted in 20,000 sq. km reverting to shifting dunes

Table 17: **Regional Distribution of Soil Erosion on Cultivated Land in the Late 1980s**

Region	Eroded area (1,000,000 hectares)	Eroded area as a percentage of cultivated area	Slope land[b] as a percentage of cultivated land
North-east[a]	7.997	37.36	16.19
North China	6.997	26.85	21.33
Loess Plateau	11.282	71.30	54.98
North-west dry	2.025	15.34	31.00
Middle and lower Chang River Valley	4.622	17.75	26.76
South China	2.124	21.97	34.35
South-west	10.168	52.35	71.44
Qinghai-Tibetan Plateau	0.191	19.75	61.75
Total	**45.406**	**34.26**	**35.09**

Notes:
a. The areal extent of these regions does not correspond to that of similarly named regions in this paper.
b. "Slope land" refers to land with a slope of eight degrees or more.
Source:
Calculated from Bi Yuyun, *Zhongguo gengdi (China's Cultivated Land)* (Beijing, Zhongguo nongye chubanshe, 1995) p. 132.

of expansion for cultivation in north China, given technology levels and water availability.

Between 1987 and 1997, China's output of pork doubled, that of eggs tripled, fresh-water fish quadrupled, and poultry output increased fivefold. Against this background, farmers now need to provide 200 million tonnes of fodder annually and estimates suggest that demand for processed fodder with balanced nutrition will increase even faster in the future.[73] Associated pressure on the grasslands suggests that even if a rational retreat of cultivation from such land can be effected – and notwithstanding plans to improve productivity on 19.5 million hectares of farm land[74]– it will be difficult to halt arid land degradation in the foreseeable future.

Water, air and solid waste pollution have also caused serious damage to crops and soils in parts of China during the last couple of decades. While the situation has improved slightly in some of the more prosperous rural areas in the 1990s, pollution levels in many middle income and low-income regions in 1998 are as high as they were in the wake of the development of township and village enterprises in eastern coastal areas a decade earlier.

Although new treatment facilities in many urban areas have facilitated more effective control of waste water, water pollution in rural areas continues to increase rapidly.[75] In addition to the removal to the countryside of dirty factories, urban water pollution is being transported directly to neighbouring rural areas. It is true that urban areas are an important source of valuable nutrients to farmers, but urban waste has also become increasingly complex as plastics and chemicals enter the sewerage waste stream. Furthermore, in coastal areas, increased pumping has exacerbated the problem of salt water intrusion into the ground water.

Use of saline waters for irrigation, lack of fresh water for flushing and improper irrigation drainage cause salinization or alkalization.[76] Since 70 per cent of grain output is produced on irrigated land, the potential for salinization and alkalization in northern and coastal China is considerable. Table 18 suggests that some progress has been made in rectifying salinized-alkalized lands since the mid-1980s. There are those who feel, however, that worsening water shortages and inadequate agricultural

73. "Ties benefit animal husbandry sector," *Beijing Review*, Vol. 40, No. 41 (1997), p. 28.

74. This is the target contained in the Ten-Year China National Action Programme to Combat Desertification, initiated in 1991.

75. The 1995 official industrial wastewater releases were 37,285 million tonnes. By contrast, in 1994 rural small-scale industries were reported to have released 4,300 million tonnes.

76. This process is often referred to as secondary salinization. Salinization and alkalization occur naturally in areas with a high water table, bad drainage and a high evaporation rate For consideration of salinization-alkalization in pre-reform China, see Eduard B. Vermeer, *Water Conservancy and Irrigation in China: Social, Economic and Agrotechnical Aspects* (Leiden: Leiden University Press, 1977), pp. 205–236. Huang and Rozelle ("Environmental stress and grain yields," p. 857) cite officials in Henan and Hebei to the effect that large increases in salinized land in their provinces during the 1980s were attributable to the reduced efficiency of irrigation systems – allegedly due, in part, to the waning influence of collective leaders.

Table 18: **The Impact of Salinization-alkalization in China**

Year	Total area salinized-alkalized land	Rectified area salinized-alkalized land	Percentage improved to total area salinized-alkalized land
	100,000 hectares		
1985	76.93	45.69	59.4
1990	75.39	49.95	66.3
1995	76.56	54.34	71.0
1996	77.25	55.13	71.4

Sources:
Modified from Guojia tongjiju (State Statistical Bureau), *Zhongguo tongji nianjian* (*Chinese Statistical Yearbook*) (Beijing: Tongji chubanshe, various years), 1992, p. 345; 1995, p. 338; 1996, p. 362; 1997, p. 374.

investment will make it difficult to maintain progress in the struggle against salinization on the North China Plain.[77]

Although salinization-alkalization is primarily a problem in northern China, Table 19 suggests that the highest rectification rate has been achieved in the centre-eastern region.[78] No less striking is the fact that as of 1995, nearly 80 per cent of salinized-alkalized land in the north – the region most seriously affect by the problem – had been improved. Significant too is the finding that in the north-west – the next most seriously affected region after the north – the rate of improvement during 1985–1995 was more rapid than in any other part of China.

In recent years, fertilizers, pesticides and herbicides have damaged cultivated land, as have the adverse effects of polluted urban industrial sludge, toxic waste dumping, and air and water pollution. In terms of its potential impact on yields, the depletion of soil nutrients is, however, likely to be as damaging as soil pollution.[79]

77. See Rozelle, Huang and Zhang, "Poverty, population and environmental degradation in China," pp. 234–35.

78. Note, however, that the estimates shown in Table 19 omit data for some provinces, while figures for others seem suspect (for example, estimates for Sichuan in 1985 and 1990 are identical). Lindert, Lu and Wu ("Trends in the soil chemistry of north China," p. 1173–1174) checked for alkalinity and discovered no increases in northern China between the 1950s and 1980s in areas of prevalent alkalinity. In contrast, they found that alkalinity had fallen along the Bohai and northern Jiangsu coastline. Salinity proved too difficult to test.

79. Chinese soil surveys suggest that most arable land lacks nitrogen, 59% is deficient in phosphorus and 23% is lacking in potassium. Note, however, the suggestion in Lindert, Lu and Wu ("Soil chemistry of south China"), that between the 1960s and 1980s there were significant differences in the levels of organic matter, phosphorous and potassium in tilled soils between different regions of southern China. Their calculations suggest that the rise in organic matter content was largest in the south-western rice-growing region (Yunnan, Guizhou and western Guangxi). Nitrogen levels also rose in this region, but declined overall. In contrast, against the background of a rising trend elsewhere, phosphorus declined in the south-western rice-growing region. While accepting the rigorous nature of the methodology used by Lindert, Lu and Wu, we would also warn against extrapolating too readily from past trends in trying to assess current conditions.

Table 19: **Regional Distribution of Salinization and Alkalization, 1985–1995**

Region	Percentage salinized-alkalized to cultivated area 1995	Percentage improved to salinized-alkalized area (Percentage of national improved area is in parentheses)		
		1985	1990	1995
North-east	7.5	49.3 (13.1)	51.2	52.3 (11.8)
North	14.2	70.9 (52.7)	77.1	79.8 (51.1)
North-west	10.3	42.7 (17.8)	53.3	63.8 (20.3)
Centre-east[a] (excluding Jiangxi, Hubei, Hunan)	8.3	81.5 (15.3)	85.3	89.7 (14.6)
South-east (excluding Guangdong and Hainan)	8.6	15.1 (1.0)	26.6	35.1 (2.1)
South-west (excluding Guizhou and Tibet)	0.07	36.4 (0.04)	50.0	51.9 (0.1)

Note:
a. 1985 data excludes Zhejiang which appears to have not had a great amount of salinized-alkalized land at that time. 1991 data was used for Zhejiang for 1990 as that year's data also was lacking.

Sources:
Calculated from Guojia tongjiju (State Statistical Bureau), *Zhongguo tongji nianjian (Chinese Statistical Yearbook)* (Beijing: Tongji chubanshe, various years), 1986, p. 158; 1991, p. 334; 1992, p. 346; 1996, pp. 355, 363.

Table 20: **Regional Consumption of Chemical Fertilizers and Agro-chemicals, 1996**

Region	Chemical Fertilizers (nutrients) Tonnes per 1,000 hectares of cultivated land	Agro-chemicals
China	**401.0**	**10.6**
North-east	201.6	3.9
North	434.0	12.6
North-west	193.7	2.3
Centre-east	612.7	23.1
South-east	689.5	28.3
South-west	377.2	8.4

Source:
 Ministry of Agriculture, *Zhongguo nongye nianjian* (*Chinese Agricultural Yearbook*) (Beijing: Nongye chubanshe, 1997), pp. 287, 433–34.

Chemical fertilizer consumption rose sharply after 1976, doubling between 1978 and 1984. It more than doubled again after 1985, reaching more than 38 million tonnes in 1996. Over 21.5 million tonnes of this were made up of nitrogenous fertilizers.[80] Similar trends are observable for agro-chemical applications, which reached 1.1 million tonnes in 1996.[81] Although the trend for increased chemical usage is common to all parts of the country, regional differences in application levels remain pronounced (see Table 20).

It is difficult to determine the impact of changing chemical usage in farming because of uncertainties about the differing quality of the product and methods of application in different parts of the country. Associated with increased applications of fertilizers, pesticides and herbicides, there

80. Ministry of Agriculture, *Chinese Agricultural Yearbook 1996*, p. 434. See Appendix Table D. Also useful is Bruce Stone, "Basic agricultural technology under reform," in Kueh and Ash (eds), *Economic Trends in Chinese Agriculture*, pp. 311–360. Chemical fertilizer use rose by more than 400% between 1978 and the mid-1990s. Some of the highest doses of nitrogen fertilizers are in areas which also have large human populations or high animal stocking rates. This suggests that part of the fertilizer pollution problem arises from the excessive application of human and animal wastes rather than just application of chemical fertilizers.

81. Ministry of Agriculture, *Chinese Agricultural Yearbook 1996*, p. 433. Todd M. Johnson, Liu Feng and Richard Newfarmer, *Clear Water, Blue Skies: China's Environment in the New Century* (Washington: World Bank, 1997), p. 90. D. W. Hollomon, Zhou Mingguo and Lu Yuejian ("Fungicide and bacterial resistance in plant pathogens in China," *China–E. C. Biotechnology Centre Newsletter*, No. 14 (1997), p. 10–11) cite an annual consumption of 850,000 tonnes of pesticide in China, of which 600,000 tonnes were insecticides and 110,000 tonnes were fungicides. Extensive use of pesticides and fungicides in the past means that pests have developed resistance to chemicals formerly used and this has encouraged the development of newer and stronger pesticides. Nanjing Agricultural University recently has established a centre for research in pesticide resistance monitoring. "The role of sustainable agriculture in China" (p. 5), recommends only two legal measures for China at this stage: protection of crop land and compliance with the International Code of Conduct on the Distribution and Sale of Pesticides. The same source (p. 11) notes that approximately 75% of domestically-produced pesticides are highly toxic and persistent insecticides.

may also be a potential trade-off between higher yields and worsening pollution, which further complicates trying to reach any definitive assessment.[82] Nevertheless, damage caused by the use of agro-chemicals is reported to have been one of the fastest growing forms of water pollution in the 1990s and a current priority is to encourage development of inexpensive, slow-release mineral fertilizers in order to minimize this damage. It is also noteworthy that the application of crop waste residue as fertilizer is once more being advocated.[83]

Although more recent data are not available, the area of polluted crop land in China in 1992 was estimated by the Ministry of Agriculture to be about 10 million hectares – equivalent to about 12 million tonnes of grain loss per annum. This is likely to be a conservative estimate. More than half of soil pollution is thought to come from pollution exhaust with another third from polluted water. Improper and over-application of pesticides and fertilizers is also a contributory factor.[84] In the 1990s, the use of polluted water for irrigation has been restricted.[85] Soil pollution in the east has persisted after sources have been eliminated, suggesting that there will be a long-term impact for areas that are now undergoing similar rapid economic growth.

Approximately one-fifth of waste released into the environment by large-scale industry is dumped directly into rivers and streams, affecting

82. The uptake of chemical fertilizers by plants is influenced by the type of fertilizer (i.e. urea versus ammonium sulphate), method of application (i.e. ammonium bicarbonate is recovered to a higher level if it is incorporated into the soil than if it is broadcast on the surface), the soil type (i.e. a considerable amount of ammonium sulphate is lost by volatilization of ammonia if applied to the surface of calcareous soils), levels of soil moisture and other factors.

83. Biogas, methane produced by the decomposition of organic matter, was often held up as a partial solution to both the solid waste and the energy shortage problems and there were 6.02 million biogas reactors in use as of the end of 1996 with 1.93 million of these in Sichuan alone. The residual sludge from this process is organic and can be used as a pest-free fertilizer. The main purpose of these reactors is to produce energy – a topic covered elsewhere in this volume by Vaclav Smil. Suffice it to say that the transformation to the family farm has hurt the production of biogas and the use of wastes as fertilizer is likely to increase further through direct application of manure on fields.

84. "The role of sustainable agriculture in China," pp. 11–12 notes that ten applications with dosage rates three to four times the recommended level to vegetables which normally should only get two to six applications is not unusual. The average fertilizer application rate is almost three times that of the U.S. Such excessive usage rates may also raise crop production costs up to threefold.

85. Institute of Soil Science (ed.), *Soils of China* (Beijing: Science Press, 1990), p. 660, notes that during the 1980s more than half a million hectares of land were polluted from irrigation with polluted water and application of urban or industrial sludge. Further problems include the use of plastic sheeting in farming which, when left in the soil, can reduce crop growth by impeding root growth and water penetration. This problem was especially serious in the 1980s when most sheeting was turned over into the soil after the harvest, thereby adding pollutants to the soil. In the 1990s, there have been campaigns launched to urge farmers to recover plastic sheeting. We cannot, however, take the levels of sheeting used as a direct sign of soil pollution. Nonetheless, even if the sheeting is removed, its disposal in rural areas still poses a long-term pollution problem. From official statistics for 1996 (Ministry of Agriculture, *Chinese Agricultural Yearbook 1997*, pp. 287, 433), we have calculated that the north-west region had the greatest percentage of plastic sheeting on cultivated fields (10.64%), followed by the south-west (9.62%), north (8.24%), centre-east (7.71%), north-east (4.70%), and the south-east (3.57). This suggests that use of the plastic sheeting is primarily to retain moisture and secondarily to retain heat.

nearby farming communities. Most urban refuse is still removed from cities by lorry or boat to farms or rural dumping sites although incineration plants which convert waste to energy are progressing in Tianjin and other cities. Meanwhile, the increase of the proportion of ash and non-organic matter in urban refuse has caused a deterioration in the quality of composting material and discouraged farmers from using urban compost.

Although there has been a decline in coverage of agricultural land by industrial solid wastes in recent years, the incidence of urban refuse deposits on such land continues to rise.[86] For example, a 1997 report notes that in the Beijing area, some 500 hectares of farmland are covered with rubbish – a figure which compares with an official estimate for 1995 of just one hectare of farmland covered with industrial waste. There are also reports of protests in the face of such dumping in Beijing Municipality.[87]

Reference has already been made to the damaging impact of air pollution on rural production, especially in economically advanced regions.[88] Sulphur dioxide, chlorine and hydrogen fluoride are said to have caused serious damage to vegetation. Research on the effects of air pollution from urban and industrial areas on agricultural, horticultural and forage crops demonstrates that the ambient concentration of both sulphur dioxide and hydrogen fluoride has been sufficient to reduce yields by five to 25 per cent.[89]

China is the largest source of emissions of primary commercial energy and the second largest producer of hard coal in the world. As a result, the susceptibility of southern China to acid air pollution is one of the highest among developing areas throughout the world.[90] Sichuan and Guizhou already face serious problems. Meanwhile, affected areas in Guangdong and Guangxi are expanding rapidly and the potential for an increase in acid pollution in south-central China during the first quarter of the 21st century is considerable. A 1988 estimate suggested that acidification affected 2.7 million hectares of farmland while a more recent source

---

86. See Appendix Table E.

87. "Beijing residents protest against garbage dump," *China News Digest*, GL97–098 (July 1997), item (4). The officially estimated proportion of arable land covered by industrial solid wastes is rather low (see Appendix Table E), although the considerable annual fluctuations which characterize such figures suggest that official figures should be used with caution. Provinces with the highest percentages in 1995 were those undergoing rapid development (Hainan and Guangdong), near to areas of rapid development (Anhui) and the largest coal base (Shanxi).

88. Eduard B. Vermeer, "Management of environmental pollution in China: problems and abatement policies," *China Information*, Vol. 5, No. 1 (1990), p. 43, cites a report from Guangdong for the late 1980s which assessed air pollution losses as 61% in forestry, 26% in crop losses and 13% in damaged farmland.

89. This is the finding of Cao Hongfa, "Air pollution and its effects on plants in China," *Journal of Applied Ecology*, No. 26 (1989), p. 767, based on data from the Baotou, Chongqing and Liuzhou areas.

90. Any pH value for precipitation which is below 5.6 can be considered to be polluted by acids.

points to annual losses of 10,197,000 million *yuan* from this process.[91] Acid pollution is not likely to become a problem in northern China due to differing natural conditions.[92]

Concluding Remarks: Global Climate Change and Chinese Agriculture

There has been considerable speculation about the impact of global warming on Chinese agriculture, although at this stage the evidence remains inconclusive. The starting point is a consensus among those who believe in global warming that mid-latitude climates are likely to become drier and differences between temperatures at the poles and at the equator reduced, thereby modifying the earth's current climatic patterns.

Chinese scholars have also looked at historical data which offer some evidence of increases in crop yield and moisture during warm periods. Some in China have used such data to argue that the earth entered a natural warming period at the beginning of the 20th century and suggest that temperatures in north China may rise by one to 2 degrees Celsius in the next century.[93] Increases of such magnitudes, however, are generally thought to have a negative impact on wheat and maize yields although depending upon local conditions, the precise effect varies – sometimes being positive for yield increases and sometimes negative.[94] There are those who argue that global warming may benefit Chinese agriculture. Ren Zhenqiu of the Chinese Academy of Meteorological Sciences has been quoted to the effect that "the warming climate can also bring benefits to China and many developing countries."[95] Ren's argu-

91. Johnson, Liu and Newfarmer, *Clear Water, Blue Skies*, p. 27; and Gu Geping [*sic*.] (Qu Geping), "China's industrial pollution survey," *China Reconstructs*, Vol. 37, No. 8 (1988), p. 17. Sulphur dioxide concentrations were positively correlated with yield reductions to varying degrees in wheat, barley, cotton, potato bean (*Phaseolus vulgaris* L., *caidou*), Chinese cabbage or pe-tsai (*Brassica pekinensis* Ruper., *dabaicai*), rice and maize. Long-term exposure to low concentrations of sulphur dioxide appears to reduce the rate of photosynthesis in soy beans, rice, potatoes and winter wheat. Exposure to sulphur dioxide and hydrogen fluoride can increase stomatal resistance, potassium leakage, superoxide dismutase and peroxidase activity and reduce chlorophyll and photosynthesis.

92. The acid problems in the north are less serious because the soil pH is generally more alkaline (greater than pH 7) and the positive ion exchange rate, levels of airborne ammonia and the rate of base absorption is generally higher, which means that the north is better able to deal with higher levels of acids. In addition, coal burned in the south generally has a higher sulphur content.

93. "China enters a warm weather stage," *Beijing Review*, Vol. 39, No. 47 (1996), p. 31.

94. Guojia qihou bianhua xietiaozu dier gongzuozu (National Co-ordinating Group on Climate Change, China), "Renlei huodong yinqi de qihou bianhua dui Zhongguo huanjing yingxiang de pingjia" ("An assessment of the impact of climate change caused by human activities on China's environment"), *Zhongguo huanjing kexue* (*China Environmental Science*), Vol. 10, No. 6 (1990), pp. 422–23. This article makes it clear that Chinese scientists do not all agree on the potential impact of global warming on Chinese agriculture. W. H. Terjung, J. T. Hayes, *et al.* "Actual and potential yield for rain-fed and irrigated maize in China," *International Journal of Biometeorology*, Vol. 28 (1989), pp. 115–135 estimate that maize yields will decline by an average of 3% per 1°C temperature increase in central China.

95. Zhou Xin, "Advantage of climate changing to warm," *Beijing Review*, Vol. 40, No. 23 (1997), p. 18. The fact that such arguments appeared in an article in the *Beijing Review* suggest that there is a political agenda underlying this debate. China is likely to contribute more than any other country to future emissions of so-called "greenhouse gases" and it is useful to argue that many developing countries may benefit from global warming.

ment is that global warming will strengthen westerly summer monsoon winds and thereby generate higher levels of summer precipitation in the interior. Associated positive scenarios include the possibility of 2 per cent yield increases in south-western China resulting from a rise of temperature by 3 degrees Celsius; increased yields resulting from wetter summers in the north-east and Inner Mongolia; and an earlier beginning to the growing season in south and central China to the benefit of wheat, rape seed, early rice and tropical and subtropical fruit cultivation. Other Chinese scientists have suggested that climate change is unlikely to significantly transform the agricultural geography of China, but may still enable certain crops to be grown profitably at up to 150 kilometres north of their current crop regions.

There are scholars whose assessment of the impact of global warming is unfavourable. Their negative scenarios predict increased evaporation cancelling out higher precipitation levels and increasing aridity in north-central and north-western China and point to a greater prevalence of seasonal drought in different parts of the country (for example, an intensified spring drought on the North China Plain and the Loess Plateau by up to 5 per cent, and more severe summer drought causing autumn harvests in eastern Sichuan and western Hubei to decline by 20 per cent). They also point to the impact of dry hot winds in reducing wheat yields in north China by 5 per cent; to a higher incidence of pests, weeds and diseases; to greater typhoon damage and to the inundation of large areas of agricultural land along the east coast under the impact of an enlarged Pacific Ocean.[96]

A report on China and greenhouse gas emissions figures published by the World Bank has indicated that a doubling of CO_2 emissions (considered highly likely by 2020) will have a negative impact upon rice, wheat and cotton production. At the same time, it predicts global agricultural production will fall by between six and 8 per cent, with the highest losses experienced in developing countries.[97] A sea level rise of 1 metre could flood 92,000 sq. km. of China's coast with much good agricultural land lost, as well as requiring the resettlement of 67 million people including the populations of Guangzhou and Shanghai.[98]

Our own view is that the effect of global warming on Chinese agriculture is likely be mixed. Warmer temperatures will mean that growing seasons will be lengthened and in many places precipitation will also increase. We also recognize, however, that high rates of evaporation

96. Han Mukang, "Sea level rise on China's coastal plains," *Tiempo: Global Warming and the Third World*, No. 6 (1992), pp. 17–21.

97. Todd M. Johnson, Junfeng Li, Zhongxiao Jiang and Robert P. Taylor, *China: Issues and Options in Greenhouse Gas Emissions Control* (Washington: World Bank, 1996), p. 1.

98. Yang Guishan ("Relative sea level rise and its effects on environment and resources in China's coastal areas," *Chinese Geographical Science*, Vol. 5, No. 2 (1995), p. 106) notes that the area susceptible to inundation in China could be greater than 125,000 sq. km and affect a population of more than 73 million. Johnson *et al. China: Issues and Options*, p. 11 points out that overall, fishery yields would be reduced, especially in the Chang River valley, where temperatures would be lower in winter and more storms and flooding would affect fish breeding.

will make soils drier and so increase the potential for soil erosion. In addition, China's relatively low level of GNP per capita will make it more difficult to undertake adequate infrastructure and technological investment to combat future climate changes.[99]

China's own ability to maintain its current level of carbon dioxide (CO_2), methane (CH_4), and nitrous oxide (N_2O) emissions into the first quarter of the 21st century appears quite limited. With 82 per cent of greenhouse gas emissions coming from energy, and energy consumption likely to double or triple between 1995 and 2020, it is most unlikely that efficiency improvement will be able to prevent an increase in greenhouse gas emissions.[100]

As one of, if not the single most significant source of greenhouse gases during the 21st century, China could do much to reduce potential global warming. However, even allowing for the adoption of techniques designed to reduce the time during which paddy is under water and the implementation of more efficient management of farms and animal husbandry, most potential problems associated with global warming lie beyond the control of the farmers themselves. In any event, the reality of China's position is captured in the Foreign Ministry's announcement in November 1997 that the nation would not accept limits on its greenhouse gas emissions.

99. Cai Yunlong, "Vulnerability and adaptation of Chinese agriculture to global climate change," *Chinese Geographical Science*, Vol. 7, No. 4 (1997), p. 296–97. Many writers have drawn attention to serious under-investment and misuse of funds in agriculture. See the work of Scott Rozelle, Carl Pray and Jikun Huang, "Agricultural research policy in China: testing the limits," (paper presented at the China Workshop – Global Agricultural Science Policy for the 21st Century, Melbourne, Australia, 26–28 August 1996) as cited in *At China's Table* (Washington, DC: World Bank), p. 15.

100. Although industry accounts for about three-quarters of Chinese CO_2 emissions, agriculture itself is responsible for some of the country's greenhouse gas production – possibly as high as 20% of China's total. Methane production accounts for 13% of China's greenhouse gases and comes largely from paddy filled with water (5%), herd animals (3%) and organic agricultural wastes. See Johnson *et al. China: Issues and Options*, p. 13. Coal-bed methane accounts for 4% of total emissions and some also comes from landfills. Fertilizers also contribute to the production of N_2O, although it is difficult to estimate by how much.[1]

Appendix

Table A: **Estimates of Regional Arable Areas** (1,000 hectares)

North-east (Liaoning, Jilin, Heilongjiang)

Year	Arable area	Net change
1978	16,330	
1980	16,530	+ 200.0
1985	16,515	-15.0
1990	16237.5	-141.5
1995	16,338.2	+ 100.7
1996	16,516.8	+ 178.6

North (Beijing, Tianjin, Hebei, Shanxi, Shandong, Henan)

Year	Arable area	Net change
1978	25.948	
1980	25.828	-120.0
1985	25.303	-525.0
1990	24.878.6	-424.4
1995	24.489.8	-388.8
1996	24.410.2	-79.6

North-west (Inner Mongolia, Shaanxi, Gansu, Qinghai, Ningxia, Xinjiang)

Year	Arable area	Net change
1978	17,369	
1980	17,287	-82.0
1985	16,491	-796.0
1990	16,435.4	-55.6
1995	16,892.7	+ 457.3
1996	17,348.2	+ 455.5

Centre-east (Shanghai, Jiangsu, Zhejiang, Anhui, Jiangxi, Hubei, Hunan)

Year	Arable area	Net change
1978	21,104	
1980	20,961	-143.0
1985	20,439	-522.0
1990	20,108.5	-320.5
1995	19,563.3	-545.2
1996	19,507.1	-56.2

South-east (Fujian, Guangdong, Guangxi, Hainan)

Year	Arable area	Net change
1978	7,154	
1980	7,125	-29.0
1985	6,859	-266.0
1990	6,792.1	-66.9
1995	6,564.7	-227.4
1996	6,562.3	-2.4

Table A: **(continued)**

South-west (Sichuan, Guizhou, Yunnan, Tibet) Year	Arable area	Net change
1978	11,543	
1980	11,575	+ 32.0
1985	11,241	-334.0
1990	11,221.7	-19.3
1995	11,125.2	-96.5
1996	11,121.9	-3.3

Sources:
1978–1986 data from Kenneth R. Walker, "Trends in crop production" in Y. Y. Kueh and Robert F. Ash, *Economic Trends in Chinese Agriculture: The Impact of Post-Mao Reforms* (Oxford: Clarendon Press, 1993). 1986–1996 data from Ministry of Agriculture, *Zhongguo nongye nianjian* (*Chinese Agricultural Yearbook*) (Beijing: Nongye chubanshe, various issues): 1988, p. 212; 1989, pp. 238–39; 1990, pp. 243–44; 1991, pp. 275–76; 1992, pp. 268–69; 1993, pp. 235–36; 1994, p. 291; 1995, p. 309; 1996, p. 279.

Table B: Flooding and Flood Prevention Measures (100,000 hectares)

Year	Total area liable to flood	Area with flood prevention measures	Area affected by floods	Percentage improved to total area liable to floods
1985	242.07	185.84	89.5	76.8
1990	244.67	193.37	56.0	79.0
1995	244.25	200.65	763.0	82.2
1996	245.82	202.79		82.5

Note:
a. The area affected by floods (*chengzai mianji*) does not necessarily bear any direct relation to the areas liable to floods (*yilao mianji*) or the areas with flood prevention measures (*chulao mianji*) in effect.

Sources:
Modified from Guojia tongjiju, *Zhongguo tongji nianjian* (*Chinese Statistical Yearbook*) (Beijing: Tongji chubanshe, various years), and Ministry of Agriculture, *Zhongguo nongye nianjian* (*Chinese Agricultural Yearbook*) (Beijing: Nongye chubanshe, various years).

Table C: **Eroded and Rectified Areas in China**

Category	Area (square kilometres)	Per cent
All China 1985 official figure	1,292,000	13.5
All China 1995 official figure	1,630,000	17.0
All China estimate for 2000	1,750,000	18.8
Official area with soil conservation measures, 1985	464,000	4.8
Official area with soil conservation measures, 1995	669,000	6.9

Sources:
   Zhongguo huanjing baohuju 1991, pp. 4–6; Zhao Qiguo. 1990, p. 156; Guo, Wu and Zhu 1989, p. 790; Zhongguo kexueyuan shengtaihuanjing yanjiu zhongxin yujingxiaozu 1989, p. 12–13; Gao Jiacai. 1989, p. 67; Guojia tongjiju, *Zhongguo tongji nianjian (Chinese Statistical Yearbook)* (Beijing: Tongji chubanshe, 1996), p. 362; Huang Heyu and Lin Zepan, "Forests, our faithful friends", *China Environment News* 15 March 1995, p. 6; "The role of sustainable agriculture in China," p. 10.

Table D: **Chemical Fertilizer Consumption**

Year	Total chemical fertilizers	Nitrogenous Phosphate (1,000,000 tonnes)		Potash	Complex
1985	17.758	12.049	3.109	0.804	1.796
1990	25.903	16.384	4.624	1.479	3.416
1995	35.937	20.219	6.324	2.685	6.708
1996	38.279	21.453	6.584	2.896	7.347

Sources:
Modified from Guojia tongjiju, *Zhongguo tongji nianjian* (*Chinese Statistical Yearbook*) (Beijing: Tongji chubanshe, 1996), p. 361; Ministry of Agriculture, *Zhongguo nongye nianjian* (*Chinese Agricultural Yearbook*) (Beijing: Nongye chubanshe, 1997), pp. 434–35.

Table E: **Agricultural Fields Occupied by Industrial Wastes**

Year	Area occupied (1,000 square metres)
1986	822.5
1987	416.3
1988	382.2
1989	357.4
1990	404.0
1991	520.9
1992	371.1
1993	407.3
1994	380.0
1995	392.7

Sources:
Modified from Guojia tongjiju, *Zhongguo tongji nianjian* (*Chinese Statistical Yearbook*) (Beijing: Tongji chubanshe, various years).

Table F: **Regional Variation in Agricultural Fields Occupied by Industrial Wastes, 1995**

Region	Area of cultivated land occupied (hectares)	Percentage of occupied to total cultivated land
North-east	30.8	0.000188
North (excluding Tianjin)	158.8	0.000660
North-west (excluding Qinghai, Ningxia, Xinjiang)	34.5	0.000280
Centre-east (excluding Shanghai)	74.4	0.000386
South-east	37.2	0.000567
South-west (excluding Tibet)	57.1	0.000524

Source:
Modified from Guojia tongjiju, *Zhongguo tongji nianjian* (*Chinese Statistical Yearbook*) (Beijing: Tongji chubanshe, 1996), pp. 355, 751.

Is China Living on the Water Margin?

James E. Nickum*

Introduction

Is there a water crisis in China? Certainly there are many sub-crises, many of them hardly new to that hydrologically complex, densely settled monsoonal landscape. Droughts, floods, befouled flows, and water-short northern cities have long been integral to the Chinese experience. The last half-century has witnessed remarkable efforts to control and reshape waters to ameliorate the traditional ravages of flood and drought. Yet many of these projects, and their water sources, are ageing at the same time that state financial capacity is diminishing. Simultaneously, economic development – especially industrialization, urbanization, chemical agriculture and livestock production – have placed increasing stresses on the quantity and quality of water.

Does all this add up to a general water crisis? Is water becoming a binding constraint on further economic growth? If not, do the growing water shortages attending the expansion of China's gross product endanger world food security, as claimed recently by Brown and Halweil?[1] The answer to all these questions, this article argues, must be "probably not," although there are a number of areas worthy of concern.

Regionalizing China

Hydrologically speaking, China is one country, many systems. Its monsoonal climate concentrates precipitation in the summer months. This effect is most pronounced in the north and north-east, where the average precipitation is lower than in the south and south-east. Except in very arid zones, summer crops such as maize and cotton can ordinarily rely on rainfall for most or all of their growing season. Winter crops, notably winter wheat and late-season rice, are more heavily dependent on irrigation. However, year-to-year variation in precipitation tends to be higher where total rainfall is lowest so supplemental irrigation may be important even in the wet season to ensure yields of summer crops in the north. The amount of supplemental water needed varies from year to year, as does the yield loss in the absence of irrigation. Hence the marginal value of irrigation water varies widely from place to place and even in the same place for the same crop, from year to year. Needless to say, this makes production function-based estimation very difficult for irrigation water.

* The work on which this article is based was supported by the Chinese and Global Food Security Project under the organizational leadership of the Millennium Institute.
    1. Lester R. Brown and Brian Halweil, "China's water shortages could shake world food security," *World Watch*, Vol. 11, No. 4 (1998), pp. 10–18.

Problems confronting irrigation are particularly pronounced in areas that, despite advances in the past two decades, are not dominant grain-producing regions. Some places, especially in the north and along the coast, have been under high levels of stress for some time; others, in the central and southern areas, remain more liable to damage from too much water than from too little. About half of China's major cities are considered to be in water deficit, but the nature and periodicity of those shortages cover a wide range of circumstances. For example, sometimes the problem is a lack of water in the supply system; other times, it is the lack of a delivery system.

The stressed areas represent water conditions "at the margins" and should not be considered representative of all China. An intense exploration of current hot spots, a task that is well beyond the scope of the present paper, would provide valuable clues as to both the pattern of future stress and the current and potential range of coping mechanisms.

There is no one best way to regionalize China from the standpoint of water, irrigation, and food production. Any of the following are possible (as well as others, such as that used elsewhere in this volume by Ash and Edmonds), depending largely on the purposes and scale of the analysis and the availability of the data. This article begins with the most aggregate, richest in available data, and least useful for considering the margins of hydraulic stress.

By dominant grain crop. Chinese statistics distinguish between paddy rice fields (*shuitian*) and dryland irrigation (*jiaodi*). This divide is of critical importance, affecting cropping, water applications, and irrigated area figures. Virtually all rice in China is considered to be irrigated. Rice dominates irrigated areas where annual precipitation exceeds 1,000 mm (south and south-east China) and in Ningxia, which relies on the Huang (Yellow) River.[2] It is also quite common in the north-east (Jilin, Liaoning and Heilongjiang).

By irrigation requirement. The Ministry of Water Resources has divided China into three zones, according to the need for irrigation, indicated by the average annual precipitation (P):[3]

1. perennial irrigation zone (P < 400 mm/year): north-west China, including the middle reaches of the Huang (irrigation always necessary);
2. unsteady irrigation zone (400 < p < 1000 mm/year): Huang-Huai-Hai Plain and north-east China (amount of supplemental irrigation varies from year to year); and

2. Over 90% of paddy irrigation: Sichuan, Hunan, Guangdong-Hainan, Jiangxi, Fujian, Guizhou, Guangxi, Zhejiang, Yunnan; over 70%: Ningxia, Shanghai, Hubei, Jiangsu, Anhui. In the north, rice uses less than 20% of irrigated area except in the north-east (Jilin, Liaoning, Heilongjiang), where it is about one-third (1978 data, but unlikely to have changed). James E. Nickum, *Dam Lies and Other Statistics: Taking the Measure of Irrigation in China, 1931–91* (Honolulu: East-West Centre, 1995), p. 80.

3. Ministry of Water Resources and Electric Power, *Irrigation and Drainage in China* (Beijing: Shuili dianli chubanshe, 1987), p. 17.

3. supplementary irrigation zone (P > 1000 mm/year): middle and lower reaches of the Chang (Yangtze), Zhu (Pearl), and Min rivers, and part of south-west China (irrigation secondary to natural supply). Most paddy land is here, and the cropping ratio tends to be higher than in the north.

Rice dominates the supplementary irrigation zone, where irrigation is a secondary source of moisture, at least for the main summer crop. Rice is also important in parts of the perennial zone along the middle reaches of the Huang River, where the flat topography, high water table, and high levels of potential evapotranspiration create a danger of salinization.

By region. Because both grain production and irrigation data are relatively abundant[4] and available at the provincial level, it is convenient and sometimes unavoidable to use these administrative boundaries as the basis of analysis. For a study of trends in irrigated area,[5] hydro-agriculturally similar provinces are grouped into seven regions: north (Beijing, Tianjin, Hebei, Shandong and Henan), north-east (Inner Mongolia, Liaoning, Jilin, Heilongjiang, and Ningxia), north-west (Gansu, Shaanxi and Shanxi), east (Shanghai, Jiangsu, Anhui and Hubei), south (Zhejiang, Fujian and Guangdong-Hainan), south-west (Jiangxi, Hunan, Guangxi, Guizhou and Yunnan), and west (Sichuan, Xinjiang, Qinghai and Tibet). With few exceptions, provincial boundaries have been stable over the past four decades, and allow for intertemporal comparison. Groupings such as these help show the considerable intertemporal variations among regions in the historical patterns of extension and decline of irrigated area. In particular, increases in irrigated area have been most striking in the formerly unirrigated north – usually (but not always) for crops other than rice (notably wheat) – and have depended in large part on the introduction of new storage and pumping technologies.

By river basin. Hydrologically, river basins are natural units of analysis. With adjustments for inter-basin transfers, they can be used to determine areas of potential abundance and stress. A large-scale assessment of China's water resources was carried out by the Ministry of Water Resources at the beginning of the 1980s using ten catchment basins (Heilong (Amur), Liao, Hai-Luan, Huang, Huai, Chang, Zhu, south-east coastal, south-west border and inland) and 77 sub-basins. The results of this survey, the only one of its kind yet published, are available in both English and Chinese.[6] Although now dated, especially in its projections

4. See, for example, the annual State Statistical Bureau, *Zhongguo tongji nianjian (China Statistical Yearbook)* (Beijing: Zhongguo tongji chubanshe), now published in both Chinese and English, and the agricultural and water resources yearbooks (Editorial Committee, Zhongguo nongye nianjian (eds.), *Zhongguo nongye nianjian* (Beijing: Zhongguo nonge chubanshe), and Editorial Committee, Zhongguo shuili nianjian (eds.), *Zhongguo shuili nianjian* (Beijing: Zhongguo shuili shuidian chubanshe)), published in Chinese.

5. Nickum, *Dam Lies and Other Statistics,* p. 81.

6. In English, see PRC Ministry of Water Resources, Department of Hydrology, *Water Resources Assessment for China* (Beijing: China Water and Power Press, 1992). A companion

of water use, this rich source of data is essential to any hydrologically-related analysis of China.

Thus catchment-based analyses can indicate specific areas of potential water stress, notably the Hai and Liao river basins. Unless broken into subunits, however, they are limited in their usefulness for looking at the large basins that include a number of agroclimatic zones. In particular, the Chang and Huang rivers dominate China's populated land mass. Yet, for example, while the Sichuan basin on the upper reaches of the Chang is prone to water shortage, the middle and lower reaches are more likely to be concerned about flooding and pollution. Some problems may also be presented by the lack of correspondence between administrative, especially provincial, boundaries, the basic unit of much reporting on agriculture, and catchment areas. Particular difficulties are presented by the major grain producing provinces of Shandong (spanning parts of the Hai, Huang, and Huai systems, together with a number of small peninsular catchments and diversions from the Huang and Chang) and Jiangsu (straddling the Huai and Chang systems).

The Biggest User: Irrigation

A thumbnail history of irrigation in the People's Republic. The first few years of the 1950s saw a restoration of the pre-war total of irrigated land (21–27 million hectares) through the rehabilitation of projects. After 1955 there was a rapid increase in irrigated area, due to the construction of new surface water systems, notably reservoirs and diversions in the previously unirrigated north. The data record is spotty and not always reliable from the initiation of the Great Leap Forward in 1957 through to the early 1970s, by which time an aggregate irrigated area of 40–44 million hectares was reported. Focus in the early 1960s was on surface pumps in southern rice-growing areas. This probably did not increase the irrigated area as much as it improved its reliability.

In the late 1960s and early to mid-1970s, a major burst in the irrigated area – in retrospect exceeding that of the Great Leap – followed the widespread installation of pump wells on previously unserved areas in north China. The nation-wide irrigated area remained basically stable at 44–45 million hectares[7] from 1976 through to 1989, although there were sometimes significant shifts in provincial totals (see Table 1). In 1990 the State Statistical Bureau reported a jump in China's irrigated area, to 47 million hectares, but this may have been a statistical adjustment rather

footnote continued

volume on water use in China, with projections to the year 2000, is available only in Chinese: *Zhongguo shui ziyuan liyong* (*Utilization of China's Water Resources*) (Beijing: Shuili dianli chubanshe, 1989). In its foreword, the latter publication indicates that the research was based on over 2,000 accounting units, aggregated into 302 tertiary zones, 82 secondary zones and nine primary basins or regions. A new, possibly more limited, nation-wide survey has been taken in recent years, but has not yet (as of 1998) been made public.

7. State Statistical Bureau figures. Ministry of Water Resources totals for effectively irrigated area varied from 45 to 49 million hectares: see Nickum, *Dam Lies and Other Statistics*, pp. 85–86.

Table 1: **Total Irrigated Area (million hectares)**

Year	SSB	MWR	Other sources
1930s			21–27
1949	16	16	
1955	25		
1965	33	32	
1975	43	48	
1985	44	48	
1989	45	48	
1990	47	48	
1994		48	

Sources:
   James E. Nickum, *Dam Lies and Other Statistics: Taking the Measure of Irrigation in China, 1931–91* (Honolulu: East West Center,1995), pp. 85–86; Ministry of Water Resources, *Zhongguo shuili nianjian 1995* (*Almanac of Water Resources 1995*) (Beijing: Zhongguo shuili shuidian chubanshe, 1996), p. 418.

than an indication of an increase in irrigation capacity. The Ministry of Water Resources figure for 1990 of 725.84 million *mu* (48.4 million hectares) was virtually unchanged from the 725.06 million *mu* reported for 1989.

The difference between the two different reporting systems illustrates one of the many problems inherent in reported figures for irrigated area, including the most commonly reported category of "effectively irrigated area." The Ministry of Water Resources receives its reports from those who administer the projects, while the figures from the State Statistical Bureau are collected from the villages which have an incentive to downplay their irrigating capacity and thus keep their tax bills down.

Another problem is that a category such as "effectively irrigated area" says nothing about the effectiveness of irrigation. For example, water supplied per "actually" irrigated hectare in 1985 varied from 3,500m³/ha in Shanxi to 30,800m³/ha in Shanghai.[8] The difference of nearly nine to one is far greater than can be accounted for by even triple cropping, and Shanghai is presumably in much less need of supplemental moisture. Moreover, the higher application rates were not restricted to southern deltas: second was Ningxia (28,000m³/ha), which diverts the Huang River to irrigate rice and which, not surprisingly, has a serious problem of salinization.

There has been a modest increase in aggregate irrigated area in the 1990s, but this has entailed the addition of relatively low yield new areas to partially offset the loss of relatively high yield fields to higher value uses such as urbanization. Although yields on irrigated land are much

8. *Ibid.* p. 36.

higher than those on dryland, yield increases have tended to be due to factors other than the presence or absence of irrigating capability, which is what irrigated area figures measure. Since at least 1975, and possibly before, there appears to be no direct correlation between grain output and irrigated area at the aggregate national level.

The enduring importance of irrigation. By any measure, and there are at least two, irrigation remains the biggest human use of water in China, consuming over two-thirds of the total.[9] Even in highly urbanized and industrialized locations such as Beijing, Tianjin and Shenyang, where water has frequently been diverted from farms to factories and households, irrigation remains the largest water demand sector. In 1993, irrigation and other farm production uses claimed 50.6 per cent of Beijing's water and 52.3 per cent of that of Tianjin. Industry's shares were 25.4 per cent and 29.6 per cent respectively, with "daily life" taking the remainder.[10]

In most of China, even in the more stressed river basins such as the Hai-Luan, Huang, Liao and Huai, water demand for irrigation is expected to decline in relative terms, but not absolutely until beyond the year 2020.[11] These projections, like those of future water "needs" in the United States, are likely to overstate increases in water use in all sectors due to underestimation of demand elasticities, structural shifts and industrial recycling needed to comply with water quality standards.[12]

Unsustainable Uses

Mining and deferred maintenance. Much current water use is "mining" either the resource or the facilities used to store and deliver it. Over-drafted groundwater aquifers are sinking (especially under urban areas, less so below irrigated farmlands), creating large drawdowns known technically as "cones of depression" in north China and suffering quality degradation from seawater intrusion near the coast. A 1991–1993 survey of the coastal areas of Liaoning, Hebei and Shandong provinces carried out by the Office of Hydrology of the Ministry of Water Resources indicated that over 2,000 square kilometres of formerly freshwater aquifers now lie below the sea level. About half of this area, which

9. Water use can be measured either in terms of withdrawals or consumption. Consumption does not include return flow, and accounts for a higher proportion of withdrawals in agriculture, largely because of evaporation from the fields, than in industry or domestic (municipal) use. Only about a quarter of the total annual supply of freshwater can be captured for off-stream uses with current technology.
10. Xu Xinyi, Wang Hao and Gan Hong (eds.), *Huabei diqu hongguan jingji shui ziyuan guihua lilun yu fangfa (Theory and Methods for Macroeconomic Water Resource Planning in North China)* (Zhengzhou: Huanghe shuili chubanshe, 1997), pp. 170–71.
11. Economic and Social Commission for Asia and the Pacific, *China: Water Resources and Their Use* (New York: United Nations, 1997), p. 18, citing Nanjing Institute of Hydrology and Water Resources, "Report on the mid- and long-term plans for water demand and supply in China" (1996: in Chinese).
12. Peter Rogers, *America's Water: Federal Roles and Responsibilities* (Cambridge, MA: MIT Press, 1993), pp. 126–27.

continues to expand, has been affected by seawater intrusion, resulting in the abandonment of over 8,000 tubewells and a cutback in pumping of 130 million m³ of water per year. This in turn has lead to a reduction in irrigated area of over 40,000 hectares and a grain crop loss of 200,000 tonnes.[13] While this may be traumatic to those concerned, the aggregate effect on irrigation and grain output is quite localized, even within the provinces concerned.

Except in a few cases – those of deep "fossil" water, a very rare condition in China, and surface land subsidence, which does occur and compresses underground storage capacity – groundwater overdraft does not deplete the water resource, which is continuously renewed. In many cases, as in London, conversion from groundwater to surface sources has led to the problem of a rising water table. Aquifers will replenish with reductions in withdrawals.

More serious problems are presented by the ageing of facilities such as dams and dikes. The relatively inexpensive and high-yield dam sites and easily accessible, comparatively unused water sources have been tapped for the most part. Many of today's projects were built in haste in the late 1950s out of earth and, sometimes, masonry. These have presented increasing maintenance and repair problems to a system that has tended to favour construction over maintenance – a world-wide phenomenon sometimes delicately labelled "deferred maintenance." New supply works, such as dams or diversions, tend to be very expensive in both financial and human terms at a time when the state is facing a chronic budgetary crisis.

Urbanization. The rapid expansion of urban areas affects irrigation and food production in a number of ways, both negative and positive. On the negative side, cities occupy nearby farmland that is often highly productive and usually irrigated; they draw off skilled and young farm labour; and they often compete with irrigation for the water sources, especially to supply industry and power.

Continuing pressure exists to transfer some irrigation water to urban and industrial uses, at least at the margin. From 1991 through to 1995 the State Statistical Bureau and the Ministry of Water Resources carried out a planning exercise to project water demand and supply situations for the years 2000 and 2010 in the 270 (out of a total of 467 in 1990) cities, mostly in the north, north-east, north-west, and south-eastern coast, that are currently considered water-deficient. One of the conclusions of this study was that 40 per cent of the projected demand gap in 2000 could be met by transferring water from agriculture.[14]

On the positive side, nearby cities provide farm households with markets and income that can be used to purchase more water-efficient irrigating facilities and to diversify into higher-value crops. Thus, both

13. PRC Ministry of Water Resources, *Zhongguo shuili nianjian 1995 (Almanac of China Water Resources 1995)* (Beijing: Shuili dianli chubanshe, 1996), p. 107.
14. *Ibid.* pp. 149–150.

grain output and overall agricultural output value have continued to increase in the suburbs of Beijing at the same time that water has been diverted to the urban core and the overall irrigated area has declined.

Upstream development. During my first visit to China in 1974, Li Jiasan, a wise water expert, summed up China's allocation rules in three words: "upstream doesn't suffer." Little has changed in the intervening years. Especially in northern rivers such as the Hai and the Huang, upstream withdrawals have reduced flows to existing users downstream, including politically-powerful Beijing (from the Guanting Reservoir). Beijing itself used its topographic advantage to cut downstream Tianjin off from the waters of the Miyun Reservoir. Tianjin was provided with another reservoir shortly thereafter, but had to endure some years of shortage. The Huang has become known as a "sick river" because of the effect of upstream diversions and effluents on downstream areas. Since 1972, it has run dry for an increasing part of the low-flow season.

Quality degradation. There are a number of quality problems which, when severe, can either reduce the effective water supply available for crop irrigation or cut yields on irrigated land. In general, where water quantity is low, water quality problems are more severe, due to the more intensive use of the water and its reduced capacity for self-cleaning. In particular, northern river systems (especially the Liao and Hai-Luan) have extensive stretches with high levels of organic contaminants (measured by biological oxygen demand (BOD), chemical oxygen demand (COD), and ammonium) and toxins, of which five have been commonly measured: mercury, chromium, phenol, cyanide and arsenic (see Table 2). Organic pollution is generally not a matter of concern for irrigation; indeed, the enriched nutrients can be used to promote plant growth. Toxins are another matter altogether. Pollution is particularly marked in and around urban areas, in the lower reaches of rivers and on tributaries.

Severe pollution, mainly industrial, is rendering many waters unusable even for irrigation. A 1984 survey by the Ministry of Water Resources found the water quality in 10.9 per cent of the 85,000-kilometre length of China's rivers it evaluated to be unsuited for irrigation (exceeding Grade V).[15] A second survey, published in 1996 and based on 1991 data, found a general deterioration in the quality of China's river water, but little increase in the total length of rivers exceeding Grade V.[16] (The paper elsewhere in this issue by Vermeer deals in detail with the problem of industrial pollution, so this particular source of China's water problems will not be dwelt on further here.)

15. PRC Ministry of Water Resources, Department of Hydrology, *Water Resources Assessment for China* (Beijing: China Water and Power Press, 1992), p. 238.

16. Zhonghua renmin gongheguo shuili bu shuiwen si, *Zhongguo shui ziyuan zhiliang pingjia tuji (Maps of China's Water Resource Quality Assessment)* (Zhengzhou: Huanghe shuili chubanshe, 1997), p. 10; and Qiao Desheng and Shi Yubo, "Woguo shui ziyuan pingjia xianzhuang yu zhanwang" ("The current situation of and prospects for water resource evaluation in China"), *Zhongguo shuili (China Water Resources)*, No. 417 (1998), p. 10.

Table 2: Grades and Criteria Used for Water Quality Assessment (in mg/l)

	BOD₅	COD	Ammonia	Phenol	Cyanogen	As	Hg	Cr
Grade I	≥7.5	≤2	≤0.5	≤0.002	≤0.02	≤0.04	≤0.0005	≤0.05
Grade II	≥4, <7.5	>2, ≤5	>0.5, ≤1.0	>0.002, ≤0.01	>0.02, ≤0.05	≤0.04	>0.0005, ≤0.001	≤0.05
Grade III	≥3, <4	>5, ≤8	>1.0, ≤2.0	>0.01, ≤0.1	>0.05, ≤0.2	>0.04, ≤0.05	>0.0005, ≤0.001	>0.05, ≤0.1
Grade IV	≥2, <3	>8, ≤20	>2.0, ≤4.0	>0.1, ≤0.5	>0.2, ≤0.4	>0.05, ≤0.5	>0.001, ≤0.05	>0.1, ≤0.5
Grade V	<2	>20	>40	>0.5	>0.5	>0.5	>0.05	>0.5
Reference Criteria								
Type 1	domestic uses, drinking water			≤0.002	≤0.05	≤0.04	≤0.001	≤0.05
Type 2	surface water			≤0.01	≤0.05	≤0.04	≤0.001	≤0.05
Type 3	fishery			≤0.005	≤0.02	≤0.1	≤0.0005	1.0
Type 4	irrigation			≤1	≤0.5	≤0.05	≤0.001	0.1
Type 5	industrial waste water			0.5	0.5	0.5	0.05	0.5

Note:
BOD₅: biological oxygen demand; COD: chemical oxygen demand; As: arsenic; Hg: mercury; Cr: hexavalent chromium
Source:
Department of Hydrology, *Water Resources Assessment for China* (Beijing: China Water and Power Press, 1992), p. 234.

Water quality since 1980 has continued to decline in many areas. A 1990 geological survey in Shandong found the water in 50.7 per cent of the 69 river stretches examined, in three of four lakes, and in one of 30 reservoirs, to be in excess of Grade V. Most of this pollution was organic, however, except for phenol, iron and fluoride (a natural pollutant in Shandong), and not necessarily harmful to irrigation.[17]

The area of cultivated land estimated to have been affected by water pollution increased from 670,000 hectares in 1980 to 1.3 million hectares in 1990. Estimated crop losses, converted to grain equivalents, were 2 million tonnes and 3.9 million tonnes respectively.[18] Again, while the localized effects may appear to be high, the aggregate losses to China seem to have been modest compared to other factors affecting grain, such as pests.

A sedimental journey and other degradations. As throughout history, the most troublesome water quality problem in much of China is sedimentation. Sediments can reduce the available water supply in two ways, by requiring a certain discharge flow to the sea for flushing (this is sometimes violated in practice, notably in the Huang) and by silting up storage facilities. The siltation that gives the Huang River (the "Yellow River") its name is legendary. The massive Xiaolangdi Reservoir now under construction in Henan is designed to silt up in about 30 years. Sedimentation is also a problem for reservoirs and river channels in parts of other northern basins, notably the Hai and the Liao, and even in parts of the south.

Still, sedimentation is a mixed curse. As in the pre-Aswan Nile, it can provide a natural replenishment of soil nutrients. The land between the wide dikes of the Huang and the river itself is prized farmland.

Data at the provincial level are reported each year by the Ministry of Water Resources for two additional categories of degraded cultivated land: that prone to flooding or waterlogging (*yilao gengdi*) and that subject to secondary salinization or alkalization (mostly salinization) (*yanjian gengdi*). Also reported is the cumulative area so afflicted that has been improved.

In general, these series indicate stability or only a slight increase in the total area subject to these ills, with a more than compensatory rise in the area improved (see the paper by Ash and Edmonds in this volume). The usefulness of these figures for assessing the impact on crop yields is uncertain at best in the absence of more specific data about the real or potential crop loss attributable to flooding or salinization.

---

17. Ke Wenwu and Tang Hao *et al. Zhongguo nongye quanshu: Shandong juan* (*Encyclopedia of China's Agriculture: Shandong Volume*) (Beijing: Zhongguo nongye chubanshe, 1994), p. 28.

18. *Shiwu shengchan di wuzhi touru yu huanjing baohu* (*Material Inputs into Crop Production and Environmental Protection*) (Beijing [?]: Nongye chubanshe, 1991), cited in Chūgoku Kenkyūjo (China Research Institute) (ed.), *Chūgoku no kankyo mondai* (*China's Environmental Problems*) (Tokyo: Shin hyōron, 1995), p. 29.

Table 3: **Reported Sources of Decline in Irrigated Area (per cent of total)**

	1984	1989	1990	1994
Structures damaged or abandoned	14	18	19	27
Tubewells abandoned	35	35	22	24
Water inadequate of which:	16	14	13	6
diverted to industry or				
domestic uses				0.8
Land occupied by construction	5	10	10	20
Converted to fishponds				3
Abandoned orchards or economic				
crops				5
Restored to lake				0.04
Other	30	23	36	15
Total (hecatres)	**1,084,120**	**750,300**	**1,263,573**	**798,560**

Sources:
Nickum, *Dam Lies and Other Statistics*, p. 18; *Almanac of Water Resources 1995*, p. 420.

Sources of decline in irrigated area. Often, irrigated farmland does not last forever. Every year, in every province, some downward adjustments are made in the reported effectively irrigated area. These are offset by gross increases in irrigated area to create a net figure, which sometimes increases and sometimes falls. The Ministry of Water Resources has reported on sources of decline in irrigated area for each province in 1984 and every year since 1989 (in the water annual *Zhongguo shuili nianjian* (*Almanac of China Water Resources*)), with increasing sophistication. These figures, which are presumably rough and subject to various reporting biases, nonetheless indicate that urbanization is far from the most significant pressure on irrigated farmland (see Table 3). Construction, which includes but is not exclusively due to urbanization effects, accounted for only 5 per cent of the total area lost in 1984 and 10 per cent in 1989 and 1990.[19] This may have been understated, as the "other" category was quite large in those years (30, 23 and 36 per cent respectively) and the construction share increased to nearly 20 per cent in 1994 while "other" fell to 15 per cent. Nonetheless, it remains relatively minor.

Recently added categories include: a breakdown of insufficient water (see above) to note the portion that has been transferred to industrial or domestic uses (less than 1 per cent of the 798,560 hectare decline in 1994); conversion to fishponds (3 per cent of the total); abandoned orchards or economic crops (such as cotton) (5 per cent); and lake restoration (300 hectares).[20] These rather minor conversions only serve to emphasize the impression that the primary pressure on irrigated area now, and probably for some time into the future, is project obsolescence within

19. Nickum, *Dam Lies and Other Statistics*, p. 114.
20. PRC Ministry of Water Resources, *Almanac of China Water Resources 1995*, p. 420.

the irrigation sector itself, much of which reflects a normal turnover in short-lived tubewells rather than encroachment from other uses. It is worth noting as well that the total area reported in decline has itself apparently diminished over time.

Hopeful Signs

Not all signs point to continued unsustainability of water use. As Liu Changming (contributor on the south-north water transfer schemes in this issue) has noted, the problems with water are threefold: shortage, wastage and quality.[21] Correcting the latter two problems can go a long way towards fixing the former.

Potential for efficiency gains in irrigation. Since irrigation dominates water uses, improved efficiency in the delivery and application of irrigation water would not only create a new source for other users, but also ensure minimal effect on crop output – other things being equal. Actual water applications to crops are well in excess of the amount absolutely needed to ensure plant growth. Low water delivery efficiencies ("canal system use efficiency rates"), defined as the percentage of water leaving a source actually reaching the crops at the end of the system, are cited for large, canal-based systems. By international standards, however, it is not clear that these loss levels are unusually high, and they may be lower than those in much of the American west. This would not be surprising as under the beneficial use doctrine ("use it or lose it") of U.S. western states, farmers have a perverted incentive to be wasteful. More importantly, water "lost" to a canal system may feed aquifers that are tapped outside the domain of the project. As Rosegrant and Meinzen-Dick have noted, actual basin-wide water use efficiency levels may be much higher than those calculated for individual projects.[22]

Still, to return to the optimistic side, there does seem to be ample room for efficiency gains in field-level application when water becomes sufficiently valuable to make the additional costs worth bearing. "Green revolution" high-yielding varieties of rice, with their short stalks and brief growing seasons, actually tend to use less water per crop than traditional varieties, but make greater demands on the timing of application. In general, if water supply can be guaranteed at the proper time, considerable water can be saved by applying smaller amounts at strategic intervals during the growing season. Heavy applications of water often reflect insecurity of supply, as well as low charges, and – at least for rice – this is often not to promote crop growth *per se* but to suppress weeds.

---

21. See, for example, Liu Changming and Cheng Tianwen, "Jiejue queshui wenti di duice" ("Countermeasures for solving the water shortage problem"), in Liu Changming, He Xiwu and Ren Hongzun (eds.), *Zhongguo shui wenti yanjiu (Studies on China's Water Problems)* (Beijing: Qihou chubanshe, 1996), pp. 19–25.

22. Mark W. Rosegrant and Ruth S. Meinzen-Dick, "Water resources in the Asia-Pacific region: managing scarcity," *Asian-Pacific Economic Literature*, Vol. 10, No. 2 (1996), pp. 36–37.

Low-water strategies require a management system that allows timely delivery and either more intensive labour input or herbicides, with their potential for environmental degradation.

Another factor inhibiting the introduction of more water-saving strategies for rice is that, except in the northern suburban areas and the north-east, rice is for the most part grown in relatively water-abundant regions. Capital-intensive application methods such as drip and sprinkler have already been widely adopted in the rural areas of many water-short urban areas in the north. In particular, in Beijing, one-third of the irrigated area (98,000 hectares out of 289,000) was outfitted with sprinklers or drip facilities in 1994. This was over one-sixth of the national total of 567,000 hectares, which was actually down from the 1989 figure of 654,000 hectares due to a large drop in Shandong province.[23] The problem inhibiting the spread of these technologies is that their expense is often well above the artificially low price charged for agricultural water, especially in surface systems. In the case of tubewells, pumping costs can be significant, particularly as aquifer levels begin to decline.

Other areas of potential efficiency gain. Aside from in-stream uses such as water needed to discharge sediments to the sea, the largest alternative source of demand to irrigation is in industry and thermal power. Here experience elsewhere and in key areas in China leads one to be cautiously optimistic about the potential for reducing consumptive use rates through treatment and reuse of abstracted water. In Japan and the United States industrial consumptive use has fallen in absolute terms since the 1970s, despite continued industrial growth. This is due to the effective imposition of wastewater discharge regulations on major emitters. Whether China can similarly let quality control reduce quantity is an open question. There are some encouraging signs: total reported industrial water use in 1988 (42.8 billion m^3 out of 498.6 billion m^3, not counting Shanghai) was actually below that of 1980 (45.7 billion m^3 out of 443.7 billion m^3).[24] Projections in China assume an increasing efficiency in industrial water use, measured both in terms of water use per unit output (e.g. of steel) and output value. It is possible that the reform and/or closure of heavy water-using state-owned enterprises in the next few years will further reduce water use by industry.

Although increased living standards will lead to rises in per capita domestic water use, they are not likely to be a major source of pressure on the water resource, at least in quantity terms. Even within the "urban daily living" (*chengzhen shenghuo*) reporting category that is comparable to municipal/domestic use, households still have a small percentage share compared to public institutions. Although in some areas, there have been

---

23. PRC Ministry of Water Resources, *Almanac of China Water Resources 1990*, p. 635; and PRC Ministry of Water Resources, *Almanac of China Water Resources 1995*, p. 941.

24. PRC Ministry of Water Resources, *Almanac of China Water Resources 1990*, p. 186. Unfortunately, more recent issues of the water annual do not seem to include comparable information.

attempts to improve the metering and pricing systems, there remains a lot of waste in domestic uses, especially in institutions.

Untapped waters within basins. Among the most stressed northern river basins, the Hai and Huang appear to be oversubscribed, mainly during the dry season when flow ceases before reaching the ocean. For most of the year, some water still flows to the sea, but this is necessary for silt discharge and to prevent erosion of the economically valuable oil-rich delta. If wet season floods and the heavy silt load they bear can be retained without appreciably damaging the delta through projects such as the Xiaolangdi Reservoir, there is still some potential for further development of water even in the Huang. New reservoirs are still being built in the Liao. The Hai has perhaps the least untapped potential, with only one additional major reservoir site under consideration.

Inter-basin transfers. Inter-basin transfers are still seen as the primary means of alleviating water shortage stresses in critical areas in the north – especially the Hai, Liao and northern Huai basins and the Shandong peninsula – in the early part of the 21st century. (The most significant of these, the south-north transfer from the Chang into the Huai and Hai basins, is covered in the article in this volume by Liu Changming.) Other significant inter-basin transfers under consideration are from the Huang into the major coal-producing province of Shanxi and from tributaries of the Sunggari (Songhua) and Yalu rivers into the Liao basin. Because of the low financial and economic value of irrigation water, these projects have to be justified primarily in terms of their benefits to industries and urban populations. For the central route, only 1.7 billion *yuan* out of total benefits of 8.8 billion *yuan* come from improved irrigation, while 6.3 billion *yuan* of benefits are estimated for industrial and urban uses.[25]

Treatment and reuse. Recycling is an option that applies primarily to non-agricultural uses. Domestic sewage can actually be applied to crops after a certain amount of treatment. Before the advent of chemical fertilizer, urban nightsoil was a significant and highly valued source of nutrients for periurban fields. Even today during the dry season, the Daqing ("Big Clean") River that drains the Haidian district of Beijing is in effect an open sewer that has been modified to provide nutrient-rich water for field use after flowing for a number of kilometres.[26] Unfortunately, at present this kind of solution only works where there is little industry, as industrial and domestic sewage systems are not separated. The percentage of urban and industrial wastewater that is treated is still quite low, but may be expected to rise with the installation of new

25. Chiu Zhongen, "Nanshui beidiao zhongxian gongcheng di jingji fenxi" ("Economic analysis of the middle route project for south-north transfer"), in PRC Ministry of Water Resources, *Almanac of China Water Resources 1995*, p. 312.
26. Personal observation.

facilities. In farm areas that rely on water containing industrial waste – such as the suburbs of Taiyuan – such treatment for reuse would improve the quality of crops.

Approaches to a Solution

Water law. The first uniform water code (*shuifa*) was promulgated in 1988 as part of an ongoing effort to rationalize the institutional framework governing China's water. Among its provisions are: (1) the first, tentative formal statement of use priorities: domestic users, both urban and rural, should have first priority, but otherwise "due consideration should be given for all concerned" when developing and using water for agriculture, industry and transportation (Article 14). In water-short regions, however, restrictions should be placed on urban growth and water-using industries and agriculture (Article 14) and water-saving techniques should be used in agriculture (Article 15); (2) the establishment of a "State Council department in charge of water administration" (the Ministry of Water Resources) entrusted with the unified management of the nation's water resources (Article 9); (3) establishment of a water permit system for withdrawals from state projects (Article 32); and (4) allowing the levy of a water resource fee (Article 34).

In practice, water management remains split as before among a number of different agencies, with the Ministry of Urban Construction in particular claiming the right to control urban water uses and the Ministry of Geology in charge of rural groundwater extraction. In the rural areas, there is a ministerial vacuum, and few if any of the provisions of the Water Code (notably, the water permit system or the water resource fee) are applied to agriculture. A proposed revision of the Water Law will attempt once again to unify the oversight of water in the hands of the Ministry of Water Resources. It will be fighting history.

Project management. The nature of management depends on the characteristics of the project. The general rule is that each project is operated under the smallest encompassing administrative unit – e.g. if it supplies more than one county, it is under the prefecture or province; if it only affects fields within a single village (pond, small pump, tubewell), it is in the "collective" sector (these days that can include de facto privatization by "specialized" households). Facilities at the next level up, the township, are in an ambivalently dual state-collective position. Reservoirs and large surface diversions ("irrigation districts") have their own management bureaus that are in the state sector but whose employees depend to a large extent on fee revenue for their income. Problems of revenue generation have tended to create staff morale and turnover problems. As mentioned, project delivery efficiency rates tend to be low, but this is due to some extent to project characteristics (e.g. long delivery lines), and does not reflect overall water-use efficiency. Although the principles of "beneficiary pays" and "use water to maintain water" have been promoted for decades, and water charge collection from agriculture has been common since the mid-1980s, fee levels tend to be set at very low uniform rates by province governments, with no automatic adjustments for inflation. The State Council's "Measures for the Appraisal, Collection, and Management of Water Fees for Water Projects" of 1985 stipulates that agricultural costs be calculated on current costs of delivery alone, with no capital recovery charge. In the economic analysis of the central route of the south-north transfer, this resulted in prospective charges to industry of between four and six times those to agriculture.[27] Collection rates also tend to be lower than for industrial and municipal uses. Hence, given the general level of revenue starvation and the procedures for sharing revenue with supervisory bodies, there is a built-in economic incentive for those projects that can do so (especially reservoirs) to switch from supplying irrigation water to slaking the thirst of the cities.

Gravity-fed surface projects also tend to suffer from problems of unreliability of supply timing, an inability to monitor actual use rates at the field level and a lack of capacity to exclude free riders. Tubewells and pumping stations operate at much higher levels of efficiency, because their management is more localized and sensitive to local conditions, supply is more likely to be on demand, conveyance routes are much shorter (especially for wells), pricing does not fall under provincial regulation (since they are in the collective sector) and costs for electricity or diesel fuel and frequent replacement of equipment create a pressing need to seek greater efficiency. The downside is that prospects for efficiency gains may therefore be much less with local projects.

Table 4 shows the relative importance of different water sources in terms of water supply to agriculture, while Table 5 breaks down effectively irrigated area by source and basin. These show that the regional distribution of different water source types varies considerably. In particular, tubewells are concentrated in the north, and dominate irrigated areas in the Hai, Luan and Liao basins. Southern areas are more reliant on state-managed large surface projects, with less resort to ground water, presumably because of its greater cost and out of concern over land subsidence in delta areas. Hence potential efficiency gains from administrative reforms in water delivery systems may be greater in the water-rich south where they are not as necessary as in the north. If this is so, improvements in water-use efficiency in northern irrigation will have to come in large part from more costly changes in on-field application methods and techniques, changes in cropping structure, or the abandonment of irrigation in marginal areas.

Demand management. A joint study of water resources management carried out by the University of Honolulu's East-West Center and the State Science and Technology Commission of China (SSTC) indicated that, at least as of the mid-1980s, demand management options had a much greater potential than new supply projects in reducing Beijing's

---

27. Chiu Zhongen, "Economic analysis of the middle route project for south-north transfer," p. 314. Nonetheless, water use rates did tend to go down in irrigation after the initiation of water charges. I do not know if anyone has calculated the elasticities, however.

Table 4: **Water Supply by Source – 1985 and 1988**

Water source	Water supplied 1985 billion m³	per cent	Area irrigated 1985 million ha	per cent	Supply 1988 billion m³
Storage	108.3	29.7	14.6	30.4	135.4
Diversion	149.9	41.2	13.5	28.1	175.6
Surface pump	41.2	11.3	9.1	18.9	52.9
Wells	57.6	15.8	8.8	18.4	123.9
Other	7.3	2.0	2.0	4.2	10.8
Total	**364.3**	**100.0**	**47.9**	**100.0**	**498.6**

Note:
  Irrigated area is "effectively irrigated area."
Sources:
  1985: Nickum, *Dams Lies and Other Statistics*, p. 26; 1988: *Almanac of Water Resources 1990*, p. 186. Data in 1988 were not available for Shanghai, Qinghai and Ningxia, but these supplied less than one percent of the national total.

projected demand-supply gap in the year 2000.[28] These included transfers from agriculture, induced by price adjustments as well as administrative fiat. In water-short areas, primary reliance will have to be placed on demand management, including more rational pricing, in the next few decades, after which interbasin transfers may provide some relief. Since Beijing is one of the areas on the hydrological margin, this lesson may be extrapolated to many of the other hot spots. Even where it is necessary to add new supply projects, as in the case of Taiyuan, it is imperative to set the price for new water at a level that at least allows cost recovery.

Water fees. Water charges are almost always below the costs of delivery, especially in the rural areas. One argument against increasing irrigation charges is that farmers cannot afford to pay full cost. The evidence for this is not compelling. A 1988–1989 farm budget survey of households in six projects (all presumably fairly well-operated) for an Asian Development Bank project estimated the total cost of water (fee plus imputed value of labour used in maintaining channels) as varying from 3.0 to 5.5 per cent of the total value of production and from 6.6 to 10.6 per cent of net household returns. Cash cost of water was sometimes much lower, ranging from 0.9 to 3.4 per cent of total value of production.[29] Since then, the price of grain has been increased significantly.
  The real problems with increasing water charges to agriculture tend to lie elsewhere, such as in the political unpalatibility of the idea. Also, despite a long-standing recognition of the economic virtues of volumetric pricing, irrigation charges for surface water tend to remain based on area. This is probably because the administrative and other transaction costs of

28. Described in James E. Nickum, "Beijing's maturing socialist water economy," in James E. Nickum and K. William Easter (eds.), *Metropolitan Water Use Conflicts in Asia and the Pacific* (Boulder, CO: Westview, 1994), pp. 37–60.
  29. Asian Development Bank, "Study on improvement of irrigation management and cost recovery" (TA No. 940) *Guidelines* (Beijing: Ministry of Water Resources, 1989), mimeo.

Table 5: **Effectively Irrigated Area by Source and Basin, 1989 (in 10,000 *mu**)**

Basin	Total	Tubewells	Fixed pumps	Mobile pumps	Reservoirs	Irrigated districts	Cross-sums
Huang	6,550	2,553	1,583	23	1,361	3,898	9,418
Huai	10,994	3,362	4,244	969	3,104	3,554	15,233
Hai	9,278	6,269	1,493	634	1,936	3,675	14,007
Luan	520	349	52	53	58	145	657
Chang	2,062	353	7,544	1,680	8,780	8,497	26,854
Zhu	4,283	7	839	80	1,621	1,462	4,009
Songhua	2,382	812	617	57	400	847	2,733
Liao	1,980	1,124	452	7	765	1,047	3,395
Total	**58,049**	**14,829**	**16,824**	**3,503**	**18,025**	**23,125**	**76,306**

			as a percentage of total effectively irrigated area within basin				
Huang	100%	39%	24%	0%	21%	60%	144%
Huai	100%	31%	39%	9%	28%	32%	139%
Hai	100%	68%	16%	7%	21%	40%	151%
Luan	100%	67%	10%	10%	11%	28%	126%
Chang	100%	2%	34%	8%	40%	39%	122%
Zhu	100%	0%	20%	2%	38%	34%	94%
Songhua	100%	34%	26%	2%	17%	36%	115%
Liao	100%	57%	23%	0%	39%	53%	171%
Total	**100%**	**26%**	**29%**	**6%**	**31%**	**40%**	**131%**

Notes:
* Divide by 1,500 to get million hectares.
Cross-sums exceed 100% for most basins, presumably because some irrigated area is served by more than one source. Total for all basins is less than the national total, as some areas are not in the seven main basins (most importantly, Xinjiang and the south-east coast).
Source:
Almanac of Water Resources 1990, p. 652–55.

monitoring and measuring and collecting water charges volumetrically exceed the benefits at the extremely low rates now allowed. Another problem is that, with the exception of a few new projects, water charge standards are usually set on a uniform basis at the provincial level, ignoring local variation.

Locating Stress

It is possible to use the sub-basin data to assess vulnerability at a relatively refined geographical level. Peter Gleick[30] developed a set of five vulnerability indicators, or "warning lamps," for sub-basins in the U.S. that Liu Chunzhen of the Ministry of Water Resources and I applied to China.[31] Gleick's indicators are: (1) the ratio between reservoir storage and runoff; (2) the ratio between consumptive water demand and water

30. Peter H. Gleick, "Vulnerability of water systems," in P. E. Waggoner (ed.), *Climate Change and U.S. Water Resources* (New York: Wiley, 1990), pp. 223–240.
31. Asian Development Bank, *National Response Strategy for Global Climate Change: People's Republic of China* (1994) TA No. 1690-PRC, pp. 8–1 to 8–15.

supply; (3) the ratio between the runoff with 5 per cent frequency and that with 95 per cent frequency; (4) the ratio between groundwater overdraft and groundwater withdrawal; and (5) the share of total electricity taken by hydroelectricity. Although we had some reservations about applying indicators and critical values based on American conditions to China – in particular, because of the highly seasonal nature of north China's monsoonal rainfall and runoff – the results were quite plausible. At a macrobasin level, the Hai-Luan River basin was the most vulnerable by our measure, followed by the Huai basin. Hot spots along the Huang and Chang rivers did not show up at the higher level of aggregation, however, indicating the value of using a more refined sub-basin unit of analysis.

At a sub-basin level, peninsular Shandong and southern Shanxi provinces proved the most vulnerable to stress of any kind, including economic development. They were followed by the much broader and more significant regions of north-east China, the North China Plain, the coastal regions of the Huang and Bohai seas, the middle and lower reaches of the Huang, Huai and Chang rivers, and the rapidly growing economic areas of coastal south-east China. Most importantly, peninsular Shandong in particular has witnessed quite high rates of economic growth in the past couple of decades. So far, water stress does not appear to have reached a level – even close to the margin of the most stressed – where it has acted as a significant brake on the economy.

Given this and the high potential that remains for water saving if it proves efficient, it would seem that the "water crisis" in China is localized, and is economic and institutional rather than one of a vanishing resource. Further economic growth and accompanying institutional change is more likely to lead to the relief of water stress than to its aggravation.

Appendix

Data sources. Since 1991, the Ministry of Water Resources has published a yearbook in Chinese, *Zhongguo shuili nianjian* (*Almanac of China Water Resources*). The earliest editions, especially *Almanac of China Water Resources 1990* (published in 1991), have quite a lot of useful information, including statistics presented on a basin basis, write-ups of developments in different provinces and river basins, the texts of laws, regulations and important speeches, and papers on topics of current interest (such as the economic analysis of the middle route cited above). More recent editions have been more modest in scope and in the number of statistics they present – *Almanac of China Water Resources 1995* is "only" 450 pages long, compared with the 724 pages of *Almanac of China Water Resources 1990* – of which 27 pages are tables of statistics, down considerably from the 86 pages of its predecessor. The monthly MWR journal, *Zhongguo shuili* (*Chinese Water Resources*), is a good source for policy-related information, but not statistics.

Environmental Issues and the South-North Water Transfer Scheme

Liu Changming*

Water Deficits on the North China Plain

China has good resources of land and water. The problem is that they are often not in the same place. The south, which is water-rich, is too hilly for extensive farming. The North China Plain is flat, like France or the Ukraine, but lacks water. It produces 27 per cent of China's grain, but at the cost of serious stresses on its water resource. Deficits in the surface water supply have led to intensified use of the groundwater well beyond the "safe yield" where recharge balances withdrawal. Hence the water table has fallen greatly under both rural and urban areas ever since electric- or diesel-powered tubewells became widespread in the early 1970s. In addition to increased pumping costs and the need to bore ever deeper wells, consequences have included land subsidence, compressing the emptied aquifer in a number of areas and salt water intrusion in coastal areas.

In addition, areas in the lower reaches of the Huang (Yellow) River that have relied on diversions of its water for irrigation have suffered from increasingly long cut-offs in the river's flow as more and more water is used upstream.[1] In 1997, a record year, the Huang failed to flow to the sea for 226 days, with the dry stretch reaching roughly 700 kilometres inland.

Water shortages affect more than crops. Pollutants from farm runoff and other sources remain highly concentrated when there is little water available to dilute them. Many people in north China drink water that is polluted by organics, minerals or nitrates. One solution to the problem of localized shortages is to transfer water from another basin. Many inter-basin diversion projects were undertaken in China prior to 1949, but for the most part these were on a rather small scale. Since the founding of the People's Republic a number of major inter-basin transfers have been developed to meet the requirements of economic development, especially those resulting from urbanization (see Table 1). Currently a number of very large transfers are being considered or developed from the Chang

* This study is supported by a key project of the Chinese Academy of Sciences, 1997–2000. I would also like to thank James E. Nickum, Robert F. Ash and Richard Louis Edmonds for their comments and suggestions.

1. Yang Chaofei, "Huanghe duanliu di shengtai sikao" ("Ecological considerations of water stoppages in the Huang River"), in Yang Chaofei *et al.* (eds.), *Huanghe duanliu yu liuyu kechixu fazhan* (*Water Stoppages in the Yellow River and Sustainable Development in the Basin*) (Beijing: Huanjing kexue chubanshe, 1997), pp. 1–9.

(Yangtze) River into the North China Plain. These are collectively known as the south-north water transfer schemes, and will be described below.

Inter-basin water transfers have mixed impacts on the natural environment. In one sense, the primary goal of south-north transfer is precisely to improve the environment in the receiving basin by providing it with a stable source of water. Yet negative environmental impacts are foreseeable. These may be very costly, but they are hard to measure in monetary terms or to anticipate with absolute certainty. To a very large extent, the success of south-north transfers will depend on the balance of environmental effects which will fall on the water-exporting region, the water-transfer region, and the water-importing region, and will result from the physical, chemical, biological and socio-economic systems.

Routes for the South-North Water Transfers

Three general routes of south-north transfer schemes are currently under consideration, depending on which part of the Chang River system the water is diverted from: the east (in Jiangsu), the centre (in Hubei) or the west (in Qinghai). The middle route, now given priority, would transfer water from the Danjiangkou Reservoir on the Han River – a large tributary of middle reaches of the Chang – to supply Hubei, Henan, Hebei and ultimately Beijing and Tianjin, as well as the western part of the North China Plain along the way.[2] In the long run, it may be necessary to divert additional water from the Sanxia (Three Gorges) Dam on the Chang River to the Danjiangkou Reservoir to meet the large water demands from the northern provinces.

The middle route. The conveyance canal of the middle route would begin at the Taocha water intake being built at the Danjiangkou Reservoir. It would then follow the southern and western edge of the Funiu and Taihang Mountains, and would terminate in Beijing's Yuyuantan Lake (see Figure 1). In order to supply water to Tianjin, a canal would have to be constructed extending eastward from Xushui county in Hebei province across the Hai River Plain.

The water source of the middle route, the Danjiangkou Reservoir, has an annual natural inflow of 41.1 billion cubic metres from a drainage area of 95,217 square kilometres. First-stage engineering works, which involve the construction of the 162-metre Danjiangkou dam with a total storage capacity of 17.45 billion cubic metres, have been completed. The second-stage engineering works, which have been approved, would raise the dam to 176.6 metres in order to increase the total storage capacity to 29.1 billion cubic metres.

Supplemental water may be pumped up to Danjiangkou from the

---

2. Yao Bangyi and Chen Qinglian, "South-to-north water transfer project plans," in Asit K. Biswas, Zuo Dakang, James E. Nickum and Liu Changming (eds.), *Long-Distance Water Transfer: A Chinese Case Study and International Experiences* (Dublin: Tycooly, 1983), pp. 127–150.

Table 1: **Main Water Transfer Works Built in China Since 1949**

Project name	Length of main canal (km)	Energy source	Annual diversion (billion m³)	Province or municipality	Exporting region	Importing region	Objective	Year of Completion
Luan River diversion	286	Gravity	19.50	North China	Luan River	Beijing-Tianjin-Tangshan	Urban water supply	1984
Huang-Qingdao diversion	262	Pump	6.85	Shandong	lower reaches of Huang River	Qingdao	Urban water supply	1990
Qinglong-Qinhuangdao diversion	63	Gravity	1.67	Hebei	Qinglong River	Qinhuangdao	Urban water supply	1991
Biliu-Dalian diversion	150	Pump	1.30	Liaoning	Biliu River	Dalian	Urban water supply	1995
Datong-Qinwangchuan diverson	70	Gravity	4.43	Gansu	Datong River	Qinwangchuan	Industry	1994
South-North transfer	400	Pump	41.00	Jiangsu	lower reaches of the Chang River	Northern Jiangsu	Industry and agriculture	1962
Dong-Shenzhen	83	Pump	6.20	Guangdong	Dong River	Shenzhen, Hong Kong	Urban water supply	1965

Source:
Liu Changming and He Xiwu (eds.), Zhongguo 21 shiji shui wenti fanglüe (Strategies for China's Water Problems in the 21st Century) (Beijing: Kexue chubanshe, 1996), p. 171.

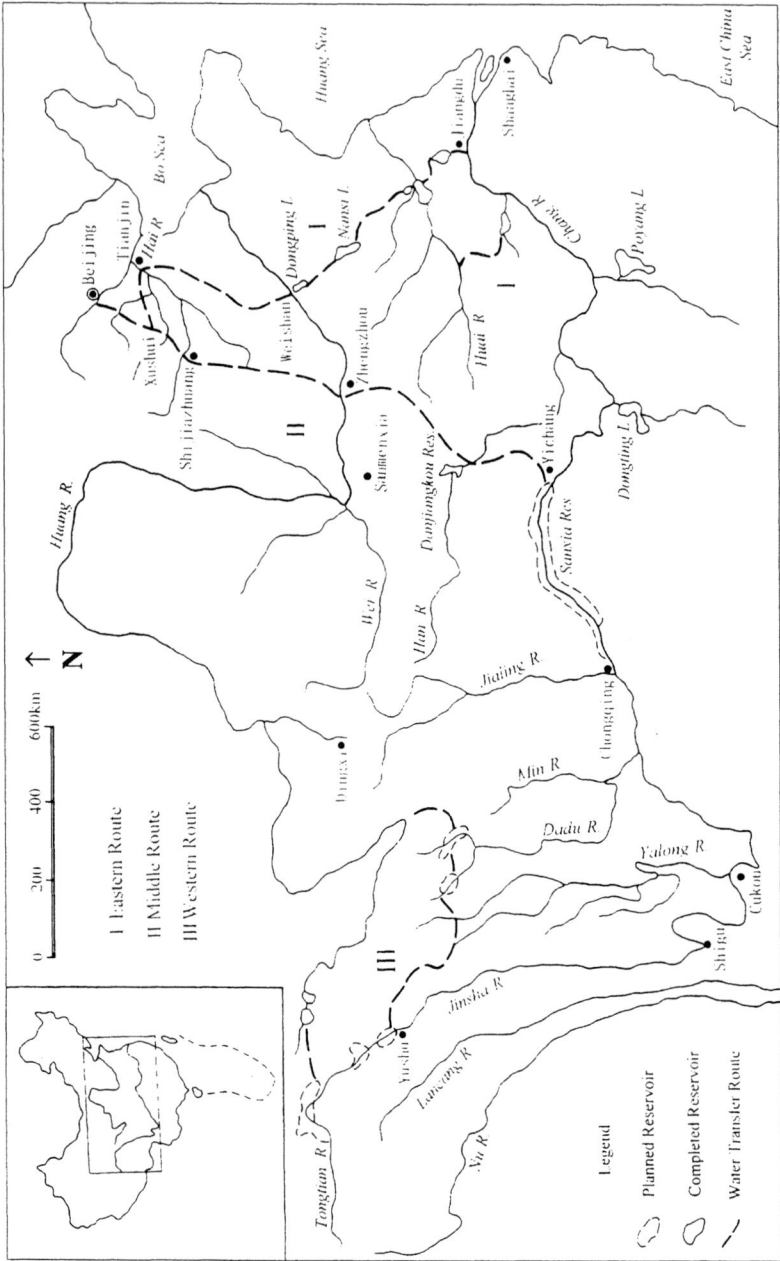

Figure 1: **Proposed Routes for the South-North Water Transfers**

reservoir created by the Sanxia Dam or from downstream Shashi. This water would flow "uphill" along the Han River into the Danjiangkou Reservoir, from which it would enter the main canal of the middle route. An alternative plan is to pump water diverted from the Han River at Xiangfan into a tributary, the Tangbai River, and then along the Bai River into the main canal. The main portion of the middle route is now at the primary design stage, with implementation likely to start in the near future.

The eastern route. The once-favoured eastern route would commence with the diversion of water from the main course of the lower Chang River at Sanjiangying in Jiangsu. Water would be diverted for use in Jiangsu, Shandong, Hebei, Tianjin and areas in the Huai River Basin located between the Bengbu Water Gate and the banks of the Xinbian River. The route would pass through four lakes: the Hongze, Luoma, Nansi and Dongping. The water would then be pumped through tunnels under the Huang River at Weishan, and flow mainly along the reaches of the Grand Canal (the Weilin, Wei and South canals), finally reaching the Beidagang Reservoir south of Tianjin (see Figure 1). In March 1983, the State Council approved the first stage of the construction of the eastern route of the south-north water transfer scheme. Further progress has been suspended due to a conflict of interest between Jiangsu and Shandong provinces. In particular, Jiangsu strongly pushed to keep more of the diverted water than it was allocated under a plan approved by the State Council.

In early 1962, before the eastern route was planned, Jiangsu built the Jiangdu Pumping Station to divert water from the lower Chang River to the province's north using the Grand Canal to send water as far as Xuzhou and the south Nansi Lake. The Jiangdu station can pump up to about 400 cubic metres per second, and would be a key structure in the eastern route transfer project. In addition, an experimental tunnel under the Huang River has been completed in Shandong. Because of these structures, some people think that the eastern route is much easier to construct than others. But poor water quality is a significant drawback, as are the large amounts of electricity necessary to pump water to the higher elevations north of the Chang River.

The western route. The western route would transfer water from the upper reaches of the Chang to the upper reaches of the Huang to provide water to north-western China.[3] The Huang River Basin Commission has been surveying possible western routes in co-operation with the Chinese Academy of Sciences since the 1950s. The investigation covered more than 600,000 square kilometres in Qinghai, Gansu, Sichuan and Yunnan that would be adjacent to a western route. Fifty lines for channelling water were investigated. A western route would be very ambitious,

3. Chen Xiande, "Water transfer along the western route," *Chinese Environment and Development*, Vol. 5, No. 2 (1994), pp. 75–85.

requiring the construction of 50,000 kilometres of canals with a diversion of 500 billion cubic metres of water from the big south-western river basins. Since the 1970s, the Commission has focused on some shorter lines, some relying on gravity and some on pumps, with a lower magnitude of diverted water (22.1 billion cubic metres) and smaller coverage of 168,000 square kilometres (see Figure 1). Feasibility studies of the western route are still being conducted. Considering the engineering uncertainties of the complex geological conditions and the very high cost of construction, a western route is unlikely to be realized before the middle of the 21st century.

The three south-north water transfer routes do not conflict with each other in the sense that they serve different areas and provide commensurately diverse benefits. The conflict lies in funding priority. For instance, the middle route can supply higher quality water to the north by gravity, while the eastern route can bring lower quality water to the large industrialized cities of Tianjin and Beijing by pumping. Yet the construction cost of the former is higher than that of the latter, since the eastern route can make use of the existing Grand Canal. An evaluation committee established under the State Council in 1995 to review the projects concluded in March 1998 that the middle route should have priority. Implementation of this recommendation must now be approved formally by the National People's Congress.

Environmental Issues and Assessment

Numerous and diverse environmental problems may arise from the diversion project. Hence decision-making requires an integrated, systematic approach that takes into account both the environment and the economic development of regions affected by it. These regions can be divided into three, according to the natural, economic and supply-demand conditions of water: the exporting region, the transfer region and the importing region.

The water-exporting region of the lower Chang River, one of China's most highly developed economic areas, would not benefit from a transfer, but may experience negative environmental impacts such as sea water intrusion. These may be mitigated using engineering and regulatory measures. Ge Weiya *et al* have estimated that the eastern route would not do appreciable damage to either the water resources of the Chang River or to the socio-economic development of the lower Chang.[4]

The transfer region south of the Huang River has experienced rapid economic development in recent years, but suffers from water shortages. Water transfer would promote the development of agriculture and industry here. In 1983, the Huai River Water Conservancy Commission

4. Ge Weiya, Luo Xueqi and Tang Peiwen, "Changjiang kualiuyu gongshui di shui ziyuan chubu fenxi pingjia" ("Assessment of the Water Resources Supplied by the Chang River in Inter-basin Transfers"), *Dili yanjiu* (*Geographical Research*), Vol. 2, No. 3 (1983), pp. 87–95.

proposed adopting the principle of "simultaneously using the water resources of the Chang River and the Huai River, taking into account both north and south, completing the scheme in phases, and getting connected first but clearing away the obstacles afterward." Following this principle, the first phase of the eastern route scheme would benefit this region without any severe negative impact on the environment initially except for possible additional damage during a high flood.

Many important cities, including Beijing and Tianjin, and numerous medium- to large-sized industrial and mining enterprises are located in the water-importing region north of the Huang River. Water shortages are restricting agricultural production and industrial development here, with severe problems such as seasonal flow stoppages in the rivers, sedimentation of estuaries, and the extension of cones of depression of groundwater aquifers. Yet while it is necessary to extend the eastern route north of the Huang River to solve the severe water deficit problem, every effort must be made to prevent a negative impact on the environment along the way, especially in lower-lying sections. The south-north water transfer scheme can yield important environmental benefits, such as improving the channel of the lower Huang River, enhancing the micro-climates of irrigated areas, ameliorating land subsidence and groundwater depletion, and replacing the poisonously fluoridated water that is now the only water available to many in southern Hebei province.

On the other hand, where the conveyance canals pass by the discharge gates of water storage facilities, and in poorly drained areas where there is a high water table, they may cause a rise in the aquifer leading to secondary salinization of the soil. The project may also have an adverse effect on fish and other aquatic life in ponds and lakes along the routes. Polluted sewage water may enter the conveyance canals as they flow northward, especially along the eastern route. Declines in flow to the estuary of the Chang River may result in salt water intrusion, affecting delta fisheries at the mouth, urban water supply and the intake to the eastern route itself.

Engineers and other researchers have suggested a number of proposals to mitigate these effects. For instance, diversion along the eastern route can be stopped when the discharge at Datong Station on the lower Chang River falls below a critical level, estimated at about 8,000 cubic metres per second, to prevent seawater intrusion. Seepage prevention measures such as lining the conveyance channel and digging drainage canals can reduce salinization. Other mitigating measures include planting forest belts, using wells and surface flows conjunctively for irrigation, regulating lake levels and treating local sewage discharges.

In general, the uncertainty of the environmental impacts of a water transfer project is in direct proportion to its scale. Therefore, from an environmental point of view, impacts may be reduced by cutting back on the size of a project. Limiting demand through water-saving measures is therefore highly advisable, and this is happening. For example, in 1995 the total output value of Beijing rose by 14.5 per cent, while water withdrawal fell by about 66 million cubic metres.

Estimating the impact of water transfer on the environment requires direct surveys, observations and experimental data. Resorting to ideas from abroad or from the past may lead to fallacious results, due to the specific nature of the contemporary natural, social and economic conditions of the areas affected. For example, in the 1980s, concern over environmental impacts of the south-north water transfer scheme focused on snail migration and soil salinization on the North China Plain. The concern over mollusc-borne schistosomiasis came from the experiences of Egypt and Pakistan; and concern about soil salinity derived from the experience of poorly-considered diversions during the early 1960s. Recent surveys and detailed experiments have concluded that neither of these problems is likely to occur with the proposed transfer. In the case of the snails, there seems to be a northern limit to their migration, and there is no evidence that they have overstepped that limit along the existing Grand Canal. As for soil salinization, the natural conditions of the water-transfer regions and technologies have changed considerably over the past three decades. With improvements in the structures for flood protection in the Huang, Hai and Huai river basins have come a higher drainage capacity from fields and in-channels. The digging of more than 1.6 million powered tubewells in these plains has resulted in a fall in the groundwater table. This has its own problems, but it does remove a precondition for salt accumulation, which is caused by evaporation from high water tables (e.g. within 3 metres of the surface). Farmers have improved the soil as they have applied conservation measures. With new sources of salinization held in check, about two-thirds of previously saline soils have been restored in the downstream areas of the three river systems. Future water transfers are unlikely to reverse this positive trend.

A large-scale inter-basin water transfer would certainly change the environment by altering hydrological processes and changing entire ecologies. On balance, however, it would probably lead to a net improvement by smoothing out the natural distribution of water both spatially and temporally. In particular, the area to the north of latitude 30° N is characterized by having a potential evapotranspiration rate that exceeds precipitation. In other words, most rainfall and much of the water stored in reservoirs goes straight up into the air. Only a small proportion goes into the rivers to form runoff, or seeps into the groundwater aquifers. Hence a transfer of flow from a hydrologically-surplus area can have a significant positive ecological impact as well as environmental impact.

Several aspects of the water transfer project deserve further study. For a start, water resources are seen as property providing benefits to regional economic development. Thus, an inter-basin water transfer implies a transfer of an economic resource from the exporting to the importing region, leading to a conflict of interest between the two. After the State Council approved commencement of the eastern route in early 1983, the project was suspended because of impasses in negotiations between Jiangsu and the northern provinces and municipalities of Shandong, Hebei, Beijing and Tianjin. Naturally the water-importing region favours transfer projects, both for economic reasons and as a matter of inter-regional equity. Yet in some cases at least, the water is not absolutely surplus in the exporting region. In particular, it is thought that for the middle route project, diverting water from the middle and lower reaches of the Han River will reduce the amount left for irrigation and navigation. In this case, the exporting region is seeking compensation.

On the other side, the diverted water may not be very clean, especially by the time it reaches its final destination. The middle route project will transfer 14.5 billion cubic metres of clean water annually, but after flowing through several cities, this is likely to create billions of cubic metres of wastewater that will have to be treated at high cost before it can be reused by those around the route in Beijing and Tianjin.

A big part of the problem is that charges remain too low for either raw water or for sewage treatment, even though cost analyses suggest that water treatment is less costly to address than water shortage. Water fees in most places in China are collected without any sewerage charges and at a rate that does not even cover delivery and operating costs. For example, the actual water cost for Handan in Hebei is calculated to be about 6 *yuan* per cubic metre, but the price charged is only one-tenth that, 0.6 *yuan*. As a result, local water demands are increasing without any connection to economic realities. This policy provides neither economical benefits nor environmental protection in the affected areas.

Institutional Implications

The Ministry of Water Resources builds projects on large rivers and manages them through seven river commissions. There is no adequate management system set up to co-ordinate regional water conflicts, how-ever. Therefore, management of an inter-basin water transfer project has to rely heavily on the central government. The south-north water transfer scheme in particular requires a high level of central involvement. Inter-regional water development and management were difficult enough before the devolution of power to local authorities in the 1980s, but those reforms have made it even more difficult to resolve provincial conflicts of interest. In the past, the costs of an infrastructure such as a large water transfer project would be borne by the central government, but more recent financial rules require co-financing by local bodies. As currently planned, 40 per cent of the total investment funding for the middle route would come from provincial governments, considerably attenuating one of the main forms of leverage in the hands of the central government. Even more foreboding, the financial responsibility for maintenance and operation of the projects remains uncertain.

Many experts have concluded that it would be best to adopt a highly unified management system for the south-north water transfer scheme. Nonetheless, this approach would result in major difficulties and is moving against the trend of reform. In this instance, it may be helpful to adopt some experiences from abroad. For instance, the introduction of participatory management has already led to more effective management.

One area that desperately needs to be addressed is how to allocate benefits and costs. These problems were often ignored in the past because large-scale water projects were mainly funded by the central budget. Although economic cost-benefit analysis has been carried out, it cannot solve all the problems. It is estimated that the benefit-cost ratio of the central route would be about 1.4 – in other words, total benefits would be nearly half as great again as total costs. The problem is that it is the water-importing regions that reap the benefits and the exporting and transfer regions that bear the costs. For example, the heightening of the Danjiangkou Reservoir will require the costly resettlement of about 224,000 people and reconstruction of navigation channels on the lower Han River. The direct cost of the middle route project is estimated at about 55 billion *yuan*, not counting indirect losses to the environment, which are not calculated. Clearly, the water-importing region should bear much or all of these costs, but there is no mechanism at present for doing this.

The water transfer projects will adopt the policy provided in China's Water Law requiring all users to pay the supply authority for water delivered. The fees are to be set according to the regulations of the State Council, taking into account project depreciation, maintenance, management and operation. Although these estimates will be calculated according to the rules of the market, water in China is still not an market enterprise. Critical issues are: how to recover full costs to allow self-financed management and operation of the project; how to ensure financial sustainability of the project finance as it is being constructed; and how to prevent the project from becoming an economic burden on the state.[5] These are difficult questions, and ones that have not been resolved in the management of water-conservancy projects completed to date. It is generally felt that new projects should not follow the old path of unceasingly begging for public funds.

The resolution of these problems requires a project's management and operation systems to devise effective financial recovery methods. They also demand that the state formulate corresponding near-term policies to serve as a guarantor to external funders, but with a realistic view of the condition of the country's economic capacity. If the state fails to deliver, it will have to pick up the economic baggage it has attempted to discard.[6]

Large-scale water-transfers differ from other hydraulic engineering projects – such as reservoirs and water gates – because of their scale. Inter-basin water transfer projects will always cross many administrative geographical units with widely differing interests. The south-north water transfer scheme would cross four large river basins. It is critical, therefore, to develop a systematic framework for creating a powerful authority to co-ordinate and manage the project in its entirety in an environmen-

5. Chen Chunhuai, "Major characteristics and problems of the south-to-north water-transfer," *Chinese Environment and Development*, Vol. 5, No. 2 (1994), pp. 20–41.
6. *Ibid*.

tally sound way. It will also be necessary to develop and apply appropriate techniques and equipment to manage the system, to allocate water according to market principles, and to involve stakeholders such as the community in management.

The Way Forward

Water use in China will continue to increase well into the 21st century, raising important questions as to its sustainability.[7] The south-north water transfer scheme has been under intense consideration for more than 40 years. The Chinese government has paid increasing attention to the project since the late 1970s and especially since 1993, because of rapid economic growth and frequent drought. Nonetheless, the south-north water transfer scheme has not been given a fully-fledged go-ahead due to uncertainty about its environmental impacts and a lack of funds.

The necessity of a water transfer project must be determined by carefully analysing the characteristics of the water shortage in the prospective importing region. Does the shortage result largely from a lack of resource or from inappropriate use of local water? We should identify characteristics of the water shortage and determine how to meet socio-economic demands in both the short- and long-term, as well as carefully analyse the regional balance of water supply and demand. A prerequisite for implementing any water transfer must be a plan that includes water-saving measures since, in most cases, imported water is only supplemental to local supplies. In addition, a feasibility analysis must determine whether the water-exporting region has a surplus available, and address the inevitable conflicts of interest between the exporting and importing regions. If the project has a significant influence on water users and their environment in the exporting region, appropriate compensation must be paid.

South-north water transfers should be seen as the principal means for reallocating China's unevenly distributed water resources, designed to solve water shortage problems in the northern metropolitan areas, where water demands exceed the capacity of local resources. Therefore, the goal of the projects is mainly to supply water to urban areas and industry. Farm irrigation and environmental improvement are secondary considerations.

Water is one of the most important environmental factors for human survival. At the same time it is also associated with natural disasters such as flooding, water-logging and drought. Human activities can benefit from water but they can also pollute it and create their own disasters. The harmonization of development and environment is no more resolved in China than anywhere else on this water planet. The evidence is that more

---

7. Asit K. Biswas, " A global perspective: water for sustainable development in the twenty-first century," in Asit K. Biswas *et al.* (eds.), *Water for Sustainable Development in the Twenty-First Century* (Delhi: Oxford University Press, 1993), pp. 7–17.

attention is given to building new water projects than to considering their subsequent management or their effects on the environment.

From a scientific point of view, the south-north water transfer scheme is likely to be environmentally-sound. Those problems that remain can be solved through inter-disciplinary research. Nonetheless, the current situation is worrying, as many of the difficult problems are not being given the attention they require.[8] Solutions can be found to the difficult problems, but only if the unrealistic optimism that pervades present decision-making is cast off. In particular, a careful and well-considered environmental impact assessment remains an undone prerequisite to the implementation of the south-north water transfer scheme.

In the waning hours of the 20th century, China's water shortage problems cannot be resolved by relying on a south-north water transfer scheme. A number of other methods are available that can mitigate matters, in particular water conservation. Water-saving should be understood in the broadest sense, including a wide range of methods to increase efficiency in urban areas, industry and agriculture. These include making greater use of sea water where possible in the coastal industrial cities; using brackish and other low quality water for purposes that do not necessitate pristine water; developing rainwater harvesting; enhancing weather modification capacities; developing high efficiency water-saving technologies such as sprinkler irrigation and water recycling; and improving conservation management. Use of these techniques could save 100 billion cubic metres of water or more each year, far more than any proposed transfer.[9]

8. Chen Chunhuai, "Major characteristics and problems of the south-to-north water-transfer," pp. 20–41.

9. Liu Changming and He Xiwu, *Zhongguo 21 shiji shui wenti fanglüe* (*Strategies for China's Water Problems in the 21st Century*) (Beijing: Kexue chubanshe, 1996), pp. 60–70.

Recent Trends in Forestry and Conservation of Biodiversity in China

James Harkness

Despite the transformative effects of millennia of human occupation, China remains a tremendous storehouse of biological diversity. The extremely mountainous terrain has fostered speciation by continuously isolating populations of plants and animals. This topography (combined with the large area of the country that is sub-tropical and tropical) also provided refuge for many taxonomic groups during the major climate change-induced mass extinctions of the Pleistocene era, as well as the more recent Ice Ages. As a result, China is one of the world's major centres of biological diversity (or biodiversity), a term which refers to the variety of ecosystem types, the number of different of species and the genetic variability within a single species. In certain respects, thousands of years of human habitation has actually enhanced this diversity. Rice, soybeans, oranges, tea and many other crops were first domesticated in China, and generation upon generation of careful selection by farmers and pastoralists have made it one the earth's richest centres of crop and domesticated animal germplasm.[1] The country's variety of wild plants and animals is greater than that of either North America or Europe, and equal to one-eighth of all species on earth.[2]

The value of this diversity of life forms to Chinese civilization throughout its history is incalculable. Plants and animals have been used for food, medicines, fuel, fibre and construction materials. The spiritual and aesthetic value of natural areas, especially sacred mountains or groves, has long been the subject of religion, art and poetry, and finds its contemporary expression in the growing domestic nature tourism market and the popularity of zoos and wildlife programmes on television. Often overlooked, however, are the "ecosystem services" provided by diverse natural communities, such as moderation of climate, absorption of pollutants and regulation of carbon, nutrient, and hydrologic cycles which are vital to human existence. The value of these functions is generally much greater than any use value that could be derived from direct consumption. China's forested uplands, for example, provide vitally important watershed protection to the country's lowland river valleys by absorbing rainfall and slowing the rate of runoff, preventing soil erosion and reducing the severity of both flood and drought, so as to make possible the country's intensive irrigated agriculture system. A recent study by Kong *et al* found that the annual added value of water and soil conservation, air purification, acid rain buffering and other functions in three forest areas was between two and ten times the gross output value of

1. National Environmental Protection Agency (NEPA), *China Country Study on Biological Diversity* (draft) (Beijing: NEPA, 12 June 1996), pp. 108–117.
2. Peter Raven, "Biodiversity and the future of China," *Pacific Science Association Information Bulletin*, Vol. 47, Nos. 1–2 (1995), pp. 1–8.

timber, wood processing and orchard production.[3] At a national level, it has been estimated that the economic value of the water storage role of China's forests is 7.5 trillion *yuan*, which is three times the value of all of the wood in those forests.[4]

Forests are the most important ecosystems in China, in terms of the sheer diversity of species they harbour and the essential goods and ecosystem services they supply. Conservation in China began with protection of forests, for good reason. Long before the concept of biological diversity came into use, China's forests were valued for their provision of raw materials for industry and role in soil and water conservation. Forests also provide 40 per cent of the fuel for rural households.[5] For these reasons, Richardson calls China the most forest-dependent civilization in the world.[6] Forests also have the richest array of species of any natural system, and China has a remarkable variety of different forest types, boasting over 2,800 tree species, a large number of other plants and the majority of the country's wildlife species.[7] However, the ecological and economic importance of Chinese forests is matched by their scarcity: forest volume per capita is one-eighth of the global average, and forests only cover 14 per cent of China's territory, compared to an international average of 34 per cent.[8]

Indeed, China's forests and biodiversity have long been under threat, both from direct uses such as logging and hunting, and from the conversion of natural habitats such as forests or grasslands to farm fields and human settlements. Forest degradation has been a concern since early imperial times,[9] and at least eight large mammal species are thought to have been extirpated in this century alone.[10] The first national nature reserve was not founded until 1956, and systematic efforts to catalogue and preserve biodiversity only began in the 1980s. In addition to being

---

3. Kong Fanwen, Dai Guangcui, Gao Lan and He Naihui, "Forest environment resource accounting and economic compensation policy," *Forestry Economics*, Vol. 1, No. 1 (1996), pp. 32–44.

4. Zhao Yining and Huangpu Pingli, "Yi ke shu ye buneng zaikanle" ("Don't even cut one more tree"), *Liaowang xinwen zhoukan* (*Outlook Weekly*), No. 18 (1998), p. 23.

5. Ministry of Forestry, Afforestation and Forest Management Section and China Forestry Association (eds.), *Quanguo xinchailin yantaohui wenji* (*Proceedings of the National Fuelwood Forest Symposium*) (Beijing: Zhongguo linye chubanshe, 1995), p. 3.

6. S. D. Richardson, *Forests and Forestry in China* (Washington, DC: Island Press, 1990), p. 14.

7. Qu Geping and Li Jinchang, *China Population and Environment* (Boulder, CO: Lynne Rienne, 1994), p. 58.

8. *Ibid.* p. 58; Zhao Yining and Huangpu Pingli, "Don't even cut one more tree," p. 23.

9. A scholarly work of the second century B.C. deplores over-harvesting and includes proposals for rational management of forests. Nicholas K. Menzies, *Forest and Land Management in Imperial China* (New York: St. Martin's Press, 1994), p. 33.

10. These include the small one-horned rhinocerous (*Rhinocerous inermis*), white-lipped macaque (*Pygathrix nenaeus*) and Xinjiang tiger (*Panthera tigris lecoqi*). The authors also include a list of 33 large mammals that they believe will become extinct during the next century. Yu Changqing and Xing Lin, "Wo guo binwei shoulei xianzhuang ji baohu duice" ("Status and conservation strategy of endangered mammals in China"), in Biodiversity Committee, Chinese Academy of Sciences and Department for Wildlife and Forest Plant Protection, Ministry of Forestry (eds.), *Shengwu duoyangxing jinzhan* (*Advances in Biodiversity Research*) (Beijing: Chinese Sciences and Technology Press, 1995), pp. 172–78.

the world's most populous country, China has for the past decade had the fastest growing economy, and the combination of these two factors has taken an increasing toll on the country's wild animals and plants. The purpose of this paper is to provide a review of the problems of forest management and biodiversity conservation in China in the late 1990s, and to assess the outlook for forests and conservation in the next century. While the principal mechanism for conservation has been the establishment of nature reserves, the entire reserve system covers less than 7 per cent of China's territory.[11] The paper therefore deals not only with this system, but also with the biodiversity implications of state and collective forest management outside protected areas. Although the large increase in resource consumption over the past two decades has clearly been an important source of pressure on the natural environment, this paper finds that threats to biodiversity in China have other, uniquely Chinese characteristics growing out of the legacy of Maoist development policies and the contradictions of conservation, marketization and decentralization in the post-Mao period.

Forests and Biodiversity Before 1976

Under Mao, resources including forests and biodiversity were treated as free goods: they had no economic value as no human labour was involved in their production. The Ministry of Forestry was organized and run principally as a supplier of raw materials for industry, rather like the ministries of coal and mining, and not as the manager of a limited but renewable resource. This led to tremendous over-exploitation with scant attention to re-planting, even in periods of relative stability. Procurement prices were set at a very low, fixed rate, which led to constant overcutting, shortages and waste at all levels of the system. Ambitious tree-planting goals were set annually, but afforestation was carried out principally through mass-mobilization style campaigns, and survival rates were low.[12] Landmark studies of forestry in socialist China by Richardson (1990) and Ross (1980) document the problems of the forestry sector during this period in some detail.[13]

While some problems inherent in the structure of the forestry system were similar to those which troubled Soviet forestry, political campaigns and policy shifts led to major episodes of deforestation with distinctly Chinese attributes. During the Great Leap Forward, huge areas were logged to fuel backyard steel smelters and build communal mess halls. In the late 1960s and early 1970s, campaigns for local self-sufficiency in

11. The figure was 6% as of 1993. John Mackinnon, Meng Sha, Catherine Cheung, Geoff Carey, Zhu Xiang and David Melville, *A Biodiversity Review of China* (Hong Kong: WWF International China Programme, 1996), p. 23.

12. Vaclav Smil, *China's Environmental Crisis: An Inquiry into the Limits of National Development* (Armonk, NY: M. E. Sharpe, 1993), pp. 59–60; Richardson, *Forests and Forestry in China*, p. 95.

13. Richardson, *Forests and Forestry in China*; Lester Ross, *Forest Policy in China* (unpublished PhD dissertation, Department of Political Science, University of Michigan, 1980).

grain led to large-scale deforestation of sloping lands for cultivation of corn and wheat. Newly reclaimed areas were more often than not abandoned after a few years due to pests, erosion and declining yields.[14] Finally, when the Household Production Responsibility System was first extended to forest land in the early 1980s, many farmers – fearful that the land use policy might change again at any time – responded by immediately felling all of the trees on their contracted land. These episodes are referred to by farmers as the *san da fa* or Three Big Cuttings.

The country's modern nature reserve system dates from 1956, when scientists made the following appeal at the Third National People's Congress: "It is hoped that the government will designate specific areas in all provinces (regions) where the felling of trees is prohibited in the interest of conservation of natural plant life and scientific research."[15] In October of that year, the Ministry of Forestry issued the "Draft Plan for the Designation of Areas for National Forestry Reserve," and over the next nine years, a total of 19 reserves were set up, covering 650,000 hectares.[16] Virtually no further expansion of protected areas occurred during the Cultural Revolution decade (1966–1976), and the conservation of biodiversity did not regain prominence until the 1980s.

Contradictions of the Post-Mao Era

Since the late 1970s, forestry and environmental conservation in China have been characterized by two diametrically opposed trends. On one hand, rapid economic growth has greatly exacerbated human pressures on natural systems. On the other hand, there has been renewed concern for forest protection and biodiversity conservation activities.

Unprecedented economic growth has entailed large increases in the absolute demand for natural resources of all kinds over the past two decades. Consumption of timber increased rapidly during the early reform period, including a dramatic rise in average annual consumption from 196 million cubic metres between 1973 and 1976 to 344 million cubic metres between 1982 and 1988.[17] Increases in the wildlife trade were even more spectacular. The number of leopard pelts sold in Yunnan rose from

14. Zuo Ting, "Forest structure change in Yunnan, China, since the 1950s: two villages investigation" (unpublished paper, Yunnan Academy of Social Sciences, December 1994).
15. Quoted in Wildlife and Forest Plants Protection Department, Ministry of Forestry, *China's National Nature Reserves* (Beijing: Arts and Photography Publishing House, 1994), p. 11. Conservation of biodiversity in modern China has largely been confined to the establishment and management of protected areas. The extent and effectiveness of efforts outside of protected areas has been very limited. There is a list of protected species, but monitoring of hunting and the wildlife trade is weak. A survey of two market towns in Yunnan found 21 protected wildlife species for sale. (See Zhao Qikun, Ma Shilai, Ma Xiaofeng, Zhu Jianguo and Ji Weizhi, "Wildlife in the frontier markets at the tri-border region in Yunnan" (unpublished paper, Kunming Institute of Zoology, 1997).)
16. Mackinnon, *et al. A Biodiversity Review of China*, p. 23.
17. Li Jinchang, Kong Fanwen, Ren Yong, Wang Xin and Feng Dongfang, *Yuanmu dingjia ji ziyuan hesuan chubu yanjiu (Initial Study on Log-Pricing and Forest Resources Accounting)* (Beijing: Policy Research Centre for Environment and Economy, NEPA, 1995) (Chinese and English).

between 5,000 and 10,000 in the 1970s to 80,000 in 1988. An illegal shipment of 700 kilograms of Chinese musk, which is extracted from the scent glands of the musk deer (*Moschus moschiferous*), was seized in Japan in 1987, an amount corresponding to 100,000 animals killed.[18]

The change in consumption has not simply been a quantitative one, however. The removal of state monopolies and the ascendancy of increasingly sophisticated markets have also brought a qualitative change – a diversification of resource exploitation and consumption. Restaurants in Guangzhou now serve wild herbs gathered on the high plains of Qinghai, children in Xishuangbanna catch endangered butterflies to sell to tourists, and the homes of Beijing's new middle class may have bamboo-tiled floors and furniture made from south China hardwoods. In short, economic growth and the re-commodification of the natural world since 1978 have greatly increased and diversified the pressures on forests and wild plant and animal populations.

Opposing, and in fact preceding this trend has been a re-emergence of environmental concern in China. This began in the early 1970s, although little was done in the area of biodiversity conservation until a decade later. Following a fish die-off in Beijing's Guanting Reservoir in 1971, Zhou Enlai ordered an investigation that eventually led to China's "first large-scale water-source pollution control project," under the direction of the newly-rehabilitated Wan Li.[19] A Chinese delegation attended the 1972 United Nations Human Environment Conference in Stockholm, and China's first National Environmental Protection Conference was convened in 1973. By 1979, an Environmental Protection Law and Forest Law were ratified, setting the stage for an explosive growth in the number of protected areas.[20] Following a national work conference on the criteria and procedures for nature reserve establishment in 1980, 2,500 specialists were sent to identify suitable sites around the country.[21] Over 100 reserves were set up in 1981 alone, and both the number of reserves and the area under protection expanded at close to that pace over much of the next decade and a half[22] (see Figure 1).

During the 1980s, there was also a major re-orientation in forestry policies in response to a drastic reduction in timber stocks and increased recognition of the environmental value of forests. The 1980s saw restrictions tightened on uses of wood for manufacturing and construction and

18. Hong Deyuan and Li Zhenyu, "Biodiversity and its conservation and management in the Hindu-Kush Himalaya region of China," in Pei Shengji (ed.), *Banking on Biodiversity: Report on the Regional Consultation in Biodiversity Assessment in the Hindu-Kush Himalayas* (Kathmandu: International Centre for Integrated Mountain Development, 1996), pp. 131–180, especially 155.

19. Qu Geping, *Women xuyao yichang biange (We Need A Transformation)* (Changchun: Jilin People's Publishing House, 1997), pp. 3–6.

20. Wang Yuqing, "Natural conservation regions in China," *Ambio*, Vol. 16, No. 6 (1987), pp. 326–331.

21. Wildlife and Forest Plants Protection Department, *China's National Nature Reserves*, p. 12. Most reserves are administered by the Ministry of Forestry, but the State Environment Protection Administration (SEPA, known as NEPA until March 1998), the Ministry of Agriculture and several other agencies also manage some reserves.

22. Mackinnon, *et al. A Biodiversity Review of China*, p. 6.

Figure 1: **Growth of China's Nature Reserve System 1956–1998**

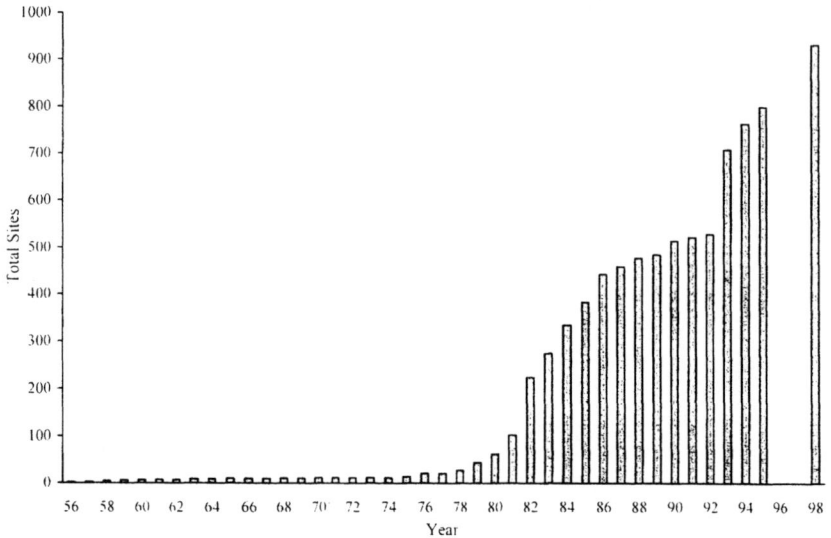

Sources:
(1956–92) John Mackinnon, Meng Sha, Catherine Cheung, Geoff Carey, Zhu Xiang and David Melville, *A Biodiversity of China* (Hong Kong: WWF International China Programme, 1996). (1993) Liu Lan and Wang Shouyi, "Proposal for strengthening management of China's nature reserves," *China's Biosphere Reserves*, Special Issue 1995, Chinese National Committee for Man in the Biosphere Programme, p. 4. (1994) Zhu Guangqing, "Historical development and improvement of China's nature reserves," *China's Biosphere Reserves*, Special Issue 1996, Chinese National Committee for Man in the Biosphere Programme, pp. 14–16. (1995) Shi Kunshan, Li Fenming and Zheng Rui, "China's country report on forestry" (Asia–Pacific Forestry Sector Outlook Study) (Rome and Bangkok: Food and Agriculture Organization of the United Nations, August 1997), p. 42. (1998) "Pollution threatens nature reserves," *China Daily*, 6 June 1998.

an intensification of efforts to find and promote substitute materials. Prohibited uses as of 1983 included mine pit props, industrial fuel, coffins, floors, stairs and bridges.[23] In 1989, there was a major effort to strengthen the regulation of logging and reduce forest losses due to fire and disease. This included an across-the-board reduction in cutting quotas, and official figures show a decline in the average annual consumption of timber from 344 million cubic metres between 1982 and 1988 to 320 million cubic metres from 1989 to 1993. Timber prices were repeatedly adjusted upward to encourage better resource management and fee systems were altered to increase incentives for replanting after logging.

A number of major afforestation projects were also initiated in order to prevent erosion, control flooding and improve local climates. The first and most famous of these is the Three Norths protection forest, also

23. Richardson, *Forests and Forestry in China*, p. 115. Richardson notes the difficulty of enforcing such rules, but points out that "the lengths to which they go indicate the concern."

known as the Green Great Wall, which began in 1978. Subsequent projects have been undertaken along the south-east coast, in the Taihang mountains and in the upper Chang (Yangtze) River watershed.[24] Survival rates for these and other recent plantations have generally been higher than for the tree-planting campaigns of the Mao era, probably due to a combination of better management, higher investment and changes in tree tenure.[25] These major state investments in "ecological forestry," combined with a national compulsory tree planting campaign initiated in 1981, make China the world leader in afforestation.[26]

By 1993, it seemed that China had achieved a remarkable turnaround in forest management and conservation. In that year, the number of nature reserves topped 760, and covered 6 per cent of China's territory.[27] The area covered by forest had increased from the 1980 figure of 12.0 per cent to 13.9 per cent of China's territory. And because the reduction in timber consumption between 1989 and 1993 to 320 million cubic metres was accompanied by an increase in the volume of annual forest growth during this period to 400 million cubic metres, there was a net increase in the actual volume of wood in China's forests for the first time since 1949.[28] However, as discussed below, these figures hide a deepening crisis in biodiversity and forest management which is both a legacy of past mismanagement and a result of new contradictions between conservation and economic reform.

The Political Economy of Protected Areas

The rapid growth of China's nature reserve system during the 1980s was not accompanied by a commensurate increase in state financial support for conservation. As in other sectors, the expansion and differentiation of state conservation activities has been accompanied by fiscal decentralization, leaving local governments with a growing burden. Although China has never had a formal budgetary channel for supporting nature reserves, the few reserves in existence before the 1980s could rely on funds from the central government.[29] During rapid expansion of the system in the 1980s, the central government only allocated a total of 290

24. Zhang Zhida (ed.), *Quanguo shi da linye shengtai jianshe gongcheng (Ten National Ecological Forest Projects)* (Beijing: China Forestry Press, 1997).

25. Qiao Fangbin, *Lindiquanshu bianhua he linyede fazhan: Yunnan linqude shizheng yanjiu (The Evolution of Forest Land Tenure and the Forest Development: The Case of Yunnan)* (unpublished MA thesis, Chinese Academy of Agricultural Sciences, 1997). As of 1990, however, Richardson quotes forestry officials as reporting that only 30% of the officially reported plantation areas could be regarded as successful. (See Richardson, *Forests and Forestry in China*, p. 95.)

26. "China now ranks first in the world in both the speed and scale of afforestation ..." in "Afforestation tops priority list among former loggers," *China Daily*, 10 June 1998, p. 3.

27. Richardson, *Forests and Forestry in China*, p. 23.

28. Li Jinchang, Kong Fanwen, Ren Yong, Wang Xin and Feng Dongfang, *Log-Pricing and Forest Resources Accounting*, p. 10.

29. Wang Long, "Nature reserves need a better management," *China Environment News*, January 1993, p. 5.

million *yuan* for reserves.[30] Now that there are over 800 reserves, most are wholly dependent on county and provincial governments for support.

Nature reserves are seen by some local governments as a source of local pride and potential tourist income, but more often they are viewed as a non-productive drain on local fiscal resources. Furthermore, most reserves are in poorer areas, where the same isolation that has slowed the destruction of natural ecosystems has also served as a barrier to economic development. (At a conference on the future of Chinese forestry held in Beijing in June 1997, an official from the Protection Division of the Ministry of Forestry stated that 30 million poor people were living in and around China's nature reserves.[31] This is a remarkable figure, given repeated government proclamations during 1997 that the country's total poverty population had been reduced to 58 million.) Under such circumstances, even a well-intentioned local government is unlikely to divert scarce funds to support conservation. As a result, many nature reserves have no physical structures or signs delineating their borders, and one-third are "paper parks" that have been formally gazetted but have neither staff nor budgets.[32]

The remoteness and poverty of the regions in which most protected areas are located, combined with the lack of any reliable outside funding, have a number of other implications for biodiversity conservation. When there are staff, they are poorly paid and even more poorly trained. In other countries, even underpaid protection staff are often highly motivated, having chosen their jobs through a personal commitment to conservation. Because of China's system of job allocation and life tenure, however, reserve staff may not have any personal interest in nature, in which case assignment to a nature reserve is an unpleasant prospect. The location of protected areas makes working in them a particularly unattractive job option for young people who need to think about finding spouses, educating their children and accessing medical care.[33] Not surprisingly, if there is a reserve management office, it is generally located in the county seat rather than inside or adjacent to the reserve itself. The meagre support provided by local governments typically covers only subsistence salary, with no support to conduct even baseline studies of biodiversity or

30. NEPA, *China Country Study on Biological Diversity*, p. 236.

31. Yan Xun, "Zhongguo shengwu duoyangxing baohu he ziran baohuqu" ("Biodiversity conservation and nature reserves in China"), in Chinese Society of Forestry and Canadian Institute of Forestry (eds.), *Mianxiang 21 shiji de linye guoji xueshu taolunhui lunwenji* (*International Symposium of Forestry Towards the 21st Century*) (Beijing: 1997), pp. 115–120

32. Han Niannong and Guo Zhifeng, "Reserves face crisis," *China Environment News*, No. 63 (1994), p. 1.

33. Ma Naixi, "Zhongguo ziran baohuqu de kexue guanli wenti" ("Problems of scientific management in China's nature reserves"), in Li Bosheng and Dan Zhiyong (eds.), *Luman Yazhou: diyi jie dongya diqu guojia gongyuan yu baohuqu huiyi ji CNPPA/IUCN di 41jie gongzuohuiyi wenji* (*The Greening of East Asia: Proceedings of the First East Asian Conference on National Parks and Protected Areas and 41st CNPPA/IUCN Working Meeting*) (Beijing: China Environmental Science Press, 1994), pp. 412–17.

regular anti-poaching patrols. There are even cases in which the reserve management office is in the county town, but has no vehicles, so staff are unable to travel to the reserve, much less carry out research or protection.[34]

The most perverse outcome of this fiscal crisis is that it spurs not just neglect, but active destruction of the resources that are supposed to be under protection. Since the central authorities are unable to provide reserve managers with regular financial support, they have urged them to diversify their funding sources and also to "fully exploit the resource advantages of nature reserves and on the basis of strengthening conservation, rationally open up utilization, develop your own industries, and increase reserves' abilities for self-accumulation and self-development."[35] And while reserve directors now spend much of their time making personal funding appeals to local and provincial leaders, the development of money-making activities *in the reserve itself* is promoted as the principal means for reserves to support themselves. Although official policy stresses that commercial activities should be subordinate to conservation, there are no clear guidelines specifying what the limits of such activities might be and no assistance in assessing which resources might be exploited without compromising the reserves' conservation function. In short, reserve directors have few, if any, incentives to conserve biodiversity, and very strong pressures to exploit the resources within the reserve for profit.

Tourism is the most frequently cited example of an environmentally-benign revenue-generating activity, and the industry has grown rapidly in the past decade, with 12 of China's nature reserves now receiving more than 100,000 visitors per year.[36] There are no enforceable guidelines for sustainable tourism development, however, so the result of this rapid growth has been widespread illegal collection of wild plants and animals, increased local demand for wood and fresh water, worsening air and water pollution and solid waste problems. In areas where road access and scenic beauty make tourism profitable, the protected ecosystems can be virtually over-run by visitors.[37] In less marketable areas, scarce conservation funds are used to build guesthouses and other tourist facilities that then stand empty.

34. Author interview, autumn 1997. Detailed citations from interviews or field notes available on request.

35. Ministry of Forestry, *Zhongguo linye nianjian 1995* (*China Forestry Yearbook 1995*) (Beijing: China Forestry Press 1996), p. 63. The Ministry of Forestry offers concessional loans for certain development projects inside reserves.

36. "Pollution threatens nature reserves," *China Daily*, 6 June 1998.

37. NEPA, *China Country Study on Biological Diversity*, p. 142; Gao Jianxin, "Bogeda shengwuquan baohuqude xianzhuang, wenti ji baohu duice" ("Status, problems and protection countermeasures in Bogeda Biosphere Reserve"), in Li Bosheng and Dan Zhiyong (eds.), *The Greening of East Asia*, pp. 284–88. Also Guan Fengli, "Guanyu Changbaishan ziran baohuqu youxiao guanli tujing de tantao" ("An inquiry into effective management techniques for Changbaishan Nature Reserve"), in Li Bosheng and Dan Zhiyong (eds.), *The Greening of East Asia*, pp. 440–444. China's mega-fauna are shy, mostly solitary inhabitants of inhospitable mountains and dense forests, so there is no possibility of developing the

Reserve managers also carry out (or contract with outsiders to carry out) more unambiguously extractive activities, such as logging, quarrying, fishing and grazing of domesticated animals.[38] The typical explanation offered for these activities is that they take place only in "buffer" or "utilization" zones of the reserve. The zoning concept is based on the principle of carrying out ecological surveys to determine which areas within a reserve can sustain varying degrees of human activity, and which areas are so fragile or valuable that they should be off-limits to human activity of any kind. Unfortunately, at least 40 per cent of Chinese reserves have had no such baseline assessment,[39] and in such places the designation of two or more functional zones – combined with the directive from above to make money – has allowed larger and larger areas to be opened to exploitation while confining protective functions to a "core zone." Even in situations where the rules are followed, therefore, the area that is actually under full protection in China's nature reserves is much smaller than it appears. The famous Wolong Giant Panda Reserve has six functional zones, only two of which are off-limits to "productive" activities.[40] A recent study by China's National Man and the Biosphere Committee found tourism development projects *inside* the core zones of 23 per cent of the reserves surveyed.[41]

The ambiguity of rules and lack of effective supervision of reserves opens up opportunities for reserve officials to secretly engage in illegal profit-making activities. What is striking is the degree to which the current incentive system allows and even *rewards* ecologically destructive activities. At Yancheng Nature Reserve in Jiangsu (an international biosphere reserve under the UNESCO Man and the Biosphere Programme), a wide variety of enterprises are underway *inside* the core area, including not only harvesting of shellfish and other wild species, but actual habitat conversion for prawn- and fish-farming. The profits from these enterprises are all invested in further money-making activities, and none of the reserve staff are reported to be working on biodiversity conservation. The reserve director has earned official praise for the reserve's positive cash flow and been held up as an example to others.[42]

---

footnote continued

high-profit safari tourism which has been so successful in Eastern and Southern Africa. The notable exception to this is the Chang Tang in Tibet, where large herds of wild ungulates remain, but it would be difficult to develop tourism on a large scale there due to the altitude and tremendous distances involved.

38. Qian Zhenyue, "Sichuan fengjing mingshengqu de baohu yu kaifa" ("Protection and development of Sichuan's scenic spots"), in Li Bosheng and Dan Zhiyong (eds.), *The Greening of East Asia*, pp. 272–74; also author's notes and interviews.

39. Han Nianyong and Guo Zhifeng, "Reserves face crisis."

40. Zhou Shiqiang, "Wolong ziran baohuqu de gongneng fenqu ji youxiao guanli yanjiu" ("Functional zones and effective management research in Wolong Giant Panda Reserve") in Li Bosheng and Dan Zhiyong (eds.), *Greening of East Asia*, p. 435–39.

41. "Pollution threatens nature reserves," *China Daily*, 6 June 1998.

42. Interview, autumn 1997.

Reserve managers not only have limited incentives for protecting biodiversity, they also have extremely limited enforcement powers. Nature reserves are a very new institution and are superimposed on a landscape already crowded with stakeholders, none of whom are willing to give up their rights to the resources in question. The most pressing prior claims on resources inside nature reserves come from local people, who experience the establishment of a reserve as a sudden expropriation of land and resource rights, generally without compensation. In extreme cases, families or communities are resettled outside of reserve boundaries. More often they remain, but with highly constrained access to natural resources which had previously been theirs. The populations in and around the newly protected areas can be very large: Caohai Nature Reserve in Guizhou has over 19,000 residents and a population density of 200 persons per square kilometres *inside* the reserve.[43]

Given the poverty and resource dependence of local people in most areas where reserves are set up, it is no surprise that resistance often damages the ecosystems in question further. When the collective forest lands of Yuhu village were incorporated into the Yulongxueshan Nature Reserve in north-west Yunnan, for example, farmers responded by cutting down trees that they had previously managed on a sustainable basis. Work teams had to be stationed in the village to prevent further damage and carry out propaganda work.[44] But despite the obvious defiance of Yuhu residents, there is more happening than simple resistance. Institutionally, setting up forest reserves in southern China has at times facilitated resource degradation as relatively effective community management institutions (*xiangguiminyue*) are replaced by extremely weak state ownership, creating a de facto open access area and inviting over use.[45] Lacking strong coercive powers, reserve managers depend largely on public education campaigns to discourage local people from illegal extractive activities. But these efforts are undermined by the reserves' own income-generating activities, especially when fishing, logging or tourism development rights are contracted out to third parties.[46]

Other challenges to the authority of reserve managers, and competition for rights to exploit resources within reserves, come from local governments and line agencies. Conflicts between vertically organized agencies,

43. Wang Wanying, "A community-based strategy for the conservation and development of the Caohai Nature Reserve, Weining county, Guizhou province, P. R. China" (unpublished ms. thesis, Asian Institute of Management, Manila, The Philippines, 1996), p. 20.

44. Author's field notes, Yunnan, November 1995.

45. Author's field notes, Yunnan, January 1996. For discussion of the theoretical implications of common property versus state institutions for management of natural resources, see Elinor Ostrom, *Governing the Commons: the Evolution of Institutions for Collective Action* (Cambridge: Cambridge University Press, 1990). Also Margaret McKean, "Is there a role for common property arrangements in privatization reforms?" presented at the International Conference on Chinese Rural Collectives and Voluntary Organizations: Between State Organizations and Private Interest (University of Leiden: Sinological Institute, 9–13 January 1995).

46. James Harkness, comments during experts' panel, "Workshop on conservation and development at Caohai Nature Reserve," (unpublished, Weining county, Guizhou province, 2–7 December 1997).

and between agencies and local governments, are a well-known feature of rural China, and are even more contentious in the complex or marginal environments where protected areas are designated. Instead of resolving such conflicts, the establishment of a nature reserve often simply drops what is fairly circumscribed authority over protected species onto an already-complex pattern of political, economic and proprietary jurisdictions.[47] The problem of lack of authority (*wuquan wenti*) and interference from other agencies was of primary concern to reserve managers at a regional conference on the problems of reserve management held in 1993.[48] While China has a Wild Animal Conservation Law, there is no systematic law covering protected areas.[49] As a result, unless they actually apprehend someone who has killed a protected species, nature reserve staff have few options when units with a strong prior claim[50] or more political power[51] make inroads into reserves. When offenders are caught, the courts are extremely lenient in all but a few highly publicized cases.[52]

Despite the attempt in the early 1980s to set out scientific guidelines for the formation of reserves, a recent audit by the Ministry of Forestry and World Wide Fund for Nature (WWF) reported serious gaps in the protected area system. The audit found that many reserves have no significant biodiversity value, and recommended downgrading their status to that of scenic areas. A number of important habitat types were found to be unrepresented or underrepresented. Many ecosystems are protected by reserves that are too small in area to remain genetically or ecologically viable in the long run.[53] If reserves are surrounded by a landscape that is essentially forested, perhaps as part of sustainable logging or multiple-use regimes, their size is not such a concern, since under these conditions plant and animal species can move between reserves, and species from relatively complete protected ecosystems can re-colonize fallow and

47. At a wetland reserve in Heilongjiang province, for example, jurisdiction is shared with five provincial departments and local governments. Protection staff have the right to punish poachers, but the fish, water, aquatic plants and subsoil which make up the habitat are not under their control. See James Harkness, "Common property, extractive economies and conservation in China: social change and sustainability at the Zhalong Nature Reserve," a paper presented at the First Conference of the International Association for the Study of Common Property (Duke University, October 1990).

48. Xie Zhixin, "Zhongguo nanfang ziran baohuqu de kunrao yu qi duice" ("Dilemmas of southern China's nature reserves and their countermeasures"), in Li Bosheng and Dan Zhiyong (eds.), *The Greening of East Asia*, pp. 251–59

49. NEPA, *China Biodiversity Conservation Action Plan* (Beijing: NEPA, 1994), p. 31–32.

50. The chief threat to the Suoluo (Tree Fern) National Nature Reserve is illegal felling by a nearby state logging company. See Fan Zuxiang, oral report at "Workshop on conservation and development at Caohai Nature Reserve" (Weining county, Guizhou province, 2–7 December 1997).

51. Provincial tourism bureau officials built a hotel inside of Lugu Lake Nature Reserve, ignoring objections by reserve staff and undermining efforts to prevent illegal logging by local people. Author's field notes, November 1996.

52. NEPA, *China Biodiversity Conservation Action Plan*, p. 32; Tom Korski, "Farmer gets life for tree cutting," *South China Morning Post*, 4 November 1996; Seth Faison, "China vows to punish wildlife poachers," *International Herald Tribune*, 16 February 1998.

53. Mackinnon *et al. A Biodiversity Review of China.*

Table 1: **Wood Consumption in China, 1994**

Use category	Volume (1,000 m³)	Per cent of total
Commercial timber	13,174.3	44.2
Fuel wood	8,593.6	28.8
Timber for farmer's own consumption	6,201.8	20.8
Destroyed by fire, pests	667.5	2.2
Other	1,192.0	4.0
Total	**29,829.2**	**100.0**

Source:
   Data compiled from Zhongguo linyebu (ed.), *Zhongguo linye nianjian 1995* (*China Forestry Yearbook 1995*) (Beijing: Zhongguo linye chubanshe, 1995), p. 80.

logged-over lands. In fact, however, the forests around China's protected areas are being converted so rapidly to other uses that they are becoming embattled islands of diversity.[54] A discussion of the large proportion of China's forests that remain outside of the protected area system altogether, and the dynamics driving forest conversion and biodiversity loss in these areas follows.

State and Collective Forests in the Reform Era

The 85 per cent of China's forests that lie beyond the protected area system, and therefore must meet the country's demands for forest products (see Table 1), can be divided into state and collective forests. Broadly speaking, there is a rough geographical division between the areas where each type of ownership predominates. Just three northeastern provinces (regions) contain state forests comprising 29 per cent of China's total forested area. In southern China, the majority of forested land is collectively owned, and collective forests in ten southern provinces (regions) comprise 37 per cent of China's forested area. Sichuan and Yunnan in the south-west are hybrids, with roughly equal division between state and collective owners, and their combined forest area is 17 per cent of the total.[55] The different functions of state and collective forests are associated with very different forest stand sizes and structures. State forests, the principal source of China's commercial timber, tend to be located in areas with lower populations, are larger in size and (before they are logged) are relatively undisturbed. Collective forests, by contrast, were so designated precisely to supply timber, fuelwood and other products to specific

54. The extreme example of this phenomenon is Hainan province. Originally almost completely forested, the island's forest cover was reduced to 7.9% by 1981. Although there are 47 forest reserves on Hainan, the Ministry of Forestry/WWF team recommended re-evaluating or de-listing half of them, citing their small size and poor condition. A depressingly typical evaluation of one reserve reads, "no forest, no conservation value." See Mackinnon *et al. A Biodiversity Review of China*, pp. 441–461.
   55. Li Yucai (ed.), *Mianxiang 21 shiji de linye fazhan zhanlüe* (*Forestry Strategies Toward the 21st Century*) (Beijing: China Forestry Press, 1996), p. 22.

communities.[56] These forests tend to occur in smaller patches, are more intensively managed and have less biodiversity than state forests. This is reflected in the very low standing wood volume of the southern collective forests compared with northern state forests, despite the fact that the former cover a much larger area.[57]

Indeed, the issue of forest area versus standing wood volume (especially commercially-harvestable volume) is at the crux of China's current forestry dilemma. As discussed above, the Ministry of Forestry reports that by 1993 strict logging quotas and regeneration of forests had ensured that more wood was growing each year than was being cut. Analysts are divided on the accuracy of Chinese forestry figures,[58] but even assuming that official figures are completely accurate, they suggest that despite these seemingly positive figures, the re-orientation of forestry policy in the 1980s came too late to prevent a crisis in the sector. Since the term "forest cover" refers to "grassland and woodland with 30 per cent canopy cover,"[59] recently planted stands may be measured as forest, even though they have much less biomass than a mature forest and will not be harvestable for 20–50 years. Because a very large area has been planted over the past 15 years, increases in forest cover have coincided with decreases in the actual amount of wood available for harvesting. Plantations account for over 26 per cent of China's forested *area*, but only 12 per cent of this is mature commercial timber, and it accounts for less than 2 per cent of China's standing wood *volume*.[60] The large areas planted in the past decade and a half will not be ready for harvest until the second decade of the next century. Currently harvestable forest plantations, on the other hand, were established before the recent improvements in silvicultural practices and are therefore so small and of such poor quality that "they are essentially ruled out from playing a significant role in timber production in the near future."[61]

By contrast, 93 per cent of China's standing wood *volume* is in primary and secondary (i.e. natural rather than plantation) forests which constitute

56. Collective forest farms in the south-east, many of which harvest timber primarily for the market, are a major exception to this characterization. See Zhang Guangzhi, Li Keliang and Song Xushan (eds.), *Nanfang jitilinqu jingji lun* (*On the Economics of Southern Collective Forests*) (Beijing: Zhongguo linye chubanshe, 1992).

57. Li Yucai (ed.), *Forestry Strategies Toward the 21st Century*, p. 23.

58. Richardson's concerns stem principally from the vagueness and inconsistency of measurement terms, as well as the lack of data. Smil finds official figures to be exaggerated at best, and in many cases fraudulent. Rozelle *et al.*, on the other hand, claim that "statistics on the status of China forests may be the most complete" available for any of the country's natural resources. Chinese forestry analysts tend to fall between these positions, accepting official figures as accurate enough for assessing trends while recognizing that they "are watered down to some extent," (*you yiding de shuifen*) and it is in this spirit that official statistics are included in the present paper. Richardson, *Forests and Forestry in China*, pp. 106–107; Smil, *China's Environmental Crisis*, pp. 59–64; Scott Rozelle, Huang Jikun and Zhang Linxiu, "Poverty, population and environmental degradation in China" (unpublished paper, January 1997), p. 5.

59. Richardson, *Forests and Forestry in China*, p. 89.

60. These are 1993 figures. Li Yucai (ed.), *Forestry Strategies Toward the 21st Century*, pp. 4, 19.

61. Yin Runsheng, *An Empirical Analysis of Rural Forestry Reform in China, 1978–1990* (unpublished doctoral dissertation, University of Georgia, 1994), p. 37.

a shrinking fraction of China's forest cover.[62] Resource economist Li Jinchang sums up the problem:

It appears that our forest resources have been developing in a healthy and sustainable way in recent years. But as a matter of fact, it is far from the truth. Actually, the structure of forest age and forest type in China is imbalanced, mature forest and over-mature forest for commercial use keep decreasing, and exploitable resources are at the edge of exhaustion ... It is estimated that exploitable mature and over-mature forests will do exhaust (sic) in six or seven years at the current utilization speed, and that things will remain such for at least ten years until the maturity of young forest.[63]

The Crisis of the State Logging Industry

The "exploitable mature and over-mature forests" Li refers to include China's healthiest and most diverse ecosystems outside of protected areas, most of which are state forests designated for logging. China's state logging industry is one of the most embattled parts of the state enterprise sector. The industry is dominated by 135 state forest bureaus, and they face almost all of the problems of other state enterprises. Ageing fixed capital and out-dated management systems raise production costs while lowering efficiency.[64] The workforce is underemployed, and there is one retiree for every three active workers. In 1995, the cost of providing housing, health care, insurance and other services amounted to 55.5 per cent of the state forest sector's profits. In that year, enterprises were unable to pay 2.05 billion *yuan* in salaries and retirement benefits.[65]

Most bureaus have attempted to deal with rising costs by intensifying logging, but because there have never been strong incentives for replanting, they have the additional problem of running out of raw materials. Of 135 state forest bureaus, 30 have virtually no forest left to cut, and this figure will reach 90 by the year 2000. The syndrome of "the poorer you are the more you log, and the more you log the poorer you get" (*yueqiong yuecai, yuecai yueqiong*) has left 85 forest bureaus in the north-east and Inner Mongolia with an accumulated debt of over 8 billion *yuan*.[66] The effect on the forests themselves has been even more devastating. Since 1977, the harvestable stumpage from natural forests under state control has fallen by nearly 50 per cent, from 1.97 trillion cubic metres to 1.04 trillion cubic metres.

The type of logging that occurs has direct implications for biodiversity conservation. The textbook harvesting procedure, strip clearcutting, leaves alleys of forest between cuts to promote rapid re-seeding and

62. *Ibid.* p. 19. A synopsis of World Bank-supported forestry projects in China states that, "natural forests ... account for 95% of standing wood volume." See Anonymous, "Briefing note: World Bank forestry projects," (1997), p. 1. Another recent report states that 88% of the wood harvested in the state sector comes from natural forests. Ministry of Forestry of the People's Republic of China, "Guoyou linqu tianranlin ziyuan baohu gongcheng jihua" ("Plan for a project to protect natural forest resources of state forest areas") (October 1997), p. 15.

63. Li Jinchang *et al. Log-Pricing and Forest Resources Accounting*, pp. 10–11.

64. Li Yucai (ed.), *Forestry Strategies Toward the 21st Century*, pp. 161–65.

65. Ministry of Forestry of the People's Republic of China, "Plan for a project to protect natural forest resources of state forest areas," p. 4.

66. *Ibid.* p. 1–5.

prevent erosion. In practice, however, once cash-strapped forestry bureaus have made the investment to build a road into a forest area, the tendency is to "shave the head bald" (*ti guangtou*), leaving at most only a few trees on ridgetops for re-seeding.[67] In the 1980s, biologists found a population of giant pandas (*Ailuropoda melanoleuca*) in forests slated for logging by the Changqing Forest Bureau. The leaders of the bureau were aware of the panda's protected status, and organized regular anti-poaching patrols in the panda habitat under their control. They also showed initial interest in experimenting with logging techniques that would preserve important habitat areas and promote more rapid regeneration. Due to financial pressures, however, these plans were never put into practice.[68]

Regeneration rates following logging vary depending on natural conditions and the type of logging. It is estimated that due to inappropriate logging practices, one-third of all forests cut before 1979 were replaced by degraded mountain slopes.[69] Where replanting occurs, it is generally of monospecific stands known in other countries as "green deserts" for their lack of biological diversity.

Like nature reserves, state forest enterprises are predominantly located in poorer areas, but whereas the former are a drain on local coffers, the latter may be the major source of tax revenue for county government. As a result, local officials, like reserve managers, have few incentives to support conservation and strong incentives to allow resource exploitation, regardless of its environmental impacts. In 1996, environmental activists from Beijing visiting Deqin county in north-west Yunnan learned that an area of forest constituting critical habitat for the endangered golden monkey (*Rhinopithecus roxellanae*, also known as the Yunnan snub-nosed monkey) was being logged by the local forest bureau. On their return to Beijing, they petitioned State Councillor Song Jian, and because of his intervention, the Ministry of Forestry issued an order for the logging to stop. The county government defied the Ministry's order, pointing out that logging was the only significant source of local tax revenue.[70] County governments also set up checkpoints along transport routes to inspect the paperwork associated with truckloads of logs. Loads that are outside the state plan are confiscated, but because they can then be resold by the county government, another perverse incentive is created: local officials have an interest in allowing over-harvesting to

67. Author interview, Beijing, autumn 1997.
68. Logging was halted in the area in 1994 and it is awaiting designation by the State Council as a national nature reserve. Funds from the General Environment Facility are being used to finance an experimental "enterprise restructuring" plan for the Changqing Forestry Bureau that includes replacement-level logging in the buffer zone, establishment of new forest-based enterprises, and relocation and re-training of some loggers. Pan Wenshi, *Qinling daxiongmao de ziran bihusuo* (*The Natural Refuge of the Giant Panda in the Qinling Mountains*) (Beijing: Beijing University Press, 1998); The World Bank, "Global environment facility: People's Republic of China nature reserves management project" (project document: May 1995); author's field notes, June 1994.
69. NEPA, *China Biodiversity Conservation Action Plan*, p. 60.
70. The Ministry eventually agreed to compensate the county budget for the lost income, but surrounding counties are now reported to have stepped up logging in an effort to gain ministerial attention; U.S. Embassy–China, "Saving the snub-nosed monkey: student environmental action in China" (unpublished report, Beijing, November 1996).

continue as long as they can earn income from confiscations, and in some locations the frequency of spot-checks has been adjusted accordingly.[71]

Collective Forests and Biodiversity

While collective forests tend to be smaller and more intensively managed than state forests, they still contain considerable biological diversity and provide vital ecosystem services. They are used for watershed protection, provision of timber for household construction, fuelwood, fodder, collection of non-timber forest products (such as medicinal plants and edible fungi) and hunting. Management of these forests may be carried out by a collective entity (team, natural village, administrative village), or by households under an arrangement similar to the production responsibility system. Almost all of China's collective forests are found in southern and south-west China, typically occupying land at higher elevations adjacent to rural communities. In areas with low population densities, especially in the south-west, state forests and nature reserves may be even farther up-slope.

The patterns of change in the composition of collective forests during the reform period show that an increase in forest area does not always mean an increase in biodiversity. In the Chinese land use classification system, the definition of the term "forest" includes not only natural woody plant communities, but also single-species shelterbelts, commercial plantations of timber, and even rubber, bamboo, fruit, nuts and other orchard crops. The latter group, known as "economic forests" (*jingjilin*), constitute a growing proportion of new "forests" which are increasingly taking the place of natural collective forests.[72] Researchers at the Kunming Institute of Zoology estimate that commercial plantations in Yunnan have 70 per cent fewer bird species and 80 per cent fewer mammal species than the natural forests they have replaced.[73] Ecosystem services suffer as well: research in Sichuan found that the spacing of plantings and removal of ground cover in orange orchards left soil exposed, exacerbating erosion during the rainy season.[74] The area covered by these "unnatural forests" has increased dramatically since the early 1980s, and at a much higher rate than the increase in total collective forest area. At the same time, there is evidence to suggest that timber species in collective forests are being harvested much earlier than during the pre-reform period. In other words, the overall increase in forest cover during the reform period has been accompanied by a decline in forest quality and diversity.[75]

71. Author's interview, autumn 1997.

72. Ministry of Forestry, *China Forestry Yearbook 1995*, p. 110. Qiao Fangbin, *The Evolution of Forest Land Tenure and the Forest Development*, p. 44.

73. Hong Deyuan and Li Zhenyu, "Biodiversity and its conservation and management in the Hindu-Kush Himalaya region of China," p. 154.

74. Personal communication, Frank Voorhies, April 1997.

75. Scott Rozelle, Vince Bezinger, Jikun Huang and Li Guo, "The rise of forests and the fall of diversity: assessing the role of tenure, policy and markets" (paper presented at the MacArthur Foundation Workshop on Biodiversity in the Himalayan Region, Kunming, China, 7–10 April 1997); Qiao Fangbin, *The Evolution of Forest Land Tenure and the Forest Development*, p. 45.

This is a result of the devolution of collective forest management to households in many areas and a variety of institutional incentives that favour economic forests over natural forests or woodlots. Frequent forest policy changes since 1949, especially the insecurity of forest and tree tenure, have left farmers wary of making long-term investments in timber management when other tree crops (such as mulberry or eucalyptus) can bring economic returns in as little as two years.[76] Timber harvesting requires a permit, even on a household's contracted forest land, and harvesting, transport and sale all entail taxes and fees that can add up to 90 per cent of the market value of the timber.[77] By comparison, farmers' property rights over cash tree crops are relatively complete and unambiguous, with few taxes and fees.

Even afforestation campaigns and wasteland auctions, both of which are primarily carried out on collective "wastelands" (huangshan, huangdi) for the express purpose of increasing forest area, tend to reduce biodiversity rather than enhance it. There is no consistent definition of what constitutes wasteland, although the term generally refers to barren hillsides or grasslands. In many cases, however, wastelands include degraded forests or scrublands that, although far from pristine, represent the last remaining native plant communities in a particular locality. Replacement of these natural communities with monospecific plantations is considered by one Forestry Ministry official to be one of the most serious threats to biodiversity in China.[78]

In addition to the direct impacts of the degradation or conversion of collective forests on biodiversity, there are also serious indirect effects. Economic plantations may increase incomes, but neither they nor monospecific shelterbelts can provide the same variety of goods and ecosystem services as diverse natural forests. Conversion to these new uses takes areas that formerly provided timber, fuel, fodder and non-timber forest products, and either eliminates access to or drastically

76. Mulberry leaves are used to raise silkworms and oil is extracted from eucalyptus leaves. The leaves of both species can be harvested within a few years of planting. Worries about tenure instability are manifested not only in the preference for establishment of cash tree crops, but also in a willingness to cut timber species at a younger age. For further discussions of forest and tree tenure, see Tang Hongqi and Du Shouhu (eds.), Lindi linmu quanshu yu shehui linye (Forest and Tree Tenure and Social Forestry) (Chengdu: Chengdu keji daxue chubanshe, 1995).

77. Most of these are imposed by local governments, making them the forestry sector component of the "peasant's burden" (nongmin fudan). See Rene Koppelman, Chun K. Lai, Patrick B. Durst and Janice Naewboonien (eds.), Asia-Pacific Agroforestry Profiles (second edition, Bangkok: Food and Agriculture Organization of the United Nations, 1996), pp. 90–95; Li Guangming and Liao Feng, "Yunnan mucai shichang tansuo" ("An exploration of the timber market in Yunnan") in He Pikun (ed.), Shehui linye: yanjiu, tansuo (Social Forestry: Research and Explorations) (Kunming: Yunnan keji chubanshe, 1995), pp. 133–38; Li Yucai (ed.), Forestry Strategies for the 21st Century, p. 367.

78. Author's interview notes, January 1995. See also Ke Wenzhong, "Ecologists promote varied afforestation," China Environment News (English edition), 15 May 1997, p. 5. A similar but even more rapid loss of diversity is occurring among domesticated crops. In response to marketization and government programmes, farmers are abandoning traditional varieties created through generations of selection in favour of higher-yielding or subsidized hybrids.

reduces the range of resources available.[79] As a result local people may simply intensify cutting, grazing and collecting in remaining nearby natural forest areas.

The importance of such a displacement should not be underestimated, especially given the tremendous dependence of rural people (especially in forest areas) on wood as a fuel source. Of 298 million cubic metres of wood consumed in China in 1994, 28.8 per cent was used for fuel. Wood supplies over 28 per cent of rural energy needs, including 40 per cent of household fuel nation-wide and a much higher percentage in upland areas. Since specially-designated fuelwood forests comprise only 3.7 per cent of forest land, most of this massive demand must be satisfied by cutting in other areas.[80] Smil makes a rough calculation that "about half of China's progressing, massive loss of natural plant cover ... could be ascribed to securing an inadequate amount of fuel for rural households."[81] Although illegal wood-cutting is one of the problems mentioned most frequently by forest reserve managers, no systematic studies on biodiversity impacts of fuelwood collection have been carried out.[82]

Looking Ahead

In the post-Mao period, there has been a remarkably rapid acceptance of emerging international norms regarding the importance of biodiversity in China, and a re-orientation of forestry policy towards conservation and sustainable use. Unfortunately, China's forests and biodiversity are doubly threatened in the 1990s, suffering from both the legacies of the planned economy and the perverse incentives of the current order. Deforestation (and ineffective afforestation) during the Mao years left the country with a seriously depleted resource base, and the wasteful, dying state logging industry threatens to take the last of China's old growth forests with it long before newly planted forests can take their place. Economic growth has brought ever more rapid depletion of wild plant and animal populations, far exceeding the state's regulatory capacity. Resource management policies and agencies have failed to take into account the social and economic landscapes of the places where forests and biodiversity are found, places where both people and local governments are poor. As a result, conservation remains a largely unfunded mandate even inside the nature reserve system, with fiscal pressures leading some reserve managers to cannibalize the very resources they are supposed to protect. Finally, because of the incentives created by state forest policies, natural forests and scrublands outside of protected areas are progressively being replaced by orchards and monospecific plantations.

79. Owners of orchards generally restrict grazing, fuelwood collection and other activities by others. Shelterbelt plantations have similar, if sometimes less strictly enforced, restrictions.

80. Ministry of Forestry, Afforestation and Forest Management Section, and China Forestry Association, *Proceedings of the National Fuelwood Forest Symposium*, p. 7.

81. Smil, *China's Environmental Crisis*, p. 106.

82. Given its importance for rural livelihoods and the amount of wood involved, the fuelwood issue is given relatively little scholarly or governmental attention in China, aside from occasional campaigns to introduce more efficient stoves.

Although much has been lost in recent decades, the state's commitment to conserving what remains continues to grow. In late 1996, during a visit to the upper reaches of the Chang (Yangtze) River, Zhu Rongji exclaimed, "if we don't protect the vegetation upstream, the Sanxia (Three Gorges) Reservoir won't last but a few years: it won't matter how many reservoirs we build. We must make up our minds and ask the 'forest tigers' to come down out of the mountains."[83] During the next year, the Ministry of Forestry carried out a study of the state forest sector which revealed the severity of the financial, social security and ecological crisis in state timber areas. The study outlines a plan to phase out logging of natural forests by 2010, and decisively re-direct the state forest sector away from unsustainable logging of old-growth forests to a combination of sustainable harvesting of plantations and a variety of alternative productive activities, such as wood processing, tourism, mining and agroforestry. The plan would cost over 2 billion *yuan* per year, and make over 600,000 forestry workers redundant by the year 2000.[84]

Provinces in the north-east and south-west have been asked to prepare their own estimates of the costs of phasing out logging in natural forests, and shortly after his ascendancy to the premiership in March 1998, Zhu visited the Sichuan delegation to the National People's Congress and discussed the issue with them. The plan was described in the press for the first time by the influential *Outlook Weekly* (*Liaowang zhoukan*) several weeks later.[85] Massive flooding in the Chang River valley during the following summer pushed ahead the timetable for implementation, and on 23 August, Sichuan governor Song Baorui announced that as of 1 September all logging and timber marketing in natural forest areas of western Sichuan would be halted.[86] If, as a result of the floods, the logging phase-out is put into effect nation-wide, it will constitute a truly remarkable re-orientation of China's forestry policy and practice.

Such is the nature of China's biodiversity crisis that even phasing out natural logging will entail risks. If the plan is announced but action is not taken quickly, logging will surely be accelerated in anticipation of the phase-out. (Even if fully funded, the plan will only provide relief for large logging bureaus, with no assistance to myriad smaller, local firms.) If the state succeeds in achieving a rapid and substantial reduction of logging in natural forests, the result will be serious shortfalls in China's ability to meet its timber demand from domestic sources. (As noted above, the amount of harvestable timber from plantations will remain small until as late as the second decade of the next century.) Forest products are already a major import commodity, and while China's imports of whole logs have decreased since the 1980s (due to price increases and log exports bans),

83. Ministry of Forestry of the People's Republic of China, "Plan for a project to protect natural forest resources of state forest areas," p. 11.

84. *Ibid.* pp. 29, 57.

85. *Renmin ribao*, 15 March 1998. p. 1. Zhao Yining and Huangpu Pingli, "Don't even cut one more tree."

86. Xiang Hong and Chao Yang, "Zhishui xian zhishan, zhishan xianzhiqiong" ("To control flooding, first control mountains; to control mountains, first control poverty"), *Qingian zhoumo* (*Youth Weekend*), 28 August 1998, p. 3.

there has been a rapid growth in imports of sawn timber, plywood, veneers and paper/paperboard.

The implications of further demand for imports are not only economic. The proportion of tropical hardwoods among China's log imports grew from 11 to 64 per cent between 1988 and 1994. These logs come from Malaysia and, increasingly, West Africa – areas with both high biodiversity and high rates of forest loss.[87] As imports from these areas grow, China's forests will increasingly be protected at the expense of forests in other countries. A similar trend is already clear in the wildlife trade between China and its southern neighbours. A 1994 study estimated that in a single day, 12 tonnes of tortoises had been brought into China from Vietnam through a single customs post. "At the same port on the same day, 13 containers of Pangolin [ant-eaters] (containing 76 individuals weighing a total of 234 kilograms) and 10 containers of Monitor lizards (150–200 individuals, weighing a total of almost one tonne) were taken across the border into Guangxi."[88]

Zhu Rongji's plans for structural reform have other implications for forestry and biodiversity conservation as well. It was announced at the NPC in March 1998 that the Ministry of Forestry (MOF) would be reduced by one rank to the level of bureau, while the National Environmental Protection Agency (NEPA) would be raised to the equivalent of ministerial rank and re-named the State Environmental Protection Administration (SEPA). It has been suggested that the Nature Reserve section of the former MOF will come under the control of SEPA, a move which some observers feel is positive, unifying China's environmental protection under a single agency. The 1994 China Biodiversity Action Plan reported that "achieving effective co-ordination (between different agencies) remains one of the most important and intransigent obstacles to effective biodiversity conservation."[89] Even the process of drafting the Plan was seriously hampered by rivalries and the unwillingness of different agencies to share data.[90] On the other hand, conflicts between protected areas and adjacent logging bureaus, which were formerly handled within a single bureaucratic system, might be exacerbated if they belong to different vertical hierarchies in the future. Many within the former MOF believe that it will retain all of its components, but simply have a lower status within the government. This would bode ill for its ability to contend for budgetary support.

The actual effects of these status changes on the power and responsibilities of these two agencies will not be known for some time, but it is clear that any changes which do occur will not alter the basic fiscal insecurity and structure of perverse incentives currently undermining China's

87. Shi Kunshan, Li Zhiyong, Lin Fenming and Zheng Rui, *China's Country Report on Forestry (Asia-Pacific Forestry Sector Outlook Study)* (Rome and Bangkok: Food and Agriculture Organization of the United Nations, 1997), pp. 53–54.

88. CCICED, "Second annual report of the biodiversity working group," in *Proceedings: The Third Meeting of the China Council for International Cooperation on Environment and Development* (Beijing: Environmental Science Press, 1995), p. 53.

89. NEPA, *China Biodiversity Conservation Action Plan* (draft, 1994), p. 29.

90. *Ibid.* p. 51.

conservation efforts. However, small but promising initiatives at the provincial and local level may pave the way for future progress along several fronts. Some reserve managers have begun experimenting with new incentive systems for field staff, with bonuses tied to time spent on patrol. Research on resource accounting has provided ammunition for advocates of green taxes which would require downstream beneficiaries of ecological services to help cover the costs of ecosystem protection and management.[91] As is often the case, provincial experiments are ahead of researchers and policy-makers in Beijing. Two upland forest reserves in Guangxi receive 140,000 and 300,000 *yuan* from surrounding counties annually as "water source regulation fee" (*shuiyuan hanyang fei*), and the city of Xi'an provides support for an important nature reserve in the Qinling mountains which protects one of the city's major water sources.[92] For many protected areas, especially montane forests, such examples may become models for long-term fiscal sustainability. A 1996 NEPA study found 17 regions which were levying "ecological environment compensation fees" of one type or another, and recommended that such policies be adopted more widely.[93]

Another issue which researchers and reserve managers are beginning to address is the conflict between protected areas and local communities. Experiments are underway in a dozen or so reserves to explore issues such as conflict management between local people and reserve staff, sustainable harvesting of non-timber forest products within reserves, the improved management of buffer zones and the direct involvement of locals in protection activities. In Guizhou, staff of the Caohai Nature Reserve hire and train villagers to monitor wildlife populations and guard against poaching, while helping to establish revolving funds within the village to promote non-degradative micro-enterprise development.[94] This "Caohai model" has recently been endorsed by the provincial government and is likely to be extended to other reserves in south-west China with support from provincial environmental protection and poverty alleviation agencies and foreign donors.

91. Research on resource accounting began in the 1980s, and has generally focused on attaching monetary values to ecological and other normally non-monetized services (such as scenic beauty) provided by natural forests. See for example, Kong *et al. Log-Pricing and Forest Resources Accounting*, p. 42; China Council for International Co-operation on Environment and Sustainable Development Biodiversity Working Group, "First report of Phase Two" (unpublished report, Beijing, 1997), pp. 2–5.

92. Chen Yalin, "Ziran baohuqu guanlizhong jingji shouduan de yingyong fenxi" ("Analysis of the use of economic measures in the management of nature reserves"), in Li Bosheng and Dan Zhiyong (eds.), *The Greening of East Asia*, pp. 428–431.

93. Also NEPA, *China Country Study on Biological Diversity*, pp. 168, 213.

94. Ministry of Forestry, "General environmental facility – China nature reserve management project: the second NGO/donor meeting document" (unpublished report, 26 February 1998); Lai Qingkui, "Conflict management and community forestry: a case of the Nangun River Nature Reserve, Yunnan, China," in J. Fox, L. Fisher and C. Cook (eds.), *Conflict and Collaboration: the Eighth Workshop on Community Management of Forest Lands* (Honolulu: Program on Environment, The East-West Center, 1997), pp. 116–135. Wang Wanying, "A community-based strategy for the CNR Office for the Conservation and Development of the Caohai Nature Reserve, Weining county, Guizhou province, P. R. China" (unpublished ms. thesis, Asian Institute of Management, 1996).

Outside of protected areas, a growing body of research is eroding the conventional assumption that upland farmers are incapable of sustainably managing forests,[95] and initiatives are underway to promote and enhance traditional forestry practices. Unfortunately, due to the sheer number of different perverse economic and institutional incentives at work, the steady loss of biodiversity is likely to continue as collective forests and "wastelands" are converted to monocrop plantations.

Finally, there have recently been promising developments completely outside of the state forestry and environment system, in the media, the legal system and in the development of non-governmental organizations (NGOs). Although China lacks a genuine environmental social movement to raise awareness, spur officials to action and monitor the behaviour of the state and private actors, the environment itself seems to be regarded as a relatively safe issue for discussion and debate.[96] Li Peng has encouraged journalists to report on environmental problems, and in the past few years, independent Chinese environmental NGOs have slowly begun to emerge. To date, these groups have operated through three main channels: raising public awareness through the media, carrying out campaigns to change behaviour (such as encouraging recycling, or discouraging the live bird trade), and making direct appeals to national leaders (for example, the petition presented to Song Jian by Friends of Nature). Leaders of these new groups are especially aware of the need to change consumer attitudes and behaviour, an area in which government appeals have had limited effect. At the same time, ordinary citizens are increasingly turning to the courts for protection against pollution. In 1995, for example, 5,000 people jointly filed an administrative lawsuit charging the Environmental Protection Bureau of Jianhu county, Jiangsu with failure to fulfil its duty in the case of an organic chemical factory that was seriously violating anti-pollution laws.[97] In another case, fish farmers from Guizhou's Hongfeng Lake district were awarded 1.68 million *yuan* by the provincial Higher People's Court as compensation for pollution from a fertilizer factory.[98] While it is difficult to gauge the magnitude and significance of such trends, the vague outlines of a more

95. Farmer management of forests has been a major theme in *Linye yu shehui* (*Forestry and Society*), a bi-monthly publication of the Institute of Scientific and Technical Information of the Chinese Academy of Forestry; Pei Shengji, Xu Jianchu, Chen Sanyang and Long Chunlin, *Xishuangbanna lunxie nongye shengtai xitong shengwu duoyangxing yanjiu lunwen bagaoji* (*Collected Research Papers on Biodiversity in Swidden Agroecosystems in Xishuangbanna*) (Kunming: Yunnan Education Press, 1997); Yin Shaoting, *Yige chongman zhengyide wenhuashengtaixitong: Yunnan daogenghuozhongyanjiu* (*A Controversial Cultural-Ecological System: Research on Slash and Burn in Yunnan*) (Kunming: Yunnan People's Press, 1991).

96. The very vocal public opposition to the Three Gorges Project in the late 1980s and early 1990s, including a campaign within the NPC which led one-third of the delegates to oppose or abstain from voting on the project, is the most famous case in point. James Harkness, "The politics of technical decision-making in post-Mao China: the case of the Three Gorges project" (unpublished ms. thesis, Cornell University, 1993).

97. Ma Xianchong, "Public participation in environmental management in China," in Xie Baodong and Li Hanying (eds.), *Environmental Management, Public Policies and Public Participation* (Beijing: China Environmental Science Press, 1995), pp. 96–102.

98. "Fish farmers win pollution payout," *South China Morning Post*, 24 September 1996.

pluralistic social landscape, in which state environmental protection is monitored and complemented by social action, are beginning to emerge.

Conclusion

Considering the degree to which the conservation of forests and biodiversity has been affected by changes to the political system, and the rapidity of those changes, one can look ahead and see reasons for both alarm and optimism. Alarm, because there are no signs of any move toward redressing the basic fiscal crises of either the nature reserve system or the poor areas where so much of China's remaining natural wealth is found. Optimism, because concern for the environment from the state and society has increased so dramatically in the past two decades, and because even in the midst of the massive problems described above, solutions are being created by the people closest to those problems: reserve managers, local officials, scientists and resource-dependent communities. The changing role of the state is key. Given the increasing fluidity and complexity of society, budgetary constraints, and the speed with which programmes are diluted and subverted as they make the long journey from Beijing to China's remaining natural areas, centrally-directed grand schemes for conservation are not likely to be effective. A more realistic strategy would recognize the legitimacy of local and non-governmental initiatives, and focus limited state resources and authority on providing a supportive legal, institutional and policy framework for conservation. Better financing of nature reserves and enforceable, basic regulatory support could relieve the pressures that undermine conservation at the local level. Moreover, tenure and tax reforms in the collective forest sector could foster a shift from unsustainable, short-term forest conversion to longer-term investments in household and collective forest management.

China's Energy and Resource Uses: Continuity and Change

Vaclav Smil

Recent writings on China's achievements during the last quarter of the 20th century stress, almost without exception, the enormity of change.[1] But, for both universal and particular reasons, this survey of the country's energy resources and uses will stress continuity as much as change. Taking the inertia of complex energy systems as the key universal given, the most important particular explanation lies in peculiarities of China's resource endowment.

Historical perspectives demonstrate that it takes a long time – usually half a century – for a new energy source to capture the largest share of a market, and the capital spent on implementing the necessary extraction, processing, distribution and conversion infrastructure is a powerful reason for maintaining existing arrangements.[2] The challenge of rising costs of extraction, transportation and conversion is mostly met through technical innovations which not only keep most of the inflation-adjusted prices from rising but often lead to impressive secular price declines.[3]

The social consequences inherent in rapid dismantling of labour-intensive industries (coal-mining is the best example) or in depriving some regions of their major source of income (oil and gas extraction in otherwise industrially undeveloped locations) make it desirable to prolong the economic viability of such operations through technical innovation (or through costly government subsidies). These virtually universal considerations exert the expected influence on China's energy industries – but the country's peculiar resource endowment is an even stronger cause of the relative stability of its primary energy supply's composition.

China's Energy Resources: Strengths and Weaknesses

Given the size of China's territory (almost exactly as large as the U.S. including Alaska), one would expect to find generous amounts of fossil fuel. The resource aggregate is, indeed, very large – but this is overwhelmingly because of China's huge coal deposits. China's global rank

1. A good example of this widespread genre is the latest World Bank review of the Chinese economy: The World Bank, *China 2020: The Development Challenges in the New Century* (Washington, DC: The World Bank, 1997).

2. For details on this inertia and on gradual transitions see: Cesare Marchetti and Nebojsa Nakicenovic, *The Dynamics of Energy Systems and the Logistic Substitution Model* (Laxenburg: International Institute for Applied Systems Analysis, 1979); Vaclav Smil, *General Energetics* (New York: John Wiley, 1991).

3. Most notably, when expressed in constant monies, the average world crude oil price in the late 1990s is no higher than it was a century ago. See: British Petroleum, *BP Statistical Review of World Energy 1997* (London: British Petroleum, 1997), p. 14.

in what is, by definition, an only imprecisely known category, is – at worst –number three behind Russia and the U.S.[4] In any case, its coal resources could last for several hundreds of years at the mid-1990s rate of extraction. Moreover, most of China's coal has a fairly high heating content, with inferior lignites accounting for only a small fraction of all resources.[5]

In terms of verified coal reserves China again ranks third in the world, behind the U.S. and Russia, with roughly 115 billion tonnes (Gt) or one-ninth of the world's total. This could support nearly a century of extraction at the current rate.[6] In contrast, at the end of 1996 the total of 3.3 Gt of China's proved oil reserve amounted to just over 2 per cent of the global total (11th largest in the world), enough for no more than two decades at the 1996 rate of extraction.[7] And the country's proved natural gas reserves are much smaller still, amounting to mere 0.8 per cent of the global total and ranking only 23rd world-wide.[8]

China's poor natural gas endowment is conspicuously out of line with the proportions of the two fuels in other major oil and gas producing countries.[9] Both American and British natural gas reserves hold about as much energy as their respective crude oil reserves, and Russia has about six times as much energy available from already discovered gas as it has in commercially recoverable crude oil. In comparison, the energy content of Chinese gas reserves amounts to mere 30 per cent of the country's verified crude oil deposits.

This unusually low natural gas endowment disadvantages China in several important ways. Natural gas is both the most convenient and the cleanest fuel for a range of uses from residential and commercial heating to electricity generation during periods of peak demand. In addition, it is also the best fuel and feedstock for numerous chemical syntheses, includ-

4. A resource category comprises the total mass of a particular commodity present in the earth's crust, regardless of technical means to recover it or the economic viability doing so. While total resources can only be estimated, reserves are the accurately known fraction of resources which can be recovered at a known cost using commercial techniques. A combination of technical innovation and higher prices constantly creates reserves out of resources.

5. The best hard (black, bituminous) coals have a heating content of between 27–29 megajoules (MJ) per kilogram (MJ/kg), typical steam coals used in electricity generation produce around 22 MJ/kg, with the poorest lignites (brown coals) being below 15 MJ/kg. Most of China's coal resources have an energy density of between 22 and 29 MJ/kg. For more details see: Vaclav Smil, *Energy in China's Modernization* (Armonk, NY: M. E. Sharpe, 1988), pp. 31–35.

6. Mistakenly, this reserve/production (R/P) ratio is often taken as an indicator of the time when a country, or the world, will run out of a particular mineral. This would be the case only for the resource/production ratio, a quotient we cannot reliably calculate because of the uncertain nature of the numerator. Higher prices and better techniques can raise R/P ratios quite rapidly: for example, the global R/P ratio for crude oil was well below 30 during the time of low oil prices in the early 1970s – but recently it has risen above 40, higher than at any time since 1945. For the latest estimates of coal reserves, and coal R/P ratios see: British Petroleum, *BP Statistical Review*, p. 30.

7. *Ibid.* p. 4.

8. *Ibid.* p. 20.

9. Crude oil contains 42 MJ/kg, one cubic metre (m³) of natural gas averages around 35 MJ with a mass of about 720 grams (g); consequently, the energy density of natural gas is nearly 49 MJ/kg.

ing plastics and nitrogenous fertilizers.[10] A high share of natural gas consumption in a country's primary energy balance thus assures lower energy intensity (the total amount of energy used per unit of GDP) while minimizing the emissions of CO_2, the world's most important greenhouse gas.[11] Because of its extensive coal deposits, China has large reserves of coal-bed methane, but this kind of natural gas is usually more expensive and less convenient to recover than the resources in hydrocarbon fields.

Fortunately, China can claim global primacy in the other most desirable clean energy resource: it has the world's highest potential for generating electricity from flowing water.[12] This potential is never easy to develop for two major reasons: hydro generation has inherently higher capital costs than thermal power plants, and expensive long-distance transmission links – needed to connect remote dam sites with populated regions – add considerably to the overall cost of hydro power.[13]

These fundamental realities mean that the dominance of coal in China's fossil fuel consumption is going to change only very slowly in the decades ahead. In fact, coal's share has actually increased since the beginning of China's post-1979 modernization: the fuel provided about 72 per cent of China's primary energy consumption in 1980, and it supplied just over 76 per cent of the total in 1996. Consequently, it is most unlikely that its share will fall below 60 per cent by the year 2010.[14] This extraordinary dependence causes a number of problems whose impact has been aggravated by the generally low technical level of Chinese mining, inadequate coal processing, underdeveloped transportation and irrational pricing.

Chinese Coal: Straddling Two Realms

China surpassed Soviet production to become the world's largest coal producer in 1989. During the 1990s production continued to grow strongly, but irregularly, by anywhere between 24 and 59 Mt a year. Extraction surpassed 1 Gt in 1989 and 1.3 Gt in 1996.[15] But the last total

10. This is a particularly important concern for China, the world's largest producer of nitrogenous fertilizers. The synthesis of ammonia requires about 50 MJ of natural gas per kilogram of nitrogen, and China has recently been using almost 30% of its total natural gas production for ammonia synthesis.

11. For example, burning typical heating coal (with an energy content of 22 MJ/kg and carbon comprising 70% of the mass) in a fairly efficient (35%) stove will release about 90g of carbon (C) for every MJ of useful energy; in contrast, burning natural gas (75% C) in a high-performance (90% efficient) household gas furnace will release a mere 17g C/MJ.

12. China's total of about 380 billion watts (GW) of exploitable power is well ahead of potential capacities in Russia, Brazil and the U.S., but the more even flow of the great Siberian rivers could eventually generate more electricity.

13. Capital costs per unit of installed generating capacity are commonly only half as much in coal-fired stations. High-voltage direct-current links are the best way to minimize transmission losses.

14. For comparison, coal holds roughly a 25% share of U.S. primary energy consumption while it supplies 20% of both Russia's and Japan's commercial energy.

15. Because of many readily available statistical sources I will not reference individual output numbers. Standard Chinese sources are State Statistical Bureau, *Zhongguo tongji nianjian* (*Chinese Statistical Yearbook*) (Beijing: China Statistics Publishing, annually), and

does not represent 38 per cent of the global coal output as a simple quotient of the two figures would indicate: Chinese totals do not refer to cleaned and sorted coal, but rather to raw fuel which contains large, and variable, shares of incombustible rocks and clay. A multiplier of roughly 0.7 has been used to convert this fuel to the standard coal equivalent – i.e. fuel with 29.3 megajoules per kilogram (MJ/kg). Typical raw Chinese bituminous coal, representing bulk of the country's solid fuel extraction, thus has an energy content of just short of 21 MJ/kg.

In reality, even this rate may be too high an average for the extraction of the late 1990s because of the rising share of raw coal comprised of more than 30 per cent incombustible waste. This qualitative decline arises from yet another long-standing Chinese peculiarity whose enormous effects go far beyond the coal industry: Chinese coal extraction originates from two very different kinds of enterprises, from large collieries owned by the state and administered from Beijing, and from a variety of local medium and small mines mostly run by counties, townships, collectives or individuals.

The first kind of enterprise, each producing more than half a million tonnes (Mt) of coal annually, is now increasingly modernized and relatively highly productive.[16] This modern sector was considerably strengthened during the 1980s when mechanization became widespread in underground mines, and when China finally began to join the other great coal powers by increasing its share of efficient surface mining. In 1979, mechanized extraction accounted for slightly less than one-third of the total output of state mines, but by 1990 the rate had reached 70 per cent. Before 1980 a handful of old small surface mines contributed less than 5 per cent of China's coal output. Then, with considerable foreign investment and technical co-operation, China decided to open several very large surface mines in Shanxi and in Inner Mongolia.[17]

Even with these innovations, international comparisons reveal the continuing inferiority of China's large-scale coal mining. Typical coal recovery rates average no more than 50–60 per cent compared to over 90 per cent in modern long-wall extraction. Even though labour productivity had risen from just 0.9 tonnes per shift in 1980 to roughly 1.4 tonnes/shift in the mid-1990s it still remains only between 30–40 per cent of European levels, and less than 15 per cent of average U.S. levels. The official target of 2 tonnes/shift by the year 2000 may not be reached.

Large Chinese mines also have a long way to go to achieve acceptable levels of coal dust and work safety. The current situation is truly shocking: chronic bronchitis and pneumoconiosis incapacitate miners in

---

footnote continued

Ministry of Energy, *Zhongguo nengyuan* (*China's Energy Sources*), containing monthly production statistics. By far the most comprehensive source in English is: Jonathan E. Sinton (ed.), *China Energy Databook* (Berkeley: Lawrence Berkeley National Laboratory, 1996).

16. For a review of recent reforms of the industry see: Elspeth Thomson, "Reforming China's coal industry," *The China Quarterly*, No. 147 (1996), pp. 727–750.

17. Eventual combined capacity of these mines was to surpass 200 Mt/year. Shanxi's Pingshuo (Antaibao) mine involved a much-publicized personal deal between Armand Hammer, the late CEO of Occidental Petroleum, and Deng Xiaoping.

their thirties, and fatal accidents are at least 30 times as frequent per million tonnes of extracted coal as in the U.S.[18] Despite an increase of more than 50 per cent in the capacity of coal processing plants during the 1980s, still little less than half of all coal produced by large mines is processed – i.e. crushed, washed in order to separate coal from incombustible waste and sorted by size according to the needs of different customers.[19]

Nothing demonstrates the inadequacy of large-scale state-controlled coal mining in China better than the fact that it no longer produces the bulk of the country's coal. Its production share slipped from 56 per cent of the national output in 1979 to half in 1984 and 40 per cent by 1995. Since 1987, collectively or individually owned local mines have been responsible for virtually all output growth. This has gone a long way towards reducing China's long-standing coal supply shortages, as well as alleviating the environmentally undesirable cutting of trees for fuel and the burning of crop residues in rural stoves.[20]

But, in line with a frequent phenomenon in China's development, this quantitative growth has not been accompanied by qualitative improvements. The race to open small mines, usually without any geological and technical evaluation, has led to an enormous waste of resources in an unco-ordinated and often illegal quest for instant profits (at least a third of some 80,000 small mines may have been opened illegally). The combination of primitive extraction methods and inexperienced operators results in very low recovery rates. Because of low productivity and insufficient profits, many small mines – in some counties a quarter or a third – have to close down within a few years, or even a few months, of opening.

Coal extracted in local mines, including those owned by the state, is sold almost exclusively in a raw state, without any cleaning or sizing. As a result (and in spite of the increased capacities of washing plants attached to large mines), the overall share of processed coal in China has remained basically unchanged during the past 20 years, fluctuating between 18–20 per cent. While the labour productivity of small mines is very low – typically just a few hundred kilograms of fuel per shift per worker – occupational risks are extraordinarily high, with fatalities two to

18. The worst accidents in large mines are caused by coal dust explosions resulting from inadequate ventilation and poor safety practices. According to the Public Works Ministry, 9,974 people died in mining accidents in 1996. With coal mining accounting for about two-thirds of all deaths, Chinese fatalities average about 5.0 deaths/Mt of coal, compared to 0.15/Mt in the U.S.

19. In contrast, basic coal cleaning, involving washing and sizing, is standard in Western mining; some coal also undergoes specialized cleaning aimed at reducing coal's sulphur content in order to meet air emission standards.

20. Besides reducing biodiversity, deforestation contributes to higher erosion rates and straw burning deprives soils of nitrogen which would otherwise be recycled. For discussion of the extent and implications of these problems see: Vaclav Smil, *China's Environmental Crisis* (Armonk, NY: M. E. Sharpe, 1993).

five times higher than in China's large mining enterprises.[21] Mine-roof collapses and landslides are especially common in the absence of operating regulations.

Given such a disregard for human safety it is hardly surprising that the operators of small mines pay scant attention to the environmental consequences of coal extraction. Predictable results include extensive destruction of arable and grazing land, accelerated erosion of exposed topsoils and increasing air and water pollution. A recent survey in coal-rich Shenmu county on the Loess Plateau illustrates these perils.[22] Streams filled with mine spoils and increased sediment aggravate local floods, and erosion caused by mining adds almost another 300 Mt of silt to the Huang (Yellow) River already overburdened with eroded loess. Local air pollution has increased 24-fold for sulphur dioxide (SO_2) and 17-fold for particulate matter.

These extraordinary increases are caused by an unusually high concentration of inefficient coking plants and industrial boilers in one of China's most polluted counties – but all of the country's industrial and urban regions have been experiencing unacceptably high air pollution levels, a state attributable to coal's dominance in China's energy supply, to inadequate coal cleaning capacities and to inefficient combustion.

Most of the inferior fuel is burned either in the small boilers that fuel local industries, service establishments and housing estates, or in even less efficient household stoves (typically they are less than 30 per cent efficient). Only modern large coal-fired power plants and a growing number of newly installed industrial boilers are equipped with electrostatic precipitators which effectively remove particulate matter from hot flue gases. Consequently, Chinese emission factors per unit of delivered useful energy are extraordinarily high in comparison with rates in Western countries,

No matter which yardstick is used – Chinese standards or the World Health Organization (WHO) levels – typical concentrations of particulate matter in Chinese cities are excessive. Indeed, they are frequently so high that their annual mean surpasses recommended daily maxima. [23] And many cities fare much worse: Taiyuan and Linfeng in Shanxi, Lanzhou in Gansu, and Mudanjiang in Heilongjiang have recorded annual total suspended particulates (TSP) means above 600 $\mu g/m^3$. Major southern cities are somewhat cleaner, with annual averages of around 300 $\mu g/m^3$– but such values are still multiples of the WHO's guidelines (maxima of 60–90 $\mu g/m^3$ as an annual average).

The average sulphur content of major Chinese coal deposits, about 1.2

21. Published estimates of local mine fatalities have ranged between 8.5–23 per million tonnes of extracted coal. Rates above 20 would clearly make this one of the riskiest occupations anywhere in the world.

22. Wei Hu and Robert Evans, "The impacts of coal mining in Shenmu county, the Loess Plateau, China," *Ambio*, Vol. 26, No. 6 (1997), pp. 405–406.

23. The capital's mean annual total suspended particulate levels are between 400–500$\mu g/$ m^3– while the WHO's daily maximum of 150–230$\mu g/m^3$ can be exceeded on only seven days (2%) each year.

per cent, is not high by international standards, and statistics for large state mines show that they produce coal with average sulphur content of just 1.04 per cent.[24] But some southern coals, most notably those from Sichuan and Yunnan, have unusually high sulphur contents (up to 5 per cent). Official estimates put sulphur dioxide emissions at 15 million tonnes (Mt) in 1990 and 19 Mt in 1996 – but these totals do not contain a sizeable contribution from the spontaneous combustion of coal seams. Mao and Li estimated that every year more than 100 Mt of coal are lost to this difficult-to-control phenomenon, releasing at least 1.6 Mt SO_2.[25] Given the anticipated increase in coal consumption it will be extremely difficult to prevent a further substantial rise in SO_2 emissions.

Annual averages of SO_2 concentrations have been above the recommended WHO levels in every northern Chinese city and, because of high-sulphur content of many southern coals, also in many centres south of the Chang (Yangtze) River. Beijing's annual means have run between 80 $\mu g/m^3$ in the cleanest suburbs and twice that much in the most polluted locations. These are low levels compared to annual means (in $\mu g/m^3$) of over 400 in Taiyuan and Lanzhou. I have estimated that at least 200 million Chinese are exposed to annual TSP concentrations of above 300 $\mu g/m^3$, and at least 20 million are exposed to twice that level.[26]

Clean coal techniques (both combustion and conversion to liquid and gaseous fuels) are seen as the best ways of reconciling China's high reliance on coal with the need for environmental protection but the short-term contributions of this approach are rather limited. Fluidized bed combustion is not commercially available at the ratings now required for China's electricity generation (with annual capacity installations surpassing 15 GW, in units of more than 300 MW) and, as the costly and aborted U.S. foray into coal conversion shows, imports of hydrocarbons are preferable.

In the future, flue gas desulphurization will thus be necessary not only in parts of southern China where highly acid rains (with pH commonly below 4.5) are already causing serious damage to forests, but also in the north. During the next generation that region will acquire the world's largest concentrations of coal-fired power plants whose emissions will be carried eastward toward Korea and Japan. Current emissions are already causing concerns in both countries, but large-scale desulphurization is an expensive proposition.[27]

Yet another lasting challenge arising from China's high dependence on

24. Dai Hewu and Chen Wenmin, "Characterization and utilization of Chinese high-sulphur coal," *Meitan kexue jishu* (*Coal Science and Technology*), No. 5 (1989), pp. 30–35.

25. Mao Yushi and Li Dazheng, *Spontaneous Combustion of Coal in China and its Environmental Impact* (Beijing: China Institute of Mining Technology, 1994).

26. Vaclav Smil, *Environmental Problems in China: Estimates of Economic Costs* (Honolulu: East-West Center, 1996), pp. 19–20.

27. Desulphurization increases both capital and operating costs by at least 20%. Japanese aid offers a perfect opportunity to channel a sizeable amount of money through the country's large chemical companies which produce and install modern flue gas desulphurization plants.

coal is the heavy burden which the shipment of the fuel places on the country's railroads and, increasingly, on its wholly inadequate road network. New electrified lines were built from Shanxi, the largest coal-producing province, to the coast to facilitate growing coal exports (rising from just 6 Mt in 1980 to over 30 Mt by 1996), but the main north-south lines of domestic coal transfers are chronically strained by the coal shipments which comprise over 40 per cent of all transported freight. The most desirable solution to this problem – burning most of the fuel in large mine-mouth power plants in China's north and north-west – is already being implemented but the high demand for cooling water needed by such plants in a region with already serious water deficits will limit the extent of this option.[28]

At least one of the Chinese coal industry's chronic problems has finally been solved. In order to make coal readily available for expanding industries, China's Stalinist planners of the early 1950s priced it so low that even the best coal mines working some of the world's richest seams of fine bituminous coal could not make any profit. This irrational underpricing meant that coal mining accounted for only about 2 per cent of China's total industrial output during the early 1990s, and a single oilfield employing several tens of thousands of people could earn greater profits than the country's two million coal miners. The Ministry of Finance introduced a two-tier price system in 1984 and by 1994 the government finally freed all coal prices.

In contrast, the prices of crude oil and refined oil products are still tightly regulated. So are the prices of natural gas which rose steeply in March 1997 when the State Planning Commission announced a 12-fold increase for fertilizer plants, a nearly five-fold increase for residential use, and a four-fold increase for other uses.[29] But it is the adequacy of domestic hydrocarbon resources rather than the pace of price reform which has become the greatest concern of China's oil and gas planners.

Oil and Gas: Strategic Contradictions

Chinese leaders and the Chinese media like to talk and write about contradictions: few of them are as acute as those presented by the country's need for crude oil and natural gas. As already noted, in spite of its large territory, and no shortage of the sedimentary basins which promise oil and gas deposits, China is a relatively hydrocarbon-poor place. The absence of substantial natural gas reserves is particularly unfortunate. More exploration may eventually modify, if not reverse, this judgement – but so far the most promising new oil and gas region has turned out to be a vast disappointment.

Quite a few enthusiasts had initially envisaged the South China Sea as a new Saudi Arabia – and this promise lured all the major multinational oil companies into an unprecedented giveaway of the results of their

28. Smil, *China's Environmental Crisis*, p. 116.
29. "SPC hikes natural gas price," *China OGP*, No. 5 (15 May 1997), p. 10.

geophysical exploration to the Chinese.[30] Disappointment came quickly once the drilling licenses were awarded in the early 1980s. Now, after 15 years of fairly extensive exploratory drilling, the area has one relatively small natural gas field in the Yinggehai Basin just south of Hainan and a smattering of small oil fields in the Zhu (Pearl) River Basin.[31] Total output from all of China's offshore fields (including about half a dozen oilfields in the Bohai Basin near Tianjin) was less than 7 Mt in 1995 – or still less than 5 per cent of China's oil extraction.

And although China is no crude oil production dwarf – in 1996 it extracted 141 Mt, enough to be the world's fifth largest producer – its rapid rate of modernization has already seen demand surpass domestic production. While the country still exports crude oil to Japan and Korea, it has been a net importer of liquid fuels since 1993. With exports declining (from 20 Mt of crude oil in 1996 to 15 Mt in 1997) and imports rising (from just 3 Mt in 1990 to 22.6 Mt in 1996), China now has a growing trade deficit in its crude oil trade. In addition, its imports of refined products are now approaching the total volume of imported crude. Except for petrol, China is now a net importer of all refined fuels, with fuel oil accounting for just over half of 15.8 Mt bought in 1996.

The potential for further increases in demand is very large as per capita consumption is still only 0.14 tonnes/year, or less than 7 per cent of the Japanese mean. Chinese projections see the need for at least 50 Mt of imported crude oil by the year 2000, and forecasts of annual imports of well over 100 Mt a decade later appear conservative.[32] Clearly, times have changed: there is no more boasting about China's imperviousness to the vagaries of the global oil market and to destabilizing threats of oil shocks. Oil security is now among the top concerns of China's energy planners as rising demand (averaging 5.5 per cent a year for the ten years before 1997), barely increasing domestic extraction (a mere 1 per cent a year for the same period) and fading prospects for discoveries of giant fields combine to create a sense of urgency.[33]

The only way to avert the need for steadily increasing imports would be to discover large hydrocarbon deposits in Xinjiang, China's final great hydrocarbon frontier. While the region already produces almost 5 per cent of China's crude oil, much of it remains to be properly explored. After years of Chinese drilling, Exxon, Agip and several Japanese companies are now active in the area, and recent discoveries of both oil and gas have been fairly encouraging. Still, no supergiant hydrocarbon

30. For details see: Smil, *Energy in China's Modernization*, pp. 162–171.

31. China OGP, *China Petroleum Investment Guide* (Beijing: China OGP, 1994), pp. 91–140.

32. Chinese imports will help to bring closer the date when OPEC is once again the supplier of the last resort – and when the world will have to pay higher crude oil prices. Will China's greater involvement in Middle Eastern affairs be a stabilizing or destabilizing influence? Plausible arguments can be made for both outcomes.

33. Xihe Yu, "Oil security risk, wolf at door?" *China OGP*, No. 10 (15 May 1997), pp. 1–3. As oil imports rise, China will also have to build sufficient storage capacity (generally, this should equal 25% of annual imports).

field has been discovered in the inhospitable deserts of Tarim in central Xinjiang or the grasslands of Junggar in the region's north.

As the Xinjiang experience increasingly mirrors the South China Sea disappointment, the country could find it difficult merely to maintain its current rate of production. Just over half of all Chinese crude comes from two ageing fields which have been remarkably successful (mainly due to improved methods of secondary oil recovery) in maintaining a fairly steady output for nearly three decades. Heilongjiang's Daqing oilfield, discovered in 1959, remains by far the largest of the country's nearly 300 fields, producing just over a third of China's crude oil total. Shengli in Shandong, another old field discovered in 1962, has recently been adding about 17 per cent.

That the Chinese oilmen do not have blind faith in Xinjiang's potential has been clear for some time. China now participates in oil extraction in Canada (its first foreign involvement began in 1993), Russia, Mongolia, Thailand, Papua New Guinea, Iraq, Sudan, Peru and Venezuela. These foreign projects are expected to supply up to 5 Mt by the year 2000, and at least an additional 15 Mt by the year 2010. In addition, China will be negotiating deals for substantial long-term imports of oil and gas from hydrocarbon-rich regions of the former Soviet Union. The first such deal, announced in August 1997, gave the China National Petroleum Corporation exclusive rights to negotiate the development of a giant Uzen oilfield on the eastern shore of the Caspian Sea in Kazakhstan. Even bigger multinational export deals involving Russia, China, South Korea and Japan are planned to take Russian gas from giant Siberian fields to energy-deficient East Asia.[34]

No matter where most of its crude oil eventually comes from, China has a great deal of work to do to improve the quality of its liquid fuels. A very important step in that direction was taken in April 1997 when it was announced that only unleaded petrol will be sold in China's major cities by the year 2000, starting with Beijing.[35]

Electricity: Doubling Decades

A universal feature of the most intensive stages of national economic modernization is the demand for electricity growing faster than the total demand for all forms of commercial energy. Historic data show typical annual growth rates of between six and 9 per cent for the former, compared to three to 5 per cent for the latter. This means that every decade (or, to be more exact, a period anywhere between nine and 12 years long) sees the demand for electricity double. China conforms closely to this pattern: installed electricity generation grew by 8.04 per

34. The Kazakh deal would involve not only a 3,000-kilometre pipeline to move some 8 Mt of crude a year to Xinjiang, but perhaps also transhipment through Iran. Detailed discussion of large-scale international oil and gas projects involving Russia, China, Korea and Japan can be found in Keun-Wook Paik, *Gas and Oil in Northeast Asia* (London: The Royal Institute of International Affairs, 1995).
35. *China News Digest*, 10 April 1997 (http://www.cnd.org).

cent between 1980 and 1995; this growth will average about 7 per cent per year until the year 2000, and is projected to remain at around 6 per cent until the year 2010.[36]

Because of China's already large generating base, this has meant a globally unprecedented spell of new power plant building activity. Annual additions to capacity are now averaging about 16 GW, and China's electricity generation, which in 1980 – at 300 trillion watt-hours (TWh) – was roughly equal to British electricity production, will be (at 1,400 TWh) the world's third highest beyond the Russian and American outputs in the year 2000.

Inevitably, coal-fired power plants dominate this expansion. Coal combustion now generates about three-quarters of China's electricity, with an increasing share coming from large modern plants, mostly equipped with units (combinations of boiler and turbogenerator) rated at 300 MW; domestic units of 600 to 1,000 MW are now under development. As a result, fuel consumption per unit of electricity has been declining, from about 450 grams of coal equivalent per kilowatt-hour (gce/kWh) in 1980 to about 380 gce/kWh by 1995.[37]

Given the country's huge water power potential it is not surprising that a massive construction programme of large hydro stations is another key ingredient in China's long-term plans. The initial goal was to quadruple the installed capacity between 1980 and the year 2000 by putting on-line some 60 GW of new hydro capacity. Actual ratings will fall somewhat short of that goal.

By far the best known, and most controversial, part of this programme is the construction of the world's largest hydro project, the Sanxia (Three Gorges) Dam across the Chang River in western Hubei.[38] In order to install 18.2 GW of generating capacity and to produce 85 TWh electricity a year, the reservoir will consume about 630 km^2 of land and displace at least 1.2 million people. Unprecedented opposition to the construction of the Sanxia Dam – both inside and outside China – has been based on a variety of environmental, engineering and economic considerations but has failed to sway the leadership.[39]

Both the U.S. and Canada, two of the Western world's most experienced builders of large dams, refused to participate in this costly project as did the World Bank. The official Chinese projection for Sanxia's total cost is 200 billion *yuan* (at its 1996 value), with a quarter of that to be spent on the dam itself and a fifth on the resettlement of one million people.[40] As we have learned from other megaprojects, this cost estimate

36. Institute of Techno-economics and Energy System Analysis, *Global Electrification: The Next Decades* (Beijing: Qinghua University, 1997), pp. 1–3.

37. *Ibid.*

38. For comparison, Itaipu, currently the world's largest hydro project on the Parana between Brazil and Paraguay has 12.6 GW, and Grand Coulee, the largest U.S. hydro station, rates 6.8 GW.

39. For detailed analyses of what is wrong with Sanxia, see: Grainne Ryder (ed.), *Damming the Three Gorges* (Toronto: Probe International, 1990); Dai Qing, *Yangtze! Yangtze!* (London: Earthscan, 1994).

40. *China News Digest*, 8 April 1996 (http://www.cnd.org).

is almost certainly an underestimate. Sanxia's construction is now well underway: the river was diverted on 8 November 1997 and completion is planned for the year 2009. The second largest hydro project now under construction – Ertan on the Yalong River in Sichuan – will have a capacity of 3 GW.[41]

Nuclear generation is China's distant third choice for large-scale generation of electricity. After years of delays, China's first domestically-designed nuclear power plant, a 300 MW facility at Qinshan near Shanghai, was completed in 1992, and two years later the six-times-larger Daya Bay station in Guangdong, equipped with light-water French reactors based on a U.S. design, began supplying Hong Kong and easing electricity supply shortages in the province. Early nuclear expectations, much like their Western counterparts, were unrealistically high, as were the latest plans calling for building of four new plants with eight reactors by the year 2001, all in the coastal provinces of Zhejiang, Guangdong and Liaoning.[42]

Long-term prospects for China's nuclear power were given a major boost by the U.S. decision, announced during Jiang Zemin's American visit in October–November 1997, allowing American companies to sell pressurized and boiling water reactors to China. French and Canadian efforts to sell their reactors will also continue, but forecasting the country's nuclear generating capacity remains a much more precarious than foreseeing its coal-fired and hydro capacities.[43]

The magnitude of the task, particularly when combined with China's still limited technical capacities, means that the expansion of the country's modern electricity generating capacity has been, and will continue to be, highly dependent on foreign participation. By 1995, foreign investors had poured almost US$15 billion into China's electricity generation, participating in more than 60 large- and medium-sized thermal and hydro projects.[44] Foreign expertise has also been important in reducing China's wasteful energy use.

Rationalizing Consumption: Efficiency Gains

The question of meeting rising demand – i.e. the matter of energy supply shortfalls that have reportedly exercised near-chronic checks on the performance of China's economy for the past quarter of a century – is more complicated than simple comparisons of official statistics would indicate. In fact, China is using too much primary energy to satisfy its current final demand. Signs of inefficient energy use abound. There are still too many old Stalinist-style state enterprises whose managers have never been concerned with optimizing energy use.

41. China's long-term hydrogeneration plans are outlined in Smil, *Energy in China's Modernization*, pp. 171–180.

42. *China News Digest*, 16 October 1996 (http://www.cnd.org).

43. Sales of Russian nuclear power plants to China are particularly uncertain.

44. This represents about 40% of total foreign direct investment received by China to the end of 1995: The World Bank, *China 2020*, p. 90.

At the same time, China has made some impressive, and too little appreciated, advances. Certainly the most encouraging indicator of its progress towards efficiency has been a rapid decline of the overall energy/GDP intensity. This measure is a powerful marker of two critical trends: lower energy/GDP ratios do not merely indicate a more efficient economy, they also mean that the economy puts, in relative terms, less burden on the environment by reducing the extent of land, water and air pollution.[45]

The long-term decline of energy/GDP intensities is expected with advancing economic modernization and it has been quite pronounced in both North America and in Western Europe – but the recent Chinese improvements have occurred at an even faster rate. If China's energy/GDP ratio had remained at the 1980 level, the country would have needed to burn twice as much coal in 1995 to produce that year's GDP, and hence also generate a much larger amount of environmental pollution.

Using the State Statistical Bureau data on energy consumption and inflation-adjusted values of the GDP, the national average of energy intensity was about 0.7 kilograms of coal equivalent (kgce) per 1 *yuan* of GDP; by 1990 the rate had declined to 0.42 kgce/1980 *yuan*, and in 1995 it was slightly below 0.35 kgce – a bit less than half its value 15 years ago.[46] Such a rate of decline is unmatched by any other major modernizing economy.

Industrial efficiencies have improved remarkably, not only because of the introduction of more efficient converters and processes but also due to the outright closure of many old plants and to a major shift from production previously dominated by inherently less energy-efficient heavy industries to light manufacturing.[47] The performance of China's cement industry, which consumes about 5 per cent of all commercial energy, is a good example of possible efficiency gains. Its output has roughly quintupled since 1980, with more than 500 Mt (nearly a quarter of the entire global output) produced in over 7,000 plants. During the same period average fuel consumption in about 60 of the largest state-run plants using rotary kilns fell from about 6.6 MJ per tonne of clinker (which is then ground to cement) to just 4.5 MJ/t.[48]

In contrast, too many small local industrial enterprises remain highly inefficient, and major efficiency gains are yet to be made in household energy consumption. Hardly any of today's Chinese apartments are built with wall and ceiling insulation or double-glazed windows, and even fewer have any individual temperature controls – fibreglass and ther-

45. For problems with determining and comparing China's energy intensity, see Smil, *China's Environmental Crisis*, pp. 72–75 and 126–28.

46. Vaclav Smil, "China's environment and security: simple myths and complex realities," *SAIS Review*, Vol. 17 (Winter–Spring 1997), pp. 107–126.

47. Lin demonstrated that energy conservation measures rather than structural changes were the leading cause of post-1980 efficiency gains: Xiannuan Lin, *China's Energy Strategy: Economic Structure, Technological Choices, and Energy Consumption* (Westport, CT: Praeger, 1996).

48. F. Liu, M. Ross and S. Wang, "Energy efficiency in China's cement industry," *Energy – The International Journal*, Vol. 20 (1995), pp. 669–681.

mostats in millions of newly built apartments would bring energy savings and environmental benefits for decades to come.

The rise in electricity consumption has been driven not only by rapidly growing industrial demand but also by an even more rapidly spreading ownership of household appliances – and this means that major efficiency gains can greatly influence future demand. Many Western utilities have become increasingly engaged in demand-side management by providing credit or offering more efficient converters at subsidized rates. China's opportunities for this kind of efficiency improvement are immense as the country now ranks as the world's largest producer of household electrical appliances and gadgets. In 1995 its annual production capacity reached 80 million electric fans, 20 million colour televisions, 15 million refrigerators, 15 million washing machines, and 8 million room air conditioners. Even small efficiency improvements translate into large capacity savings when multiplied by tens of millions of various appliances.

These savings could be particularly impressive for whitegoods such as refrigerators. In 1989, China surpassed the U.S. to become the world's largest producer of refrigerators but the insufficient thermal insulation, inefficient compressors and poor-quality gaskets of typical Chinese-made refrigerators make them up to 50 per cent less efficient than optimized redesigns which are also chlorofluorocarbon-free.[49] Similarly, better designs could cut the electricity demand of a wide variety of smaller gadgets, ranging from electrical fans – now ubiquitous in all affluent urban households – and rice cookers to hair driers and curlers.

Looking Ahead: Difficult Challenges

Even the most desirable combination of trends reducing the growth of China's energy demand – further industrial restructuring complemented by persistent and aggressive energy conservation campaigns – would not prevent significant increases in China's primary energy consumption and electricity generation. As always with Chinese output statistics, impressive growth rates and huge absolute totals still hide only very modest per capita consumption rates.

China's annual per capita consumption of fossil fuels and primary (hydro and nuclear) electricity now averages about 25 gigajoules (GJ). This is more than the Indian rate, but only about half of the global mean, and – to indicate the distance separating China from its great East Asian example – still less than a fifth of Japanese consumption.[50] Numerous national peculiarities – environmental, economic and cultural – make it impossible to offer a definite value of per capita energy use that would indicate a high quality of life in a modernized economy. However,

49. David G. Fridley, "U.S.–China super-efficient CFC-free refrigerator project," *LBNL Energy Analysis Program 1995 Annual Report* (Berkeley: Lawrence Berkeley National Laboratory, 1996), pp. 24–25.

50. The gap is even wider for average annual electricity use: China's 1995 rate of about 800 kWh/capita was only a tenth of the Japanese mean, and only 10% of that low total was accounted for by household use.

international comparisons show that the promise of economic security, good health care and broadly accessible educational opportunities does not come with annual rates below at least 50 GJ per capita.[51]

Consequently, it is easy to make a case for yet another doubling of China's per capita energy use, and because of the expected addition of at least another 250–300 million people during the next two generations the fulfilment of this goal would require a 2.5-fold increase of today's total consumption. Even if no insurmountable extraction and transportation problems accompanied this growth (most unlikely given, above all, China's deepening involvement in the global oil market), one trend is already causing a great deal of concern.

With about one-eighth of the global total, China is currently the world's second largest producer of greenhouse gases, its emission rates are greater than Russia's and a bit over half as large as America's. But while Russian emissions have actually been declining with the post-Soviet collapse of industrial production, and while the U.S. emissions are growing only very slowly and, given political will, could be stabilized at current levels or even cut, China's emissions will increase substantially during the coming generation.[52]

Rapid economic expansion and the continuing reliance on coal can be expected to more than double China's current carbon dioxide emissions, and large increases in the other important greenhouse gases are forecast as well. As China develops its natural gas reserves, methane losses will rise. In the agricultural sector, more rice will mean more methane from rice paddies, and more nitrous oxide from the denitrification of synthetic fertilizers. Nitrous oxide is 200 times more effective at trapping heat than carbon dioxide, and China is already responsible for more than 20 per cent of the world's nitrous oxide emissions.

The question is thus one of when, not if: China will become the world's largest emitter of greenhouse gases, but it may be as early as 2010 or as late as 2025. At this time, official policy offers no hope for remedial action. As expressed in the Beijing Declaration of 1991, China believes that the rich countries are responsible for the rise in greenhouse gases both in terms of current emissions and in a cumulative sense, and hence it concludes that the developing countries need not do anything to limit their emissions until they reach the developed world's level of per capita emissions, as well as its historical cumulative emissions.[53]

Chinese energy would face many challenges even if there were no signs of relatively rapid global warming during the coming generation. Judging by the Western experience, dealing with a truly runaway demand for transportation fuels will be particularly problematic. Expected conse-

51. Vaclav Smil, "Elusive links: energy, value, economic growth and quality of life," *OPEC Review*, Vol. 16, No. 1 (Spring 1992), pp. 1–21.

52. Vaclav Smil, "China's greenhouse gas emissions," *Global Environmental Change*, Vol. 4, No. 4 (1994), pp. 279–286.

53. Although China strongly objects to the imposition of binding obligations on developing countries, it is now prepared to make (unspecified) efforts to reduce greenhouse gas emissions: *China News Digest*, 5 November 1997 (http://www.cnd.org).

quences will be rising concentrations of ozone (the most aggressive air pollution oxidant created by complex reactions in photochemical smog), excessive losses of highly productive farmland, huge economic penalties for time wasted idling in stalled traffic, further degradation of urban environments, a rising toll of deaths and injuries in car accidents – and greater dependence on oil imports.[54]

Although it is not yet too late to avoid the worst and follow the *shinkansen* model of transportation by developing a network of efficient rapid train links throughout its densely populated provinces, Chinese planners are most inappropriately bent on following the American example: the official policy is for every family to eventually have a car.[55]

While this article has focused on China's commercial energy, the country's non-commercial rural fuel supply does remain precarious: in many areas peasants have barely enough to support a minimal existence.[56] The combination of small local coal mines, private fuelwood lots and more efficient stoves has gone a long way towards easing widespread energy shortages in village households. Mass adoption of improved stoves – with some 100 million installed since the early 1980s – has been particularly helpful,[57] but this alone cannot propel rural populations to modernity.

Nor will the role of renewable energies be as helpful as envisaged by many uninformed enthusiasts. Two of China's showcase renewable programmes of the 1970s – small-scale hydro stations and biogas digesters – have been reduced to modest proportions as technical problems and economic realities have exposed their limitations.[58] China has considerable wind energy (particularly in Inner Mongolia), geothermal energy (in more than a dozen provinces, and especially in Tibet) and solar energy (everywhere in its arid interior) potential but, so far, these sources have made only very limited, local difference, and their future contributions remain highly uncertain.

A quarter of a century of frequent long-term energy forecasts have taught us the perils of such exercises. Even when the numbers click, the realities do not agree. In my first book on China's energy, written in 1975, my median forecast of the country's primary energy demand had an error of a mere 2 per cent for the year 1985, and only 10 per cent for the

54. The effects of ozone on China's food production capacity may be the most worrisome long-term problem: Vaclav Smil, *Energy and the Environment: Challenges for the Pacific Rim* (Vancouver: Asia Pacific Foundation of Canada, 1996).

55. This unwise goal would eventually mean between 300–400 million vehicles – compared to about 500 million cars registered world-wide in 1995: American Automobile Manufacturers Association, *Motor Vehicle 1996 Facts and Figures* (Detroit: AAMA, 1996), p. 44. Even if the average fuel consumption of Chinese cars could be just half the current U.S. mean, China would need about 300 Mt of petrol a year, roughly twice as much as its current annual crude oil consumption.

56. For basic numbers see Smil, *China's Environmental Crisis*, pp. 101–110.

57. Kirk R. Smith *et al.* "One hundred million improved cookstoves in China: how was it done?" *World Development*, Vol. 21 (1993), pp. 941–961.

58. For details on these programmes see: Smil, *Energy in China's Modernization*, pp. 54–69.

year 1990.[59] Yet, although I was certain that major changes were inevitable, I could not have predicted the reality of post-1979 modernization with all of its complex implications for energy demand, economic expansion and environmental degradation. Inevitably, there are more surprises ahead.

Industrial Pollution in China and Remedial Policies

Eduard B. Vermeer

Introduction

This paper presents an analysis of the adoption and implementation of Chinese environmental policies and pollution abatement measures. It sketches the role of the State Environmental Protection Administration (SEPA) and the recently adopted Five-Year Plan for the years 1996–2000 in coping with China's increasing problems of water, air and soil pollution. Remedial measures, which could be legal, administrative or economic, are analysed both as part of more general programmes of legal and economic reform, and as specific designs for local or sectoral problems. In previous articles, I have discussed several major environmental concerns: environmental damages, scarcity of water, control over emissions by township and village enterprises (TVEs), investments and management methods.[1] The present contribution will focus on wider political issues, such as participatory policies, differences in implementation between regions and sectors, and most recent developments in industrial pollution problems and abatement measures. This survey cannot be complete: the limitations of space and the need to give some concrete examples make it necessary to be selective. Therefore, while some problems will be highlighted – such as water treatment in the Huai River basin, sulphur dioxide emissions, and pollution by TVEs – other problems such as noise pollution will be omitted.

The scope of environmental policies and the definition of environmental degradation differs from place to place. Most people are concerned primarily about the effects of pollution on their immediate environment and health, and global issues such as global warming, depletion of the ozone layer, oceanic pollution, loss of biodiversity and nuclear radiation are now receiving more and more attention from governments and the public. The actual efforts of countries and governments vary. In developing countries – and China is no exception to this – there are clear links between poverty, lack of awareness of environmental degradation and threats to human health, limited capacity to sacrifice present consumption on behalf of future generations, and lack of political concern for the environment.

China is a large, polluting country, with rapidly increasing industrial production, domestic and foreign trade and investment, and a central

1. E. B. Vermeer, "Management of environmental pollution in China: problems and abatement policies," *China Information,* Vol. V, No. 1 (1990), pp. 32–65 and "An inventory of losses due to environmental pollution: problems in the sustainability of China's economic growth," *China Information,* Vol X, No. 1 (1995), pp. 19–50.

government determined to catch up with international standards. Some enlightened politicians, government officials and industrial managers in China have demonstrated their active concern for reducing pollution and encouraging cleaner production, and environmental protection has recently been elevated to the status of "national fundamental policy." However, economic growth still has priority. More fundamental than shortages of capital or trained manpower are institutional and mental limits. The communist government lacks the capacity for self-regulation and does not allow media and action groups to further environmental causes. Society at large has little awareness of the threats of environmental pollution to human health and future resource availability, and does little to restrain individual pollutive behaviour. Weak and uneven enforcement of environmental laws and protectionism in local markets discourage industries from reducing pollution and increasing efficiency – which should be the twin goals of any industrial policy. The present crisis in the old industrial areas and sectors, and the booming success of the TVEs have made it difficult to adopt the more advanced and environmentally friendly technologies from the modern sectors, coastal cities and foreign-invested enterprises on a national scale. Such political, institutional and economic barriers and differentials between the economic sectors in China are major impediments to the spread of advanced technologies and management practices.

International Agreements, Investments and Trade

China has subscribed to most international treaties in the environmental field. In return, it expected – and to some extent received – foreign support for many of its environmental goals. Between 1991 and 1995, US$1.2 billion worth of foreign capital was invested in environmental protection. Since the 1980s, the World Bank has been a major source of support, and, together with the Asian Development Bank, it now provides some US$800 million in environmental loans to China annually.[2] There are bilateral co-operation agreements with aid organizations from the U.S., Korea, Canada, Japan, Germany, Finland, Denmark and the Netherlands. Between 1996 and 2000, China expects considerably more foreign funds, to a level of about US$4 billion.[3] The Chinese government

2. At the Houston summit meeting in mid-1990, leaders of the G7 countries added two additional criteria (apart from basic human needs) for support of loans to China: facilitation of economic reform and benefit to the environment. Thereafter, over the years 1993–1996, roughly two-thirds of a total US$9 billion of IBRD loans to China was spent on infrastructural projects (mainly transportation and electrical power) and 11% was spent on the environment. Of an approximate total of US$3 billion of IDA loans, 22% was spent on the environment, but less than 7% of US$4.5 billion of ADB loans was spent in this area. (The World Bank, *World Tables 1995–1997* (Washington DC: The World Bank, various years); The Asian Development Bank, *Emerging Asia: Changes and Challenges* (Manila: The Asian Development Bank, 1997).) As it has been agreed that, by 1999, China will no longer be eligible for the concessional IDA loans, the financing of environmental projects will become more difficult when it has to be arranged at market-based rates.
3. Guojia Huanbaoju *et al. Guojia huanjing baohu jiu wu jihua he 2010 nian yuanjing mubiao (Ninth Five-Year Plan for Environmental Protection and Targets for the Year 2010)*

maintains that China is entitled to foreign support because it lacks the financial, organizational and technical capacity to single-handedly deal with international environmental demands for projects such as the reduction of sulphur dioxide emissions, and the protection of the ozone layer and biological diversity. This view is shared by environmental experts. In 1996, China's own expenditure on the environment was only US$6.3 billion – twice that of Taiwan but less than one-tenth of Japan's. Its domestic environmental protection equipment industry is underdeveloped and cannot compete with foreign companies.[4]

Environmental protection has become a factor in foreign trade and investment,[5] as China learned when, for instance, the EU restricted imports of refrigerators using CFCs as a coolant in 1990, and the U.S. restricted imports of textiles which carried heavy metals and other pollutants in 1993. On the one hand, China protests that "foreign countries should not impose trade restrictions on China under the pretext of the environment, impose environmental standards on our products or other 'green' taxes. Green signs, packaging or recycling should not bring additional burdens to developing countries ... Because economic development is uneven, countries have different environmental policies, and their different standards should be accepted."[6] On the other hand, it realizes that environmental measures are necessary for the health of its own population and part of a global process of technological modernization. Some officials are willing to accept that free trade has a positive effect on environmental protection.[7]

In 1996, China imported environmental equipment and services worth US$1.8 billion.[8] Its own environmental industry is small, but expected to

---

footnote continued

(Beijing: Zhongguo huanjing kexue chubanshe, 1996), pp. 4 and 46. US$1 is equivalent to about 8.30 *yuan*.

4. As the prices of most goods and services are lower in China, international comparisons understate the Chinese effort. At the end of 1993, China had 8,651 enterprises (half of which were TVEs) in this sector, with over 45 billion *yuan* in fixed assets, 31 billion *yuan* turnover (11 billion from product sales), 4.1 billion *yuan* profits and 1,882,000 employees. Only 370 of these enterprises were of any great size. Xu Shufan and Liu Xianhua, "Woguo huanbao chanye fazhan xianzhuang ji duice" ("The state of development of China's environmental protection industry and countermeasures"), *Huanjing baohu (Environmental Protection)*, No. 2 (1997), pp. 39–41; NEPA (ed.), *Disi zi quanguo huanjing baohu huiyi wenjian huibian (Collection of Documents from the Fourth National Environmental Conference)* (Beijing: Zhongguo huanjing kexue chubanshe, 1996), p. 297; NEPA, the State Planning Commission and the State Economics and Trade Commission, *Ninth Five-Year Plan for Environmental Protection and Distant Targets for 2010* (Beijing: Zhongguo huanjing kexue chubanshe, 1996), p. 3.

5. For example, Qu Ruyao, "Guoji huanbao da qushi dui woguo waimaodi yingxiang ji duice sikao" ("The effect of international trends in environmental protection on foreign trade of our country and countermeasures"), *Jingji lilun yu jingji guanli (Economic Theory and Economic Management)*, No. 1 (1997), pp. 70–74.

6. NEPA (ed.), *Documents from the Fourth National Conference*, pp. 363–64.

7. Liu Min, "Maoyi ziyouhua dui huanjingde yingxiang he woguode lifa duice" ("The effect of trade liberalization on the environment and legal countermeasures of our country"), *Huanjing baohu (Environmental Protection)* No. 10 (1997), pp. 29–32, 35.

8. The U.S. Department of Energy has estimated that the Chinese market for environmental goods and services is US$15 billion, and grows by 30% annually: see U. S. Department of Energy, *China Country Review* (Washington: Government Printing Office, 1996).

grow by 20 per cent or more per year. In China's view, developed nations have the greater responsibility for the solution of global environmental problems – especially because they have been, or still are, the greatest polluters – and should give support to other countries. By stressing that environmental policies cannot be divorced from the economic development which is necessary to fulfil the basic needs of the poor people of this world, China lays a double moral claim on the rich countries.

Problems of National Leadership and Control, the Plan and Citizen Involvement

The various sectors and levels of the Chinese government are not equally supportive of domestic or foreign projects in environmental protection and abatement of pollution. The honeymoon period of the 1980s, when pollution abatement could make rapid advances at low costs, is over. The dominant political group stresses economic growth over environmental quality, even if official policy is that "economic growth and environmental protection should go hand in hand, and the one should not go at the expense of the other." The National Environmental Protection Agency (NEPA, renamed the State Environmental Protection Administration or SEPA in March 1998) built up a nation-wide control network in the 1980s, benefiting considerably from foreign project funding and technical assistance, and the establishment of a co-ordinating Environmental Protection Commission under the State Council has further enhanced its status. The number of its employees at all levels has doubled between 1985 and 1995 to 88,000 people. However, it has become difficult to maintain high standards of staff quality and performance as salaries were eaten away by inflation and environmental protection became an unrewarding, low-status job. Moreover, the political tendency of the 1990s is towards smaller government, devolution of central controls and liberalization. In consequence, while SEPA has continued its pressure for more environmental policies and investments (and thereby is a natural partner for foreign assistance), its powers have remained very limited, notably over chemical and other large industries, and in rural areas. Writing in January 1997, Kley and Thomas noted that "there are few clear areas where [NEPA] has the final say, and for the most part, each ministry is responsible for implementing industry-specific legislation. The result is a considerable degree of overlap."[9] Over the past two decades, NEPA and Chinese environmental scientists have urged publicly on many occasions that China should spend at least 1.5 per cent of its GNP on measures to protect the environment.[10] In fact, China

9. Julia E. Kley and Felicity C. Thomas, "An evolving environmental framework," *The China Business Review* (Jan–Feb 1997), pp. 34–40.

10. Most recently, at the Fourth National Environmental Conference, "we should increase investment in environmental protection from the present 0.7–0.8% of GNP to 1.5%, and from 4–5% of investments in capital construction to 7%; ... the percentage of technical transformation funds which are used for environmental protection should be increased from the present 1% to 7%. In urban construction, it should be increased from the present 25–30% to 40%." See NEPA (ed.), *Documents from the Fourth National Conference*, p. 326.

Table 1: **Investment in Prevention and Treatment of Pollution, 1991–1994**

	1991	1992	1993	1994
Investment (billion *yuan*, current prices)	17.0	20.6	26.9	30.7
% of GDP (current prices)	0.84	0.86	0.86	0.68
% of GDP (1990 prices)	0.81	0.75	0.68	0.63
% of social investment	3.09	2.62	2.16	1.88
% of EP investment used for:				
- old enterprises	41	38	33	34
- new businesses	26	27	28	29
- urban construction	33	35	40	37
% of EP investment originating from:				
- base state allocation	58	59	60	62
- renewal state allocation	19	18	20	18
- retained profits from recycling	1	1	1	1
- refunded pollution fees	12	12	11	11
- other	10	10	8	8
EP as % of total investments in:				
- new projects "3S"	4.2	4.0	3.5	3.7
- renewal projects	1.7	1.2	1.0	0.9
- urban construction	32.6	25.2	20.4	17.0

Source:
    The China Environmental Yearbook Editing Committee and Society (eds.), *Zhongguo huanjing nianjian 1996* (*China Environmental Yearbook 1996*) (Beijing: Zhongguo huanjing kexue chubanshe, 1996), pp. 112–14, 137.

has never spent more than half of that, and the figure is not rising (see Table 1).

At the local level, priorities, projects and implementation of national regulations are decided by municipal and county governments, and standards vary widely. In 1997, the adoption of the *Ninth Five-Year Plan for Environmental Protection and Distant Targets for 2010* (hereafter the Plan) illustrates this. The Plan was drawn up under the joint responsibility of NEPA, the State Planning Commission and the State Economics and Trade Commission, with cautions from the State Council to co-operate in its implementation. Concrete goals were set and over 1,500 projects listed. However, it stated that "the necessary capital should be provided mainly by local governments and enterprises. The state will provide loans, use of foreign capital and economic policy support. For the strengthening of their capacity for environmental monitoring, all government levels should request support from the financial departments."[11]

The Plan's targets are rather ambitious. Urban concentrated water treatment facilities should increase by 20 million tonnes per day, with a chemical oxygen demand (COD) reduction of 4 million tonnes. About 5

11. State Council Notice [1996] No. 72, d.d. 3 September 1996, in Guojia huanbaoju *et al. Ninth Five-Year Plan for Environmental Protection*, pp. 1–2.

Table 2: **Discharge of Main Pollutants in 1995, and Plan for 2000 (all sources, all levels)**

	1995	2000 (planned)
Fly ash (million tonnes)	17.4	17.5
Sulphur dioxide (million tonnes)	23.7	24.6
Industrial dust (million tonnes)	17.3	17.0
Industrial fixed waste (million tonnes)	61.7	60.0
COD (million tonnes)	22.3	22.0
Oils (tonnes)	84,400	83,100
Cyanide (tonnes)	3,495	3,273
Arsenic (tonnes)	1,446	1,376
Mercury (tonnes)	27	26
Lead (tonnes)	1700	1668
Cadmium (tonnes)	285	270
Cr6 (tonnes)	669	618

Source:
   The China Environmental Yearbook Editing Committee and Society (eds.), *China Environmental Yearbook 1996*, p. 115.

and 7 per cent, respectively, of these will be realized in the coastal cities and three lakes (Tai, Chao, Dianchi). Through various measures, such as installation of desulphurization facilities and precipitators, washing of coal and increased supply of gas and central heating, sulphur dioxide emissions are to be reduced by 1.8 million tonnes and dust by 1.6 million tonnes. Treatment capacity of industrial solid waste will be increased by 40 million tonnes.[12] As Table 2 shows, these measures will result in a stabilization rather than a decrease of pollutants between 1995 and 2000. Also, only 12 pollutants have been subjected to quantitative control of discharges (three for air, eight for water, and solid waste), and almost all pertain to industry only (and none to agriculture, although nitrate pollution of surface and ground water is most serious, and pesticides are a major threat to health).[13] Therefore, main achievements are likely to be in the urban and state-owned industrial sectors. The rural industrial and agricultural sector will further deteriorate, as the improvement of standards in some areas will be offset by increased pollutive activities, both from displacement and from economic growth, in most other areas.

   The case of other socialist countries such as the Soviet Union has proven beyond doubt that state-planned economies tend to waste resources and have little regard for the quality of life of individual

   12. NEPA, the State Planning Commission and the State Economics and Trade Commission, *Ninth Five-Year Plan for Environmental Protection*, p. 72.
   13. Since the use of pesticides was limited in the early 1980s, not much has been published about their effects. Annual affected people and deaths fell to some 100,000 and 10,000, respectively. Studies in the 1990s showed that suburban rice and vegetables had high levels of contamination: see *Huanjing baohu* (*Environmental Protection*), No. 7 (1997), p. 43.

citizens, and that without a free press, independent political parties or action groups, the environment receives insufficient attention.[14] Lothspeich and Chen mention three systemic features of centrally-planned economies which threaten the environment: limitations of citizen involvement in environmental issues, an obsession with growth and industrialization, and the high material intensity of production methods promoted at the expense of natural resources.[15] In China, the absence of democratic processes to reach consensus over environmental policies, and the distrust of civil protest or action in any form further hamper the efforts to increase public awareness and political support for environmental actions. It should be recognized that although state-imposed mass mobilization campaigns, such as that for tree planting, may have been very effective, modern society requires public participation based on adequate information, open exchange of views, transparency of the decision-making process and early involvement of interested parties.

The National People's Congress and other law-making bodies have followed foreign examples and passed many environmental laws, and these have been backed up by many directives from the State Council and detailed regulations passed by local governments.[16] However, their enforcement and coverage has been rather uneven. In June 1997, NPC Chairman Qiao Shi denounced the illegal conduct of leading cadres and pressed for a greater role for people's congresses, the people and mass media in supervision of the environmental work of local governments, but his subsequent removal from the Politburo and Central Committee has ended his influence.[17] Others have advocated the introduction of hearings in the course of environmental impact assessments, where local residents might have their say.[18] Recently, NEPA, the Communist Party and the Department of Education have jointly launched an "Action Plan for Environmental Publicity and Education," which emphasizes

---

14. D. J. Peterson, *Troubled Lands: The Legacy of Soviet Environmental Destruction* (Boulder, CO: Westview, 1993); V. Sobell, "The systemic roots of the East European ecological crisis," *Environmental Policy Review*, Vol. 1 (1990), pp. 1–10.

15. R. Lothspeich and A. Chen, "Environmental protection in the People's Republic of China," *Journal of Contemporary China*, No. 14 (1997), p. 47.

16. By 1995, China had formulated five environmental laws, eight related laws, more than 20 regulations and 364 environmental targets. More than 600 local regulations had been passed. For central regulations and directives, see *Guowuyuan huanjing baohu weiyuanhui wenxian xuanbian* and *Guowuyuan huanjing baohu weiyuanhui wenjian huibian (er)* (*Selected Documents of the State Environmental Protection Committee* and *Collected Documents of the State Environmental Committee (Vol. II)*) (Beijing: Zhongguo huanjing kexue chubanshe, 1988 and 1995, respectively), and the China Environmental Yearbook Editing Committee and Society (eds.), *Zhongguo huanjing nianjian* (*China Environmental Yearbook*) (Beijing: Zhongguo huanjing kexue chubanshe, various years).

17. "Leading cadres … should strengthen legal awareness on protecting the environment and resources, administer affairs according to law, and resolutely stop such behaviour where their words replace the law, their powers supersede the law, and where they violate the law while enforcing it," Qiao Shi, speech at the 1997 NPC meeting on protecting the environment and resources on 18 June 1997, *Xinhua News Agency*, 18 June 1997, as translated in British Broadcasting Corporation, *Summary of World Broadcasts, Part 3: Asia Pacific* (BBC/FE/2955).

18. Clause 22 of the Water Law provides room for such a hearing, *Huanjing baohu* (*Environmental Protection*), No. 4 (1996), p. 28.

of environmental knowledge in regular curricula.[19] Very little has been written about environmental action groups in China, with the exception of those involved with the giant Sanxia (Three Gorges) hydropower station, for the simple reason that they hardly exist. Only the official *China Environment News*, which caters to the foreign community, highlights "green" activities by concerned citizens. Most concern conservation of wildlife resources, such as the panda, white dolphin, golden monkey and crane – easy themes to catch the interest of children – but (like tree-planting) these issues are also the most innocuous, the furthest from urban pollution and the least threatening to polluting industries. Participation by non-government organizations and concerned individuals, which is almost completely non-existent in China, is an essential condition for increased environmental awareness and activities and pollution abatement programmes.[20]

Increasingly large parts of industry, particularly those managed by township and village governments, have been outside of the control of SEPA and are hardly monitored, if at all. This is a severe handicap for pollution abatement programmes, whether instigated by national agencies or more or less directly by foreign donors. The absence of reliable data, and resultant official disregard of their contribution to pollution, has resulted in statistical confusion and overly optimistic pictures of achievements in environmental improvements.[21] Inspection is uneven and infrequent, and reported data often represent the design capacities of equipment rather than actual measurements.[22] This is the more regrettable

19. *CCICED Newsletter*, Vol. 3, No. 1 (1997), p. 2.

20. Dai Qing and Eduard B. Vermeer, "Do good work, but do not offend the 'old communists': recent activities of China's non-governmental environmental protection organizations and individuals," paper presented at the ECAN Workshop in Hamburg, 17–18 October 1997.

21. Data carried by the *Statistical Yearbook of China* are incomplete, and often inconsistent with those published in NEPA journals. For instance, a table in the 1995 yearbook gives figures of 5.83 million tonnes of discharged industrial dust and 18.25 million tonnes of discharged SO_2; the first figure disregards TVEs and therefore covers only one-third of total industrial discharge, while the second does include TVE emissions. Conclusions based on such data (such as by R. Lotspeich and A. Chen, "Environmental protection in the People's Republic of China," pp. 33–59) are not valid.

22. Statistical materials on China's environment are incorrect for several reasons: their scope is limited to enterprises of county-level and above, and some of the most seriously polluting organizations and TVEs. But very few TVEs, private companies and companies belonging to urban street committees, tertiary and service industries report data, and pollution by urban households is not included. Reporting is incomplete or fraudulent, in order to avoid pollution charges or fines. People concerned have inadequate knowledge and training, and measurements are taken infrequently. "Inspection of sources of industrial pollution happens two to four times annually for wastewater, one or two times for waste gases and noise, and for fixed waste even less often. Whether this really reflects the emission levels of the enterprises is difficult to say. Regulations on where to have sample spots, how often to sample and with which equipment are lacking. This is particularly serious for waste gas measurements, which last only a few minutes ... There should be a three-level network of inspection. Industrial wastewater inspection by the enterprise itself should occur once a week (and follow the production cycle) ... and waste gas once a month (and a sample be about one cubic metre) ... Inspection by the branch station should be once every quarter for wastewater and twice a year for waste gases, fixed waste and noise. The higher-level stations should inspect a sample of 30 to 50%:" Lin Chaoyang, "Lun zongliang kongzhidi paiwu

because many of the small-scale industries not covered by official statistics are highly pollutive and treatment measures would yield immediate and high returns. However, for the same reason that TVEs are beyond the reach of the government, they are difficult for remedial programmes to access.

Chinese Citizens' Perceptions of Pollution Problems

According to most domestic experts, China's environmental situation is seriously deteriorating. Major causes given are population growth, the limited per capita availability of resources, fast economic growth, wasteful production methods and lack of concern from government or public. As Shen Yimin has written, "China is one of the worst polluted countries in the world. On a whole, our environmental conditions resemble those of the developed countries in the 1960s when their environmental pollution was the gravest."[23] Even the Plan admits that, "generally speaking, environmental pollution centred around cities is still increasing, and creeping into the villages. The scope of environmental destruction is increasing, and its seriousness, too. More and more, environmental pollution and ecological destruction become major restricting factors influencing economic and social development, and of great concern to the people."[24]

There is little information about the environmental awareness of the ordinary Chinese citizens or their willingness for action, although two recent opinion polls provided some indications. Major concerns, according to an urban survey, were water pollution and air pollution. Pollution from residential waste was mentioned by half of the respondents, noise and lack of green areas by one-third. About a quarter mentioned the dirtiness of public places, damage from pesticides, and problems of solid waste. Only about 10 per cent cared about forest destruction, wildlife losses and dust storms. Desertification was mentioned by only 3 per cent, and sea pollution by less than 1 per cent: people seemed most concerned about the problems which touched them personally.[25] Another sample showed that most people had little awareness of environmental problems. Their main sources of information were television, cinema and radio. Similarly, they saw water and air pollution and garbage as the main problems. Most did not recognize that fast economic development has a direct bearing on environmental pollution. While acknowledging the

---

footnote continued

jiankong" ("Discharge monitoring under quantity control"), *Huanjing baohu* (*Environmental Protection*), No. 3 (1997), pp. 5–7.

23. Shen Yimin, "An initial look into China's population, environment and sustainable development," in China Population and Environment Society (ed.), *China Population and Environment* (Beijing: Zhongguo huanjing kexue chubanshe, 1996), pp. 35–48.

24. NEPA, the State Planning Commission and the State Economics and Trade Commission, *Ninth Five-Year Plan for Environmental Protection*, p. 3.

25. Yang Chaofei (NEPA), "Zhongguo ziran baohu wenti ji duice" ("China's problems of natural protection and remedies"), *Huanjing baohu* (*Environmental Protection*), No. 10 (1996), pp. 24–27.

importance of individual behaviour, they had little confidence in individual action. More than 70 per cent were willing to contribute some money to actions that were well-organized. There was a close relationship between level of education and environmental awareness. Eleven per cent of respondents felt that the government stressed economic development but neglected environmental protection, 23 per cent that the government paid the environment insufficient attention, and 31 per cent that the government had made some efforts, but without good results. Only 35 per cent were positive or very positive about government actions in this field. As many as 90 per cent of people surveyed agreed that in the present society, the words of many people with regard to the environment were not consistent with their actions.[26] These responses may seem obvious in Western democracies, but they are unusual for Chinese citizens, who tend to be very polite and positive in the views they express about government.

The apparent lack of concern about conservation of resources and wider environmental issues, lack of confidence in individual actions, and lack of trust in the authorities' readiness to improve the environment should all be matters of serious concern to both Chinese authorities and foreign donors. These two polls suggest that the Chinese authorities need not expect much pressure from concerned citizens. Moreover, non-state organizations and the media are under tight control. More remote problems, such as emissions of greenhouse gases (China's carbon dioxide emissions are expected to more than double between now and 2020, and its world share to increase from 13.6 per cent to 19.3 per cent)[27] receive very little public attention. Thus, the willingness to invest in environmental protection has to come mainly from within China's political system itself.

Political Debates on the Environment: Views at the 1996 Fourth National Conference, Priorities and the "Model" Approach

China's political debate about environmental policies and investments takes place almost exclusively behind closed doors. At the national level, the Politburo, the State Planning Commission, the Environmental Committee of the National People's Congress, SEPA and various ministries are predominantly involved. Only SEPA brings its demands for a higher political priority for environmental measures into the open through its

26. China Environmental Yearbook Editing Committee and Society (eds.), *China Environmental Yearbook 1996*, p. 248.

27. DRI/McGraw Hill in "Earth summit: dire about hot air," *Financial Times, Power in Asia: The Asian Electricity Market*, No. 230 (1997), p. 4. Of course, it is often pointed out that China's per capita outputs of CO_2 and NO_x are many times lower than those of Western countries. Most likely, increased emissions will produce considerably higher temperatures and precipitation and higher agricultural output in north China and the mountain regions. T. M. Johnson *et al. China: Issues and Options in Greenhouse Emissions Control* (Washington, DC: The World Bank Discussion Paper No. 330, 1996). The Fourth National Environmental Conference document did not refer to the CO_2 problem at all, a fact pointed out by a representative of the State Meteorological Bureau.

journals and other publications, often receiving support from academics and environmental specialists. The lack of response from other departments has prevented an open debate. In the past, the three national conferences about the environment held in 1973, 1983 and 1989 provided the main occasions for Chinese politicians and domestic experts to engage in statements of position and an exchange of views. Each conference marked new long-term policies and set the tone for subsequent government measures. Therefore, it is worthwhile considering the debate at the 1996 Fourth National Environmental Conference in Beijing, and then studying participants' reactions to the *Ninth Five-Year Plan and Targets for the Year 2010*, a separate section of which was titled *China's Trans-Century Green Project Plan*. The first phase of that project plan (till 2000) has 1,591 projects, with an emphasis on water pollution treatment (comprising half of all projects, 282 of which are for the Huai River) and provincial projects (three-quarters of all projects).

One important concern was with the personnel of the local environmental protection bureaus (EPBs) and their effective execution of duties. The Shaanxi vice-governor said the Plan neglected this problem: while calling for an increase of the EPB staff at the county level from 19,000 in 1995 to 30,000 by the year 2000, and for some staff where needed in townships, as well as the strengthening of monitoring, information, education etc., the Plan gave no indication how this should be either organized or paid for. The vice-chairman of the Inner Mongolian government argued that the EPBs should be upgraded (as Inner Mongolia had done), in line with the elevated position of environmental protection in national policy. The Henan vice-governor remarked, somewhat optimistically, "if officials are clean, water will be clean," and complained that because there were few staff at county and *xiang* levels, they could not handle the pollution problems of TVEs. A representative from Guangxi pointed out that the recent reforms in government organization had weakened the county-level environmental offices; most did not have even one full-time official, nor did they collect any pollution charges.[28] A similar reduction of personnel was noted in the industrial ministries, meaning that "there was no way in which they could do their work properly." An official from Hainan remarked that at county-level, the amalgamation of urban construction, environmental protection, land management and mining into one bureau had hindered independent implementation of environmental laws by the environmental protection

---

28. Staffing problems are most serious in underdeveloped inland areas such as Yunnan and Guizhou, where many counties have only one or two people, sometimes less, in charge of environmental protection. However, the same is true for some counties in the developed coastal provinces of Jiangsu and Zhejiang. In Sichuan and some other provinces, most counties and municipalities do not have an independent environmental protection organization. See NEPA (eds.), *Documents from the Fourth National Conference*, p. 324. Yunnan, Guizhou, Sichuan, Guangxi, Tibet and Anhui have less than half the national average of environmental staff per capita, according to data from State Statistical Bureau, *China Statistical Yearbook 1995* (Beijing: China Statistical Publishing House, 1995), pp. 60 and 691.

departments.[29] Most participants felt that implementing the Plan would be most difficult, as it did not specify which ministries were responsible for what, nor which kind of control structures should be established.

A second point of criticism at the Conference was the absence of concrete control targets in some vital areas. The vice-mayor of Chongqing wanted specific water quality demands for the Huang (Yellow) River and Chang (Yangtze) rivers, ensuring that their water quality did not get worse. Other high-level participants demanded definite targets for oceanic pollution, CO_2 reduction and emissions by vehicles and boats. Most voiced their concerns about issues relating to their own province or department. These criticisms were taken into account by the State Council, which wrote in its Notice endorsing the Plan that control targets should be specified for place and period and management mechanisms be established.

A third major concern was investment. Participants from Inner Mongolia and Ningxia pointed out that investments in environmental protection had not been quantified in terms of percentage of GDP, or with other set targets. The Jiangsu governor claimed that his province would reach its target of 1.5 per cent of GDP by 2000, the Shanghai CCP vice-secretary that Shanghai would achieve 3 per cent by then, but representatives from poor provinces expressed the need for subsidies from the central government. An engineer from the Construction Bank of China remarked that environmental protection measures increase enterprise costs, and that strict quantification and application of the law on an objective basis were necessary in order to justify investments.[30] He implied that any planning without such concrete guidelines would not convince local economic committees and enterprises to invest in abatement measures.

The discussions demonstrated a major gap between coastal and inland areas in their capacity to invest in pollution abatement projects. Many old, polluting, loss-making heavy industries are located inland, and local governments depend on budgetary support from the central government for their improvement. Partly for that reason, the Plan has adopted a graded approach with different goals: by 2000, "national keypoint areas" (the Huai, Hai and Liao river basins in north China; the Dianchi, Chao and Tai lakes; acid rain areas; the Sanxia power station; the industrial and mining triangle of Shaanxi-Shanxi-Inner Mongolia; the Alashan steppe; the Zhu (Pearl) River Delta and Hainan) should achieve considerable recovery; provincial capitals and the large coastal and tourist cities should reach state environmental standards for ambient air and surface water quality; other developed cities should show improvement. Only a few "model" cities and lakes will obtain financial support from the central

29. NEPA (eds.), *Documents from the Fourth National Conference*, pp. 167–170, 174, 182–85; NEPA, the State Planning Commission and the State Economics and Trade Commission, *Ninth Five-Year Plan for Environmental Protection*, pp. 40–42.
30. NEPA (eds.), *Documents from the Fourth National Conference*, p. 173.

government, with the largest of these the Huai River basin, which was severely hit by floods and pollution accidents in the early 1990s.[31]

The "model" approach was not disputed by any of the Chinese participants. It is dictated by budgetary shortages and limited organizational capacities and, moreover, it reflects the political desire (which is shared by foreign donors) to tackle some of the worst environmental disaster areas first, achieving the greatest immediate and visible benefits. But while the political and technical advantages of such examples are obvious, there are drawbacks, too. For example, funds may be drawn away from other areas where investments would have been more cost-effective. Studies in Europe have shown that people attach three times as much value to prevention of further deterioration of their environment than to its improvement,[32] so politically it seems wiser to concentrate on the former. There is also the danger that selective local "clean-ups" will drive polluting factories and equipment to other, less controlled areas. A representative from Wuhan (also a paper-producing area) urged the government to stop the (more than 400) water-polluting paper factories which had been closed in the Huai River area from selling their equipment to other areas.[33] However, the government does not have the legal authority to restrict the movement of polluting equipment. As long as capacities for control and political priorities differ between regions and sectors, urban and regional clean-ups are bound to (and to some extent, and for good reasons, are intended to) displace rather than stop pollutive industries.

The State Council's imposition of stricter standards on the industries in the Huai River and other priority basins will increase pollution elsewhere, at least in the short-term. Its effect on industrial development is uncertain. In the medium- and long-term, industries should benefit from the weeding out of small pollutive competitors and from their own more efficient processes, but only if the government creates a level playing field by imposing the same environmental standards on all – and monitoring compliance. So far, this has not happened. The most recent recommendations for new environmental standards in China's main industrial sectors

31. In 1991, more than 4 million hectares of farmland in the Huai River basin were flooded, striking more than 50 million people and causing direct economic losses of more than 30 billion *yuan*. The next year, the river's main stream was seriously polluted by a wastewater spill of 150 million cubic metres, making the water unusable for industry and drinking. Nevertheless, more than a million residents in three cities had to drink seriously polluted water for more than half a month. The pollution lasted for two-and-a-half months, affecting 350 kilometres of the river's course as well as part of the Hongze Lake. See Pan Tiensheng *et al.*, "Inspection of and reflection on the ecological background of Huai River calamity during 1991–1992," in China Population and Environment Society (eds.), *China Population and Environment*, pp. 125–129.

32. David W. Pearce and R. Kervy Turner, *Economics of Natural Resources and the Environment* (New York: Harvester Wheatsheaf, 1990), pp. 142–48.

33. NEPA (eds.), *Documents from the Fourth National Conference*, p. 182. In 1990, Chinese paper industries released 4 billion tonnes of wastewater, with 8 million tonnes of organic matter, 800,000 tonnes of residual alkali, and 2 million tonnes of biological oxygen demand (BOD) (1990); by 1996, Chinese paper industries were responsible for one-sixth of China's industrial wastewater and one-quarter of its BOD, *Huanjing baohu* (*Environmental Protection*), No. 7 (1997), p. 9.

differentiate between large-, middle- and small-scale industries, between different technological processes, and again between high, medium and low technological levels.[34] From the point of view of treatment, this is a sensible and practical approach, as it allows local EPBs to urge all sorts of factories to improve their environmental performance. However, at the same time, it justifies and perpetuates large differences in emission standards, discouraging the adoption of the most advanced but more expensive technologies at the expense of those enterprises (generally, large state-owned enterprises, foreign companies and those in coastal cities and developed areas) which have included full treatment costs.

Investment Issues

Investment levels in environmental protection differ significantly between China's provinces (see Table 3, column 7 and 8). Per urban capita, 1995 investment in treatment of pollution caused by existing enterprises (which are mainly urban and industrial) was highest, at 64–75 *yuan* in Henan, Hebei and Gansu, but only 15–23 *yuan* in Guangdong, Hubei and Jiangxi; when measured per employee in the state manufacturing and mining sector, differences were slightly less but still higher than a factor of two. Because about 80 per cent of investments in environmental protection originate from allocation by the state and its enterprises (see Table 1 above), such differences primarily reflect national subsidy programmes to selected regions (such as Xinjiang, Henan and Gansu) and different degrees of local political support for abatement of pollution. Investment seems unrelated to the seriousness of pollution as measured in terms of untreated or insufficiently treated wastewater, emissions of fly ash or untreated waste gases from production (see Table 3). This is a disturbing finding, as it seems to indicate that investment priorities are not dictated by objective needs or maximal effect. In this respect, little should be expected from enterprises themselves, except for the largest and foreign-invested ones. Even if environmental laws were to be applied more fully, and compliance were better monitored, present pollution charges are so low that, generally speaking, it is much more expensive for an enterprise to pay for treatment measures than to continue to pollute.[35] Although the Chinese government has claimed that "the polluter pays" is a leading principle, in reality it still pays to pollute.

34. Wang Jinnan *et al. Gongye wuranyuan quanguocheng kongzhi yu guanli* (*Total Process Control and Management of Industrial Pollution Sources*) (Beijing: Zhongguo huanjing kexue chubanshe, 1997).

35. The main problems are that they are levied on the single highest pollutive element only, charges are only half or less of treatment costs, costs may be passed on, and control of actual levels of emissions is weak. See, for example, Ran Shenghong, "Huanjing baohu jizhong jingji shouduandi bijiao" ("Environmental protection and comparison of its economic methods"), *Huanjing baohu* (*Environmental Protection*), No. 4 (1996), pp. 30–32, and Wu Bangshan, "Qianxi woguo paiwu shoufei zhidu shishizhongdi wenti" ("Problems in the implementation of our country's pollution discharge fee system"), *Huanjing baohu* (*Environmental Protection*), No. 10 (1996), pp. 11–12.

Therefore decisions to invest in pollution abatement facilities have to be taken (as they mostly are) by planning bodies at the municipal or industrial branch level.

The question of how to solve the problem of inadequate investment is crucial. The Plan states that China will invest 450 billion *yuan* (in 1995 prices) or 1.3 per cent of its GDP in environmental protection during 1996–2000. This already seemed overly ambitious by 1996, implying a doubling within five years, and by now it is quite clear that this target will not be met.[36] The Plan assumed that a foreign contribution of US$4 billion would cover around 7 per cent of the necessary investments, but a year later, Chinese insiders were quoted as saying that only 1 per cent of GDP could be gathered within the country, necessitating a greater contribution of foreign capital.[37] It is questionable whether actual investments will reach even 1 per cent of GDP; in 1996, at least, investment in pollution control projects alone declined instead of going up.[38] How much of the funding will come from central and provincial government budgets is not clear – possibly, 188 billion *yuan* or about 40 per cent of the total required.[39] The central government contribution will be mainly in the form of loans.

A breakdown of environmental investments shows where the problems are. The system and sources of funding are divided into the so-called "three-synchronous funds" for new projects (most of which have undergone an Environmental Impact Assessment (EIA) before obtaining approval),[40] technical renovation and transformation projects, projects financed through refunded pollution charges (see Table 4 for their origin and use), enterprise- or bank-financed treatment projects, urban construction projects, and foreign enterprises.[41] Pollution reduction in existing enterprises used to be the main component of environmental investment, but its share declined from 41 per cent in 1991 and 34 per cent in 1994 to only 23 per cent in the Plan. The valuation of the cost embedded in

36. Nevertheless, the investment projections of US$6.3 billion in 1996 rising to US$15.2 billion in 2000 have been taken seriously by some. See, for example, Trish Saywell, "True grit," *Far Eastern Economic Review*, 26 June 1997, quoting Environmental Business International (San Diego) and a report by Sofres Consulting Asia Pacific (Hong Kong); also quoted in *China Trade Report*, April 1997.

37. *China Daily Business Weekly*, 11–17 May 1997.

38. Such investments totalled 3.78 billion *yuan* in 1995 and 3.66 billion *yuan* in 1996. As these were calculated at current prices, the real decrease may have been about 10%. State Statistical Bureau, *Zhongguo tongji zhaiyao 1997 (A Statistical Survey of China 1997)* (Beijing: Statistical Publishing House, 1997), p. 149.

39. *CCICED Newsletter*, Vol. 3, No. 1 (1997), p. 4, quotes *China Environment News* as to what "China will invest in environmental protection."

40. By the end of 1995, 61% of the new industrial projects initiated at the county-level and above went through EIA, and 87% applied the "three-synchronous" procedure. 480 cities (out of 640) registered discharges of pollutants, of a total of 77,000 enterprises; 240 cities (out of 640) issued discharge permits to a total of 14,000 enterprises. NEPA (eds.), *Documents from the Fourth National Conference*, p. 290.

41. See E. B. Vermeer, "An inventory of losses due to environmental pollution: problems in the sustainability of China's economic growth," *China Information*, Vol. X, No. 1 (1995), pp. 19–50.

Table 3: **Indicators of Pollution Treatment in 17,590 Industries and Units of County-level and Above in All Provinces, and Their Investments per Urban Capita and Industrial Employee, 1995**

	1.	2.	3.	4.	5.	6.	7.	8.
National total	**55**	**77**	**90**	**71**	**43**	**9,875**	**38**	**156**
Beijing	66	88	90	89	65	223	33	151
Tianjin	73	90	94	89	73	254	51	175
Hebei	68	89	94	84	44	438	64	142
Shanxi	50	77	93	69	24	291	44	129
Inner Mongolia	40	73	85	60	21	196	29	133
Liaoning	66	83	83	73	35	617	36	121
Jilin	52	72	91	53	48	462	45	185
Heilongjiang	54	81	87	69	59	411	28	102
Shanghai	77	86	94	84	83	491	56	205
Jiangsu	65	74	95	82	78	534	35	123
Zhejiang	72	76	93	59	59	363	47	165
Anhui	47	69	84	83	54	449	48	213
Fujian	41	64	94	67	58	344	53	222
Jiangxi	49	70	87	68	20	155	23	87
Shandong	48	85	92	72	62	824	46	196
Henan	49	84	94	59	44	947	75	284
Hubei	62	75	94	78	56	274	20	92
Hunan	56	83	91	75	40	377	38	160
Guangdong	56	81	87	85	54	300	15	89
Guangxi	44	70	93	78	42	332	52	288
Hainan	56	56	96	84	29	30	21	191
Sichuan	39	56	76	46	39	473	27	112
Guizhou	39	77	85	61	24	118	26	138
Yunnan	30	63	82	71	23	215	48	219
Tibet	0	2	85	0	3	1	5	67
Shaanxi	63	78	94	41	17	169	27	100
Gansu	47	69	93	55	26	264	69	243
Qinghai	44	45	89	82	27	43	40	192
Ningxia	50	67	92	15	32	41	33	146
Xinjiang	35	58	85	71	41	239	51	312

Notes:
1. % of up-to-standard treated wastewater
2. % of industrial wastewater treated
3. % of fly ash removed
4. % of waste gases from production cleaned
5. % of comprehensive use of fixed waste
6. investment funds in enterprises and organizations for pollution treatment (million *yuan*)
7. investment per urban, non-agricultural capita (*yuan*)
8. investment per employee in the state manufacturing and mining sector (*yuan*)

Sources:
   The China Environmental Yearbook Editing Committee and Society (eds.), *China Environmental Yearbook 1996*, pp. 488, 509. Population and labour data from State Statistical Bureau, *Zhongguo tongji nianjian 1996* (*China Statistical Yearbook 1996*) (Beijing: China Statistical Publishing House, 1996), p. 84 and SSB, *Zhongguo renkou tongji nianjian 1995* (*China Population Statistical Yearbook 1995*) (Beijing: China Statistical Publishing House, 1995), p. 381. Investments per urban capita and employee in state manufacturing and mining calculated by author.

"cleaner" processes and preventive equipment in newly-established enterprises or their expansion (the "three-synchronous") has risen from 26 per cent in 1991 to 29 per cent in 1994 and 45 per cent in the Plan. This rise may be partially attributed to greatly increased Chinese investment in joint-ventures. It is partly a statistical artefact, measuring the difference between rapidly advancing production technologies and outdated and abandoned technologies. The share of urban environmental infrastructural facilities, which had risen from 33 per cent of total investment to as much as 40 per cent in 1993, was reduced again to 32 per cent in the Plan (see Table 1 above).

It is difficult to see how the downward tendency (in terms of percentage the of GDP) of investments in the reduction of *existing* sources of pollution will be stopped. The Plan aims to bring up the share of environmental investment in new project investment to the 1991 level of 4.2 per cent, to triple the environmental share (exclusive of energy savings) in renovation project investment to 3.6 per cent, and to double the environmental share in urban construction project investment to 35 per cent. The latter two targets require such major turnarounds,[42] most of which depend on local government finances, that they are not realistic without a new and full commitment from local authorities and enterprises to environmental goals at the expense of other priorities. They might be interpreted as a compromise between the much higher levels of investment demanded by the National People's Congress Environmental Committee and SEPA[43] and what the government believed to be maximum credible targets. One may conclude that the financial underpinning of the Plan is weak, and government commitment to its indicated environmental priorities and projects is political rather than financial.

Water: Increased Shortages and the Possible Impact of New Legislation and Other Measures

China has become increasingly short of water. Demand is rising, quality of supply is deteriorating, and underground stocks are being over-exploited. More than three-quarters (78 per cent) of river sections near cities are polluted and unfit for use as drinking water – demand for which is rapidly increasing. Between 70 and 80 per cent of shallow and 30 per cent of the deep underground water layers below China's cities are polluted[44] (see Table 5). Difficulties are greatest in the north and in large coastal cities. More than a hundred cities are seriously short of water. Coastal regions are predicted to be short by 40 billion cubic metres of

42. The first indicators are encouraging. 1995 and 1996 realized investments in pollution abatement measures financed from technical transformation funds were 5.4 and 6.2 billion *yuan*, respectively, increasing from 1.6 to 1.7% of total expenditures from these funds. However, the share of energy saving projects declined from 2.3% to 2.1%. See State Statistical Bureau, *A Statistical Survey of China 1997*, p. 43.

43. NEPA had demanded increases to 7%, 7% and 40%, respectively: NEPA (eds.), *Documents from the Fourth National Conference*, p. 324.

44. *Huanjing baohu (Environmental Protection)*, No. 5 (1996), p. 20.

Table 4: **Pollutant Emission Charges, China 1991–1995 (million *yuan*, current figures)**

	1991	*1993*	*1995*
Paying units (1,000)	206	254	368
Total charge revenues	2,010	2,680	3,710
(a) provincial and above			24%
(b) municipal, prefectural			33%
(c) county			42%
of which:			
1. emissions above standard	1,571	1,946	2,487
i.e. % of total	78%	73%	67%
(a) wastewater	996	1,228	1,504
(b) waste gases	494	561	743
(c) waste sludge	40	38	48
(d) noise	41	119	190
(e) radiation	0	1	2
2. polluted water discharges	62	13	25
i.e. % of total	3%	5%	7%
3. income from 4 items	372	608	972
i.e. % of total	19%	23%	26%
Use of funds from these charges:			
supplementary capital for EP	1,764	2,451	3,185
of which: pollution treatment	1,199	1,510	1,771
for EP service units*	564	1,047	1,414
EP Fund	1,438	2,104	2,932
outstanding loans	248	320	545

Notes:
* "for development of environmental protection organizations"
   Current figures. If corrected for price changes, real revenues dropped. Before 1988, most of the emission charges were refunded to the paying enterprises for pollution reduction investments. New regulations adopted by the State Council in 1988 stipulated that charges should be put into a fund for support of treatment measures in keypoint polluting units. However, these were only partially implemented. The main problems were that only part but not all enterprises received such preferential treatment, and that interest rates on loans were too low, so that the environmental fund capital was insufficiently accumulated and recouped. In 1993, a revision process was started and new draft rules were submitted by the SEPB to the State Council in 1995.
Source:
   The China Environmental Yearbook Editing Committee and Society (eds.), *China Environmental Yearbook 1996*, p. 211.

water by 2010.[45] The main polluters are industry and agriculture, and water shortages, pollution and treatment needs are closely linked. Moreover, precipitation seems to be more variable and to be decreasing in north China. Consequently, as water volumes in rivers decrease and industrial and residential discharges increase, water quality suffers.

   More than a thousand industries directly discharge their polluted water

45. The shortage will be 15 billion cubic metres of water by 2000, *China Environment News*, September 1995, p. 6.

Table 5: **Urban Air, Ground and Surface Water in China, 1995 and 1996**

	1995	1996	unit
Urban air suspended particles, north	392	387	mu/m^3
Urban air suspended particles, south	242	230	,,
Monthly urban dust fall, north	24.7	23.2	tonne/km²
Monthly urban dust fall, south	10.2	9.1	,,
Average SO_2 in urban air, north	81	83	mu/m^3
Average SO_2 in urban air, south	80	76	,,
Average NO_x in urban air, north	53	53	,,
Average NO_x in urban air, south	41	41	,,
Polluted groundwater, all cities	n.d.	50	% of total
Urban river sections unfit for drinking	n.d.	78	,,
Chang River Basin, below standard III	24	27.5	,,
Huang River Basin, below standard III	60	65.4	,,
Zhu River Basin, below standard III	22	19.3	,,
Huai river basin, below standard III	51	51.2	,,

Sources:
 "Report on the state of the environment in China, 1996," pp. 3–6; "Report on the state of the environment in China, 1995," pp. 3–7.

into the Huang River on its 500-kilometre stretch from Togtoh (Inner Mongolia) south to Longmen. Their sewage constitutes 5 per cent of the average daily runoff, and half or more during the dry season. At this very place, Shanxi is constructing a giant irrigation project which will draw its water here. Downstream past Sanmenxia reservoir, the 700 km-long lower reaches of the Huang River dried up for 122 days in 1995, 136 days in 1996 and more than 200 in 1997. Only 8 per cent of the river basin is up to the state-prescribed first- and second-class standards, and 65 per cent is in the worst two categories. The main pollutants are ammonia, nitrates and phenols. In its middle reaches, the Huang's function as a source of irrigation and industrial water has been seriously impaired, and the lower reaches are a dirty sewer during much of the year. There is no solution in sight. Before 2020, what used to be called the Huang's lower reaches will be a stretch of polluted sand, parts of which may eventually be planted with trees, with a lined sewer in the middle.

Other, smaller rivers in the north, such as the Liao and Hai, have fared even worse. Annual average densities of volatile phenols are 69 times the standard in the Liao River and 7 times in the Hai River; biological oxygen demand (BOD) between two and seven times; permanganate between two and 29 times, and nitrogen between 16 and 36 times. Mercury and other heavy metals are also serious threats.[46] These smaller

46. Yang Chaofei, "China's problems of natural protection and remedies," pp. 24–27; "Communiqué on 1996 Environmental Status," *China Environment News*, July 1997, p. 3. Detailed figures on pollutants in the worst sections show average annual values 54 times the norm for suspended particulate matter and six times the norm for nitrogen. Similar high values for nitrogen of 3 to 4 grams per litre occur in the Pearl, Huai and Huang rivers, and 19 grams per litre has been measured in the Hai River. China Environmental Yearbook Editing Committee and Society (eds.), *China Environmental Yearbook 1996*, pp. 200–202.

northern rivers will receive priority treatment under the Plan. In much of north China, as the climate becomes drier, run-off more variable, and almost all water is diverted for agriculture, industrial and urban users will no longer be able to rely on river water for their needs. The only solution is a more economical use of water, including recycling techniques, and adequate treatment of wastewater.

To turn to the Huai River floods and pollution accidents in 1992 and 1994 mentioned above: according to a subsequent survey, 75 per cent of the river sections in the Huai River basin are seriously polluted and have lost all function. Eighty per cent of its tributaries have black/green water. Millions cannot use drinking water from nearby, and factories have had to close. The most serious pollution is caused by the paper, chemical, dyeing, leather and liquor factories. In 1994, only 12 per cent of the 2.5 billion cubic metres of wastewater was treated. Death rates are several times higher than elsewhere. In 1995, temporary regulations were issued by the State Council. It adopted the Huai River Water Pollution Prevention and Control Plan the next year, which stated that, by the end of 1997, all factories in the basin should meet standards of discharge, and that the Huai River should be clean by 2000. Local authorities were ordered to close down all small paper, leather and dyeing factories as well as chemical, electroplating, asbestos and other factories with pollutive technologies. The obligation to take measures was placed on the four provinces, and strict rules were passed, with charges and fines for non-compliant industries and government officials. Almost all financing had to be local. In 1995, clean-up costs of the Huai River which would advance it to standard 3 were estimated to be 12 billion *yuan*, or 0.77 per cent of the region's GDP in the previous year.[47] However, Henan province indicated that it would have great difficulty in providing its share of 5 billion *yuan*,[48] and the clean-up costs seem to be seriously underestimated.

The Tai Lake is one of three singled out for an immediate clean-up. It is seriously eutrophic with industrial pollutants and chemical fertilizers. As with the Huai River, one source of pollution used to be paper industries, which produced most of the BOD. In both areas, those with a size under 5,000 tonnes/year were closed in 1996, and larger factories have been made to undergo treatment. Next, there are breweries, most of which use maize or sugar cane. Chemical fertilizer plants, leather tanneries, electroplating and textile dyeing factories all have high emissions of chemicals and heavy metals. Most facilities are too small for treatment measures to be economic, and should be shut down. However, with

47. *Huanjing baohu gongzuo quanshu* (*Compendium of Environmental Protection Work*) (Beijing: Zhongguo huanjing kexue chubanshe, 1997), pp. 337–340; Li Liangyi, "Huaihe liuyu shuiwuran xianzhuang yu fangzhi chanwang" ("Present situation and prospects for treatment of water pollution in the Huai river basin"), *Huanjing baohu* (*Environmental Protection*), No. 11 (1996), pp. 6–9, 34; *China Environment News*, May 1995, p. 1.

48. NEPA (eds.), *Documents from the Fourth National Conference*, pp. 232–36.

adequate investment, the larger facilities can be upgraded and controlled at a net profit.[49]

The city of Guangzhou suffers from serious deterioration of the Zhu River water, which is now in the most polluted categories of 4 and 5. Pollution affects the water intake of five drinking water plants, including sometimes the largest one at Xicun, and also industrial and agricultural production. Citizens and officials are worried: how can Guangzhou become an international city under these conditions? The sources of pollution are well-known. Industries in Guangzhou municipality release almost 1 million tonnes/day of wastewater, carrying heavy metals, phenol, benzene and carcinogenic substances like polycyclic aromatic hydrocarbons. More than 1 million tonnes of residential sewage flow into the Zhu River every day, with an annual increase of 10 per cent. Moreover, there are 500,000 tonnes of organic manure from animal husbandry every day, pollution from ships and boats and chemical fertilizers. These organic pollutants have resulted in serious eutrophication of the Zhu River's water, which is now down to 3.2 mg/l of dissolved oxygen. Nitrates, permanganates and arsenicals surpass state standards. Solutions could be found in a variety of measures: clean production and reduction of pollutants, to be achieved first by 12 large factories which produce 47 per cent of all industrial wastewater; relocation of factories; expansion of sewers (at present there are only 2–3 metres per person); less use of nitrogen fertilizers; construction of additional water treatment facilities; higher investments in pollution abatement (more than 1.5 per cent of GDP); and the establishment of total quantity control and discharge

49. For treatment of black wastewater in a typical 10,000 tonnes/year paper factory, with an investment of 12 million *yuan* and annual operating costs of 3.8 million *yuan*, 70 to 72% of the alkali can be recovered and net profits are 1.26 million *yuan* and a decrease of chemical oxygen demand (COD) of 6,000 tonnes, and recovery of 2,800 tonnes of alkali. For treatment of intermediate water, a 5,000 tonnes/year factory needs 2 million *yuan* investment and annual operating cost of 570,000 *yuan* to achieve 80% COD reduction and water recovery rate. For the treatment of white water, the usual techniques reduce suspended matter (generally 0.8 to 1 gr/l) by 90% and COD by 60%; if the entire Taihu Lake area used this technique, it would need an investment of 40 million *yuan* in water fees, reduce suspended matter by 100,000 tonnes, and create an annual net profit of 52.4 million *yuan*. For maize, in a 10,000 tonnes/year brewery, an investment of 7.5 million *yuan* and annual operating costs of 4.4 million *yuan* result in 95% reduction of COD and net annual profits of 2.1 million *yuan* and 10,000 tonnes of feed. Sugar cane treatment is less profitable: annual treatment of 70,000 tonnes of distillery waste requires an investment of 1.7 million *yuan*, with operating costs of 195,000 *yuan*, and annual profit of 175,000 *yuan*. Compound fertilizer plants using the level balance technique which produce 10,000 tonnes/year need an investment of 150,000 *yuan* and 96,000 *yuan* annual operating costs, with a net profit of 540,000 *yuan* and ammonia waste reduction of 79%. Those using prill towers and producing 20,000 tonnes need an investment of 1,930,000 *yuan* and annual expenses of 630,000 *yuan*, with annual profits of 1,290,000 *yuan*, thereby reducing 5 million tonnes of water per day, sulphates by 45,000 tonnes/day, phenol by 2,000 tonnes/day, and increasing ammonia compounds by 2,000 tonnes/year. Leather industries with a new technique requiring 100,000 *yuan* investment can obtain annual profits of 137,000 *yuan* and reduce chromium waste by 312 tonnes. For electroplating industries, various techniques result in very high profits with very low investment. Ke Yongchao, "Sanhu shui wuran zhuangkuang ji wuran fangzhi jishudi fenxi" ("Analysis of water pollution in the three lakes and pollution treatment techniques"), *Huanjing baohu* (*Environmental Protection*), No. 1 (1997), pp. 44–46.

Table 6: **Waste Treatment Rates in Different Branches of Industry, 1994** (%)

	Gases	Water	Of which, to standard	Solid
Defence industries	74.0	51.3	76.9	76.7
Metallurgical industries	93.0	81.2	90.1	28.0
Oil and gas industries	78.0	92.5	50.0	52.0
Shipping industries	80.4	30.8	80.0	63.7
Airline industries	70.4	73.7	98.8	88.7
State building materials bureau	96.9	90.0	84.0	100.0
Coal industries	83.0	41.0	72.0	54.0

Source:
The China Environmental Yearbook Editing Committee and Society (eds.), *China Environmental Yearbook 1996*, p. 117.

permit systems.[50] The example of this, the richest city of China, shows that the problems of pollution reduction are again mainly political and organizational – investment funds could be mobilized. Choices have to be made about industrial relocation, levies on pollutive factories and heavy chemical fertilizer use, and urban infrastructure facilities.

This underlines the urgent need for revisions to the 1984 water pollution law. The relevant proposal by the State Council in 1995 called for regions and cities to draw up pollution control plans and institute a pollutant-discharge permit system. This includes centralized treatment of urban sewage, protection of water intake areas and handling the problem of nutrification of water by agriculture. The State Council has forbidden the establishment of any further small pollutive factories which do not treat their wastewater. It also invites industrial ministries to set time limits for backward pollutive technologies. Legal actions should be taken against those companies and individuals who do not use water treatment facilities in a regular way, but shut them off or neglect them. Instead, provincial governments are permitted (but not obliged) to establish total quantity controls, and asked to monitor water quality levels at their borders, so as to determine their respective responsibilities. This represents a devolution and also a strengthening of regulatory powers.[51] As with many other Chinese laws, the proposed new law leaves much – maybe too much – room for local differentiation, and enforcement is problematic.

50. Wei Chaohai and Qian Yu, "Zhujiang Guangzhou heduan shuiwuran zonghe zhengzhidi tantao" ("Study of comprehensive treatment of water pollution in the Guangzhou section of the Pearl River"), *Huanjing baohu* (*Environmental Protection*), No. 10 (1997), pp. 5–7.
51. Sun Youhai, Environmental and Resource Commission of the National People's Congress, "Xiugai 'shuiwuran fangzhi fa' di biyaoxing he zhongdian" ("The urgency and focus of revising the Water Pollution Law"), *Huanjing baohu* (*Environmental Protection*), No. 8 (1996), pp. 38–40.

Table 7: Industrial Pollutants Discharged by SOEs in 1996 and Previous Years and by TVEs in 1995 (million tonnes, unless otherwise indicated)

	County and above, 1996	Change from 1995	Change in 1995 from 1994	TVEs, 1995
Fly ash	7.58	-9.5 %	+4.7 %	9.93
Dust	5.62	-12.1 %	+8.1 %	13.58
Sulphur dioxide	13.97	+0.1 %	+4.1 %	5.49
Discharged wastewater COD	7.04	-8.4 %	+13.1 %	6.70
" suspended particulates	7.8	-3.5 %	—	n.d.
" heavy metals (tonnes)	1,541	-14.3 %	+7.4 %	n.d.
" arsenic (tonnes)	1,132	+4.2 %	+4.4 %	n.d.
" cyanide (tonnes)	2,504	-1.8 %	-1.7 %	n.d.
" volatile phenols (tonnes)	5,710	-10.0 %	+17.7 %	n.d.
" oil pollutants (1,000 tonnes)	61	-5.0 %	+15.4 %	n.d.
" sulphides (1,000 tonnes)	32	?-25 %[a]	—	n.d.
Discharged solid waste	16.9	?-34 %[a]	+15.3 %	n.d.
of which: dangerous	0.22			n.d.

Notes:
a. "?" signifies that figures have been inflated because of definitional changes.
Sources:
"Zhongguo huanjing qingkuang baogao (1996-nian)" ("Report on the state of the environment in China, 1996"), *Huanjing baohu* (*Environmental Protection*), No. 6 (1997), pp. 3–6; "1995 Report on the state of the environment in China," *China Environment News*, July 1996, pp. 3–7.

Table 8: **Means and Rates of Pollution Control in Industries at County-level and Above, 1995 and 1996**

	1995	1996	
Soot and dust removal facilities for fuel emission	89.7	90.0	% of all industries
Up-to-standard boilers	78.0	80.0	% of all industries
Production gas purification facilities	70.8	75.0	% of all industries
Up-to-standard furnaces, kilns	54.3	62.1	% of all industries
Treatment rate of wastewater	76.8	81.6	% of all wastewater
Discharged wastewater up-to-standard	55.4	59.1	% of all wastewater
Treatment of solid waste	142.0	115.0	million tonnes
Comprehensive utilization of solid waste	43.0	43.1	% of all solid waste

Source:
"1996 Report on the state of the environment in China," *China Environment News*, 15 July 1997.

The fact that industrial water tariffs and pollutant release charges have been fixed too low, while residents pay nothing at all, has been a major constraint on the capacity to invest. In 1988, NEPA began trials for polluted wastewater discharge permits in 18 cities, which took three years to complete. In 1995, a nation-wide wastewater discharge permit system was set up. However, not many regions actually implement it. Some still use the original concentration system. The main reason is that the existing system of pollution charges does not correspond with the new total quantity release permit system.[52] The inadequacy of water treatment measures is apparent both in existing and in new industries. Tables 6, 7 and 8 (which do not include TVEs) show that treatment rates of wastewater by industrial sectors vary between 30 and 90 per cent, only part of which treat water up to standard. In the state-invested projects which started production in 1995, on average only 69 per cent of wastewater is treated, and removal rates are 72 per cent of COD, 82 per cent of oil, 33 per cent of heavy metals, and 84 per cent of suspended solids, 88 per cent of fly ash, 42 per cent of SO_2, 82 per cent of dust and an unknown percentage of solid waste.[53] Between provinces, up-to-standard industrial wastewater treatment rates vary between 30–40 per cent in west China and 55–65 per cent in most coastal provinces. Provincial capitals in the interior have treatment rates of around only 50 per cent (see Tables 3, above, and 9). It should be noted that most have at least some modern water treatment facilities (usually secondary-level), which use air blow aeration tanks, with a capacity of 50,000–150,000 tonnes/day. Beijing,

52. Yan Qingwei, "Zongliang kongzhi yaoqiu xianxing paiwu shoufei tizhi gaige" ("Total quantity control demands application of systemic reform in levying pollution charges"), *Huanjing baohu (Environmental Protection)*, No. 12 (1996), pp. 35–36.
53. China Environmental Yearbook Editing Committee and Society (eds.), *China Environmental Yearbook 1996*, p. 138.

Table 9: **Pollution Prevention and Treatment in Key Chinese Cities, 1995**

	1.	2.	3.	4.	5.	6.
Beijing	66	73	0.094	0.123	4.6	44.01
Shanghai	77	123	0.053	0.075	—	44.69[c]
Tianjin	73	89	0.082	0.050	2.9	43.38
Taiyuan	48	22	0.211[a]	0.055	5.3	40.16
Datong	50	19	0.192	0.043	4.7	>22
Shenyang	48	25	0.105	0.074	4.3	42.09
Nanjing	70	59	0.062	0.049	3.0	39.13
Suzhou	77	61	0.071	0.049	—	44.64
Hangzhou	77	61	0.068	0.054	3.4	42.43
Changsha	60	6	0.113	0.041	3.5	43.23
Chongqing	—	—	0.338[b]	0.069	6.6[c]	35.72
Guangzhou	64	56	0.057	0.129[c]	3.8	42.69
Nanning	49	125	0.070	0.013	2.5	37.62
Urumqi	50	44	0.060	0.070	4.4	30.99
Average 47 cities	67					
Total 47 cities		1,744				

Notes:
1. Up-to-standard water treatment rate of main industries (national total: 26,795) (%)
2. COD release (1,000 tonnes)
3. Average daily value of SO_2 (mg/m^3)
4. Average daily value of NO_x (mg/m^3)
5. Comprehensive air pollution index (includes, besides 3. and 4., suspended particulate matter and dustfall)
6. Comprehensive pollution control score (on 10 items; does not include quality of the urban environment and urban facilities)
   a. highest of 44 northern cities
   b. second highest of 44 southern cities, after Guiyang
   c. highest of all cities
Source:
Various tables and data in The China Environmental Yearbook Editing Committee and Society (eds.), *China Environmental Yearbook 1996.*

Tianjin and Hangzhou have larger facilities. There is considerable room for technical improvements: valves, pumps and silt removers should be brought to international levels of efficiency and energy consumption.[54] Of course, all this is end-of-pipe treatment, and industries are increasingly directing efforts towards cleaner industrial processes.

Over the 1992–1996 period, China promoted 140 best applicable techniques in order to reduce water pollution; 72 concerned end-of-line treatment, 52 were recovery techniques, and only 16 advocated control of origin. This distribution shows the backward state of production technologies and pollution control, with the emphasis on end-of-pipe

54. Zhou Guocheng, "Woguo chengshi feishui chuli gongchengzhong yinjin jishu he shebeidi xianzhuang yu jidian kanfa" ("Present situation of imported techniques and facilities in water treatment projects in China's cities and some views"), *Jishui paishui (Water Supply and Drainage)*, No. 22 (1996), p. 6.

treatment. Chemical and physical methods predominate, and the more difficult and capital-intensive biological methods are mainly used in recovery and large-scale water treatment projects. Adoption rates of best applicable techniques have increased, and so have their economic efficiency. On average, capital investment is recouped within three to four years, and profits are more than four times higher than operating costs. Most were developed by central and local industrial departments, and to a lesser extent by the provincial EPBs, while the contribution of Academy of Science institutes and SEPA has been negligible. The development of best applicable techniques seems to be market-driven, rather than funded from the central budget, and might profit from more central support and co-ordination.[55]

Air: SO₂ Emissions, and What SEPA and the Plan Will Achieve

Acid rain affects between 30 and 40 per cent of China's territory.[56] The main cause is SO_2 emitted from the burning of 1.3 billion tonnes of coal annually, much of which is burned directly without any treatment. Although industrial emissions of SO_2 were subjected to pollutant discharge fees in 1982, trials with actual enforcement only started in nine cities in 1993. In south and central China, acid rain had become a major problem (responsible for 16 billion *yuan* in annual economic losses in 1991). In 1992, NEPA had indicated that 0.30 *yuan* per kg of coal was necessary in order to finance desulphurization measures which would keep emissions in 2000 at the 1990 level; it demanded only 0.20 *yuan*/kg, as this would keep product price increases below 1 per cent. The latter was supported by the State Council Environmental Committee, but to no avail. The discharge fee was again proposed for 1996.[57] In the meantime, emissions have continued to increase; in 1995, the SO_2 removal rate in new projects was 42 per cent. In the state sector, half of the sulphur dioxide emissions come from power industry.

55. Li Yiping and Wan Qiushan, "Woguo shui wuran fangzhi zuijia shiyong jishudi fazhan fenxi" ("Analysis of the development of best applicable techniques in water pollution treatment and control in our country"), *Huanjing baohu (Environmental Protection)*, No. 6 (1997), pp. 10–12.

56. The area affected by acid rain (pH below 5.6) increased from 1.75 million square kilometres in 1985 to 2.8 million in 1993. Acid rain is expanding northward and westward. Over 1 million square kilometres are affected by acid rains with pH value below 4.5, *China Environment News*, August 1995, p. 5. Most seriously affected are central China and Sichuan (Chongqing), but also some coastal cities. Forty-three out of 84 monitored cities in China are affected. Acid rain is worst in Changsha, with an annual average pH value of 3.54, and in Xiamen, Ganzhou and Yibin, all with average values below 4.5, *China Environment News*, October 1995, p. 6, and July 1997, p. 2.

57. "Guanyu zhengshou gongye ranmei eryanghualiu baiwufeidi qingshidi puchong shuoming" ("Clarification of the request for instruction about sulphur dioxide emission charges for industrial burning of coal"); preceded by summary of discussion and letter, *Collected Documents of the State Environmental Protection Committee (Vol. II)*, pp. 288–307; China Environmental Yearbook Editing Committee and Society (eds.), *China Environmental Yearbook 1996*, p. 210.

In 1995, the power industry planned that the proportion of coal in primary energy would decrease slightly in the medium- to long-term, that annual energy savings would be 4.3 per cent, and that SO_2 emissions would increase by 3.9 per cent per year until 2000.[58] In the eyes of NEPA, this was not good enough, and it successfully demanded that the power industry should not increase its 1995 discharge of 7 million tonnes of SO_2. The power industry argued that this was impossible. The average amount of sulphur in the coal used by China's power plants decreased only slightly from 1.2 per cent in 1988 (already below the world average of about 2 per cent) to 1.1 per cent in 1994. The ceiling for 2000 not only meant that all new power plants should have desulphurizing facilities, with an efficiency above 95 per cent, and extra investment costs of 50 billion *yuan* (for 60 GW), it also required installation of desulphurizing facilities (in addition to existing plans of the Ministry of Power for 10 to 12 GW) in another 25 to 30 GW of existing units or units under construction. How to find the necessary investment funds, and approvals to include the costs in electricity prices? Moreover, most desulphurization equipment would have to be imported, as it would take five to eight years for China to be capable of producing this plant itself. The power industry made counterproposals, such as the inclusion of environmental costs in the electricity price, more investments, balancing regional differences in environmental loads, and so forth.[59]

The eventual Plan seemed to be a compromise: it did not mention a specific control target for the power industry and allowed a small increase for the entire industrial sector. Total SO_2 emissions were planned to increase from 23.7 million tonnes (including 14 million from urban industries, including power plants, and 5.5 million from rural industries) in 1995 to 24.6 million tonnes in 2000. The Plan allows increases to 15.5 and 6.5 million tonnes, respectively, for urban and rural industries in the year 2000 (see Tables 2 and 7 and the Plan, pp. 14–15). These increases of between two and 4 per cent[60] annually are about half the expected increases of energy consumption.[61] The Plan included considerable increases in the coal-washing capacity, which should increase from 320 to 500–550 million tonnes, the removal of 100,000 tonnes of sulphur from coal, a restriction on pollutive small-scale power plants, and other

58. Zhang Kunming *et al.* "Woguo nengyuan huanjingdi xingshi yu duice" ("The shape of China's energy environment and remedial measures"), *Huanjing baohu* (*Environmental Protection*), No. 4 (1996), pp. 2–4.

59. NEPA (eds.), *Documents from the Fourth National Conference*, pp. 199–201.

60. The quantities emitted by TVEs in 1995 had to be estimated, as they were not included in regular statistical reporting, and the scope of data differed between provinces. When it was decided to control emissions by the year 2000 at the 1995 level, the problem of measurement of the base year became acute. In April 1996, a new control plan was drawn up. See China Environmental Yearbook Editing Committee and Society (eds.), *China Environmental Yearbook 1996*, p. 115.

61. Between 1990 and 1996, energy consumption, almost 75% of which was in the form of coal, increased by 41.4% and energy elasticity of demand was 0.4 (calculated from *A Statistical Survey of China, 1997*, p. 109). The share of coal is expected to drop to 71.6% of primary energy, and its elasticity from the present 0.38 to 0.32 by 2000. *Xinhua*, 28 May 1997.

supportive measures. Even so, the power industry still feels it has been put under too much pressure, as stricter emission standards, and particularly specific control targets for SO_2 emissions, have been handed down to local authorities, who have in turn been made responsible for their realization. As the Ministry of Energy has commented, "this has put the development of new thermo-power plants under great pressure, and recently five projects have met with difficulties in getting environmental approval."[62]

Other control measures are aimed at China's 430,000 industrial boilers, which are responsible for 20 per cent of SO_2 emissions. A hundred boilers have been selected in three cities each for a trial, with Japanese assistance, and three projects involving domestic production of desulphurizing equipment have been funded by German government loans.[63] Most highly pollutive (in terms of SO_2/product value) are coal production itself, coking and electricity generation, followed by cement-, fertilizer- and brick-making and smelting. With the exception of brick-making, all are within the scope of the state-planned economic sector. A prohibition on burning raw coal and the use of mould coal for households (one-third of urban households have not yet converted to gas for cooking) might cut urban SO_2 emissions in half. Also, sulphur fixing agents could be added.[64] The earliest and most common flue gas desulphurization technique is the limestone technique. However, it is fairly complicated and expensive, using much water and power, for only 80 per cent reliability. In the late 1970s, the spray-drying process was introduced, with savings of 10 to 15 per cent over the previous wet processes. In the 1980s suspension techniques were used. Electric beam irradiation is in the trial stage (at one Chengdu plant); it uses waste as fertilizer instead of dumping it. The recovery of sulphur, instead of disposal, is still uneconomical.[65] Foreign examples of clean coal technologies such as integrated gasification combined cycles (IGCC) are unlikely to be adopted, as they are similarly expensive. Introduction of pressurized fluidized bed combustion (PFBC) technology from Asea-Brown-Boveri or other companies is likely only after China accepts that it will need to pay adequate license fees.

Pollution problems have forced some local planners to reconsider their energy strategy. In Guangdong (and other coastal cities are likely to follow suit) hopes are pinned on nuclear power, hydropower and supply of electricity from elsewhere. No more small thermopower stations will be constructed, as they cause the most pollution.[66]

62. Planning Department of the Ministry of Energy, "The implementation of the 1996 power plan and some ideas on arrangement of the 1997 plan," *Zhongguo nengyuan* (*Energy of China*), No. 5 (1997), pp. 10–15.

63. Planning Department of the Ministry of Energy, *ibid.* pp. 10–15; Zhang Kunming *et al.*, "Woguo nengyuan huanjingdi xingshi yu duice," pp. 2–4.

64. Li Li, "Energy consumption in the Chinese economy and sulphur dioxide," in China Population and Environment Society (ed.), *China Population and Environment*, pp. 74–83.

65. Wang Po, "Yanqi tuoliu jishudi jingji bijiao" ("Economic comparison of desulphurization techniques"), *Huanjing baohu* (*Environmental Protection*), No. 10 (1997), pp. 36–38, 41.

66. *Zhongguo xinwenshe* (*China News Service*), 28 August 1997.

The Plan has three weak elements, pertaining to the entire energy sector and its emissions of pollutants. First, it has little or no control over coal use and SO_2 emissions by small-scale industries and households. It has already been doubted whether TVEs will meet their planned target. Their base-year figures may have been seriously underestimated.[67] The conversion programme from coal to gas for urban residents has a long way to go.[68] The second weakness is energy pricing. The very low coal and oil prices in China, compared to international prices, make it difficult to include full treatment cost in the price (as suggested by the Ministry of Energy), or to make energy saving programmes both cost-effective and attractive to enterprises. In 1997, Li Peng reconfirmed the government policy of keeping energy prices low.[69] Thirdly, it does not solve the problems of monitoring and sanctions. For many years, SEPA has been advocating the introduction of an SO_2 release permit system, and an SO_2 reduction fund.[70] So far, few areas have adopted quantity controls.

Solid Waste: Unknown Quantities, Unknown Qualities

Management of solid waste in China is extremely weak. A law relating to pollution from solid waste was adopted in 1996, but without any standards for storage, treatment or disposal. A technological policy for prevention and treatment of solid waste and preferential policies for recycling are badly needed. Sub-standard treatment facilities, if inspected at all, are free to continue operation. Local governments may subsidize recycling, but consistent economic and fiscal policies to stimulate recycling and reuse are still to be formulated. Only the construction sector utilizes solid waste on a large scale, but not all of this is useful from an environmental point of view. For instance, by 1995 China had reused almost 40 per cent of its slag for road-building, more than twice as much as in 1990. Inspection and registration of some 40 dangerous chemical substances, and an approval system for imports have been set up recently.[71]

---

67. One author estimates that TVEs will be responsible for about 35% of industrial emissions of SO_2 in 2000, implying a total of 8.4 million tonnes. Cao Fengzhong, "Woguo xiangzhen qiye daqi, shui wuran ji duice" ("Air and water pollution by our country's TVEs and remedies"), *Huanjing baohu* (*Environmental Protection*), No. 5 (1997), pp. 3–6. This estimate may have been based on the findings (so far, unpublished) of the 1995 national survey of pollution by TVEs, which came too late to be incorporated in the Ninth Five-Year Plan.

68. Even in Shanghai, about half of all households still use small coal stoves to cook their meals. "This contributes to chronic bronchitis, pulmonary emphysema, and lung cancer," *China Environment News*, August 1995, p. 7.

69. Report by Premier Li Peng "China's policy on energy resources," *Xinhua* news release dd. 25 May 1997, tr. in BBC FE/2956 S1. The electricity price was raised to 0.36 *yuan* per kWh in May 1997.

70. NEPA (eds.), *Documents from the Fourth National Conference*, pp. 311–323. Both had already been proposed by NEPA chief Qu Geping in 1991: see his series of articles in *Huanjing baohu* (*Environmental Protection*), Nos. 3–5 (1991).

71. *Huanjing baohu* (*Environmental Protection*), No. 1 (1997), p. 41; China Environmental Yearbook Editing Committee and Society (eds.), *China Environmental Yearbook 1996*, pp. 154–155.

The Plan aims to reuse 45 per cent of industrial waste and treat 50 per cent of residential solid waste by 2000, while limiting industrial solid waste disposal to 60 million tonnes. These figures are not very different from those suggested in 1995. National data collection is uneven and figures are sometimes contradictory and hard to interpret. According to NEPA, industrial waste from SOEs was 645 million tonnes in 1995 – most of which came from power generation and mining. About 70 and 30 million tonnes, respectively, were from metallurgical and chemical industries. 142 million tonnes of this total were treated, of which a quarter was handled by storage. Twenty-two million tonnes were released into the environment with 6.5 million tonnes going into water bodies. Interior provinces (particularly Sichuan, Yunnan and Shaanxi) were the worst offenders.[72] In 1996, NEPA added that another 410 million tonnes of solid waste had come from TVEs that year. Dumping by SOEs had been reduced to 16.9 million tonnes, and 20 per cent less solid waste had been treated than in the year before. Most ashes were used in construction projects, or, as with other solid waste, were deposited at the industrial site. Rates of reuse of industrial waste now vary from between 65 per cent or more in cities (and 83 per cent in Shanghai) to 20 per cent in some provinces (see Tables 3, 7 and 8).

Treatment rates vary between 0 and 30 per cent. There is no information available on storage locations, conditions and possible leaks of substances to the surroundings. Good locations for land-fills are increasingly scarce, and some have been relocated around major cities. The drinking water supplies of coastal areas with high ground water tables are particularly vulnerable to poisoning. While some provinces still store more than half of their industrial waste (Hainan, Jiangxi, Shaanxi and Inner Mongolia), and most store at least a third,[73] places such as Shanghai and Tianjin cannot do so any more.

China is just beginning to realize the dangers, and future costs, of dumped industrial waste, particularly toxic waste. Several factors have made prevention, treatment and control very difficult. Many factories have ample room to store their waste on their own grounds, where they are not likely to be strictly controlled by the EPB. The value of land is insufficiently appreciated, most having been allocated for free or rented at a very low price. Expert knowledge about toxic substances is limited, and the effects on workers' or residents' health may be masked by generally poor health conditions. The costs of cleaning up, polluted soils in particular, are prohibitive. Therefore, progress can only be slow.

For materials savings, the record is not any better. According to one author, the recovery rate in mining is only 30 per cent (as against a world average of 50 per cent); also, the level of reuse of resources is 70 per cent less than the world advanced level, resulting in annual losses of more than 25 billion *yuan*. Forty billion *yuan* of waste and old materials might

72. China Environmental Yearbook Editing Committee and Society (eds.), *ibid.* pp. 483–85.
73. *Ibid.* pp. 483–88.

be reused.[74] In 1995, China recycled only 15 per cent of its paper, 10 per cent of its plastics, and 1 per cent of its aluminium cans. Almost none of the annual quantity of 13 million tonnes of packaging materials were recovered.[75] To quote one local example: in Beijing, only 10–12 per cent of glass is recycled, a far cry from the city's goal of 50 per cent by 2000. The main cause is the lack of protection for the glass recovery industry, which consequently has insufficient capital and uses old equipment. Moreover, the number of collection points has been decreased and people's awareness of recycling needs improvement. The percentage of glass in the city garbage has more than doubled from less than 0.5 per cent in 1978 to about 1 per cent in 1995.[76] There have been several local initiatives to reduce waste. For example, the Tianjin EPB has listed the quantity of refuse per product, and uses this list to calculate discharge fees.[77]

Combustion of Chinese city garbage has always been difficult. It has a low content of paper, plastics, textile fibres, metals or glass, but very high content of ashes and fruit peels. A recent survey shows great variation between north and south, particularly due to heating practices. In cities with household gas, 72 per cent of the garbage is organic, but in cities which use coal, 70 per cent is anorganic. Most garbage is dumped, and the average amount of garbage produced daily per capita is almost 1 kilogram, rising by 8–10 per cent per year.[78]

Regional and Sectoral Differences in Pollution Problems and Treatment Measures

As noted above, there are considerable variations in political support for greater environmental efforts in China, with the demands of SEPA meeting with resistance, and problems of implementation in other departments and at provincial and local levels. This is not just because the industrial ministries and local governments have to provide most of the necessary investments as owners of industries. Market barriers and technological gaps are contributing factors as well. Within and between industrial sectors, great differences persist in levels of technology, owing to a continued tradition of market barriers and state subsidies, and to low or absent penalties on uneconomical resource use. There is a great technological and environmental gap between the developed areas along the coast and interior provinces. New industrial sectors (such as consumer

74. Zhao Jiarong, "Nuli kaizhuang ziyuan zonghe liyong gongzuodi xin jumian" ("Strive to make a break-through in comprehensive utilization of materials"), *Huanjing baohu* (*Environmental Protection*), No. 2 (1997), pp. 36–37. The author sees major problems with awareness and understanding, stagnating legislation, weak management (notably on standardization, inspection and reporting) and the absence of an information network.

75. NEPA (eds.), *Documents from the Fourth National Conference*, p. 411.

76. Hu Xiuren, "Feiqi boli huishou liyongdi diaocha yanjiu" ("Investigation of recovery and use of waste glass"), *Huanjing baohu* (*Environmental Protection*), No. 1 (1997), p. 43.

77. *Huanjing baohu* (*Environmental Protection*), No. 2 (1996), pp. 43–45.

78. *Huanjing baohu* (*Environmental Protection*), No. 7 (1997), pp. 16–17. The survey has data for individual cities.

durables) and those with foreign competition are much less wasteful and pollutive than traditional sectors.

Tables 5, 6 and 9 show major differentials between industrial branches, some cities, north and south China, and main river basins, respectively. As a vast country, China has very different geographical conditions, population densities and levels of industrial development. Within the state sector, local industries have less concern about environmental standards than provincial or national industries.[79] However, by far the major distinction is between state-owned urban industries and township- and village-owned rural industries – a difference which is rooted in China's institutional and economic division of city and country. This merits some attention.

A 1989 survey of 573,000 industrial TVEs showed a dismal record on all environmental indicators. Only 22 per cent of their wastewater was reused, only 16 per cent of discharged wastewater was up to standard, and 70 per cent of pollutive industries did not treat their wastewater at all. 72 per cent of their boilers were not up-to-standard, and 86 per cent did not remove dust from their flue gases. 76 per cent did not treat their solid waste, while 77 per cent worked without environmental impact approval. Their total payment of pollution charges – 169 million *yuan* – was less than 0.1 per cent of their turnover, and their fines were only 21 million *yuan*. Only 1.4 per cent of the value of their fixed assets was related to environmental measures.[80]

By 1995, these rural industries accounted for 45 per cent of China's industrial output value and 30 per cent of its added value, and their pollution had reached alarming levels. On the basis of a new survey (not yet published) which tried to establish 1995 as a bench-mark year, NEPA concluded that, by the year 2000, these rural industries would be responsible for 50 per cent of pollutants. In most coastal medium- and small-size cities, rural areas and towns, they were already the main polluters.[81] Current predictions are that without restrictive measures they will be responsible for 35–40 per cent of industrial wastewater and 60–70 per cent of COD by 2000, 35 per cent of SO_2, and 48 per cent of fly ash. The paper and building materials industries create the most pollution. Annual economic losses from their pollution are estimated at 100 billion *yuan*, or 2 per cent of GDP. As noted above, the State Council very belatedly

---

79. According to a 1995 study, compliance rates for implementation of the "three-synchronies" varied between 95.2% for provincial-level projects to 90.4% and 84%, respectively, for municipal- and county-level projects. Of those where it was implemented, 95% of the provincial-level projects were up to standard, but only 84 and 82%, respectively, of municipal- and county-level projects. China Environmental Yearbook Editing Committee and Society (eds.), *China Environmental Yearbook 1996*, p. 137.

80. Guojia huanbaoju ziran baohusi, *Zhongguo xiangzhen gongye huanjing wuran jiqi fangzhi duice (Environmental Pollution by Township and Village Industries and Remedial Treatment Policies)* (Beijing: Zhongguo huanjing kexue chubanshe, 1995), pp. 18–19.

81. China Environmental Yearbook Editing Committee and Society (eds.), *China Environmental Yearbook 1996*, p. 172.

decided to restrict the so-called "15 small industries."[82] Officially, 57,330 enterprises (81 per cent of the target) were closed down in consequence. However, SEPA and the inspection departments still have to send teams to inspect their closure, and "seriously deal with leaders who do not comply or change their course of action."[83] The new restrictions may later be applied more universally, but, as discussed above, water pollution in the Huai River basin has been singled out for attention.[84]

Conclusion: Further Development of Incentives and Environmental Awareness

Summarizing the main pollution control problems of China in future years, it is clear that major efforts will be needed to improve industrial production processes and reduce pollution. The growing shortage of water, land and other resources will force society into producing in a less wasteful manner. The alternative will be to accept increasing damages to health in many regions of China, deviance from international and advanced standards of industrial production and quality of life, loss of biodiversity and a rapid and unbalanced depletion of precious resources. All these will raise costs for the future generations. Even under the right set of priorities and measures from central government, many poor and industrially backward local communities will continue to cause environmental damage in their efforts to achieve economic growth. Here lie the real tests of governmental authority and responsibility for present and future generations, and for the quality of its organizations and foreign donor programmes. Some time ago, a report[85] by environmental specialists advised that emphasis should be placed on changing local governments' behaviour, and that a target responsibility system should be developed. It recommended reinforcing county EPBs, extending their scope to townships with serious pollution. Inspections and fines were to be stepped up, and more detailed environmental regulations drawn up and applied. The production structure should be improved, and technical improvements made. While incentives should be offered for the reduction of pollution, environmental costs should be internalized. Obviously,

---

82. In August 1996, the State Council ordered local authorities to close down small paper factories (output below 5,000 tonnes/year), leather factories (output below 30,000 hides/year), dyeing factories (below 500 tonnes/year), and chemical, electroplating, asbestos and other factories with antiquated polluting technologies. Local leaders of government and companies were threatened with prosecution if they did not comply. *Huanjing baohu* (*Environmental Protection*), No. 9 (1996), pp. 2–4.

83. Cao Fengzhong, "Air and water pollution by our country's TVEs and remedies," pp. 3–6.

84. 17,000 enterprises were shut down in Henan province alone. 259 seriously pollutive larger industries (mostly in paper and alcohol) in the Huai River basin were warned that if they could not meet discharge-standards before a certain date. or if they "illegally change their names, or shift the pollution problems to other enterprises, people can report them to the local EP bureaus." *Xinhua*, 6 January 1997 and 17 March 1997.

85. Guojia huanbaoju, *Zhongguo xiangzhen qiye diaocha baogao* (*Report on an Investigation of China's TVEs*) (Beijing, 1995). See also *Zhongguo gongye jingji* (*China's Industrial Economy*), No. 12 (1996).

the report concluded, an all-out approach of educational, legal, administrative, economic and technological measures was needed.

However, some powerful factors work against any fast improvements. Some are physical, such as the water shortage and the heavy reliance on coal for energy. Others are an inescapable part of economic progress, such as rapid urbanization and industrialization. Many, however, are political. The present government apparatus is neither strong nor equally motivated. The tradition of political bargaining, and huge differences in levels of technological development and environmental awareness work against the strict application of environmental laws. The government's very limited direct involvement in the rural economy makes it easy to lay down strict standards, but difficult to see to monitoring and control. Even if the central government perceives the need for action now, it cannot subsidize projects on a large scale from its own budget. In contrast, county and township authorities thrive on the income generated by their industries, often through personal involvement. Their legitimacy is based primarily on economic success and, as yet, environmental concerns do not have much local support or their own political platform.

The main challenges for China are to raise environmental awareness, to train and expand a core apparatus of experts, to promote participation in environmentally-friendly policies and activities, and to phase out polluting and wasteful enterprises using a combination of legal and economic measures. China may be better positioned to achieve this than many other countries. Its high economic growth permits the rationalization of industrial production and greater investments in the environment by government and companies without having to sacrifice income growth. In almost all regions and sectors, major technological and managerial improvements are possible, which will bring immediate and visible gains in terms of resource savings and health improvement, and build up political and popular support. The wave of foreign industrial investment in 1993–1995 has produced standards of advanced technologies and management methods which may serve as examples. However, their effect on the production practices of small and rural enterprises is likely to be indirect and slow. The most direct way to influence pollutive behaviour would be to have all polluters pay, irrespective of whether they are a foreign company or TVE, a defence industry or hotel, an urban resident or private farmer, poor or rich. That is to say, the economics of pollutive behaviour have to be changed, costs of pollution internalized, and a level playing field established and enforced. Of course, this is an ideal which can never be realized in any country. Yet it is the direction one should go. Such environmentally-motivated industrial policies would do away with local protectionism, directly influencing the economics of production and causing massive dislocations. The question is to what extent China is prepared and able to accept temporary and local reductions of economic activities for the benefit of qualitative improvements to its national production structure and the quality of life for future generations.

Population, Public Health and the Environment in China

Judith Banister

Introduction

To the extent that China's population size or population growth rate causes environmental destruction, such damage has already been done over the last several centuries, especially in the most recent 50 years. The impacts of China's large population and continuing population increase are basically irreversible in the medium-term. But in the coming decades, the relatively low PRC population growth rate will be a minor continuing environmental problem. Other environmental effects associated with population will be twofold. First, China's current age structure is strongly skewed toward the working age groups, and the population aged between 15 and 64 will increase dramatically in the coming decade. This contributes to huge unmet current and future demand for employment. Because the legitimacy of the PRC government depends in part on its success in generating jobs, it will continue to endeavour to meet the challenge of employment generation. This imperative, aggravated by the age structure changes, can be expected to take precedence over environmental considerations where these goals conflict. Secondly, the rising living standards of China's population will contribute to further environmental deterioration. When an enormous population rapidly multiplies its per capita income, the impacts can be massive and ecologically destabilizing.

The pressure of population on China's environment is intensifying today, but this is not a new phenomenon. For nearly one and a half millennia, the total population of China fluctuated around the total of 60 million people counted in the censuses of 2 A.D. and 1381 A.D.[1] From the early Ming Dynasty, however, slow population growth became the norm. The subsequent 500 years saw China's population multiply about 10 times to the count of 583 million people in the first modern census conducted under the People's Republic of China in 1953. China's population, due to its growth by the middle of the Han dynasty, and again during the Ming and Qing dynasties, constituted 28–30 per cent of the world's total population in A.D. 2, 1750, and 1900 respectively.[2] China's mainland population today comprises 21 per cent of the total global population.

As the numbers grew during the last two dynasties, the area of land

---

1. John D. Durand, "The population statistics of China, A.D. 2–1953," *Population Studies*, Vol. 13, No. 3 (1960), pp. 209–256.

2. John D. Durand, *Historical Estimates of World Population: An Evaluation* (Philadelphia: University of Pennsylvania Population Studies Center, 1974), mimeo.

under cultivation also multiplied, reducing the area of forest and grass-lands. When the dominant Han-Chinese people spread out, they displaced smaller groups, pushing ethnic minorities into mountains and hills and other marginal lands where the environmental impact was sometimes great. China's historical record includes periodic mention of the need to deal with the effects of food cultivation and fuel gathering by Han and minority peoples, including severe deforestation, eroding hillsides and loess lands, siltation of rivers and resultant flooding.[3]

PRC Population – The First Half Century

Until 1949, population changes in China[4] had occurred slowly, except for periods of massive intentional slaughter and warfare. But the pace quickened immediately after the founding of the PRC. Most developing countries at the time experienced similar trends of sudden mortality decline and population growth of unprecedented speed. But in China, the shift from decades of invasion and civil war to comparative security for most people triggered an even sharper demographic transition during the 1950s.

Trends in illness and survival. China's death rate dropped by almost half between 1949 and 1957.[5] This extraordinary mortality decline was caused by the cessation of warfare, the maintenance of public order, the redistribution of access to agricultural land, and government storage and distribution of grain. Also very important were the public health measures and immunization programmes implemented from the beginning of the 1950s. Increased environmental sanitation played no small part in this transformation of health conditions and survival chances. The "patriotic public health campaigns" targeted filth and disease-carrying pests, promoted the building of latrines and taught peasants about composting human waste to kill parasites before using it as fertilizer.

These great successes of the 1950s were temporarily reversed by the ideology-driven policies of the Great Leap Forward. In the years 1958–1961, the death rate skyrocketed and 30 million excess deaths occurred – probably more than from any other famine in human history.[6] The

3. For details see Mark Elvin, "Three thousand years of unsustainable growth: China's environment from archaic times to the present," *East Asian History*, Vol. 6 (1993); Richard L. Edmonds, *Patterns of China's Lost Harmony, A Survey of the Country's Environmental Degradation and Protection* (London: Routledge, 1994); and Wen-Yuan Niu and William M. Harris, "China: The forecast of its environmental situation in the 21st century," *Journal of Environmental Management*, No. 47 (1996), pp. 101–114.

4. In this paper, the analysis is based entirely on data from the mainland of China excluding Hong Kong and Taiwan. Therefore, the terms "China" and "PRC," for reasons of convenience, do not include Taiwan or Hong Kong in this report. No political statement is implied.

5. Details of China's health and mortality transition from early in this century to the late 1980s are found in Judith Banister, *China's Changing Population* (Stanford, CA: Stanford University Press, 1987), pp. 50–120.

6. *Ibid.* pp. 85, 118; Basil Ashton *et al.* "Famine in China, 1958–61," *Population and Development Review*, Vol. 10, No. 4 (1984), p. 614; Ansley J. Coale, *Rapid Population Change in China, 1952–1982* (Washington, DC: National Academy Press, 1984), pp. 69–70;

breakdown of public health measures increased the devastating effects of the lack of access to food.

Once food supply was restored in 1961–1962, the death rate dropped rapidly again. During the Cultural Revolution of the late 1960s, hundreds of thousands of people died in political conflict, and again many lost their lives through the withdrawal of medical care or food. But these numbers were small compared to China's normal annual deaths. Meanwhile, the expansion of the production brigade co-operative health systems and the training of barefoot doctors probably increased survival chances in rural areas. By the mid-1970s, expectation of life at birth was about 64 years, unusually high for a country as poor as China.

Rapid population growth. China's low death rate for most of the PRC years was not followed by sharp fertility decline until the 1970s. High natural growth rates of population were produced by comparatively high birth rates combined with low mortality. In the century between 1851 and 1953, China's population had grown only 0.3 per cent a year on average, but by the 1960s the annual rate of population growth was almost 3 per cent. During a demographic transition from high to low death and birth rates, it is unavoidable that there will be a period when birth rates are higher than death rates and the population grows quickly. In China's case, had the government steadily encouraged fertility control and provided contraceptives to rural as well as urban populations from the 1950s, rural fertility decline might have started earlier than it did. Without compulsion, the urban and rural fertility transitions would have been more gradual than they were.

Fertility control. China's government began implementing a forceful, required family planning programme in the 1970s. The total fertility rate, a period measure of average births per woman, dropped from six in 1970 to three during 1976–1979. The compulsion intensified with the implementation of the one-child policy in 1979 and a national campaign of forced sterilization, abortion and intra-uterine device (IUD) use that peaked in 1983. Required family planning continues. The decline in fertility reduced China's population growth rate to about 1 per cent per year in the late 1990s, which is very low by developing country standards.

Environmental impacts of rapid population growth. For two and a half decades from the beginning of the 1950s, China's fast-growing population put further pressure on the environment. In particular, it was necessary to increase food production by several per cent a year just to supply the same per capita calories and nutrients as in the early 1950s. This clear need led to an intensification of agriculture on already-tilled

footnote continued

Sheng Luo, *Reconstruction of Life Tables and Age Distributions for the Population of China, by Year, from 1953 to 1982* (Ann Arbor: U. M. I. Dissertation Services, 1990), p. 141; Penny Kane, *Famine in China, 1959–61: Demographic and Social Implications* (New York: St. Martin's Press, 1988).

land, and to the expansion of farming into former forests, grasslands, hillsides, deserts and swamplands. If the increase in agricultural production had been achieved in the most enlightened and feasible manner, China could have minimized the environmental damage during this inevitable period of rapid population growth. But in the early PRC decades, the government engaged in careless destruction of the environment in its drive to speed the economic and industrial transformation of China. The blame for this devastation is usually laid on China's large and rapidly increasing population, but the primary cause was policy decisions that could have been avoided. For instance, the worthless backyard steel furnaces of the Great Leap Forward were fuelled by massive deforestation, and the leadership decided to require that grain be grown in places where other food production (aquaculture, fruit and nut trees, grazing animals) could have been carried out with less environmental damage.[7]

Economic reform and public health. The current economic reform period that began in 1978 included the abandonment of communal farming and with it the rural co-operative health systems. Public health experts and other specialists abroad feared that the loss of health insurance and the implementation of fee-for-service medical care would cause deterioration of public health, and perhaps even a rise in China's level of mortality.[8] Reports of weakened and neglected disease control systems in the early reform years were alarming.

Meanwhile, both before and during the economic reform decades, another factor has been impacting health and survival – increasing pollution of air, water and other aspects of the environment such as soil. It might be assumed that deteriorating public health programmes and worsening environmental conditions would have serious health effects.

Air Pollution and Public Health in China

Some pollution of the air people breathe comes from the direct release of noxious chemicals and gases. However, in China as elsewhere, most pollution of outdoor air and the air inside dwellings is caused by the combustion of biofuels and fossil fuels in home cooking and heating stoves, industrial boilers, power plants and vehicles. The burning of coal – widespread in China – releases a different mix of pollutants depending on the type of coal (e.g. anthracite or bituminous) and on whether the coal is raw or washed, high-sulphur or low-sulphur, smoky or less smoky. In general, coal-burning releases large amounts of suspended particulates, sulphur dioxide (SO_2), carbon monoxide (CO) and nitrogen oxides.

Respiratory illnesses and irritation of air passages, eyes and skin are the main health effects of air pollution. Long-term exposure to polluted

7. For examples, see Vaclav Smil, *The Bad Earth, Environmental Degradation in China* (Armonk, NY: M. E. Sharpe, 1984).

8. Dean T. Jamison *et al. China, The Health Sector* (Washington, DC: The World Bank, 1984), pp. xvi-xvii; Amartya Sen, "Food and freedom," *World Development*, Vol. 17, No. 6 (1989), pp. 776–79.

air can cause chronic bronchitis, asthma, chronic obstructive pulmonary disease (COPD), pulmonary heart disease and lung cancer. High concentrations of air pollution can cause acute respiratory illness and the deaths of vulnerable individuals. All these morbidity and mortality effects can be seen in China today.

Health effects of China's ambient air pollution. Before the founding of the PRC, atmospheric pollution was not a problem in most of China. Just one-tenth of the population lived in urban places, and the only industrial areas were Shanghai and parts of Manchuria. But since 1949, China has emphasized heavy industry, paying little attention to the effects of air pollution until the 1980s. The urban proportion of the population rose to almost one-fifth in the 1950s, and during the economic reform period has continued its climb to 29 per cent by 1995. Severe urban air pollution has characterized most of China's cities for decades, mostly due to the burning of coal for industrial, municipal, utility and household uses. In urban areas, the population's exposure to particulates and sulphur dioxide is exceptionally high.[9] Measured air pollutants in China's cities rival the worst cities in the world, past or present; particulates are especially high in northern cities due to the burning of unwashed coal for industrial, municipal and household uses, including winter heating. Sulphur dioxide emissions are a problem in cities throughout China, including the south where high-sulphur coal is burned. The explosive growth of rural industries has now caused ambient air pollution in some rural areas.

Data linking sickness and deaths to ambient air pollution in China are usually weak and indirect, but a few sophisticated studies provide more convincing evidence. One Chongqing study found a significant association between ambient air pollution and reduced pulmonary function; there was a strong correlation between high concentrations of particulates and sulphur dioxide, on the one hand, and increased hospital admissions, emergency room visits and deaths on the other. A Shenyang study calculated mortality increases as a function of higher concentrations of suspended particulates and of sulphur dioxide. A Beijing study linked higher particulate concentrations with increased mortality from COPD and pulmonary heart disease.[10] In Shanghai, detailed mapping shows that the incidence of lung cancer is highest in industrial parts of the city.[11] Finally, when a temperature inversion combines with high ambient air pollutant concentrations to cause a city medical emergency, there is little doubt of the cause of the health problems. For example, during 28–30 March 1998, residents of Tianjin experienced this combination of factors: 14 people died of ambient carbon monoxide poisoning before they could

9. Vaclav Smil, *Environmental Problems in China: Estimates of Economic Costs* (Honolulu: East-West Center, 1996), East-West Center Special Reports No. 5.

10. These three studies are reported in Todd M. Johnson, Feng Liu and Richard Newfarmer, *Clear Water, Blue Skies: China's Environment in the New Century* (Washington, DC: The World Bank, 1997), p. 18.

11. World Health Organization and United Nations Environment Programme, *Urban Air Pollution in Megacities of the World* (Oxford: Blackwell, 1992), p. 210.

reach hospital, and another 1,126 were rushed to hospitals for treatment of acute symptoms of air poisoning.[12]

One of the most serious contaminants in China's air today, especially in urban and suburban areas, is lead. Lead has irreversible effects on children's intelligence, neurobehavioural development and physical growth, even at low doses. Seventeen recent studies in cities of China have detected dangerous levels of lead poisoning in children.[13] The causes are leaded petrol, industrial emissions, coal combustion and lead added to products such as toys, food, traditional medicine and paint. China has barely begun to address this critical issue, but has recently announced that leaded petrol will soon be phased out.

During the 1980s and 1990s, China has been implementing policies to reduce ambient air pollution with some success, presumably reducing the associated morbidity and mortality in the process. In large cities, which have the highest levels of particulate and SO_2 pollution, average ambient particulate concentrations reportedly fell by 40 per cent from 1985 to 1991, then levelled out during 1991–1995; average ambient sulphur dioxide concentrations stabilized from 1987 to 1993, then declined to 1995. In medium-sized and small cities, average ambient particulate concentrations also declined by a similar percentage from 1985 to 1991 before levelling out, while sulphur dioxide concentrations have been stable and much lower than in large cities during 1985–1995.[14]

Health effects of indoor air pollution. In developing countries throughout the world, households primarily burn biofuels (fuelwood, crop residues, dung, grasses, leaves, twigs) in inefficient, usually unvented stoves for cooking and heating.[15] Household concentrations of indoor air pollutants, such as fine particulates, gaseous hydrocarbons and carbon monoxide, are extraordinarily high, especially in cold climates where the stoves are kept burning for warmth. Throughout history, families have burned biofuels for household energy needs, which helps to explain why respiratory diseases were and are a major cause of death. Children living in these households can die of acute respiratory illnesses and adults can develop COPD, chronic bronchitis, pulmonary heart disease or respiratory system cancers from the smoke and fumes.

Indoor air pollution and health trends. In China, as of 1989, biomass supplied almost three-fifths of all rural energy and coal about one-third.[16] In most rural homes, the fuel is wood or crop residues such as stalks; in some dwellings in grassland areas, the main fuel is dried animal dung.

12. Chan Yee Hon, "Air poisoning victims out of danger," *South China Morning Post*, 4 April 1998, p. 8.

13. Xiao-ming Shen *et al.* "Childhood lead poisoning in China," *The Science of the Total Environment*, No. 181 (1996), pp. 101–109.

14. Johnson, Feng Liu and Newfarmer, *Clear Water, Blue Skies*, p. 9.

15. Details in this paragraph are from Kirk R. Smith, *Biofuels, Air Pollution, and Health, A Global Review* (New York: Plenum, 1987).

16. Vaclav Smil, *China's Environmental Crisis: An Inquiry into the Limits of National Development* (Armonk, NY: M. E. Sharpe, 1993), p. 102.

Through the 1970s in China, few improvements were made in rural residential stoves or fuels. The continuing prevalence of respiratory disease illness and deaths in rural areas was probably caused in part by rural indoor air pollution, as well as by lack of timely treatment for acute respiratory infections.

During the last two decades, however, the PRC has aggressively attacked the problem of indoor air pollution in rural areas. The Ministry of Agriculture has popularized more efficient stoves (higher efficiency produces less indoor air pollution), with the important addition of flues to vent the dangerous gases. By 1992, about 150 million households (approximately two-thirds of the total number of village households) were using these improved stoves for biofuel or coal-burning.[17]

Urban households have benefited from cleaner stoves and fuels.[18] Indoor air quality has improved as gas, electricity and central heating have partly replaced solid fuel and coal stoves and as kitchen ventilation has increased. Between 1989 and 1996, the proportion of the urban population using gas for fuel reportedly increased from 39 per cent to 68 per cent.[19] Many of those still using coal now burn cleaner and more efficient briquettes in specially designed stoves.

Trends in respiratory disease morbidity and mortality. We would expect that rates of illness and death from respiratory diseases might reflect the combined effects over time of indoor and outdoor air pollution plus any other important causes of respiratory ailments such as cigarette smoking. Data are sparse on the morbidity (illness incidence and prevalence) of respiratory diseases in China over time; levels and trends of respiratory illness might be different in urban and rural areas. Surveys in the mid-1980s showed that during a two-week period, 4 per cent of the urban population and 2 per cent of the rural population were ill with respiratory diseases. In city hospitals from the mid-1960s to mid-1990s, 16–19 per cent of inpatients were treated for respiratory diseases with no clear trend. Of inpatients in county hospitals from the mid-1970s to the mid-1990s, 17–19 per cent were admitted for respiratory system diseases, again with no trend.[20] One study based on 65 rural counties in 1983 reported that chronic lung disease rates were extraordinarily high for reasons that seemed to have little to do with tobacco smoking, especially among females.[21] A 1993–1994 survey found that respiratory ailments

17. Edmonds, *Patterns of China's Lost Harmony*, p. 151; Johnson, Feng Liu and Newfarmer, *Clear Water, Blue Skies*, p. 10.

18. Johnson, Feng Liu, and Newfarmer, *ibid.* p. 10.

19. The Editorial Board, *China Environment Yearbook 1996* (Beijing: China Environment Yearbook Inc., 1996), p. 30.

20. Chen Minzhang (ed.), *Yearbook of Health in the People's Republic of China, 1997* (Beijing: People's Medical Publishing House, 1997), pp. 309–311, 314.

21. Chen Junshi *et al. Diet, Lifestyle, and Mortality in China, A Study of the Characteristics of 65 Chinese Counties* (Oxford: Oxford University Press, 1990), p. 76.

were still the main illnesses reported by respondents for the prior two-week period.[22]

Data are available on respiratory disease as a cause of death in China (see Table 1). In 1973–1975, according to a comprehensive national survey of causes of death, respiratory diseases were the second leading cause of death for both sexes, causing 16 per cent of all deaths; half of the respiratory disease deaths were due to pneumonia. (Poverty and lack of timely and skilled medical care are important causes of pneumonia deaths; breathing polluted air may only be a minor contributing factor.) Cardiovascular diseases were the leading cause of death for both sexes, and over 40 per cent of these deaths were caused by pulmonary heart disease, with no significant difference between the sexes. Adding figures for death rates from respiratory disease and pulmonary heart disease results in very high death rates from indoor and outdoor air pollution in combination with general poverty. In the mid-1970s, respiratory disease death rates were twice as high in rural areas as in urban areas for both sexes.

The Chinese Academy of Preventive Medicine in the Ministry of Public Health collects cause-of-death data from 145 disease surveillance points that are designed to be nationally representative (Table 1). Nation-wide respiratory disease death rates reportedly declined somewhat between 1973–1975 and 1995 (from 118 to 99 deaths per 100,000 population per year). The comparatively low urban rate rose slightly from 60 to 66 during these two decades, while the high rural rate dropped from 126 to 109.[23] Meanwhile, the pneumonia component of respiratory disease deaths dropped stunningly, which implies that death rates from some other respiratory diseases have risen.

The respiratory disease death rate today is about 65 per cent higher in rural than urban areas. In particular, chronic obstructive pulmonary disease, including bronchitis and emphysema, kills people at a far higher rate in rural than in urban areas.[24] The rural causes of respiratory disease deaths, including indoor air pollution, remain serious, while urban populations are apparently more readily surviving their combination of ambient and indoor air pollution.

Water Pollution, Unsafe Food, and Health Effects in China

Water and food contamination from bacteria, viruses, parasites and other disease vectors characterizes underdeveloped places. In pre-1949 China, poor sanitation and the use of untreated nightsoil on crops spread

22. "Public health survey findings reported," *JPRS Epidemiology*, No. JPRS-TEP-95-002, 17 January 1995 (Beijing: Xinhua, in English).

23. The definition of respiratory disease appears to be comparable in the 1973–1975 and 1995 data shown in Table 1. MOPH has another reporting system for recent years which is not comparable to the 1970s data because pulmonary heart disease has been shifted to the respiratory disease category since the late 1980s. This paper uses recent cause-of-death data in ICD-9 categories.

24. J. Richard Bumgarner *et al. China, Long-Term Issues and Options in the Health Transition* (Washington, DC: The World Bank, 1992), pp. 13, 16–24.

Table 1: China: Causes of Death, 1973–1975 and 1995

Causes of Death	1973–1975 National		Urban		Rural		1995 National		Cities		Rural	
	Rate	Rank	Rate	Rank	Rate	Rank	Rate	Rank	Rate	Rank	Rate	Rank
Cardiovascular	192	1	208	1	189	1	187	1	187	1	186	1
of which:												
pulmonary heart disease	(79)						(26)		(9)		(31)	
cerebrovascular disease	(63)		(88)		(60)		(90)		(98)		(88)	
hypertensive disease	(14)						(18)		(14)		(19)	
Respiratory	118	2	60	3	126	2	99	2	66	3	109	2
of which:												
bronchitis, emphysema, asthma							(73)		(51)		(80)	
pneumonia	(59)						(18)		(6)		(21)	
Communicable	107	3	49	4	116	3	14	7	9	8	15	7
Neoplasms (cancer)	77	4	87	2	78	4	90	3	107	2	84	3
Injuries	71	5	48	5	80	5	56	4	32	5	63	4
Digestive	67	6	32	6	71	6	21	6	14	6	23	5

Notes:

Death rates are cause-specific deaths per 100,000 population per year. Data for 1973–1975 are from a nation-wide collection of data on cause of death for almost all deaths in China in a three-year period. Data for 1995 are from the 145 disease surveillance points of the Ministry of Public Health, Chinese Academy of Preventive Medicine, for 1995. All data are reported, not adjusted. The 1995 data are defined according to the ICD-9 (international classification of diseases) system. Classifications for 1973–1975 may not be exactly comparable to 1995. For 1973–1975, "cerebrovascular disease" was reported separately from "heart disease"; they are combined here under "cardiovascular" to accord with ICD-9. Similarly, for 1973–1975, "tuberculosis" was reported separately from "communicable disease"; they are combined here under "communicable" as in ICD-9.

Sources:

Public Health Ministry, *Public Health in the People's Republic of China (1986)* (Beijing: People's Medical Publishing House, 1986), pp. 93, 95; Weishengbu jibing kongzhi si, Zhongguo yufang yixue kexue yuan (Ministry of Public Health, Department of Disease Control, Chinese Academy of Preventive Medicine), *1995 nian Zhongguo jibing jiance nianbao (1995 Annual Report on China Disease Surveillance)* (Beijing: Renmin weisheng chubanshe, 1997), pp. 104–111, 145–150; personal communication, Chinese Academy of Preventive Medicine.

waterborne and foodborne diseases through the faecal-oral route, contributing to the high levels of mortality from infectious and digestive diseases. Water pollution then was probably a more localized phenomenon than today.

Water pollution from industry. China's industrialization since 1949 has increased the inorganic pollution of rivers and lakes through the release of industrial wastewater; this has escalated since the 1970s as urban industry and township and village enterprises (TVEs) have expanded.[25] Industrial processes can release harmful metals, minerals and other effluents into water supplies, which can cause neurological and brain damage, paralysis and other serious health conditions. In recent decades, China's government has been pushing industries to treat their wastewater before releasing it. By 1996, 82 per cent of industrial wastewater was reportedly treated.[26] The amounts of eight major harmful substances (heavy metals, lead, oil, etc.) discharged into industrial wastewater peaked in the 1980s and have since declined markedly, according to the available statistics.[27] However, these data refer only to factories managed at or above county level, and therefore the figures exclude the wastewater discharges from TVEs that would be expected to affect the rural population. Though the relevant morbidity data are lacking, it is likely that the dangerous substances in industrial effluents are harming the health of some people in urban and rural areas.

Organic pollution of water. In urban areas, much of the untreated sewage that used to be collected and taken to rural areas for agricultural fertilizer is being dumped into rivers and lakes instead. Since 1980, surface water and groundwater have grown progressively more polluted because of increased emissions consisting of municipal sewage, agricultural runoff, and industrial waste.[28] Municipal wastewater discharges nearly tripled between 1981 and 1995, yet only 7 per cent of this discharge is treated. Nation-wide, by 1996, half the ground water had been polluted and 40 per cent of water sources were declared undrinkable.[29]

Waterborne diseases in China. Data on the health effects of water pollution in China are weak. By 1984, dysentery and viral hepatitis (hepatitis A) were not yet under control, although rates of infection of most other acute communicable diseases had declined markedly.[30] In 1985, China reported 650 cholera cases, 3,280,000 cases of dysentery,

25. Edmonds, *Patterns of China's Lost Harmony*, pp. 133–145.
26. The Editorial Board, *Zhongguo huanjing nianjian 1997 (China Environment Yearbook 1997)* (Beijing: Zhongguo huanjing nianjian chubanshe, 1997), p. 467.
27. Edmonds, *Patterns of China's Lost Harmony*, pp. 133–145.
28. Johnson, Feng Liu and Newfarmer, *Clear Water, Blue Skies*, pp. 6, 11–15.
29. *China Environment Yearbook 1996*, p. 24.
30. Public Health Ministry, *Public Health in the People's Republic of China (1986)* (Beijing: People's Medical Publishing House, 1986), p. 84.

790,000 cases of viral hepatitis and 86,000 typhoid cases, with reported deaths from these diseases totalling 5,000.[31] It is probable that organic water pollution and food contamination were responsible for these diseases. Shanghai, the major city with the worst drinking water contamination, had half a million cases of hepatitis A in 1988.[32] By 1996, nation-wide cases of intestinal infectious diseases had declined in incidence, according to the National Reporting System on Infectious Diseases, but there were still 3,500 cases of cholera, 708,000 cases of viral hepatitis, 747,000 cases of dysentery and 60,000 typhoid cases reported for that year, resulting in a thousand deaths.[33] Viral hepatitis declined in incidence from 1992 to 1995 nationally and in both rural and urban areas, according to the Chinese Academy of Preventive Medicine disease surveillance system data.[34] But dysentery incidence showed no clear trend during 1990–1995, and diarrhoea incidence dropped from 1990 to 1991 and then showed no clear trend.[35]

Digestive diseases in China. Surveys in the mid-1980s discovered that in a two-week period, 1.2 per cent of the urban population and 1.3 per cent of the rural population were ill with diseases of the digestive system.[36] A similar survey in 1993–1994 found that intestinal ailments (such as gastroenteritis) were still among the most common during a two-week period.[37] Nevertheless, in the last two decades, there has been clear improvement in mortality rates from digestive diseases. In 1973–1975, digestive disease was the sixth leading cause of death: 9 per cent of deaths were attributable to this cause.[38] The rural death rate from digestive diseases was more than twice the urban rate. Data since the 1970s are for only a portion of urban and rural locations, yet the trend seems definitive even if the exact levels of mortality are incorrect. By 1988, cities of different sizes had reduced – but not much reduced – mortality from digestive diseases.[39] Rural areas, however, had made great progress. Even the poorest category of rural counties had a much lower death rate from this cause in 1988 than China's overall rural digestive disease death rate of 1973–1975. By the mid-1990s, 3 per cent of urban deaths and 4 per cent of rural were due to digestive

31. *Ibid.* p. 218.
32. Johnson, Feng Liu and Newfarmer, *Clear Water, Blue Skies*, p. 142.
33. Chen Minzhang (ed.), *Yearbook of Health in the PRC, 1997*, p. 67.
34. Weishengbu jibing kongzhi si, Zhongguo yufang yixue kexue yuan (Ministry of Public Health, Department of Disease Control, Chinese Academy of Preventive Medicine), *1995 nian Zhongguo jibing jiance nianbao (1995 Annual Report on China Disease Surveillance)* (Beijing: Renmin weisheng chubanshe, 1997), pp. 57–61. The reported incidence of 24 infectious diseases at the 145 disease surveillance points of the Chinese Academy of Preventive Medicine, MOPH, is twice as high as in the MOPH National Reporting System on Infectious Diseases. *Ibid.* p. 28.
35. *Ibid.* p. 62.
36. *Ibid.* p. 314.
37. "Public health survey findings reported," *JPRS Epidemiology*.
38. Public Health Ministry, *Public Health in the PRC (1986)*, pp. 93–95.
39. James S. Lawson and Vivian Lin, "Health status differentials in the People's Republic of China," *American Journal of Public Health*, Vol. 84, No. 5 (1994), p. 738.

ailments.[40] Comparing this with the mid-1970s data, the urban cause-specific death rate had dropped by more than half and the rural rate by two-thirds (see Table 1). Life-threatening contamination of water and food supplies in China had been reduced greatly during these decades.

Water shortages and sickness. Disease organisms and industrial contaminants are not the only water problems that affect health; a shortage of water itself can cause illness. When the supply of water is inadequate for personal cleanliness, people can be sickened by "water-washed" diseases such as diarrhoeal diseases and infections of the skin and eyes. The provision of a single tap, bringing increased supplies of water, can increase health substantially even if the quality of that water has not improved.[41]

The PRC has emphasized greater convenience of access to water in recent decades for both the urban and rural populations. By the end of 1991, public health officials reported that water treatment projects had upgraded the quality of water supply for 666 million of China's 880 million rural population. "As a result, the farmers' health has improved. Water-related diseases, especially intestinal disorders, are now under control."[42] As of 1996, 87 per cent of the rural population had benefited from improved (more convenient and/or safer) drinking water supplies, and of these beneficiaries, 45 per cent received tapwater service near their homes.[43] At the same time, however, increasing water shortages in north China would be expected to cause illness in the affected areas. A dearth of water makes sanitation more difficult and concentrates pollutants. For example, the Huang (Yellow) River partially dries up between July and November and the water quality deteriorates sharply; nevertheless, the annual average Water Quality Index for the Huang River improved measurably from the 1980–1984 period to the years 1985–1989, probably due to anti-pollution efforts.[44]

Food safety in China. Much of China's food is grown and consumed in villages without the involvement of a market, so it is only localities and households that can prevent its contamination. In addition, the Chinese government has begun to pay attention to the safety of food that is sold raw or is prepared for sale. The number of foodstuffs under surveillance increased from 850,000 in 1986 to 1,265,000 in 1996; reported cases of food poisoning dropped from 76,000 in 1985 to 24,000 in 1996.[45]

40. Chen Minzhang (ed.), *Yearbook of Health in the PRC, 1997*, pp. 319–320.
41. David Bradley, "Health, environment, and tropical development," in Bryan Cartledge (ed.), *Health and the Environment* (Oxford: Oxford University Press, 1994), pp. 131–33.
42. Wang Wenli, "Pure water supplied to more rural residents," *China Daily*, 6 December 1991, p. 1.
43. Chen Minzhang (ed.), *Yearbook of Health in the PRC, 1997*, p. 323.
44. Xu Youyun (ed.) *Huanjing weisheng gongzuo shouce (xiu ding ban)* (*Handbook of Environmental Health Work, revised edition*) (Beijing: Renmin weisheng chubanshe, 1992), pp. 395–99.
45. Chen Minzhang (ed.), *Yearbook of Health in the PRC, 1997*, pp. 322–23.

General Mortality and Morbidity Trends During Economic Reform

For the last two decades, in contrast to earlier periods, analysts have had available death data representing all China from a national mortality survey (referring to 1973–1975), two censuses of the whole population (referring to 1981 and 1990) and a by-census or 1 per cent sample census (referring to 1995).[46] Even though there is some underreporting of deaths in infancy and at old ages, trends in mortality levels can be derived with reasonable confidence from these death statistics. Table 2 displays age-specific death rates from these four successive enumerations. The data show that since just before the economic reform period began, death rates have fallen for both sexes at most ages. Accordingly, life expectancy has continued to increase for both sexes.

Figures 1 and 2 show the reported changes in age-specific mortality rates for males and females from before the beginning of the economic reforms (1973–1975) to 1990. It is immediately visible that death rates at most ages for both sexes declined during this decade and a half. Much of the credit must go to the rapid rise in the incomes and living standards of most of China's population in both rural and urban areas. The multiplication of real per capita incomes meant increased quantities of food, a more varied and better balanced diet, improved housing conditions and greater spending on health care.

It is noteworthy that child and adult mortality dropped more for girls and women than for boys and men. Why? Generally speaking, both sexes are living in the same environments with the same economic conditions, food supply and public health situation. It appears that China's historic severe discrimination against females has continued to decline at most ages. In addition, the sharp drop in fertility has reduced deaths associated with pregnancy and child-bearing. Also important is the possibility that men are engaging more frequently in activities that cause their premature death: cigarette smoking has increased in China, with far greater proportions of men than women smoking, and smoking heavily. Similarly the use and abuse of alcohol and some forms of violence could be increasing among men. Rising geographical mobility has seen a rise in transport-related deaths, with men travelling more than women. And, finally, rapid economic growth has increased male self-employment in which occupation hazards are great.

Mortality changes in the early 1990s give further clues regarding what to expect in the coming decades (see Table 2). Toddler and young child mortality reportedly continued to drop for both sexes. But improvements in survival chances stagnated for other girls and for women in their twenties. Boys and men reportedly experienced increased death rates in age groups 10–14 through to 35–39, but especially in their twenties. Finally, for the first time since the early 1970s, reduced death rates were reported for elderly age groups of men and women.

46. For details see Judith Banister, "Perspectives on China's mortality trends," *International Population Conference, Beijing 1997*, Vol. 3 (Liege, Belgium: International Union for the Scientific Study of Population, 1997), pp. 1335–1351.

Table 2: China, Mortality Trends as Reported, 1973–1975 to 1995

MALE Age	Central death rates m(x) as reported				Percentage change, unadjusted data			
	1973–1975	1981	1990	1995	1973–1975 to 1981	1981 to 1990	1990 to 1995	1973–1975 to 1995
0	0.05097	0.03940	0.02895	0.02805	-23	-27	-3	-45
1–4	0.00906	0.00400	0.00236	0.00184	-56	-41	-22	-80
5–9	0.00231	0.00128	0.00079	0.00073	-45	-38	-7	-68
10–14	0.00101	0.00078	0.00059	0.00062	-23	-25	6	-39
15–19	0.00110	0.00106	0.00103	0.00110	-4	-3	7	0
20–24	0.00148	0.00142	0.00140	0.00167	-4	-2	19	13
25–29	0.00157	0.00146	0.00140	0.00178	-7	-4	27	13
30–34	0.00200	0.00176	0.00179	0.00194	-12	2	8	-3
35–39	0.00286	0.00243	0.00228	0.00235	-15	-6	3	-18
40–44	0.00411	0.00351	0.00329	0.00327	-15	-6	-1	-20
45–49	0.00622	0.00535	0.00513	0.00491	-14	-4	-4	-21
50–54	0.00985	0.00873	0.00833	0.00758	-11	-5	-9	-23
55–59	0.01539	0.01434	0.01372	0.01248	-7	-4	-9	-19
60–64	0.02532	0.02444	0.02336	0.02099	-3	-4	-10	-17
65–69	0.03763	0.03830	0.03785	0.03374	2	-1	-11	-10
70–74	0.06064	0.06357	0.06366	0.05451	5	0	-14	-10
75–79	0.09478	0.09639	0.09759	0.08161	2	1	-16	-14
80–84	0.14575	0.15634	0.15571	0.12552	7	0	-19	-14
85+	0.23697	0.23725	0.23353	0.19277	0	-2	-17	-19

Table 2: Continued

FEMALE Age	Central death rates m(x) as reported				Percentage change, unadjusted data			
	1973–1975	1981	1990	1995	1973–1975 to 1981	1981 to 1990	1990 to 1995	1973–1975 to 1995
0	0.04435	0.03726	0.03377	0.03743	-16	-9	11	-16
1–4	0.00928	0.00444	0.00252	0.00171	-52	-43	-32	-82
5–9	0.00211	0.00105	0.00059	0.00058	-50	-43	-2	-73
10–14	0.00085	0.00065	0.00045	0.00046	-23	-30	1	-46
15–19	0.00096	0.00092	0.00087	0.00078	-4	-5	-10	-19
20–24	0.00146	0.00134	0.00121	0.00122	-8	-10	1	-16
25–29	0.00171	0.00148	0.00117	0.00117	-13	-21	0	-32
30–34	0.00208	0.00168	0.00135	0.00117	-19	-20	-13	-44
35–39	0.00280	0.00216	0.00165	0.00146	-23	-24	-11	-48
40–44	0.00374	0.00291	0.00231	0.00201	-22	-21	-13	-46
45–49	0.00512	0.00421	0.00364	0.00305	-18	-13	-16	-40
50–54	0.00776	0.00659	0.00581	0.00501	-15	-12	-14	-35
55–59	0.01153	0.01018	0.00913	0.00781	-12	-10	-14	-32
60–64	0.01916	0.01713	0.01549	0.01235	-11	-10	-20	-36
65–69	0.02886	0.02685	0.02537	0.02140	-7	-6	-16	-26
70–74	0.04627	0.04583	0.04400	0.03791	-1	-4	-14	-18
75–79	0.07258	0.07062	0.07006	0.05882	-3	-1	-16	-19
80–84	0.11275	0.12107	0.11635	0.09719	7	-4	-16	-14
85+	0.19920	0.19991	0.18947	0.15976	0	-5	-16	-20

Sources:

Rong Shoude et al. "Woguo 1973–1975 nian jumin pingjun qiwang shouming de tongji fenxi" ("Analysis of life expectancy in China, 1973–1975"), *Renkou yu jingji (Population and Economy)*. No. 1 (25 February 1981), pp. 25–26; China State Council Population Census Office and State Statistical Bureau Department of Population Statistics, *Zhongguo 1982 nian renkou pucha ziliao (dianzi jisuanji huizong)* (*Data from China's 1982 Population Census (Results of Computer Tabulation)*) (Beijing: China Statistical Publishing House, 1984), pp. 272–281, 320–27; China State Council Population Census Office and State Statistical Bureau Department of Population Statistics, *Tabulation of the 1990 Population Census of the People's Republic of China* (Beijing: China Statistical Publishing House, 1993) Vol. 2, pp. 2–5 and Vol. 4, pp. 8–13; Quanguo renkou chouyang diaocha bangongshi bian, *1995 Quanguo 1% renkou chouyang diaocha ziliao* (*1995 Nationwide 1% Population Sample Survey Data*) (Beijing: Zhongguo tongji chubanshe, 1996), pp. 512–17.

Figure 1: **China, Male Mortality as Reported 1973–1975, 1981, 1990**

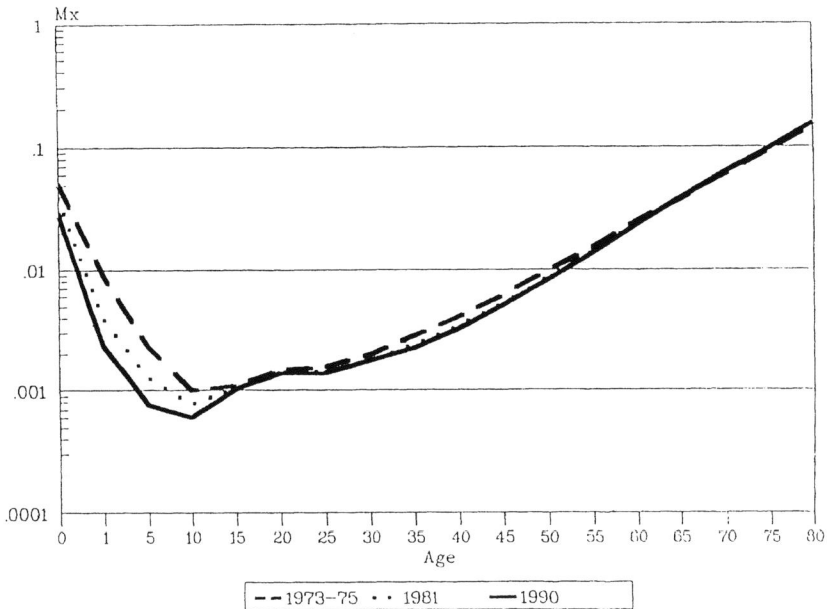

Sources:
Rong Shcude *et al.* "Analysis of life expectancy in China, 1973–1975," pp. 25–26; China State Council Population Census Office and State Statistical Bureau Department of Population Statistics, *Data from China's 1982 Population Census,* pp. 272–281, 320–27; China State Council Population Census Office and State Statistical Bureau Department of Population Statistics, State Statistical Bureau, *Tabulation of the 1990 Population Census,* Vol. 2, pp. 2–5 and Vol. 4, pp. 8–13.

Environment and mortality. We have seen that China has had some forms of environmental deterioration or lack of improvement in the economic reform decades that might affect health and survival – urban ambient air pollution, urban organic water pollution, rural contamination of air and water from TVEs. Respiratory disease morbidity and mortality have remained stubbornly high, reflecting perhaps continued indoor air pollution with the addition of more tobacco smoking plus ambient air pollution. But overall survival chances at most ages for both sexes have risen spectacularly in rural as well as urban areas. There have been considerable improvements in China's human environments in these decades, such as higher incomes, better housing, improved rural water supplies, immunization programmes, and targeted government-directed attacks on the remaining preventable causes of illness and death. The environmental problems that do exist have not blocked China's progress in improving public health and raising life expectancy.

Figure 2: **China, Female Mortality as Reported 1973–1975, 1981, 1990**

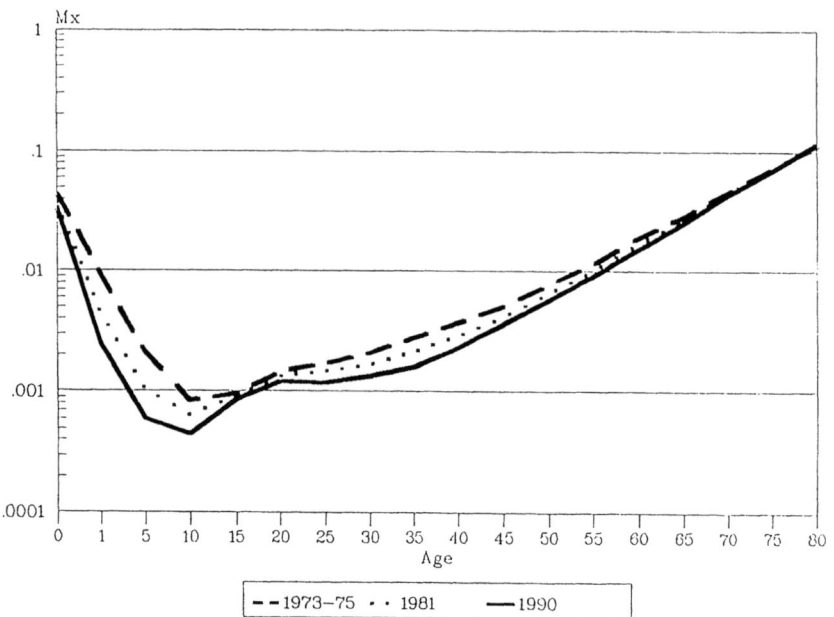

Sources:
    Rong Shoude *et al.* "Analysis of life expectancy in China, 1973–1975," pp. 25–26; China State Council Population Census Office and State Statistical Bureau Department of Population Statistics, *Data from China's 1982 Population Census,* pp. 272–281, 320–27; China State Council Population Census Office and State Statistical Bureau Department of Population Statistics, *Tabulation of the 1990 Population Census,* Vol. 2, pp. 2–5 and Vol. 4, pp. 8–13.

Survival of young children. Death rate trends for some age groups are particularly meaningful. When infants are breastfed, their survival depends strongly on perinatal and congenital conditions and the health of the mother. But after weaning begins, young children are especially vulnerable to environmental pathogens and dangers – contaminated water and food, filth surrounding them, unsafe items in their homes and immediate neighbourhoods, and diseases spread by the greater numbers of people they come in contact with. In the early 1970s, while death rates at most ages were lower than would have been expected at China's level of development, child death rates were still high. This signified that environmental causes of disease and death were still relatively poorly controlled.

Figure 3 shows the phenomenal change in mortality rates of young children of both sexes aged from one to four years between 1973–1975 and 1995. Their death rates halved in the seven years from 1973–1975 to 1981. A further halving of the age-specific death rates occurred between 1981 and 1995. Some of the credit for this great success goes to a national programme to immunize very high proportions (85 per cent or

Figure 3: **China, Reported Central Death Rates m(x) at Ages 1–4, 1973–1975 to 1995**

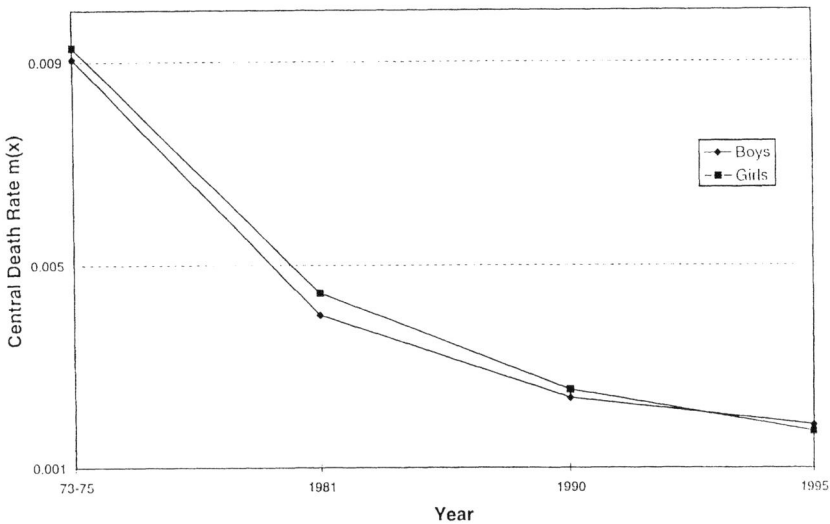

Sources:
   Rong Shoude *et al.* "Analysis of life expectancy in China, 1973–1975," pp. 25–26; China State Council Population Census Office and State Statistical Bureau Department of Population Statistics, *Data from China's 1982 Population Census,* pp. 272–281, 320–27; China State Council Population Census Office and State Statistical Bureau Department of Population Statistics, *Tabulation of the 1990 Population Census,* Vol. 2, pp. 2–5 and Vol. 4, pp. 8–13; Quanguo renkou chouyang diaocha bangongshi bian, *1995 Nationwide 1% Population Sample Survey Data,* pp. 512–17.

more) of children against six, and now more, major diseases of childhood (tuberculosis, polio, measles, diphtheria, pertussis or whooping cough, and tetanus; followed more recently by encephalitis, meningitis and hepatitis B immunizations). The Expanded Programme of Immunization was launched in 1979 and has been vigorously pursued with funding from UNICEF and the World Health Organization (WHO). As a result, China has reported sharp drops in the incidence of these diseases and in deaths from vaccine-preventable diseases.

The improvements in rural water supplies during the 1980s and 1990s surely contributed enormously to the enhanced survival of young children, who are especially susceptible to waterborne diseases including dysentery, diarrhoea, typhoid, cholera and intestinal parasites. For example, the mortality rate from diarrhoea among children under five years of age decreased by 57 per cent between 1991 and 1995, according to the national network of surveillance points covering young child mortality.[47]

By 1990, the leading cause of death of Chinese toddlers in cities and developed areas of the countryside was "external causes," meaning accidents and injuries. In the "undeveloped countryside," however, respir-

47. Chen Minzhang (ed.), *Yearbook of Health in the PRC, 1997,* p. 114.

atory diseases were still by far the leading cause of toddler deaths (30 per cent), followed by digestive system diseases (22 per cent), external causes (15 per cent), and infectious and parasitic diseases (13 per cent).[48]

China's Ministry of Public Health conducted a national survey in 1993–1994 on the frequency and types of illness (morbidity) in China's population.[49] The survey found that the incidence of infectious and parasitic diseases had dropped considerably compared with the mid-1980s. The most common ailments reported were respiratory (colds, tonsilitis and tracheitis) and intestinal (gastroenteritis). But "the main diseases in China's underdeveloped rural areas are still infectious diseases and diseases resulting from malnutrition, according to the investigation report." Another health and nutrition survey confirmed that, as of 1989, China still had a sizeable population of undernourished children; one-third of children aged from one to six in the sample were stunted in stature from under-nutrition, and about 8 per cent of children that age were suffering from acute malnutrition.[50]

Nature strikes back. Public finance for epidemic prevention stations declined from 0.11 per cent of GDP in 1978 to 0.04 per cent in 1993; absolute funding levels (in 1993 constant *yuan*) declined from 1.5 billion in 1986 to 1.3 billion in 1993.[51] Tuberculosis was thought to be the main cause of death in China as of 1958.[52] Great progress was made in tuberculosis control by 1979–1980, when a nation-wide pulmonary tuberculosis survey found that only 1 per cent of China's population was infected.[53] During the economic reform period, however, treatment programmes began to deteriorate. TB patients were not being cured and were spreading the disease, because of the weakened public health system and the prohibitive cost of the required medicines. Among rural men and women in the early 1990s, tuberculosis was the major infectious cause of death.[54] Since late 1990, a concerted effort funded partly by the World Bank and WHO has discovered how to cure China's TB patients; this TB control project was implemented in half of China by 1995.[55] As an overall cause of death, tuberculosis dropped from 10th place in 1986 to 12th in 1995, but TB still causes 1.3 per cent of all deaths and 53 per cent of deaths from infectious diseases.[56] Meanwhile, illness from tuberculosis

48. *Chinese Medical News Archive*, Issue 3 (17 December 1995), internet.
49. "Public health survey findings reported," *JPRS Epidemiology*.
50. Barry M. Popkin *et al.* "The nutrition transition in China: a cross-sectional analysis," *European Journal of Clinical Nutrition*, Vol. 47 (1993), pp. 342–43.
51. Winnie C. Yip and William C. Hsiao, "Intended and unintended consequences of market reform for health care," presented at the conference on "Unintended Social Consequences of Chinese Economic Reform," Harvard, May 1997, p. 17.
52. Editorial, *Chinese Journal of Tuberculosis*, Vol. 6, No. 4 (11 July 1958), p. 273, cited in Banister, *China's Changing Population*, p. 56.
53. *Ibid.* p. 63.
54. Bumgarner *et al. China, Long-Term Issues and Options*, p. xii.
55. http://www.who.org/programmes/gtb/tbrep_95/china.htm
56. Chen Minzhang (ed.), *Yearbook of Health in the PRC, 1997*, pp. 79–80.

did not decline during the early 1990s. Annual incidence was 50–80 cases per 100,000 people per year.[57] Nevertheless, the future looks hopeful because 97 per cent of newborns in China now receive BCG immunization to prevent tuberculosis.[58]

Mortality and Health – Future Prospects

China's health and sanitation goals for the 21st century emphasize the need to provide basic preventive and primary care as well as more advanced curative medical care to the entire rural population as well as the urban population.[59] Control of infectious and endemic diseases is envisioned. Because the main causes of death in China are now chronic diseases, the government's goals include research on preventing and curing chronic disease. Control of tobacco smoking is mentioned. One prominent goal is to minimize the impacts of environmental pollution on people's health by reducing air pollution, water pollution and occupational disease. These ambitious health goals for the coming century are muted, however, in the Ninth Five-Year Plan (1996–2000) and the Long-Term Target for the Year 2010. This document includes only a brief mention of emphasizing rural health and preventing disease.[60]

Prospects are good for further control of infectious, endemic and vaccine-preventable diseases. The government has shown its determination in this area, and international organizations continue to assist in the process as part of a co-ordinated focus on the remaining areas of absolute poverty. But the main causes of death in most of China today are heart disease, stroke, cancer and respiratory disease.[61] The public health and medical systems were not designed to deal with the prevention, postponement, control, and cure of chronic diseases, and they are only adapting slowly to this need.[62]

There may have been some success in the early 1990s. Mortality data from the 1995 sample census indicate that after decades of little or no improvement, age-specific mortality rates in late middle age and old age have begun to decline (see Table 2, above). We cannot yet be certain of the validity of this trend, however. China's best national life tables routinely omit about 10 per cent of elderly deaths, and it is possible that omissions were worse in the 1995 by-census.

Some factors point to the future worsening of certain chronic diseases. China's people are rapidly increasing their dietary intake of animal fats and alcohol. Nutritional experts are concerned about these trends away

57. Weishengbu jibing kongzhi si, Zhongguo yufang yixue kexue yuan, *1995 Annual Report on China Disease Surveillance*, p. 65.
58. Chen Minzhang (ed.), *Yearbook of Health in the PRC, 1997*, pp. 79–80.
59. China State Council, *China's Agenda 21: White Paper on China's Population, Environment, and Development in the 21st Century* (Beijing: China Environment Science Press, 1994), pp. 65–80.
60. "PRC: Ninth Five-Year Plan, Long-term Target," *Foreign Broadcast Information Service*, No. FBIS-CHI-96-070 (18 March 1996), p. 49.
61. Lawson and Lin, "Health status differentials in the PRC," pp. 737–741.
62. Bumgarner *et al. Long-term Issues and Options*.

from a grain-and-vegetable diet to a diet more typical of Western countries, because they expect higher cardiovascular disease to follow.[63] So far, however, most of China's population is still struggling to get adequate dietary variety. In the late 1980s, four-fifths of food energy in the Chinese diet still came from direct consumption of grains.[64] To get the full range of nutrients in adequate supply, China's people need to eat greater quantities and more varieties of fruits, nuts, legumes, vegetables, seafood, dairy products, eggs and meats.

Tobacco smoking grew at a prodigious rate after the economic reform period began. As early as 1984, 75 per cent of Chinese men in the age groups 30–34 to 55–59 were smokers. The proportion was over half in every male age group from 20–24 and up. Of women, 14–19 per cent were smokers in each age group from 45–49 and older, but smoking was minimal among younger women. Total consumption of cigarettes continued to increase rapidly in the late 1980s.[65] The increased tobacco use in the early economic reform period will be followed in another decade or so by increases in the chronic diseases caused or exacerbated by tobacco.

China's goal for the next century is to "control the proportion of male smokers above 15 to below 50 per cent."[66] Some efforts are now underway to limit smoking. For example, smoking is banned on at least some domestic flights and in the public places of many cities. A 1996 national survey of smoking prevalence found that only 4 per cent of adult women aged below 55 were smokers, and the current smoking rates for middle-aged men ranged from 65 to 71 per cent.[67] This suggests some reduction in male smoking rates compared to 1984, but it is likely to be some time before the PRC is able to greatly reduce the proportions of men who are smokers. In general, prospects are not good for reducing chronic disease in China by 2010.

Injuries and occupational diseases. During the early 1990s, the age-specific death rates of young adult men reportedly rose in cities, towns and rural areas (see Figure 4). If these data prove to be correct, the cause is not broadly environmental because women are barely affected. These figures suggest that injuries, accidents and life-style factors associated

63. Popkin *et al.* "Nutrition transition," pp. 343–45; T. Colin Campbell *et al.* "Associations of diet and disease: a comprehensive study of health characteristics in China," presented at the conference on "Unintended Social Consequences of Chinese Economic Reform," Harvard, May 1997.

64. Smil, *China's Environmental Crisis*, p. 81.

65. Bumgarner *et al. Long-term Issues and Options*, pp. 32–36.

66. China State Council, *China's Agenda 21*, p. 79.

67. Chinese Academy of Preventive Medicine, Chinese Association of Smoking and Health, Department of Disease Control in the Ministry of Health and Office of the Committee of the National Patriotic Health Campaign, *1996 National Prevalence Survey of Smoking Pattern* (Beijing: China Science and Technology Press, 1997).

Figure 4: **China, Male Central Death Rates at Ages (a) 20–24 and (b) 25–29, City, Town and Rural, 1981–1995, as Reported**

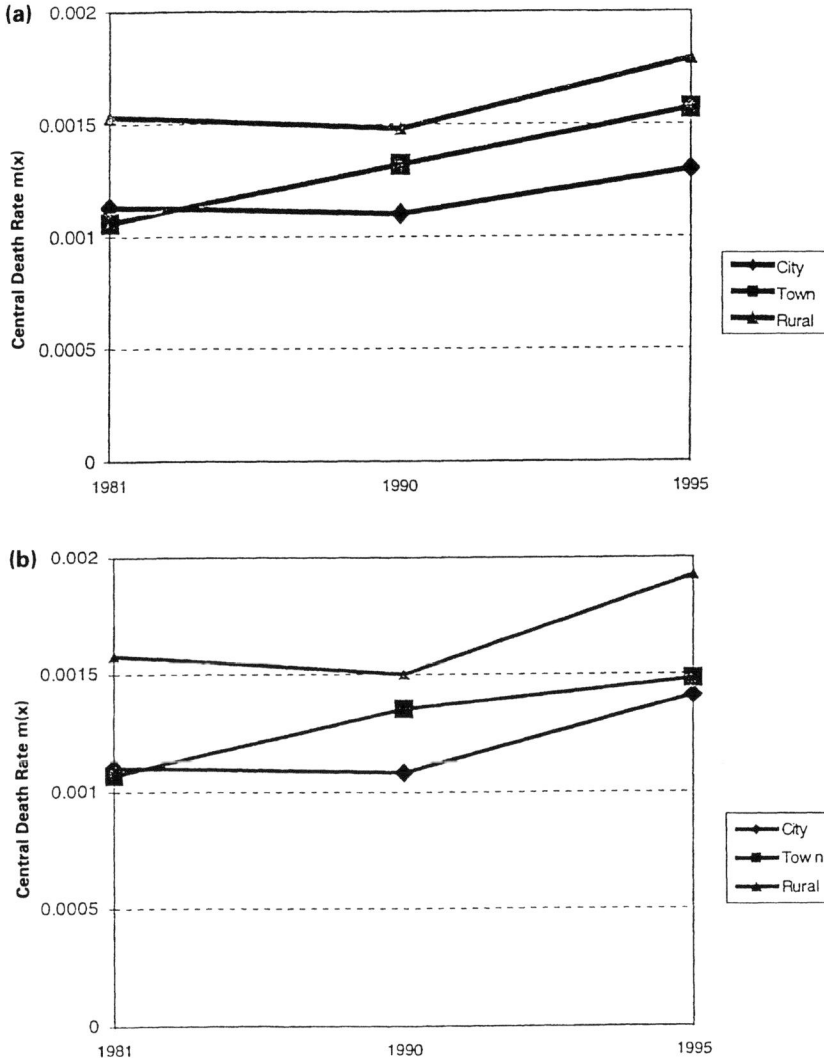

Sources:
Rong Shoude *et al.* "Analysis of life expectancy in China, 1973–1975," pp. 25–26; China State Council Population Census Office and State Statistical Bureau Department of Population Statistics, *Data from China's 1982 Population Census,* pp. 272–281, 320–27; China State Council Population Census Office and State Statistical Bureau Department of Population Statistics, *Tabulation of the 1990 Population Census,* Vol. 2, pp. 2–5 and Vol. 4, pp. 8–13; Quanguo renkou chouyang diaocha bangongshi bian, *1995 Nationwide 1% Population Sample Survey Data,* pp. 512–17.

with male work, transport and leisure activities in urban and rural areas are causing increased death rates. For 1995, injuries were the fourth leading cause of death for both sexes, but the male death rate due to injuries was 52 per cent higher than the female rate, and in cities it was

68 per cent higher.[68] In 1996, the Minister of Labour noted "the lack of improvements in work-place safety."[69]

Future Fertility and Population Growth

China's low death rates are expected to remain low. The factor that most affects China's population growth rates today is fertility. Do we know the true levels of China's birth rates and other measures of fertility today? Some observers think that public and local officials underreport births all the time, that fertility is much higher than any estimate, and that no-one has an accurate idea of how high China's fertility actually is.[70]

Recent fertility levels and trends. It is indeed true that registered births in China have never been usable for measuring fertility levels; these data have been especially useless since the beginning of the compulsory family planning programme in the 1970s. In addition, during the 1990s, one fertility survey (in 1992) and the 1 per cent sample census of 1995 clearly underreported fertility. Data from these two sources resulted in a total fertility rate of only 1.4–1.7 births per woman in China; hardly anyone believes these figures.

Fortunately, we do have usable data from other sources. China's censuses in 1982 and 1990, and national fertility surveys in 1982 and 1988 obtained rather complete reports of births. In retrospect, minor upward adjustments have been needed in the fertility levels reported from those sources, and such small corrections are well within the standard repertoire of demographers. Also, since 1982, China's State Statistical Bureau (SSB) has conducted a large annual survey early in each calendar year investigating the births and deaths of household members during the previous calendar year. After the survey is completed, the SSB carries out a more intensive post-enumeration survey of a sample of the households to estimate the percentage of births that were missed in the survey. Each year the percentage missed has been from 6 to 15 per cent. The SSB adjusts the national birth rate by that amount before reporting China's official national birth rate for the previous calendar year. It is important to keep in mind that the SSB adjusts the national birth rate for under-reporting in the survey because it has evidence for the amount of adjustment needed, but no corrections are made to the provincial birth rates reported in the survey. Finally, when a full census is taken, for example, in 1990 or 2000, the counts of children aged from about seven and above tend to be more complete. At that time it is possible to go back and make any further corrections to the official birth rates for earlier years.

68. Weishengbu jibing kongzhi si, Zhongguo yufang yixue kexue yuan, *1995 Annual Report on China Disease Surveillance*, p. 29.

69. Li Baiyong, "Objectives of labor work in the new century," *Renmin luntan* (*People's Forum*), 8 January 1996, No. 1, pp. 13–14, tr. in *Foreign Broadcast Information Service Daily Report*, No. FBIS-CHI-96–060, 8 January 1996.

70. For example, Mark Hertsgaard, "Our real China problem," *Atlantic Monthly*, Vol. 280, No. 5 (1997), pp. 105–106.

Consequently there are some relatively high quality data on fertility in China to work with. What emerged after 1984 was a rise in the national birth rate to 1987, caused by increasing numbers of women in the peak childbearing age range, declining marriage age and a rise in marital fertility.[71] Some increase in the rate of births to married couples occurred because of a popular backlash against the most extreme year of coercive campaigns in family planning, 1983, which induced the government to ease its restrictions a little.

By 1986–1987, however, China's leaders had reacted to the rising birth rate with alarm. They reversed the moderate relaxation in required family planning, and, for the last decade, the government has mandated escalating compulsion in family planning.[72] The result has been annual reductions in the proportion of married couples with one child having a second, the proportion with two children having a third, and so forth.[73] Based on the official annual birth rates from the SSB (already adjusted for underreporting), the fertility level of China's population dropped below replacement level in 1991, and for 1996 the PRC had a total fertility rate of 1.8 births per woman.[74] The crude birth rate was 17 births per thousand of population, the crude death rate was 7, and the difference was a natural population growth rate of 10 per thousand of population or 1 per cent annually. This is very low for a developing country. By the middle of 1998, the total PRC population was about 1.24 billion people, more than double the population of the 1953 census.

China's population objectives. China's Agenda 21 stated: "Every effort will be made to keep the average annual rate of population growth within 1.25 per cent by the year 2000. The total fertility rate will be reduced from 2.3 in 1990 to below 2.0, the average fertility rate in developed countries at present. It is expected that the Chinese population will be stabilized at around 1.5 or 1.6 billion by the middle of next century."[75] These total fertility rate and population growth rate goals had already been met by the time the objectives were approved and published. In reviewing the achievements of the Eighth Five-Year Plan (1991–1995), the government reported: "New success was achieved in planned parent-

71. Zeng Yi *et al.* "A demographic decomposition of the recent increase in crude birth rates in China," *Population and Development Review*, Vol. 17, No. 3 (1991), pp. 435–458; Nancy Riley and Robert W. Gardner, *China's Population, A Review of the Literature* (Liege: International Union for the Scientific Study of Population, 1997), pp. 15–36.

72. John S. Aird, *Slaughter of the Innocents: Coercive Birth Control in China* (Washington, DC: American Enterprise Institute Press, 1990); Susan Greenhalgh, Zhu Chuzhu and Li Nan, "Restraining population growth in three Chinese villages, 1988–93," *Population and Development Review*, Vol. 20, No. 2 (1994), pp. 365–395; Riley and Gardner, *China's Population*, pp. 31–54; and John S. Aird, "Human rights and family planning in China," in Commonwealth of Australia, Senate Foreign Affairs, Defence and Trade References Committee, *Australia's Relations with the People's Republic of China* (Canberra: Government of Australia, September 1995).

73. Griffith Feeney and Yuan Jianhua, "Below replacement fertility in China? A close look at recent evidence," *Population Studies*, Vol. 48 (1994), pp. 381–394.

74. U.S. Bureau of the Census, International Programmes Center, *World Population 1998*, forthcoming. Replacement level fertility would be about 2.1 births per woman on average.

75. China State Council, *China's Agenda 21*, p. 51.

hood, excessive population growth was brought under control, the natural population growth rate declined from 14.39 per thousand in 1990 to 10.55 per thousand in 1995."[76] The Ninth Five-Year Plan included the goal that "by the year 2000 China's population will be controlled within 1.3 billion," and the Long-Term Target for the Year 2010 said that "China's population will be controlled within 1.4 billion." Also, "in the period of the Ninth Five-Year Plan, we must maintain a natural population growth rate of 1.083 per cent through control measures." [77] These goals are all being over-fulfilled. With hardly any further decline in fertility, the population of the PRC will be about 1.26 billion in the year 2000 and 1.33 or 1.34 billion in 2010.

The size of China's population when it peaks in the coming century is of course much less predictable. The one-child policy is now tightly implemented in most of China's urban areas and in many populous rural areas. If the government decided to revert to a two-child limit in those places, China's peak population size would be higher. Alternatively, if required family planning were abolished or phased out, population growth and peak population size would also be larger than otherwise. Many Chinese and Western demographers argue that a two-child policy would be beneficial, and some of China's cities are concerned about future ageing of the population structure if the one-child limit is maintained. Nevertheless, there is little evidence that the PRC government has any intention of abandoning the one-child policy at any time soon.

If the current fertility level of 1.8 births per woman were to decline very gradually to 1.7 in the year 2050, and if increases in life expectancy were roughly as expected, then China's population (not including Hong Kong and Taiwan) would stabilize at 1.35–1.42 billion during 2012–2047, declining slowly in size thereafter. Assuming that China's current population continues this slow increase as projected, and that China's economy continues growing even half as fast as it has in the last two decades, then national population growth by itself is not a serious concern. Greater income and wealth give the PRC a variety of options for ameliorating the ecological impacts of the added people.

Population Distribution and Movement

Regional population distribution. Ever since the founding of the PRC, China's leaders have lamented the "uneven distribution" of the population over the national land mass. The half of China's territory that includes the western and north-western provinces and autonomous regions has for this half-century housed far less than 10 per cent of China's population. Well over 90 per cent of the people live crowded into China's southern, central, eastern and north-eastern provinces. This basic situation has not changed even though the government has vigorously pursued directed migration from the crowded half to the uncrowded half

76. "PRC, Ninth Five-Year Plan," p. 6.
77. *Ibid.* pp. 12–13, 19.

of the territory. China's government has promoted animal husbandry as well as irrigation and tilling in the deserts, grasslands and arid plateaus of the west. Economic development of the sparsely populated regions has been pushed and subsidized. People living in the less populated provinces, especially minority nationals, have been allowed more births than people in densely populated regions. Yet the basic distribution of China's population has changed little.

There are good geographical reasons for this situation. The arid west can support few people. The well-watered south and east can support huge numbers. The people live where they live because the climate and soil can sustain intensive cultivation, or at least extensive cultivation as in the north-east. The environments in China's less populated areas are more fragile. Decades of overuse of the western lands by people and livestock have caused severe erosion and desertification.[78] Now the stated goal is to move people out of those poverty-stricken areas that do not have "subsistence conditions to the places with a potential for development." [79]

Migration and urbanization. During the 1960s and 1970s, the PRC government blocked China's expanding urbanization, tying people to where they were born or where the authorities sent them. People's jobs, rations, housing, benefits and legal right of abode were linked to their permanent residential location. The main purposes of this system were to keep rural people out of urban places and to prevent spontaneous migration. One result of this system was to hold 83 per cent of China's total population in villages engaged primarily in agriculture – a policy which held back the economic development of the countryside.

During the economic reform period, some of these restrictions have been lifted. Millions of rural workers are now allowed to move to cities and towns, but they are usually not allowed to stay. The official concept is that they will go to the urban areas to work for some years, then go back to the villages. Other workers from rural areas will take their places. This system is designed to prevent over-urbanization while providing employment to rural surplus labourers.

Even though this movement is considered temporary or provisional, it adds to China's urban population because workers do stay – at least for many months and some for years. The total urban population increased to 21 per cent of China's total population in 1982, 26 per cent in 1990 and 29 per cent by 1995, based on successive censuses. In 1995, those who had been living in a city or town for six months or more were counted as part of the urban population, whether or not they had been able to relocate their permanent registration. Each recent census has attempted to count the migrants for the prior five-year period, and all have found the numbers surprisingly small.

Compared to most developing countries, the speed of China's urban-

78. China State Council, *China's Agenda 21*, pp. 180–191.
79. *Ibid.* p. 62.

ization is moderate. Nevertheless, this greater concentration of China's population in urban places also concentrates pollution and infrastructure problems.[80] Also important is the fact that urban expansion takes place in the midst of China's richest agricultural lands, permanently taking high-yield agricultural fields out of the production cycle.[81] As some of the most productive fields are lost to food production, they are replaced by "wasteland" opened up as arable lands.[82] The concentration of China's population into cities and towns, an inevitable part of development, is diminishing the quantity and quality of China's arable land. Arable land has been lost in most years of the 1980s and 1990s.

Population Age Structure and its Impacts

The pressure of China's population on China's environment is caused partly by huge population size, large annual increments in absolute numbers even when the population growth rate is low, the distribution of the large rural population over the arable land in the populous provinces, and increasing population concentration in cities and towns. In addition, perhaps the key variable to watch in the coming decades is not population size or growth but population age structure. As shown in Figure 5, the PRC population age-sex structure in the year 2000 is characterized by a low dependency ratio,[83] with low aged dependency and low child dependency. The elderly make up only 7 per cent of the population. Children aged from 0 to 14 years, thanks to low fertility, now constitute only 27 per cent of the total population, down from 40 per cent in 1975. China's age structure now has a bulge in the population of the most productive working ages. The age structure is beneficial in that it promotes productivity, savings and investment, and minimizes consumption needs for education and health care.

This type of age structure, however, indirectly causes environmental neglect and deterioration. Why? The government of the PRC has been scrambling during the entire economic reform period since 1978 to increase the numbers of jobs as the working age population has increased in number. In the period 1978–1988, as the total population grew by only 1.5 per cent annually, the population aged from 15 to 64 grew at a rate of 2.5 per cent a year. Because of its booming economy, China succeeded in increasing the number of jobs faster than the rising number of working age adults. But this left little room for re-employing the huge surplus rural and urban workforce.

Much of the employment generation was accomplished in rural areas through the establishment of township and village enterprises. These have

80. For details see Qu Geping and Li Jinchang, *Population and the Environment in China* (Boulder, CO: Lynne Rienner Publishers, 1994).

81. Smil, *China's Environmental Crisis*, pp. 55–58.

82. Tim Hanstad and Li Ping, *Land Reform in China: Auctioning Rights to Wasteland* (Seattle: Rural Development Institute, 1995), RDI Reports on Foreign Aid and Development No. 88.

83. The "dependency ratio" is defined as the number of persons aged between 0 and 14 plus the number aged 65 and older, per 100 persons in the age range 15–64.

Figure 5: **China 2000 Age-Sex Structure**

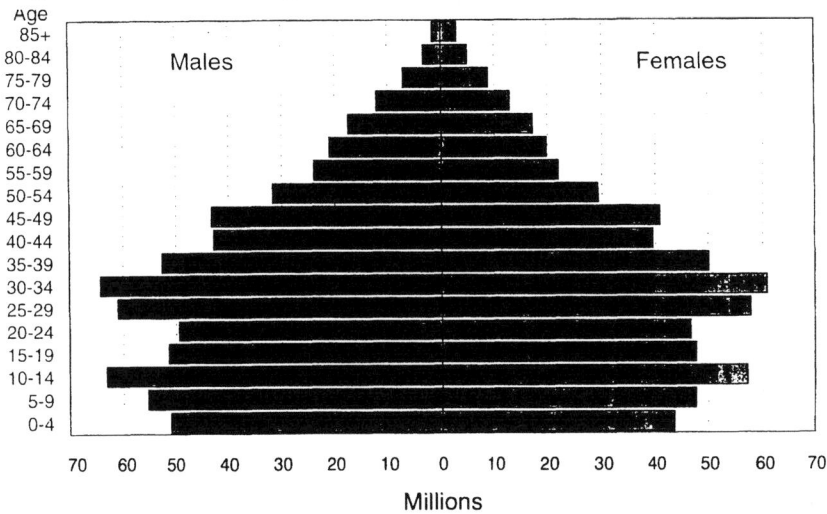

Source:
Projected at the International Programs Center, U.S. Bureau of the Census, *World Population 1998* (Washington, DC: Government Printing Office, 1998).

benn critical to creating rural jobs, but have a low technical level, are inefficient, waste energy and resources and are massively polluting. Yet closing them down means laying off workers, and this is often politically unacceptable.[84] For instance, as China's reported national unemployment rate approached 5 per cent in mid-1998, President Jiang Zemin reaffirmed support for rural township enterprises, saying they were an important source of jobs.[85] In urban areas, the same contradiction is encountered. Some polluting state-owned industries are not closed down because of fear of laying off the workers.[86]

During the five years from 2000 to 2005, the PRC population aged between 15 and 64 years will increase from 856 million to 922 million, a staggering 66 million increment. China may be able to generate that many new jobs in only five years, but to simultaneously provide more productive jobs to the millions of surplus workers will be less feasible. During China's economic reform period, the emphasis has been on economic growth and employment generation, with environmental considerations taking a distinct second place. This situation is likely to get worse before it gets better. The perceived legitimacy of China's govern-

84. Jiang Zhixue and Huang Xianfeng, "The restraints of population on the implementing of sustainable development strategies of the township and village enterprise in China," presented at the 23rd General Population Conference of the International Union for the Scientific Study of Population, Beijing, October 1997.
85. Daniel Kwan, "'Rudimentary' relief plan for laid-off staff," *South China Morning Post*, 24 April 1998, p. 9.
86. Hertsgaard, "Our real China problem," pp. 97–114.

ment depends in part on its ability to deliver jobs and prosperity. Environmental impacts are not as salient. Therefore, it is likely that for some decades, the environment will receive less attention while the real push continues to promote rapid economic development and to create employment.

Population and Prosperity – Environmental Impacts

Population growth alone is no longer a major contributor to China's ongoing environmental deterioration, since the population growth rate is now quite low and is likely to drop further, even without a change in the level of fertility per woman. Population age structure is very important, because of the imperative to create jobs despite environmental costs. In addition, the rise in prosperity since 1978 multiplies the impact of each person on China's environment.

The rise in living standards has meant demand for more and higher quality food. Agricultural production has to further intensify, and this means more fertilizers and pesticides and more contamination of water from nutrient and chemical runoff into rivers, lakes and the ocean. The strong demand for food and other agricultural products makes it difficult to divert land out of agriculture for less environmentally destructive uses. More people with higher living standards also means more demand for water, electricity, heating, air conditioning, appliances and transport. Also, rapid industrial growth causes huge direct damage to air and water through the release of untreated pollutants.

China's huge and growing population combined with rapidly increasing prosperity means there is great potential for further environmental impacts. Yet not all aspects of increased per capita income are harmful to the environment. In some ways, increased prosperity in rural areas reduces environmental stress as people replace biofuels with electricity, natural gas, or coal, and as the quality of housing and sanitation improve. Also, with greater wealth, the PRC has more options for targeting some of the environmental destruction for correction or alleviation.

China's fertility level probably cannot be reduced much more in the coming decade. It is also not realistic to tell the people of China that they do not have a right to the same sort of prosperity that developed countries have. The solution is to direct resources to minimizing the negative environmental impacts of the Chinese population's growth and rapid development.

Conclusions

The PRC has the world's largest population, constituting 21 per cent of the global total. This population has exerted pressure on its environment for the last half millennium, and to a lesser extent for two millennia before that. The main effects were deforestation, erosion, loss of plant and animal species and the use of comparatively fragile arable land for food production.

After the PRC was founded, population growth escalated due to the success of mortality reduction. A period of rapid population growth was an unavoidable part of China's historic transition from high to low mortality and fertility. There was no way to prevent either an associated reduction in per capita arable land in China or the need to increase the intensity of production on the agricultural lands. Much of the environmental destruction of the PRC decades was, however, policy-driven and was not a result of China's large and rapidly growing population.

Increased industrialization and urbanization in the PRC have been accompanied by rising ambient air pollution and increasing water pollution. Resulting public health effects are complex and not well documented. Respiratory diseases were a major cause of illness and deaths in the 1970s, prior to the escalated economic, industrial, and urban growth of the reform period. There has been some reduction in respiratory disease mortality. While pneumonia deaths have declined in the last two decades, death rates from pollution-related respiratory diseases may have risen.

It is still true that the death rate from respiratory diseases is 65 per cent higher in rural than urban areas, and far higher in very poor rural counties than in comparatively well-off rural counties. This suggests that continuing poverty and indoor air pollution are maintaining the high respiratory disease mortality in less advanced rural areas. In cities and prosperous rural areas, some reduction in indoor air pollution may be counteracted by rising ambient air pollution and increased tobacco smoking.

Pollution of rivers and lakes has reportedly increased in the economic reform period. Industrial effluents rose alarmingly during the 1980s, but a concerted effort to treat industrial wastewater has been partially successful. Meanwhile, the dumping of untreated urban sewage into water bodies has escalated, so far without abatement. The feared increase in waterborne disease morbidity and mortality has not materialized – at least it is not evident in the available data. Rather, national policies of improving rural and urban water supplies and promoting food safety and hygiene have apparently succeeded in reducing illness and mortality from digestive and intestinal infectious diseases.

China's compulsory fertility control policy has reduced population growth to an unusually low level. Given the rapidly growing economy, growth of population is not causing grave problems for China today. In the future, it is likely that population growth will be slow enough and economic growth brisk enough to continue this manageable situation.

The public health situation in China has improved dramatically since 1949, and also since the beginning of the economic reforms. Survival chances have risen greatly for both sexes at most ages. Environmental threats to health have lessened enough to allow remarkable reductions in child mortality. Though considerable environmental hazards remain and cause continuing ill health, the main causes of death today in China are chronic diseases. China has only begun to address the prevention and cure of these health problems.

Business Opportunities for Foreign Firms Related to China's Environment

Bruce Tremayne and Penny de Waal

Introduction

The world's environmental technology and service industry, although comparatively young, is already important in global terms. In 1992 the value of the world market was estimated at US$210 billion, which was comparable to the global aerospace and pharmaceutical industries. By the year 2000 the market is expected to have grown to around US$335 billion and to have reached a value of US$640 billion by 2010.[1]

Within this context many of the world's environmental technology and service companies are showing an increasing interest in the Chinese market and China's approach to the challenge of environmental degradation associated with its industrial revolution. This paper examines the current status of the market and future trends, highlighting key issues which foreign companies should address when assessing and developing business opportunities in China.

National and Local Environmental Plans and Policies to 2010

Central, provincial, and municipal five-year plans and related programmes act as the mechanism to release funds for environmental projects. Thus they are the key drivers of state spending on environmental technologies and services, and also indicate how foreign finance will be allocated. The Chinese government has adopted a range of policies and programmes for controlling environmental pollution and ameliorating resource shortages to 2010, although detailed implementation is still largely undertaken within the five-year planning framework. Table 1 lists the key environmental initiatives and planning documents underpinning China's environmental policy since 1992.

Foreign environmental businesses should be particularly aware of three important current environmental policies and plans:

1. Five-Year Plans, the latest being the Ninth (1996–2000), which identify government policy and priorities for environmental spending during each five-year period. The five-year planning cycle is duplicated at the provincial and municipal levels. The Ninth Five-Year Plan includes specific targets for control of a range of key pollutants and overall treatment of wastewater, air emissions and solid waste. Increasingly

1. Ecotec Research and Consulting Ltd, *Global Environmental Markets, An Update* (London: JEMU DTI Export Publications, May 1997).

Table 1: **Key Initiatives and Policy Documents**

Countermeasures, programmes and plans	Approving agencies and dates	Main contents
Ten Countermeasures in China's Environment and Development	Central Committee of CPC, State Council, August 1992	A programme document guiding China's environment and development
China's Environmental Protection Strategy	NEPA, SPC, 1992	A policy document about environmental protection strategies
China's National Programme for Gradually Phasing Out Ozone Layer Depleting Substances	State Council, January 1993	A concrete programme for implementing the Montreal Protocol
China's National Environmental Protection Plan (1990–2000)	State Council, September 1993	Ten-year action plan on China's environmental protection in different fields
China's Agenda 21	State Council, March 1994	White Paper on national pollution, environment and development at a national level
China's Biodiversity Conservation Action Plan	State Council, 1994	An action plan implementing the Convention on Biodiversity
China's Urban Environmental Management Study (Sewage and Garbage)	NEPA, MOC, 1994	A study on environmental management focusing on urban sewage and garbage
China: Issues and Options in Greenhouse Gas Emissions Control	NEPA, SPC, 1994	An analytical study on greenhouse gas emission inventories, with suggested control measures and costs
China's Agenda 21 for Environmental Protection	NEPA, 1994	A ministry-level iteration of China's Agenda 21
China's Agenda 21 for Forests	MOF, 1995	A ministry-level iteration of China's Agenda 21
The Ninth Five-Year Plan and Long-Term Programme Compendium by 2010 for National Environmental Protection	July 1996	A plan guiding national environmental protection in the coming five and 15 years

Source:
National Environmental Protection Agency, *Executive Summary of China's Trans-Century Green Plan* (Beijing: 1997). (NB. NEPA was officially renamed and redesignated as the State Environmental Protection Administration (SEPA) in March 1998.)

municipalities are also required to adopt environmental quality targets for improvement, which are specific to local conditions;

2. The State Environmental Protection Administration's (SEPA) *Trans-Century Green Programme for Environmental Protection to 2010*, which identifies over 1,000 national projects for environmental improvement during its first phase 1995–2000. Two conferences were held in November 1997 to clarify areas of potential foreign co-operation during the first phase of the programme. The main focus during this first phase (relevant to the scope of this paper) is on: water pollution control in seven major

river basins, three lakes and key coastal cities and seas; air pollution control in acid rain control regions; improved solid waste management in main cities; and pollution control and process upgrade in priority energy and industry sectors; and

3. China's Agenda 21 *Plan for Sustainable Development into the Next Century*, completed in March 1994 following the Rio Conference on Environment and Development in June 1992. This White Paper is supported by an Action Plan which identifies foreign co-operation as a means of raising finance for projects. According to China's Agenda 21 Office, over US$2 billion has been pledged by foreign governments and companies for implementing projects under the Plan to date.

The latter two programmes were developed at a different stage to serve particular functions, and are under the jurisdiction of different government departments. The Trans-Century Green Programme is administered primarily by SEPA, whereas the Agenda 21 Programme is co-ordinated by the State Science and Technology Commission (SSTC) through the Agenda 21 Office. There is strong competition between these two agencies. The two programmes address the same issues to a large extent, although Agenda 21 has a much broader remit and covers a wide range of topics outside of environmental pollution control and is less integrated into the five-year planning framework.

Government programmes and plans are useful in providing foreign companies with an overview of priorities for spending on environmental protection, and these in turn can help to identify an appropriate sectoral or geographical focus for market entry. In assessing sales potential related to a particular programme or project, there are two main issues to consider:

wide range of implementing agencies: although projects are drawn together under umbrella programmes as described above, implementation falls under the jurisdiction of a wide range of different ministries and different levels of government (national, provincial and municipal). In most cases, an effective sales strategy necessitates developing a relationship with the final purchaser. It is important, though often very difficult, for companies to identify the relevant project implementing authority and establish contact early in the project cycle; and

availability of finance: there are severe limitations in access to finance in general and foreign exchange in particular, the latter determining the potential for import of environmental equipment and services. The *renminbi* is not yet fully convertible; only those projects earmarked to receive foreign funding have the potential to purchase foreign equipment or services. While central government and many local governments have developed impressive improvement targets and action plans, the funds are often lacking to be able to implement these. Table 2 shows a breakdown of proposed funding sources for the Trans-Century Green Programme.

Administrative and Regulatory Framework

China has traditionally adopted a command and control approach based on end-of-pipe solutions. The regulatory framework has developed since

Table 2: **Funding Sources for China's Trans-Century Green Programme (Stage I) (billion *yuan*)**

Project	Investment	No. of projects	Foreign loans	Bank loans	Local funds	Funds raised by industry	Fines for pollutant discharge
Urban infrastructure	100.4	434	22.8	2.5 (c) 7.5 (l)	67.6		
Industrial pollution, prevention and control	61.5	786	6.4	2.0 (c) 3.1 (l)		40.0	10.0
Ecosystem protection	14.6	106	1.8	1.0 (c) 4.0 (l)	7.8		
Global environmental problems	3.25	70	1.4		1.85		
Total	**179.75**	**1,396**	**32.4**	**20.1**	**77.25**	**40.0**	**10.0**

Notes:
(c) = central bank
(l) = local bank

Source:
National Environmental Protection Agency, *Execuive Summary of China's Trans-Century Green Plan* (Beijing: 1997).

the 1970s and there is now a fairly comprehensive set of environmental legislation in China covering water, air and, more recently, solid waste. Of these the regulation of water pollution has traditionally been strongest and most comprehensive, reflecting national priorities.

Table 3 lists the main government agencies with responsibility for environmental protection and Table 4 lists key legislation and environmental quality and discharge standards related to air, water, and solid and hazardous waste. Although there are problems with enforcement (see below), China's environmental market is regulatory-driven. In general discharge standards are comparable with international standards, although the majority of domestic enterprises do not meet these standards. There have been major revisions to national legislation since 1995 with an increasing trend toward strengthening enforcement, implementing mass loading control and exploring the use of market incentives.

Enforcement

Despite significant recent developments in legislation, enforcement still remains weak. This limits the effectiveness of the regulatory system to foster demand for the environmental pollution control technologies necessary to comply with local standards. Moreover, charges and fines levied on industrial emissions do not reflect the marginal costs of pollution control so that the potential for economic incentives to act as a catalyst for spending on industrial pollution abatement is largely untapped.[2] Increases in levies are proposed to address this problem as well as initiatives to regulate total pollution loading.

Enforcement is not uniform and varies across different sectors of the economy. Three major categories emerge:

state enterprises and other large pollution sources: in practice enforcement activities are focused on larger polluting sources, which mainly comprise the larger state owned enterprises. SEPA has drawn up a black list of 3,000 major polluters and specified time limits for compliance to several hundred of these. However, state industries wield considerable power within the municipal government and it is often difficult for the environmental authorities to force compliance. The state enterprises pollute more than their non-state counterparts and generally have a lower operating efficiency and older technologies. In addition, they have privileged access to funding for environmental upgrades from the state (through the five-year planning mechanism);

town and village enterprises: the vast majority of these collectives are rurally based. As such they fall under the jurisdiction of county-level environmental protection offices which are ill-resourced, and most receive little or no regulation. Many TVEs use highly polluting outdated technologies with little or no environmental control. It is likely that

---

2. The recent World Bank report (The World Bank, *China 2020: Clear Water, Blue Skies* (Washington, DC: World Bank, 1997)) does, however, draw a positive correlation between the current fines and fees systems and reduced pollution intensity in five cities.

Table 3: **National Environmental Administrative Framework**

National Environmental Authorities:

State Council: China's highest legislative body with authority over all Ministries and sub-Ministry government bodies. The Council plays a pivotal role in shaping policy and adopting legislation.

State Environmental Protection Commission (SEPC) makes recommendations regarding new environmental policies and settles disputes among conflicting interests.

State Environmental Protection Administration (SEPA) is the secretariat to the SEPC, drafts laws, regulations and standards, and administers environmental management, environmental publicity, international exchanges, research and education. Known as NEPA until March 1998.

State Science and Technology Commission (SSTC): responsible for supervising and financing key national environmental projects.

Environmental Protection and Natural Resources Conservation Committee of the National People's Congress is a policy think-tank established in 1993. The committee is playing an increasingly influential role in drafting new environmental legislation.

Local Environmental Authorities:

Environmental Protection Bureaus (EPBs) and Environmental Protection Offices (EPOs): enforcement of legislation (notably of Three Synchronies Policy, the primary environmental management tool in China), setting local standards, approving EIAs, administering the discharge regulation system, investigation and response to pollution accidents.

Source:
    Shelley Clarke and Felicity Thomas, *Pollution Control in the PRC: An Investors' Guide* (London: Environmental Resources Management, 1997).

increasing pressure will be put on TVEs to bear the costs of pollution control or to close down. A recent and much publicized example was the closure of thousands of small-scale pulp and paper plants along the Huai River and the requirement for all such medium and large plants to control pollution within a limited period.[3] However, due to poor enforcement, even where ultimatums are issued, this does not necessarily translate into action;[4] and

foreign invested enterprises: the experience of foreign investors in China shows that in most cases foreign invested enterprises are more

---

    3. However in the case of the Huai River it is important to note that the action was prompted in the wake of a disaster situation and that there is international finance available to support the costs of upgrade under the Huai River Project.
    4. Reportedly 80% of the 1,036 factories in Henan province which were required to meet discharge standards by the end of 1997 have not reached the treatment targets, and 60% of the 1,036 have not started treatment projects at all (*China Environment News,* 17 June 1997).

Table 4: **Key Legislation, Regulations and Standards**

General:
Trial Environmental Protection Law 1979 (ratified 1989)

Water:
PRC Water Pollution Prevention and Control Law 1984 (amended 1996);
PRC Environmental Quality Standard for Surface Water (GB3838–88);
Combined Wastewater Effluent Standards for Type 1 and Type 2 Pollutants (GB8978–96);
Quality Standard for Ground Water (GB/T 14848–93).

Air:
PRC Air Pollution Prevention and Control Law of 1987 (amended 1995);
National Ambient Air Quality Standard (GB 3095–82);
Comprehensive Air Emission Standard (GB 16297–96);
Emission Standard of Air Pollutants from Industrial Furnaces (GB 9078–96);
Emission Standard of Odour Pollutants (GB 14554–93);
Administrative Regulations for Urban Smoke and Dust Control Zones 1987;
Emission Standard of Air Pollutants from Thermal Power Plant (GB 13223–96);
Emission Standard of Air Pollutants from Chemical Furnaces for Coking (GB 16171–96);
Emission Standard of Air Pollutants from Cement Industry (GB 4915–96).

Waste:
Prevention and Control of Solid Waste Pollution 1995;
Regulation on the Control of Chromium Pollution 1992;
Control Standard on Poly-Chlorinated Biphenols (PCBs) for Wastes (GB 13015–91);

Other:
Regulations for Radiation Protection (GB 8703–88);
Regulations for Environmental Management on the First Import of Chemicals and the Import and Export of Toxic Chemicals 1994.

Source:
   Shelley Clarke and Felicity Thomas, *Pollution Control in the PRC: An Investors' Guide* (London: Environmental Resources Management, 1997).

---

strictly regulated than their domestic counterparts[5] since they are seen as having the finance to install and operate appropriate environmental controls. Some multinationals operate to stringent internal global company standards as a matter of policy.

   Improving enforcement will require significant changes in the institutional framework for environmental management, continued improvement in regulations and the regulatory process, as well as extension of

---

5. Case examples are discussed at length in Shelley Clarke and Felicity Thomas, *Pollution Control in the PRC: An Investors' Guide* (London: Environmental Resources Management, 1997).

control over all polluting sources to include TVEs. As such, progress is unlikely to be fast.

New Legislation, Regulations and Directives[6]

Several innovative programmes have been implemented recently and are collectively referred to as the "Five New's." The Five New's represents an attempt to translate legislative goals (found in the Environmental Protection Law) into more effective and enforceable regulatory and policy instruments. Proposed changes to the pollution discharge regulation system include adding an additional chapter to the criminal law to cover environmental crimes. New regulations for discharge fees have been proposed for air pollution including a new fee for excessive emissions of sulphur dioxide. In the area of solid waste, a law on the Management of Toxic Wastes has been drafted, but has currently not been approved by the State Council. Following the Solid Waste Prevention and Control Law (1995), new standards and regulations are expected to cover registration of solid wastes, transportation, and disposal. It is unclear when these standards will be issued.

New legislation is proposed for noise pollution, nuclear power generation, coastal zone management, fisheries, prevention and control of desertification and natural disaster prevention. Amendments are proposed for the Natural Resources Law, Soil and Water Conservation Law and the Forestry Law. Draft regulations, under consideration by the State Council, will address nature reserves, pesticides and agricultural environmental protection, rural enterprises (TVEs) and environmental accidents.

Issues of Special Interest to Foreign Companies

Implementation of structural changes within government. Following the 15th Party Congress (September 1997), sweeping changes to governmental structure have been approved by the National People's Congress (March 1998), including the downsizing and merging of a number of ministries. Conversely, the National Environmental Protection Agency was upgraded to the level of Commission and is now the State Environmental Protection Administration, which will strengthen its influence in relation to other government departments. SEPA's resources are likely to increase with a view to improving its monitoring and enforcement function. Proposed structural changes will also tend to separate industry from the state and make enterprises more responsible for their own profits and losses. This has implications for environmental management.

Issuing of new national regulations and laws. While the main framework laws have been enacted, many implementing regulations still require detailed clarification. In the first instance it is important for

6. *Ibid.*

foreign companies to identify whether legislation and standards exist relevant to their particular technologies/products, and whether modification would be required to meet the needs of potential end users in the domestic market. At the same time it is also important to appreciate that many regulations are not implemented, either due to poor enforcement or because legislation, designed in the absence of dialogue with regulated parties, proves impossible to implement in practice – either on technical or financial grounds.

Increases in pollution fines and fees, and the possible introduction of pollution taxes. Currently fines and fees are too low to act as a significant incentive for industry to adopt environmental controls. Proposals for a tenfold increase in pollution levies have been made by SEPA, and if implemented could be expected to have a significant impact on industry spending on environmental protection. However, SEPA concedes that such large increases are unlikely to be approved in the foreseeable future.

Pilot programmes for trial implementation of new policies and regulations. China typically adopts a policy of trial implementation of new regulations and policies in selected locations prior to general implementation. Obtaining information on the location and progress of pilot programmes allows the likely impact of a new programme on a company's business prospects to be assessed. For instance the trial implementation approach is being used for key initiatives such as sulphur emission fees in 14 key cities and provinces; wastewater discharge, mass loading controls and zoning restrictions – the Shanghai Upstream Water Resources Protection Programme, for example; and an Ecological Environmental Compensation Fee levied on industry has commenced trial implementation in Yulin, Tongchuan and Xiaoqinlin in Shaanxi province.[7] According to SEPA's pollution levy department, pilot programmes are also underway to experiment with a more comprehensive pollutant charge system covering all pollutants discharged (as opposed to charges which are only levied on the major pollutant discharge as is currently the case).

Performance of individual municipalities. There is a wide variation in the effectiveness of policy implementation and regulatory enforcement at the municipal level. The performance of individual municipalities depends on a range of factors including availability of local finance (in general, municipalities in the more affluent eastern coastal areas are more

---

7. According to the Protocol of Levy Ecological Compensation in Yulin and Tongchuan, Shaanxi province, which became effective from 1 January 1997, 11 industries which engage in mining, mineral resources supply and processing must pay ecological environmental compensation amounting to a certain percentage of the local price of the products. A total of 90% of the levied fees will be used for environmental protection (*China Environment News*, 20 February 1997).

advanced in environmental control than their inland counterparts); availability of local expertise; political will within the municipal government, particularly that of the mayor; and the structure of the local economy. Enforcement of standards is difficult where one large, uneconomic, state enterprise employs a significant proportion of the local population, as occurs for example in Anshan in Liaoning province. Municipalities have the power to implement local environmental standards, regulations and policies, provided these are at least as stringent as the national equivalent.

Reforms in Pricing of Utilities and Investment Environment

Underpricing of water and minimal fees for sewerage and municipal waste collection have resulted in a lack of investment in urban infrastructure, hampering its ability to keep pace with economic development and population growth. Efforts to raise prices of utilities are most advanced in the electricity and water supply sectors. According to the World Bank:

> the Ministry of Water resources has recommended freeing water prices starting with all new water projects ... More aggressive local governments have already started to allow fully self-financed water projects to set their own prices ... In Taiyuan (Shanxi province) the Price Bureau has announced that water prices will increase from an average of 1.24 *yuan* per cubic meter to 4.94 *yuan* over the next five years in order to recover supply costs."[8]

Similarly, allocated central/local government revenues will not be enough to meet investment needs for urban wastewater treatment and it will be necessary to raise sewerage and waste management fees in order to recover costs and raise funds for investment in new facilities. The legal basis for such price increases was established in the Revised Water Pollution Law (1996), but they have only been implemented in some locations.

It would be unwise to oversimplify the problem. China is in transition from a socialist economy. In addition to price increases, significant legal, institutional and financial reforms will be necessary to facilitate the participation of the private sector in infrastructure development, which is seen as a major source of funding in the future, and to decentralize the process of project approval, which can currently delay projects by several years. Government policy prioritizes use of foreign investment and funding in urban infrastructure, environmental industry and advanced technology. A large portion of the concessional finance from bilateral government arrangements is used to finance water supply and sewage treatment facilities and, to a lesser extent, waste disposal. In the case of industry, current utility prices are too low to act as a significant incentive to adopt technologies for waste minimization or water/energy conservation. However, continued increases in prices, which can be expected in the medium term, should gradually influence industry performance, particularly in under-resourced areas.

8. The World Bank, *China 2020: Clear Water, Blue Skies.*

Growing Public Awareness and Development of Media Attention

Public pressure to improve environmental performance is emerging in some locations but is as yet relatively insignificant as a market force. Public demand for environmental improvement is increasing as environmental quality deteriorates, but this tends to be restricted to educated urban residents in the more affluent areas and in the wake of localized pollution incidents. Indeed there appear to be emerging opportunities for foreign firms in the area of environmental public relations. Some locally based foreign public relations firms are already undertaking environmental PR activities for multinational clients.

Experiments are being made with public consultation in planning decisions during the Environmental Impact Assessment (EIA) process for internationally funded projects in line with donor agency requirements. Media coverage of environmental issues has increased in recent years and there is growing recognition of the need to raise public awareness and improve environmental education in schools. SEPA has also stepped up its awareness-raising activities. Examples include routine publication of lists of non-compliant factories by local environmental authorities, experiments involving members of the public in monitoring local industries, and publication of a rating list of the environmental performance of municipalities. The Shanghai Environmental Protection Bureau has established a website, "Shanghai Environment Online," to enhance public awareness of environmental protection, providing information and encouraging citizen participation.

It is difficult to anticipate how important the role of the public will become in environmental matters in the future. On the one hand, China is traditionally unaccustomed to public consultation and public relations as experienced in developed Western countries. On the other hand, China's centrally controlled administration enables it to initiate nation-wide awareness-raising campaigns that would be difficult to effect in other countries. According to RSA, a locally based media company, all local television stations were recently ordered to devote a specific proportion of prime viewing time to environmental programmes.

Overall Market Size

The above discussion indicates that the long-term growth potential for China's environmental market is significant although the existing financial, structural and administrative barriers will continue to impede development in the short- to medium-term. Many different estimates of the current size of China's environmental market have been developed, however the assumptions upon which they are based are often not clear. At best such figures should be taken as indicative of general trends.[9]

9. For instance, large increases predicted in industry spending may be based on an assumption that a new standard will be fully enforced, while this is unlikely to occur in practice. Similarly, anticipated macro-investment plans, such as provincial or municipal five-year plans, may also be based on requirements to meet targets which may contain a shortfall in terms of actually available finance.

Table 5: **Planned Expenditure 1996–2000**

	Billion yuan	*US$ billion*
Investment in new projects, expansion and renovations	200	24
Pollution treatment for existing plants	105	12.6
Urban environmental structure	145	17.4
Total	**450**	**54**

Source:
State Council, *PRC Ninth Five-Year Plan* (Beijing: 1996).

Under the Ninth Five-Year Plan a total of 450 billion *yuan* (US$54 billion) is earmarked for pollution control (see Table 5).

Unofficial estimates are much lower than this. For example the U.S. Embassy estimates the figure at closer to US$15 billion during 1995–2000 based on current growth rates.[10] In Ecotec's latest study of the global market for the UK government, China's expenditure on the environment is estimated at US$3.5 billion for 1997 rising to US$5 billion in 2000 and US$15 billion by 2010. This extrapolates to US$20 billion for the period 1996–2000.[11] However, only an estimated 15 per cent of the total is likely to be open to foreign companies through direct sales. Ecotec estimates therefore translate actual direct business available to foreign firms of US$525 million in 1997, rising to US$750 million by 2000.

In addition to hard currency restrictions, barriers to the import of foreign technology include: high import duties (25–30 per cent) which makes it difficult to compete on price; limitations on the right of foreign companies to directly access China's wholesale and retail markets; difficulties in ensuring adequate after-sales service; an inefficient banking system; product standards and quality control requirements;[12] lax enforcement of intellectual property laws; and an inadequate system for dispute resolution. In the short- to medium-term, import of foreign environmental technologies can be expected to increase as overall spending increases. However, it should be noted that the government is pursuing an aggressive policy to develop its local environmental industry and localize production of key technologies in order to reduce the overall share of imports. This is discussed below in relation to China's domestic technology base. Companies looking to participate in China's environmental

10. U.S. Embassy, Beijing, Commercial Section, *Impact of Foreign Bilateral Development Assistance on the Competitiveness of U.S. Firms in the Chinese Environmental Market* (Beijing: U.S. Embassy, 1996).

11. Ecotec Resources and Consulting Limited, *Global Environmental Markets, An Update*.

12. For example, from 1 October 1997, China enforced its safety quality licensing system for imported boilers and pressure vessels as mandatory. All importers must register for a licence at a fee of US$15,000 plus expenses (70 companies have registered since 1995).

Table 6: **China's Environmental Industry by Activity**

Activity	% of Total
Environmental equipment manufacture	32
Comprehensive utilization	29
Consulting	12
Engineering design and construction	11
Product distribution and sales	6
Research and development	6
Natural resources protection	4

Source:
   National Environmental Protection Industry Survey Project Office, *Quanguo huanjing baohu chanye jiben qingkuang diaocha* (*National Survey of the Status of the Environmental Protection Industry*) (Beijing: 1995).

market in the longer term would be well advised to develop a local base, either through co-operation with a local partner or independently.

Domestic Technology Base

According to a national survey initiated in 1994,[13] the China Association for Environmental Protection Industry estimates that domestic sales of environmental protection equipment totalled US$1 billion in 1995, including US$8.7 million exports. This survey identified over 9,000 enterprises involved in the environmental protection industry nationwide. The survey's breakdown of China's environmental industry is shown in Table 6.

The overwhelming majority of domestic manufacturing companies are small scale TVEs; less than 500 are classified as large.[14] The privately-owned sector constitutes about 20 per cent of the total, of which around 1 per cent is associated with foreign investment. Data from the survey indicate a steady increase in production value, profits and the number of enterprises and employees over the last ten years. However, the industry as a whole is subject to several limitations including a generally low level of technology, over-production and duplication, particularly in the waste-water treatment sector, problems in quality control of products, lack of product standards and the inability to service large-scale turnkey projects.

The statistics from the 1994 survey on domestic production capability for different media are shown in Table 7.

In terms of the level of technology, only around 4 per cent of products

13. National Environmental Protection Industry Survey Project Office, *Quanguo huanjing baohu chanye jiben qingkuang diaocha* (*National Survey of the Status of the Environmental Protection Industry*) (Beijing: The Project Office, 1995).
14. Large-scale enterprises are defined as having fixed assets of greater than 50 billion *yuan* (US$6 million).

Table 7: **China's Environmental Industry by Medium**

Medium	Number of companies	Annual output (million yuan)	Annual profit (million yuan)
Water pollution	1,386	3,822	481
Air pollution	1,371	4,527	508
Solid waste	100	238	37
Noise control	408	620	79
Radiation/magnetic	4	21	3
Monitoring	138	225	30
Other	238	944	201
Total	**3,645**	**10,397**	**1,339**

Source:
National Environmental Protection Industry Survey Project Office, *Quanguo huanjing baohu chanye jiben qingkuang diaocha* (*National Survey of the Status of the Environmental Protection Industry*) (Beijing, 1995).

reach international standards, around 20 per cent are up to 1980s standards with the remainder at 1960–1970s standards. Moreover, the research and development base is underdeveloped, so that there is considerable impetus for transferring technology from overseas. As a result the government is pursuing an active programme to improve the domestic technology base. Key policy recommendations resulting from the 1994 survey include measures to improve management and quality control within the industry, prioritize the types of technology being imported, establish specialized environmental engineering technology centres, promote international co-operation and exchange (including developing the international market) as well as the transfer of advanced technologies from other countries, and foster development of 100 "super" environmental manufacturing companies.

In 1994 the State Science and Technology Commission (SSTC) approved a loan to SEPA of over 100 million *yuan* for the development of the environmental protection industry. The loan covered 40 items, including projects for comprehensive utilization of resources[15] (37.5 per cent), development of new and advanced low polluting technologies (10 per cent), and environmental demonstration projects (10 per cent). In 1996 the government announced further preferential policies to encourage development of its environmental protection industry and to support companies producing high quality products. These included favourable policies on tax and financing and classification of the environmental protection industry to receive favourable support as part of China's adjusting industrial structure. There are also exemptions on import duty and VAT for environmental equipment and technology which form part

15. A catch-all term which includes recycling and reuse of waste materials among other things.

of a capital contribution to an investment in an encouraged or restricted sector, and preferences and tax holidays for recycling and other environmentally related activities.[16]

Foreign Funding Sources

An estimated 15 per cent of total spending on the environment originates from multilateral and bilateral lending programmes and aid budgets. An estimated US$3–4 billion in environmental spending from these sources is predicted during 1995–2000.[17]

China is now the World Bank's largest borrower. Although the overall level of lending is not likely to increase, there has been an increased emphasis on environmental projects in recent years, with over US$2 billion of environmentally connected projects in various stages of development in 1995. The Bank is primarily involved in urban infrastructure and tends to be technology oriented. It has been active in all aspects of environmental infrastructure (water supply, wastewater treatment and waste management) with major projects in Beijing, Shanghai, Jiangsu and Liaoning. Environmental projects are also under preparation in Hubei, Yunnan, Guangxi, Sichuan and Shandong, as well as assistance with the clean up of the Huai River. The World Bank lends from two different funds: the International Bank of Reconstruction and Development (IBRD) and the International Development Association (IDA). It is also an implementing agency for the General Environmental Facility (GEF) and Montreal Protocol trust funds. During its pilot phase (1991–1994), approximately US$45 million of GEF projects were funded in China, with a further US$50 million of projects related to the Montreal Protocol.

The Asian Development Bank (ADB) also concentrates on infrastructure, and has been increasing loans to the environmental and social sectors in recent years. In 1995 the ADB had over US$2 billion of projects in the pipeline. ADB also funds more technical assistance (TA) projects than the World Bank, providing opportunities for international consulting firms. Often these will lead to loan projects with a major technology component. Current and pending projects include assistance to Anhui, Fujian, Hainan, Jilin and Shanxi provinces and Beijing (including TA for various central government agencies).

Both Asian Development Bank and World Bank bids are conducted through the China National Technical Import Corporation and the China National Import and Export Corporation, with bids announced in the national press. However, a successful bidding strategy requires establishing contact with the relevant local project authority much earlier in the project cycle, usually at the feasibility stage.

The United Nations Development Programme (UNDP) is a major provider of grants for environmental projects in China, mainly for

---

16. Ministry of Foreign Trade and Economic Co-operation, *Revised Guidance Catalogue for Foreign Investment in Production* (Beijing: MOFTEC, 1998).

17. United Nations Development Programme.

training, international consulting and some equipment procurement. Projects are administered through the Ministry of Foreign Trade and Economic Co-operation's (MOFTEC) China International Centre for Economic and Technical Exchanges (CICETE). The UNDP Office for Project Services conducts the international procurement for equipment valued at over US$40,000. UNDP also acts as an implementing agency for the GEF, Montreal Protocol and Agenda 21 trust funds.

Main bilateral donors include Japan, Germany, Australia, Canada, Britain and the Scandinavian countries. Japan has by far the largest bilateral aid programme to China (US$800 million per annum under its OECF Fourth Yen Loan Programme), and a significant number of these projects contain an environmental component. In the case of the U.S., assistance from the U.S. Agency for International Development (USAID), Trade Development Alliance (TDA) and United States–Asia Environmental Partnership (USAEP) was prohibited by statute in 1989. The European Union has two major environmental programmes to implement over the next five years, providing mainly technical assistance, as well as some equipment. These are the Environmental Management Co-operation Programme between the European Union and China's Agenda 21 Office (18 million ECU), and the EU–China Liaoning Integrated Environmental Programme (37 million ECU).

With the exception of Japan, which operates an untied aid programme administered through public tender, bilateral aid is required to use the services and equipment originating from the donor country. Bilateral aid falls into two categories. The first comprises technical assistance grants, which constitute the main market opportunity for consulting firms and include training programmes, exchange missions, feasibility studies, environmental centres, capacity building in Chinese ministries and institutions and environmental education. These grants often have a modest budget for the purchase of imported equipment (particularly monitoring equipment). Secondly, there is concessional finance (CF), where loans of typically US$10–15 million are provided to finance equipment and plant construction. These loans incorporate an effective grant element of around 35 per cent and there is intense competition among Chinese end-users to access these funds. Currently around 60 per cent of such loans are used for water supply and wastewater treatment facilities, and effective use of these facilities has helped many foreign companies to develop projects in China and establish their reputation locally.[18]

Estimates of the total value of different types of bilateral aid and sectoral distribution are shown in Tables 8 and 9.

The last few years have seen developments in policy and legislation to facilitate use of foreign commercial loans for developing environmental (water supply, wastewater treatment, waste management) and energy infrastructure in China through investment, project financing, Build-Operate-Transfer and joint ventures. While the overwhelming

---

18. Examples in the water sector include DHV (Holland), Kruge (Denmark), Chiyota and Tsurumi (Japan), and ITT Flygt (Switzerland).

Table 8: **Bilateral Assistance Summary 1993–1996**

Aid type	Amount (US$ million)
Concessional finance loan	1,096.75
Concessional finance grant	200.85
Memoranda of Understanding between donor governments and the Chinese government	86.64
Technical assistance	193.15
Total aid	**1,577.4**

Source:
Unpublished internal document, U.S. Embassy Beijing Commercial Department, 1997.

majority of foreign funded infrastructure projects are currently financed with concessional loans, there are some commercially financed ventures being implemented or in negotiation. Reported examples include: the sale of 60 per cent of three water supply facilities to foreign investors by the Guangzhou Water Corporation; the signing of a 30–40 year co-operation contract between the Harbin Water Corporation and the French Urban and Rural Construction Corporation; and the 25-year municipal water supply plant in Shanghai by Thames Bovis. Many proposed projects are experiencing delays over mutually agreeable rates of return[19] and tariffs, as well as problems with guarantees. Moreover the lead times to gain necessary approvals for Build-Operate-Transfer projects can extend to several years. This may change pending reform of the project approval system and as precedents develop, but is unlikely to develop significantly in the short-term.

Best Sales Prospects for Foreign Companies

Wastewater treatment, sewerage and water supply. Demand for potable water equipment in 1993 was US$886 million, of which US$98.4 million was supplied through imports.[20] Total demand for wastewater treatment equipment rose from US$487 million in 1994 to US$761 million in 1996, approximately 22 per cent of which was met with imported goods.[21]

The domestic technology base includes the manufacture of physical, chemical and biochemical wastewater treatment equipment, aeration equipment, oil water separators, ion exchange equipment, hospital sewage treatment equipment and environmental monitoring instrumentation. Higher technology products however are imported for their quality and

19. As a rule of thumb 18% IRR is preferred as a minimum by foreign investors whereas the Chinese imposed maximum rate at project approval stage in China is currently 15% IRR.
20. U.S. Department of Commerce, *China Industry Sector Analysis: Potable Water Technologies* (Washington, DC: Government Printing Office, 1993).
21. Christine Huang, *Wastewater Treatment in Guangzhou, Guangdong* (Beijing: U.S. Embassy Commercial Section, 1996).

Table 9: Number of Bilateral Assistance Projects by Sector

Aid type	Solid	Water	Air	Energy	Resource management	Capacity building	Planning management	Cleaner production	Total
Technical assistance	2	34	12	12	19	29	11	2	121
Concessional finance	5	78	16	25	7	—	2	3	136
Memoranda of understanding	—	1	—	6	4	4	2	1	18
Total	**7**	**113**	**28**	**43**	**30**	**33**	**15**	**6**	**275**

Source:
Unpublished internal document, U.S. Embassy Beijing Commercial Department, 1997.

Table 10: **Value of Solid Waste Market**

| | US$ million | | |
	1994	1995	1996
Import market	68.2	103.5	155.3
Local production	60.0	65.0	70.0
Total market	**128.2**	**168.5**	**225.3**

Source:
Unpublished internal document, U.S. Embassy Beijing Commercial Department, 1995.

reliability and include screening presses, digester agitators, aerating brushes for oxidation ditches, shaftless screw conveyors, methane generators and motors, large pumps, adjustable outlet weirs, automatic monitoring instruments and automatic control systems, disinfection systems, sludge scrapers, suction and aeration equipment and sludge mixing and dewatering plant, and various pipes and parts.[22]

The end users for large-scale water supply systems include municipal water supply and wastewater organizations, as well as large industrial establishments such as petrochemical complexes or iron and steel works. There are also opportunities for sales of medium- and small-scale water treatment equipment to hotels, villas, large working complexes and residential developments which are not connected to the municipal water supply system, although smaller scale plants are more likely to be serviced with local technology.

Waste management. Estimates of the market for equipment sales for solid waste management over three years are shown in Table 10.

Domestic companies currently produce equipment for primary waste collection and transportation, but they lag behind international competitors in treatment capacity, key parts, automation and auxiliary equipment. For newly constructed projects, imported products usually account for 50 per cent of the total equipment investment. The best sales prospects include auxiliary equipment and technology for landfill, incineration equipment, waste collection vehicles, and recycling and comprehensive utilization.

Industrial pollution control. It is less easy to develop a specific picture of sales prospects for foreign firms in this area. The Trans-Century Green Programme assigns an overall budget of around 2–3 billion *yuan* for each industry sector to fund projects to 2000, however it is not clear where funding will be drawn from to implement these. For instance, a certain

22. List as identified in U.S. Trade Promotion Co-ordination Committee, *China Environmental Technologies Export Market Plan* (Washington, DC: Government Printing Office, 1996).

proportion of projects will be funded through the World Bank Huai River Clean Up project, which includes funding for 20 industrial projects and 130 industrial wastewater treatment and upgrade recycling/recovery projects[23] covering the sectors outlined in Table 11. In other cases, foreign funding may be sought but is not yet secured, as indicated during the First International Co-operation Conference of Environmental Protection Projects in November 1997, which put forward 70 projects seeking foreign funding. These were mainly industrial pollution control and infrastructure projects.

Energy. The priorities for spending on environment-related energy technology focus mainly on technologies to reduce pollution from coal combustion, particularly desulphurization technology. These include: high efficiency sulphur scrubbers; efficient boiler technology and related dust control equipment; fluidized bed combustion boilers which remove 50–80 per cent of the sulphur; combined heat and power; utilization of gangue and coal ash; coal-washing facilities; and low NO_x burners (for plants over 300MW in size)

Other energy sector priorities identified in the Trans-Century Green Programme include: research and development of pilot projects for low- or zero-emission energy alternatives for rural energy supply (biogas, liquefied petroleum gas, small hydropower, solar and wind energy); treatment of wastewater and sludge resulting from the exploitation and processing of oil and gas, and sulphide containing gas in natural gas; and monitoring of (civil) nuclear facilities and nuclear waste disposal. China has also developed a list of priority technologies which it wishes to introduce in order to reduce greenhouse gas emissions. These include:[24] IGCC; direct reduction technology; coal gasification for ammonia synthesis; vapour emission control systems; biomass gasification and gas cleaning; fuel cells; smelting reduction technology; production of organic compound fertilizer from animal wastes; and solar water heaters.

Environmental monitoring and analytical equipment/analytical services. There is a buoyant market for environmental monitoring and analytical instruments reflecting the environmental authorities' initiatives to increase supervision of pollution sources, and to support data collection activities for producing environmental management planning and project feasibility studies. A major proportion of multilateral and bilateral technical assistance funds support this type of work and these invariably contain a budget for the purchase of foreign equipment (including mobile laboratory facilities). Many foreign suppliers of monitoring and analytical equipment have established agents in China.

---

23. Huai River Basin Pollution Prevention Plan, Editorial Group, *Huaihe liuyu shui wuran fangzhi jihua* (*Huai River Basin Pollution Prevention Plan*) (Beijing: The Editorial Group, 1997).

24. National Climate Change Co-ordinating Group, 3rd Working Group, *Zhongguo wei nuan wen shi qi ti pai fang suo xu de ji shu zhuan rang qing dan* (*List of Technologies to be Popularized to Reduce Greenhouse Gas Emissions in China*) (Beijing: The Working Group 1996).

Table 11: **Priorities for Industrial Pollution Treatment and Clean Technology (Trans-Century Green Programme)**

Iron and steel industry
Clean technology: adopt advanced technologies for sintering, desulphurization of coal gas from coking furnaces, replacement of wet coke extinguishing with dry process, heat recovery, increase overall proportion of co-casting. End-of-pipe: particulate control, wastewater and recycling systems for various processes.

Non-ferrous metals industry
Clean technology: improve ore dressing, increase grade of concentrate, promote cyanide-free ore dressing, flue gas recovery from SO_2 concentrated smelting for acid production, renovation of copper smelting process. End-of-pipe: waste gas treatment, electric furnace dust emission control, and comprehensive utilization of SO_2, wastewater and waste sludge.

Construction materials industry
Cement: adopt dry cement process and increase use of rotary kilns to 25 per cent by 2000. Brick and tile: develop new product lines for wall materials including hollow brick, waste residue brick, concrete lay brick, aerocrete and various types of slab materials.

Chemical industry
Cleaner production technology for pharmaceutical, coating, dioxide, inorganic salts, calcium carbide, basic organic raw materials, synthetic materials, rubber processing and carbon black. Chlorine alkali industry: treatment and reuse of acid alkaline wastewater, waste gas, alkali containing waste liquid and salts. Sulphuric acid: technologies to eliminate SO_2, fluorine and arsenic pollution. Nitric acid: control of NO_x. Nitrogen fertilizer: reduce loss of ammonia and nitrogen by 30 per cent. Phosphate fertilizer: control of fluorine.

Petrochemical industry
Upgrade open type wastewater treatment equipment and adopt closed process reactors. Adopt bio-membrane separation and combination technology. Recovery of flare gas and sulphur recovery from waste gas and wastewater (for high sulphur crude oil processing).

Light industry
Pulp and paper: alkali recovery, centralized treatment for alkali chemical pulp enterprises over 17,000 tons capacity. Brewing and fermenting: utilization of high protein/alcohol containing organic wastewater for forage production (DDGS). Sugar refining: recovery and recycling of wastewater/waste residue from beet sugar refining, granular dregs production and production of aldose, alcohol carbohydrate and yeast with waste from sucrose refineries. Leather and fur production: adopt low chromium and chromium liquid recycling process technologies and centralized treatment of wastewater.

Textile industry
Treatment and recycling of wastewater from printing and dyeing plants; cycling utilization of water from air conditioners; treatment of chemical fibre starch wastewater and resource recycling.

Pharmaceutical industry
Adopt clean low-polluting technologies and technologies for treatment and recycling of concentrated organic wastewater with anaerobic process; adopt catalysis, oxidization, desulphurization and dust emission control technologies. Develop new approaches to the production of antibiotics and forage additives and comprehensive utilization of waste residue from production of synthetic medicines.

Source:
   National Environmental Protection Agency. *Executive Summary of China's Trans-Century Green Plan* (Beijing: 1997).

Environmental consulting. Although China's emphasis has always been on acquisition of equipment ("hardware"), there is increasing awareness of the need for improving environmental management, both within the environmental protection administration and in industry. Consulting in China has traditionally focused on two main areas: Environmental Impact Assessment (EIA) as part of the local project approval process; and design and engineering services. The main domestic providers of these services are research and design institutes and companies attached to government ministries and departments. In both cases these institutions must hold government certification to conduct their work, and there are different grades of certification depending on the capability of an organization, which determines the type of project it is permitted to evaluate (based on a scale of overall investment). For domestically-funded projects both of these areas are effectively closed to foreign consulting companies, although foreign agencies are usually used where foreign funding is involved. For example, in the case of the EIA process, while it is possible for a foreign company to gain *de facto* EIA accreditation through a joint venture with a local institution, the project opportunities are limited in practice since the EIA must be approved by the relevant environmental authority, and it is customary for the project proponent to use the services of that authority's own research institute to conduct the EIA.

In recent years domestic interest has grown in environmental management consulting, environmental auditing, ISO 14000 certification, and international standard EIA techniques and procedures (which differ from Chinese EIA techniques and procedures in both content and function). The National Technology Supervision Bureau has issued standards to implement ISO 14000 in China. As with EIA, it is likely that foreign companies will not be able to participate in this market without appropriate accreditation which can only be gained through joint ventures with a locally accredited company or institution.

Although the government's stance with regard to contaminated land liability is still unclear, previous poor industrial practices carry a high risk that a company may invest in a property which has been contaminated to some degree. This provides an added incentive to conduct environmental investigation prior to acquisition and establish baseline data. There are many domestic laboratory facilities supporting environmental departments at different levels of government. As with EIA, the market is effectively closed to competition with local environmental authorities routinely contracting their own agencies to conduct sampling and analysis. However, there may be opportunities for co-operative ventures to bring analytical procedures in line with international standards.

Sales by foreign consulting firms are therefore funded almost exclusively through bilateral and multilateral aid channels or foreign companies investing in China. Opportunities for consulting to locally investing multinationals include advising on regulatory issues and local permitting requirements, as well as pre-acquisition auditing. Local capability in this area is almost non-existent and it is mainly foreign consulting companies who are servicing demand either from a local base in China, or through their regional/head offices. Demand for such services seems set to remain consistent in the short term, although overall foreign investment levels are likely to decrease over the coming two years.

Accessing the Market

Successful entry strategies pursued by foreign environmental firms in China combine the following elements: early market entry; effective utilization of available government support (such as mixed credits for infrastructure projects); reasonable prices and flexibility in negotiations; reputation for high quality and good after-sales service; and an emphasis on developing and maintaining good relationships with end-users and decision-makers. Conducting a successful business in China, whether through a co-operative venture or direct sales, generally requires long lead times and careful positioning to develop the necessary local relationships upon which the success (or not) of the business will depend. This requires a willingness to take a longer term view, and necessitates a commitment from top management to travel to China to deal directly with potential clients and develop relationships with them over time. Companies usually have to expend much effort to achieve their first sales since Chinese buyers invariably prefer to purchase technology which is already proven in China; an established record in other countries will be a lesser contributing factor. Utilization of available concessional finance to fund demonstration projects is an effective strategy for entry into the local market. As might be expected, competition for these resources is intense.

Another crucial consideration is that companies wanting to do business in China will often find themselves actively involved in identifying or arranging finance for the purchase of their goods or services. This is particularly true with infrastructure projects where it may be necessary to raise finance for the overall project either through accessing available concessional finance or arranging commercial loans. Often Chinese project proponents do not understand the restrictions and banking criteria applicable to such funds, and it is usually up to the foreign company or consortium to advise on this. It is therefore vital for foreign companies to be aware of sources of funding and how to access these effectively.

The majority of equipment sales to end-users are influenced by provincial or municipal governments. Companies must therefore establish and maintain good relationships with key officers, either directly or through an agent. It should be noted that China is increasingly moving towards use of public tender procedures for public sector projects and regulations on this are pending.

Since the environmental industry is characterized world-wide by small- and medium-sized companies, most cannot afford to set up their own representative offices and must rely on a local agent. Finding (and keeping) a good agent is therefore crucial and is usually the decisive factor in whether or not a company is successful in the China market. There are four types of agent:

1. state trading enterprises: these are typically buyer's agents who are

authorized to engage in foreign trade, can conduct their own transactions, and usually have the necessary connections to conduct relevant paper-work. However, such agents are unlikely to actively market a product and will need considerable input from the foreign partner to define a market-ing programme and monitor results;

2. independent private enterprises: these are satellites of state enter-prises or independent private companies which are responsible for their own profits and losses. They may not be authorized to engage in foreign trade and must entrust final negotiations to an authorized company. Such companies are more likely to engage in proactive marketing, although they may lack technical expertise and require assistance with marketing techniques;[25]

3. manufacturers/service centres: some local manufacturing companies may act as an agent whereby a company can access their knowledge and networks within the local market, with the possibility of establishing an after-sales service centre.[26] Although such companies have technical expertise, training usually needs to be provided. Engaging this type of agent can also constitute the first step in developing a co-operative venture, whereby a relationship can be developed over time to assess the local partner's capabilities and interests, and whether they can adequately market and service the company's products and protect the company's technology; and

4. representative offices of overseas trading or consulting companies: many existing general trade and consulting companies are seeking to represent foreign environmental firms in China. To achieve economies of scale these companies will usually target a group of technology suppliers serving a particular sector. Contracts with such usually include a combi-nation of retainer and commission.

Whichever route is chosen, there are some essential factors to take into consideration prior to selecting an agent. It is advisable to obtain an independent understanding of market opportunities in order to define an appropriate geographical and sectoral focus. There is a growing number of locally-based consultants who can provide this type of service, includ-ing screening and shortlisting appropriate agents. Through such advance preparation the foreign company is better placed to assess the likely effectiveness of an agent, based on the strength of their connections in the relevant sectors/locations. China is a large country and in reality few agents will be able to cover all areas and sectors. It may be desirable to engage more than one agent to cover different areas. It is also important to understand clearly (and verify) the legal status of the agent and permitted scope of business. To ensure that the most effective use is made of an agent's services it is necessary to foster a close relationship through

---

25. It should be noted here that mass marketing techniques are not as yet considered to be particularly effective in China with sales still dominated by personal relationships and networks.

26. Such centres must be set up in the name of the Chinese company and require approval from MOFTEC.

regular communication, and to provide training to ensure that technology is understood.

The National Survey of the Status of the Environmental Protection Industry (1995) identified over 150 environmental ventures in China with foreign investment. No further details have been published on the nature of these (which may include representative offices, agents, joint ventures and wholly foreign owned enterprises). Domestic environmental technology companies are currently very enthusiastic about forming joint ventures with foreign companies. The incentives are numerous but usually involve some or all of the following opportunities: to improve technology and gain an edge over domestic competition; to obtain finance for business development through the investment of a foreign partner; to access internationally-funded projects through joint bids through association with foreigners; and to access overseas markets. These objectives reflect the government's policy of developing China's environmental industry as discussed above. A market strategy based on direct sales alone will be difficult to sustain in the long term. Using a co-operative venture with a local partner, foreign companies can improve and sustain participation in the market by reducing product cost, accessing market sectors denominated in local currency (although this will be less relevant when the *renminbi* becomes fully convertible), accessing the partner's existing sales and distribution networks and providing a base for after-sales service.

There are various types of investment vehicles which are appropriate to the manufacturing or services sectors. Options include wholly foreign-owned enterprises and various forms of joint venture including equity joint ventures, and co-operative or contractual joint ventures. The choice of vehicle depends on the nature of the business and the extent to which a local partner is required. In general either equity joint ventures or wholly foreign-owned enterprises could be appropriate for manufacturing, whereas a contractual joint venture may be more appropriate for an operating contract or a project with minimal capital contributions. There is much scope for mutual benefit through joint ventures, however there is also the potential for conflict of interest and differing views on management and development. In 1997 wholly foreign-owned enterprises became the most popular form of foreign investment for manufacturing. However opportunities for obtaining licences for wholly foreign-owned enterprises for consulting are restricted, but vary depending on location.

Intellectual Property Rights (IPR) are currently a high profile issue with respect to both direct sales of technology and the Chinese government's policy of attracting foreign co-operation to develop China's domestic environmental industry. At worst, companies run the risk of finding copies of their own products competing on the international market. Where contract breaches occur, enforcement may be difficult – due mainly to the relatively recent and evolving nature of legislation and judicial processes (both specific to IPR as well as in general in China). There is also a lack of clear precedents as well as a lack of resources within enforcement agencies to adequately cover the number of cases which arise. As always with IPR issues, the solution lies in effective management of the process at all levels.

Conclusion

In analysing the many opportunities in the Chinese market, foreign environmental technology and service companies need to establish where there is a determination to achieve international solutions and standards, and above all where financial resources are available. Often at the most senior levels the will to act appears resolute but is dissipated when choices are required against financial constraints. As environmental degradation mounts, the balance in favour of expenditure to resolve the situation should increasingly move in favour of imported technologies and services. However China is aggressively building its own environmental technology base, and foreign companies may need to obtain a stake in this to secure a future market share. As elsewhere, real opportunities will expand as the wealth of a particular sector or province increases. Even when this occurs the unique nature of approaching business in China will remain. Successful companies will adopt a local mantle, focus on a particular sector or province, and devise strategies that do not demand immediate returns but aim at long-term rewards.

Index